C0-AWN-117

Community Organizing:
Canadian Experiences

68884

Wharf, Brian, ed.

Community organizing

FOR USE IN LIBRARY ONLY

DATE	NAME / NOM
Se 26	P Burman
Sept 2	

68884

Community Organizing: Canadian Experiences

Edited by Brian Wharf
and Michael Clague

BRESCIA COLLEGE
LIBRARY
68884

Toronto New York Oxford
Oxford University Press
1997

Oxford University Press
70 Wynford Drive, Don Mills, Ontario M3C 1J9

Oxford   New York
Athens   Auckland   Bangkok   Bombay
Calcutta   Cape Town   Dar es Salaam   Delhi
Florence   Hong Kong   Istanbul   Karachi
Kuala Lumpur   Madras   Madrid   Melbourne
Mexico City   Nairobi   Paris   Singapore
Taipei   Tokyo   Toronto

and associated companies in
Berlin   Ibadan

Oxford is a trade mark of Oxford University Press

Canadian Cataloguing in Publication Data

Main entry under title:
Community organizing: Canadian experiences

Includes bibliographical references and index.

ISBN 0-19-541226-5

1. Community organization — Canada. I. Wharf, Brian.
II. Clague, Michael, 1940–   .

HN110.Z9C6 1997   361.2'5'0971   C96-932192-9

Editor: Valerie Ahwee
Text & cover design: Brett Miller
Formatting: Janette Thompson (Jansom)
Cover photos: Women's demonstration (Canapress Photo Service/Tom Hanson);
Native march (Canapress Photo Service (Wayne Glowacki)

Royalties from this book will go to Campaign 2000 to end child poverty.

Copyright © Brian Wharf and Michael Clague 1997

1 2 3 4 — 99 98 97
This book is printed on permanent (acid-free) paper ∞.
Printed in Canada

Contents

Section III

Section IV

Art Stinson, Community Worker

In December 1995, community workers in Canada lost a friend and colleague. Art Stinson died in his seventy-ninth year in Ottawa after a lifetime in community development. He exemplified praxis in community work—the application of knowledge through action, reflection, revision of knowledge, and re-engagement. Art's work spanned two-thirds of this century:

- developing a community YMCA without walls in Toronto

- working in the public affairs department of the CBC to plan programs on social affairs with national voluntary organizations for broadcast on 'Citizen's Forum', linked to discussion groups across Canada

- working with the Royal Commission on Bilingualism and Biculturalism

- developing a proposal, as the director of the Canadian Citizenship Council, to transform it into the Canadian Institute for Social Development

- founding, with colleague Alan Clarke, the Centre for Community Development within the Continuing Education division of Algonquin College, Ottawa

- teaching community development in the School of Social Work at Carleton University, Ottawa

During these many phases of his career, Art was always close to the practice of community development. He developed the first and, to date, only compilation of case-studies in community development in Canada, *Canadians Participate: An Annotated Bibliography of Case Studies*.

Art Stinson thought and wrote passionately about community, about the future directions of our society, and about the role of community development in this process. Long before many of us, he was arguing 'for a new model of community development' (Stinson 1978:8). He challenged a preoccupation with theories of social change that sought redistributive justice within the prevailing view that economic progress, the consumer society, and the good life were synonymous: '*more* of everything was needed for the client constituency: more education, more even-handed justice, more equitable distribution of opportunity, wealth, resources and power. There were few who questioned that this was possible within the modern industrial state' (Stinson 1978:6).

Art was one of those who argued early for a 'paradigm shift' in our thinking before the term became abused. More important than theories of social change, he believed, was a 'theory of changing'.

> I wish to comment that writing in Canada about community development appears not to be influenced to any significant degree by the literature of social transformation. Theory about community development is repetitive and moribund in comparison with the startling perceptions which abound on the macro level. If we are concerned with developing a 'theory of changing' we must surely relate community work to the macro concepts of change (Stinson 1978:8).

Characteristic of his eclectic mind and intuitive sense for ideas before they became fashionable, Art identified what was necessary for a theory of change in his writings about the concept of 'personhood' (what it means to be human), the concept of a conserving society, the concept of appropriate technology, and the work in conceptual mapping to develop a new paradigm or model for society and our social relations.

Art was always concerned with the link between local action and the larger picture. He recognized that local action could produce meaningful change in the lives of people, groups, or perhaps even communities. He believed that lasting change requires us to question our assumptions about modern society and its values and replace them with vision and values that encourage the best in the human spirit.

Art will always be remembered for how he influenced individuals and helped people discover and mobilize their energies. His recollection of his first community development experience is illuminating:

> It was during 1938–39 that I had my first community development experience. I was teaching in one of those typical rural, one-room schools, my first job. By a combination of chance, intuition and inclination I became involved in a process which, in retrospect, was consistent with all the principles of community development. . . . In a community which had done nothing for itself for years, we ended up with a rink, a clubhouse and an active, varied, social and recreation program. The community, poor as it was, did it all on its own with its own resources. There was a surprising serendipity effect. During the first few months in the school it became obvious the pupils were dedicated to running the teacher out as they had the previous one. During the community development process the situation became

completely reversed. All my problems in the school disappeared and the school became the animation centre of the process (Stinson 1977:1).

Art, you are missed, but your legacy will endure.

References

Stinson, A.

   1977. 'A Brief, Personalized, Historical View of Community Development in Canada.' Unpublished paper presented at the School of Social Work, University of BC.

———— .

   1978. 'Community Development in an Era of Paradigm Search'. Unpublished paper presented at the 17th Conference on Comparative Community Development, University of Missouri.

Acknowledgements

We want to thank the authors of the chapters, who remained committed to their work despite the numerous requests for revisions. We are grateful to Professor Brad McKenzie of the Faculty of Social Work at the University of Manitoba for his perceptive review of the manuscript.

Negotiations regarding the publication of the book began with Al Potter, college editor of McClelland and Stewart. Al authorized publication despite some initial misgivings about the anticipated sales. Given that royalties from the book will support Campaign 2000, we hope that the initial estimates of the sales prove to be wrong! Following the sale of McClelland and Stewart's college list to Oxford University Press, Euan White was extremely helpful in the early stages of the book, and Valerie Ahwee provided exemplary editing.

Particular thanks go to Barbara Egan at the University of Victoria for collecting and formatting the chapters.

Chapter One

Community Organizing: Canadian Experiences

Brian Wharf

This introductory chapter outlines the organization and objectives of the book, which is divided into four sections. The first consists of this introduction, chapters that portray the history of community development in Quebec and anglophone Canada, and chapters that examine current activities in Quebec and British Columbia.

The second section presents four chapters on unemployment. Three case-studies describe the federal government's attempts to involve communities in tackling unemployment, particularly among youths. These efforts included the Company of Young Canadians, the Opportunities for Youth Program and the Local Initiatives Program, and regional and economic development. In contrast to these federal, top-down initiatives, the fourth chapter argues the case for economic development, which is not only located in but controlled by communities.

The third section considers social movements as examples of development and change. The chapters include discussions of the First Nations, feminist, environmental, and poverty movements.

The concluding section consists of a chapter on who participates in community development activities, and a chapter that sums up the lessons and legacies discussed in the preceding chapters.

The objectives of this book are to tell some stories about community development in Canada, and to determine if there are any lasting legacies of the many and varied experiences portrayed here. Telling the story of community development is a worthwhile enterprise in its own right since there have been no previous attempts to trace the history of community development in this country from its early days to the present. Indeed, as Jim Lotz, Jean Panet-Raymond, and Robert Mayer point out in their chapters, little has changed since Tony Lloyd claimed almost thirty years ago that: 'As far as it is possible to ascertain no one has yet undertaken a survey of community development in Canada, and there are few people who are aware of the extent of community development activities throughout the country' (Lloyd 1967:6).

Although some useful books, monographs, and articles have been written, ranging from in-depth case-studies of particular activities to annotated bibliographies covering a wide range of projects and experiences (Draper 1977; Keating 1975; Stinson 1975; Wharf 1979), none of them provide a description and analysis of four decades of community development in Canada. We acknowledge that this book falls short of portraying a full account of community development activities (for example, coverage of current activities is restricted to two provinces). While it would have been desirable to include similar accounts from other provinces, the limitations of space precluded this option. Other omissions include examples of community development activities in direct service agencies despite the long record of community work in some Children's Aid Societies in Ontario and more recently by the provincial Ministry of Social Services in BC.

The second objective of the book is to make some judgement calls about the legacies of community development. Can significant changes at any level (local, regional, provincial, or national) be credited to the community development activities described in this book? A confident assumption is that changes such as the establishment of locally relevant services and the blocking of unwanted high-rise projects have occurred. These 'ordinary issues of social policy' (Lindblom 1979:523) are of immense importance to residents of affected neighbourhoods. However, the question of whether changes resulting from community development projects and activities have had greater than local impact must still be raised.

Some forms of community development (like the environmental, women's, and First Nations movements) seek changes in the 'grand issues of social policy which pertain to the fundamental structure of political life. These issues include those on the distribution of income and wealth, on the distribution of political power and on corporate prerogatives' (Lindblom 1979:523). Indeed, the grand issues concern not only governance but societal norms about such matters as the definition of work and what forms of work are payable from the public purse. Why, for example, do we pay for building helicopters and destroyers but not for child care?

Thus our inquiry is concerned with determining if any changes in the distribution of power, governing structures, and societal norms can be attributed to community development. As will become evident in the following chapters, community development is based on values that include social justice and the equitable distribution of power and resources. Given this value base, is there any evidence that the wide variety of community development activities have influenced who rules and how in Canadian society? This inquiry into power and who rules intrigued the authors of a recent text on community organization and the state:

> This collection of papers has posed a challenge to how we think about the 'community' and the 'state'. We suggest that the way in which these concepts are traditionally defined have restricted our ability to look beyond the confines of what constitutes the 'community' and community development. . . . In closing we want to emphasize the fluidity of the boundaries between community and the state. How these boundaries are defined and constituted must be a subject of critical exploration at all times (Ng, Walker, and Muller 1990:318).

One significant contribution of Ng, Walker, and Muller's text is its criticism of the notion held by many on both the right and left of the political spectrum that the state is rigid and inflexible, while the community is seen as representing 'the good and the benevolent sphere of social life' (Ng, Walker, and Muller 1990:316). While acknowledging the need for continuing inquiries, Ng, Walker, and Muller end their search with a confirmation of their original assumption about power: Canada is a patriarchal society in which a relatively few men rule in their own interests. If this ruling arrangement does not apply with regard to the ordinary issues as completely as it does to the grand issues of social policy, it is only because ordinary issues do not disturb the overall distribution of wealth and power.

We begin our work with similar assumptions, such as the following. First, ruling arrangements in Canada are dominated by clusters of élites whose interests are sometimes aligned with the public interest but more often serve their own ends. Opportunities, wealth, and power are still distributed unequally and subject to the disproportionate influence of men. This view supports the contention of Ng, Walker, and Muller and that of many other critics of Canadian society that state-sponsored community development activities represent approved aberrations in otherwise closely controlled ruling arrangements.

Second, it is important not to embrace 'community' as a solution to counter the state's failure to meet its social obligations adequately. Like families, communities can be places of support, nourishment, and refuge, or, on the other hand, places of intolerance and oppression. The current rediscovery of community and community development cannot be at the expense of national social policies that provide equitable access to health, education, and employment programs, protection in times of economic hardship, and the maintenance and enforcement of human rights.

Finally, the subject of rights and community development merits clarification. Because community development is grounded in social justice, it is frequently associated with the advancement of rights, particularly those of marginalized groups. A current prevalent view is that society has become too rights-centred, and that individuals and groups are advancing their interests at the expense of the greater public good. It is indeed ironic that this criticism is led by the neoconservatives among us, a group that has previously profited enormously from the ethic of individualism. Equally disturbing is that the neoconservatives have been successful in eroding the middle's class's sense of obligation for building a more equitable society. Increasingly vulnerable itself, the middle class has turned against programs that are seen to benefit the marginalized, blaming victims for circumstances beyond their control.

One question that has been raised repeatedly throughout the history of community development is whether a process of change that is grounded in and controlled by communities can be initiated and funded by senior levels of government. As the history chapters make clear, community development emerged as an instrument of national policy in undeveloped countries, and 'first saw the light of day in the British Colonial Office in 1948' (Lagassé 1967:19). At that time, the essential (if not always manifest) objective was to modernize Third World countries and recreate the British institutions of capitalism and systems of government. As the authors of the chapter on First Nations argue, this objective has continued with respect to First Nations peoples in Canada.

Another perspective on this question looks at whether senior levels of government with the mandate and resources to deal with social problems across the country should have the sole responsibility of planning programs that ultimately have to be implemented in local communities. Can programs be implemented from the top down? If not, can communities play a useful role in a plan conceived elsewhere? As noted earlier, it is our view that senior levels of government can and should play a leadership role in addressing issues such as poverty and unemployment. Until recently the federal government demonstrated leadership by developing programs such as the now disbanded family allowances, the Canada Pension Plan, and unemployment benefits. Such benefits can be managed and distributed without any local involvement. On the other hand, many programs affecting children and families have both cultural and community traditions that require the active participation of residents and community associations. One of Paul St Pierre's stories about ranching in northern BC describes such an example.

Without having time to consider and without having asked for anything the Namko Cattlemen's Association was informed that Namko was to become an Agricultural Redevelopment Area. This would be a major range improvement program, the draining of wet meadows and the irrigation of dry ones by damming creeks. They would be employed by government to do this work, on their own lands at staggering rates of pay.

The ranchers responded gravely, softly, even courteously but in manner totally unexpected. They voted an absolute and unequivocal rejection of the offer on the principle that governments knew bugger all about ranching and were best kept far away from where anything useful was to be done (St Pierre 1985:4).

The troubling issue of who is responsible for addressing social problems is addressed in a number of chapters and the final chapter offers a resolution.

What Do We Mean by 'Community'?

While we do not intend to explore exhaustively the many definitions of community—ninety-four, by Hillery's count (Hillery 1955)—it is useful to present the range and variety of definitions as well as our own. The case for defining community as a locality is argued by theorists such as Edwards and Jones.

> The term community refers in this textbook to such varied settlements as the plantation, the farm village, the town and the city. What is common to all of these and what is considered essential to the definition of community used here is that in each case there is a grouping of people who reside in a specific locality and who exercise some degree of local autonomy in organizing their social life in such a way that they can, from that locality base, satisfy the full range of their daily needs (Edwards and Jones 1976:12).

Edwards and Jones's assertion that a community has 'some degree of local autonomy' may overestimate the degree of control in many communities, given the limited resources available to local governments and community organizations (Edwards and Jones 1976:12).

These authors defend their interpretation by claiming that the four components of their definition, 'people, location in a geographic space, social interaction and common ties is in line with a majority of the ninety-four definitions of community analysed by Hillery' (Edwards and Jones 1976:13). However, the assumption that common ties bind some communities together does not take into account the divisions of class, race, and gender in other communities.

Criticism of the common ties theme has come from a variety of sources. Some have attacked the concept for its tendency to 'assume a classless society at the local level where people of all classes work towards a common goal' (Repo 1971:61). Repo's argument is supported by Warren, whose research showed that neighbourhoods differed in the dimensions of identity, interaction, and linkages with the larger community (Warren 1980). There are six types of neighbourhoods, but only three share common interests. Warren describes the remaining three as 'stepping stone', 'transitory', and 'anomic', and these neighbourhoods lack identity and cohesion (Warren 1980). Hence in at least some neighbourhoods, common ties do not distinguish community life.

More recently feminist scholars have pointed out that the traditional definitions of community are based on a conception that 'community is a local space which is small enough for people to interact with each other. These definitions have a further common characteristic. Until feminists redressed the balance they ignored gender. This is strange for women have always been present and active in the community' (Dominelli 1989:2).

A more expanded conception of community comes from Ross, who includes both geography and function in his definition of community, yet it is clear from the following quote that he favours the geographic aspect.

> 'Community' is used here also to include groups of people who share some common interest or function, such as welfare, agriculture, education, religion. These interests do not include everyone in the geographic community but only those individuals and groups who have a particular interest or function in common.
>
> Some of these functional communities, it should be said, fail to identify their true nature and confuse themselves with the geographic community (Ross with Lappin 1967:42).

The prominent scholar and practitioner, John McKnight, argues that the way to improve the human condition is not through social policies at the national level but by 'centering our lives in community' (McKnight 1987:54). Clearly for McKnight, even if common ties do not currently bind communities, they can and should be developed.

For Williams and many others, 'the term community seems to have a warmly persuasive tone to it, whether this describes an existing set of relationships or a preferred set' (Williams 1976:65–6). In her chapter in this book, White comments:

> . . . the word community is an emotionally powerful one, for it signifies, on the one hand, a sense of belonging and on the other, the local, immediate,

and familiar social environment. . . . Despite its conceptual promiscuity . . .
and the vagueness of the term, community groups seem to have maintained
an identifiable ethic that they practise, whether or not they articulate it.

Despite the disagreement over the definition of community, the term is
used in common parlance to refer to both geographic areas and functional or
special interest groups, and this dual interpretation is used throughout this
book. Our understanding of community is that it represents shared relationships and common interests among people (Wharf 1992). Indeed, we are not
so much interested in pursuing the definitional issue as we are in determining who controls the community development enterprise. Can community
development be an instrument of national policy? Should it be restricted to
ownership by communities? Or is some partnership arrangement possible?

On a more philosophical level, we are interested in examining the relationship between community and citizenship. For example, some communities may have few obvious common ties, but there is nevertheless some concern for the well-being of others in the neighbourhood from time to time,
for example, shovelling snow for an elderly neighbour. Citizenship may
include a commitment to others' well-being and, if so, how does it differ from
membership in a community?

What Is Community Development?

Just as community has a number of different interpretations, so does development. However, there is no disagreement about the importance of bringing about change in communities. Indeed, many will agree with Ross that
process is more important than outcomes. 'What community organization as
a conscious process is directed at achieving is not simply a new nursery, water
system or housing project, but more important, an increased capacity to
undertake other cooperative projects in the community' (Ross with Lappin
1967:49). Others maintain that process and outcome are equally important,
and that attention to one to the exclusion of the other damages both.

The widespread agreement about the significance of process breaks down
when it comes to *how* the process should unfold. Is the process based on
cooperation, confrontation, or on a rational, research-based approach to problem solving? Is the process based on all of these at different times, depending
on the circumstances and challenges? The earliest attempt to resolve this disagreement was proposed by Rothman in a conceptual framework that distinguished between approaches to bringing about change in communities
(Rothman 1974). This framework and some more recent ones are briefly dis-

cussed. The discussion will be particularly useful to readers who are not familiar with the literature.

Rothman's article, 'Three Models of Community Organization Practice',
has become a classic in community and social work literature. He established
twelve characteristics of community work and distinguished between locality development, social planning, and social action. These approaches have
opposing assumptions about the nature of society, particularly about the distribution of power. In addition, Rothman's framework connects the three
approaches to change strategies, agency auspices, and practitioner roles.

Locality development represents the attempts of definable localities, such
as neighbourhoods, to identify and resolve problems cooperatively. It is based
on an essentially benevolent understanding of society and the use of power.
The prevailing assumption is that those in power at municipal or provincial
levels will respond positively to proposals from neighbourhoods. Typical
agencies engaged in locality development are neighbourhood associations
and ratepayer associations.

Social action is rooted in a contrary assumption. It assumes that some
individuals, groups, and communities are oppressed, and that the oppression
is deliberate. Change will occur only with a redistribution of power. Given
oppressed communities' lack of power and resources, they must use the only
strategies available to them, such as demonstrations and tactics aimed at
embarrassing those in power. The late Saul Alinsky was the most famous practitioner of social action. He received national and international attention
because of his imaginative strategies aimed at embarrassing municipal politicians and local institutions. Perhaps the best known was his warning to
Chicago Mayor Richard Daly that the members of the Woodlawn
Association would occupy all the toilets in O'Hare airport until the mayor
agreed to meet with the association (Alinsky 1946). Needless to say, the
mayor quickly agreed to a meeting.

Social planning, which relies on research and a rational approach to problem solving, follows the tradition of urban planning and assumes that problems can be resolved by gathering information and presenting solutions based
on the facts. It represents the science of social problem solving, which takes a
neutral position to politics and power.

Rothman identified a fourth approach to social reform that combines
social planning and social action. However, his discussion of social reform is
brief and is not included as an approach to change in his framework. It is surprising that social reform was not accorded a more prominent place given
that it represents a pragmatic and often used approach that acknowledges the
need to confront power in bringing about change.

The identification of three approaches to practice does not suggest that they are separate and distinct from each other. A combination of these strategies is often necessary. Thus neighbourhood groups often begin by using the social planning approach when preparing briefs for city council or a provincial ministry. Gathering information and presenting it in an orderly fashion is the usual starting-point for all community work activities. However, if neighbourhood associations receive a negative response to an important issue, they may then engage in social action.

The Rothman framework has been criticized by a number of authors despite its contribution to clarity and the acknowledgement of the need to use a combination of strategies. Perlman and Gurin claim that the framework links models to strategies of change. Thus locality development is restricted to consensus approaches, whereas social action requires tactics of confrontation (Perlman and Gurin 1972). O'Brien carries the argument even further:

I believe the Rothman framework invites the creation of practice enclaves which reinforce the tendency to partialize and segment. Can anyone not be impressed with the frequent and often bitter exchanges among community practitioners as to which brand of practice is most relevant. All too often we have been treated to scenarios which pitted those advocating social action and locality development roles against those brandishing his own version of ultimate truth. My opinion is that any approach which contains the potential of reinforcing the already existing tendency toward fragmentation is undesirable (O'Brien 1979:234).

A second criticism of the Rothman framework comes from feminists, who are concerned that the discussion of assumptions about society and strategies ignores the role and contribution of women: 'Yet women have played a major role in sustaining community action through their domestic labour, their organizing skills, their commitment to community values and their capacity to innovate' (Dominelli 1989:2). In order to recognize women's role and the class- and race-based divisions within society, Dominelli has proposed six models of community work: (1) community care, (2) community organization, (3) community development, (4) class-based community action, (5) feminist community action, and (6) community action from a Black perspective (Dominelli 1989:7).

There is some agreement between these models and Rothman's approach, and indeed Dominelli notes her obligation to the earlier conceptual work. Thus community development is virtually identical to locality development, class-based community action bears a close resemblance to social action and community organization, and the organization of agencies towards some common goal has some similarities to social planning. The differences between the two frameworks are in Dominelli's creation of three new models: community care, feminist community action, and community action from a Black perspective. These are briefly described below.

Community care establishes relationships and resources to support and care for people, particularly those with special needs. The inclusion of this model is required from a feminist perspective since women are often the workers in and the organizers of paid and unpaid community care, which is an essential component and characteristic of a community that looks after its residents. However, it is often consumed by incessant demands and does not address the larger issues of inequality and injustice.

Feminist community action, which focuses on gender as a central organizing theme, has attended to both private troubles and public issues (Mills 1959).

> Feminist community action has transcended the boundaries of traditional community work by challenging fundamentally the nature of capitalist patriarchal social relations between men and women, women and the state, and adults and children through action which begins in the routine activities of daily life. By picking up on the specific needs of women as previously excluded in community work, feminists have developed theory and practice, new understandings of the concept 'community' and revealed the political nature of the social relations embedded with it (Dominelli 1989:12).

The final model in the Dominelli framework, community action from a Black perspective, recognizes the particular needs of Black people in Britain. It recognizes that attention to class, gender, and race is necessary in community work, and that the differences between these divisions require a separate model. The correspondence between community action from a Black perspective and action by First Nations peoples in Canada is addressed in the chapter by Absolon and Herbert.

A third framework for community development focuses on the activity of organizing and identifies seven forms (Miller, Rein, and Levitt 1990): (1) the organization of organizations, (2) grassroots organizing, (3) organizing around consumption, (4) the organization of identity, (5) advocacy organizing, (6) self-help and mutual aid organizing, and (7) mixed approaches.

Again there are some similarities between Miller, Rein, and Levitt's framework and other frameworks, particularly Dominelli's. The organization of organizations corresponds to her category of community organization, grassroots organizing to community development, and the organization of identity to class-based community action. The organization of identity is intended to include feminist and race approaches, although feminists and First Nations peoples will, with justification, argue against incorporating their approaches within a more inclusive category. However, Miller, Rein, and Levitt's framework ignores the important category of community care, but includes self-help and mutual aid, which Dominelli and Rothman omit.

The final approach to community development discussed here differs from the others because it does not represent a conceptualization of different ways of working but sets out a particular understanding of the process of community development. Paolo Freire and Gustavo Gutierrez are the best-known exponents of conscientization, an approach that is anchored in the belief that 'we shall not have our great leap forward . . . until the marginalized and exploited become the artisans of their own liberation—until their voice makes itself heard directly, without mediation, without interpreters' (Gutierrez 1983:65). For Freire and Gutierrez, the oppressed, not the professionals, are the agents of change. The professional's role is to provide information about oppression and strategies of change, but not to be the architect of change. These writers' insights have inspired many working in First Nations communities, as discussed in the chapter by Absolon and Herbert.

Frameworks are intended to clarify what defines 'community development', yet it is far from clear as to whether they have achieved this objective or simply added to the confusion. Community development is still used as a synonym for locality development and grassroots organizing, and in common usage it is even more inclusive and subsumes social action, community organization, and social reform. Some have argued that community work is the more appropriate umbrella term since it allows for a distinction between 'development', 'organization', 'action', and 'reform' (Dominelli 1989; Wharf 1979 and 1992).

Recognizing that the more elaborate the framework, the greater the chance of confusion, Perlman and Gurin argue that various labels are not particularly important, but that the essential tasks regardless of approach and label are to 'strengthen social provisions and to improve people's problem solving capacities' (Perlman and Gurin 1972:58). The issue of labels and frameworks is rejoined in the final chapter. However, the term development is offensive for many since it conveys the image of outsiders coming to develop an undeveloped (if not primitive) community: 'Community development has gained such a paternalistic reputation in the Third World that the term has been effectively abandoned in some circles in favour of community participation. Despite this, however, the term is still used in other contexts and so it will reappear in this and other chapters in spite of these understandable efforts to kill it off' (Mayo 1994:65).

The term development has also become problematic in an age of environmentalism as we struggle to deal with the exploitation and depletion of the world's natural resources. The struggle is more than an issue of conservation or of trying to find the alchemist's formula for sustainable development. Rather it is about what constitutes human progress. As Tester makes clear in his chapter, one of the environmental movement's contributions has been to challenge the previously unquestioned assumption that development equals progress. Two unresolved questions of enormous importance are 'What are we developing communities for?' and 'How optimistic can we be about our capacity to live peacefully and democratically when resources are scarce and inequitably distributed?' Our responses, based on the case-studies presented in this book, are in the final chapter.

We began writing this book with the assumption that as the most frequently used term, community development is also the most appropriate. Most of the chapter authors use community development, but organizing is the preferred term in Chapter 10 and in Chapter 11 development is replaced by action. While we agree with Mayo that it will be difficult (if not impossible) to strike development from our lexicon, we plead the case for the term organizing in the final chapter. Like Miller, Rein, and Levitt, we argue that organizing is the key activity and it can take place in a number of venues and around a number of issues and causes.

References

Alinsky, S.D.
   1946. *Reveille for Radicals*. New York: Random House.

Draper, J.A.
   1971. *Citizen Participation in Canada*. Toronto: New Press.

———.
   1977. *Community Development at the Crossroads*. Toronto: Canadian Association for Adult Education.

Dominelli, L.
   1989. *Women and Community Action*. Birmingham: Venture Press.

Edwards, A.D., and D.G. Jones.
   1976. *Community and Community Development*. The Hague: Mouton.

Freire, P.
   1985. *Pedagogy of the Oppressed*. New York: Continuum Publishing.

Gutierrez, G.

1983. *The Power of the Poor in History*. New York: Orbis Books.

Hillery, G.

1955. 'Definitions of Community: Areas of Agreement'. *Rural Sociology* XX, no. 2:118–19.

Keating, D.

1975. *The Power to Make It Happen*. Toronto: Green Tree Publishing.

Lagassé, J.

1967. 'A Review of Community Development Experiences in the World'. *Anthropologica* IX, no. 2:15–28.

Lindblom, C.

1979. 'Still Muddling, Not Yet Through'. *Public Administration Review* (Nov./Dec.):517–26.

Lloyd, A.J.

1967. *Community Development in Canada*. Ottawa: Canadian Research Centre for Anthropology, St Paul University.

McKnight, J.L.

1987. 'Regenerating Community'. *Social Policy* 17, no. 3:54–8.

———.

1992. 'Redefining Community'. *Social Policy* (Fall/Winter):56–62.

Mayo, M.

1994. *Communities and Caring*. New York: St Martin's Press.

Miller, S.M., M. Rein, and P. Levitt.

1990. 'Community Action in the United States'. *Community Development Journal* 25, no. 4:356–68.

Mills, C.W.

1959. *The Sociological Imagination*. New York: Oxford University Press.

Ng, R., G. Walker, and J. Muller, eds.

1990. *Community Organization and the Canadian State*. Toronto: Garamond Press.

O'Brien, D.

1979. 'Documentation of Social Need, a Critical Planning Activity: Variations on an Old Theme'. In *Community Work in Canada*, edited by B. Wharf, 225–40. Toronto: McClelland and Stewart.

Perlman, R., and A. Gurin.

1972. *Community Organization and Social Planning*. New York: John Wiley & Sons.

Repo, M.

1971. 'The Fallacy of Community Control'. In *Participatory Democracy for Canada*, edited by G. Hunnius, 55–97. Montreal: Black Rose Books.

Ross, M., with B. Lappin.
    1967. *Community Organization: Principles and Practice*. New York: Harper and Row.

Rothman, J.
    1974. 'Three Models of Community Organization Practice'. In *Strategies of Community Organization*, edited by F. Cox et al., 22–39. Itasca, Illinois: Peacock Press.

St Pierre, P.
    1985. *Stories of the Chilcotins*. Vancouver: Douglas & McIntyre.

Stinson, A., ed.
    1975. *Citizen Action: An Annotated Bibliography of Canadian Case Studies*. Ottawa: Community Planning Association of Canada.

Warren, D.
    1980. 'Support Systems in Different Types of Neighbourhoods'. In *Protecting Children from Abuse and Neglect*, edited by J. Garbarino and H. Stocking, 61–93. San Francisco: Jossey Bass.

Wharf, B., ed.
    1979. *Community Work in Canada*. Toronto: McClelland and Stewart.

————.
    1992. *Communities and Social Policy in Canada*. Toronto: McClelland and Stewart.

Williams, R.
    1976. *Keywords*. London: Croom Helms.

Chapter Two

The Beginning of Community Development in English-Speaking Canada

Jim Lotz

Canada has a long, strong tradition of community action and local initiative. Self-help and mutual aid ensured community survival in the pioneer years. Acadians came together to build *aboiteaux* (dikes or dams) to protect fertile farmland around the Bay of Fundy. They have continued this cooperative tradition in communities such as Chéticamp in Cape Breton. The first cooperative in Canada opened in 1861 in Stellarton, Nova Scotia, only seventeen years after the Rochdale pioneers started their venture in Toad Lane in England, the event usually taken as marking the beginning of the modern cooperative movement. In 1862 the Abbé Georges A. Belcourt, recognizing local farmers' need for credit, founded the Farmers' Bank in Rustico, Prince Edward Island. This first 'people's bank' in North America inspired Alphonse Desjardins, who launched the first *caisse populaire* in Quebec in 1900, to extend credit to poor people.

As urbanization and industrialization accelerated, affluent and middle-class women organized to meet needs that governments were unwilling or unable to tackle. The Young Women's Christian Association began in Saint John, New Brunswick, in 1870, and became a national body in 1895. In 1893 the National Council of Women was established to champion the cause of women and children. In 1895 Mabel Bell, wife of Alexander Graham Bell, and a handful of women came together in Baddeck, Nova Scotia, and voted to buy books and globes for the community's academy. This meeting marked the beginning of the Canadian Home and School Association. A group of women came together in Stoney Creek, Ontario, in 1897 to form the first Women's Institute, and every Canadian province had a branch by 1913. It was estimated that by 1912 one of every eight women in Canada belonged to a women's organization. These bodies focused on a wide range of concerns, from ensuring the safety of milk to pressing for women's suffrage. These indigenous initiatives are part of the legacy of community development in Canada.

The Lost Canadian Legacy of Community Development

As noted earlier, the first cooperative store in Canada opened in Stellarton, Nova Scotia, in 1861. At least ten others came into being in mining areas of the province over the next forty years. Mining communities in British Columbia and Alberta also started co-op stores in the 1880s and 1890s. The widely used slogan of the cooperative movement, 'Each for all and all for each', reflects the basic value of community development.

The cooperative idea spread rapidly in the early part of this century (MacPherson 1979). In the west and in Nova Scotia, co-op stores offered alternatives to the company stores and exploitive independent merchants. In Ontario and the Prairies, farmers joined together to buy their supplies more cheaply. In manufacturing cities, co-op stores arose as a reaction to inflation and received support from trade unions.

During the years of the Great Depression, Saskatchewan became a seedbed of ideas on effective ways to cooperate. In 1934–5, B.N. Arnason, the newly appointed commissioner of cooperatives, incorporated thirty-six new consumer associations in the province. Most of them developed around wheat-pool locals. Other groups developed community halls, community pastures, and public restrooms. In 1934 representatives of cooperatives met in Regina to create the Saskatchewan Conference of Co-operative Trading Associations. Over the next two decades, fieldmen from wheat-pools became the most zealous promoters of cooperative activities. The conference became the most important annual meeting in Canada for different types of collective ventures and a source of new ideas on how to start and run them.

Cooperative ventures in Canada in the first half of this century showed the necessity for government support. Strong and enlightened leadership, effective management, and ongoing coordination were vital for the survival of these self-help collective ventures.

Postwar community development in Canada was influenced by international developments, particularly that of British decolonization. One of the earliest definitions of community development was provided at a conference of African administrators in Cambridge, England. They defined community development as: 'A movement designed to promote better living for the whole community with the active participation and on the initiative of the whole community' (Central Office of Information 1966:6). This same definition, changed only slightly, appeared in *Social Progress Through Community Development*: 'Community development can be tentatively defined as a process designed to create conditions of economic and social progress for the whole community with its active participation and the fullest reliance upon the community's initiative' (United Nations 1955:1). This claim, with its emphasis on 'progress' and the involvement of the 'whole community', haunts practitioners still. While the British viewed their community development efforts as a prelude to decolonization, new and old nations leapt into community development after the Second World War, seeing the process as a way of bringing about change in measured ways, especially in rural and 'disadvantaged' areas. However, the rhetoric of community development in Canada and elsewhere never matched the reality when governments sought to involve people in the decisions that affected them. There was no argument about the goals of community development as outlined in the United Nations document, but how could they be best achieved?

Between 1919 and 1939, British influences on Canadian society waned, and those influences from the United States did not dominate life here then as they do today. These were the years of indigenous social and cultural innovation, when the Canadian Broadcasting Corporation was founded, and the Group of Seven began to paint our home and native land. Three university-based initiatives from the interwar years illustrate the forces, factors, personalities, and process that encouraged people in rural and urban areas to solve problems together that they could not tackle on their own. They also reflect the importance given to education as a means for enriching isolated lives and helping people mobilize for action on community issues. At the University of Alberta, the arts became a powerful tool for educational and community enrichment.

Drama and Development in Alberta

The University of Alberta came into being in 1890, three years after the province became a separate entity. Henry Marshall Tory, its first president, worked hard to take education to Albertans—to homes, churches, schools, and small and large communities—and faculty members gave public lectures on topics ranging from Shakespeare to sewage treatment. In 1912 the university appointed Edward Ottewell as secretary of the extension department. Ottewell established a travelling library to supplement the public lectures, as well as a publishing program focused on women's suffrage, consolidated schools, immigration, and other issues. In the winter of 1914–15, he distributed scripts for thirty plays suitable for amateur theatrical production. They proved popular among isolated people who were deprived of culture and entertainment, and provided a way for community groups to work together in creative ways.

In 1921 Ottewell hired E.A. (Ned) Corbett as his assistant. By the end of the decade, the extension department had its own radio station, a large collection of films and slides, travelling libraries, and other resources. Word of the University of Alberta's innovative approach reached New York. In 1931 Dr William Learned of the Carnegie Corporation visited the campus. The corporation had become the prime mover in adult education in North America, and Learned suggested that the university apply to the foundation for funds to expand its extension program in the fine arts. A grant of $10,000 allowed the extension department to hire Elizabeth Haynes to work with theatrical groups to improve their performances and skills. In 1933 Alberta had nearly 300 small drama groups. Scattered across the province and isolated from each other, the members had little opportunity for professional development or mutual learning, which Ned Corbett believed could be achieved through a summer school. With $1,000 from the Carnegie grant, Corbett drove to Banff, met with key community leaders, and secured their agreement to host the summer school. To everyone's surprise, 190 people enrolled.

In 1936 Corbett moved to Toronto and became the first director of the Canadian Association of Adult Education, handing over responsibility for the drama program to Elizabeth Haynes. She gathered a remarkable group of gifted people, but left the university when the Carnegie grant expired. In 1935 the summer venture became the Banff School of Fine Arts. It received a Carnegie grant of $4,000 in 1941 for programs in applied arts, and five years later acquired a site in Banff for a dollar a year. From these small beginnings came the Banff Centre, an international focus for culture and management training, a major employer in the community, and a contributor to all aspects of its economic and social life.

Beginnings on Prince Edward Island

John Tougas Croteau held a chair in economics and sociology, endowed by the Carnegie Corporation, at Prince of Wales College and St Dunstan's College from 1933 to 1946. Croteau played a central role in encouraging community development on the island. He taught a generation of students, helped to develop the province's library system, and set up study clubs through which local people could learn about the origins of their problems and what could be done to alleviate them. He also organized the Adult Education League, the Credit Union League, and the Co-operative Union on Prince Edward Island.

Although economic times were tough on the island, encouraging fishermen and farmers to cooperate to improve their incomes proved to be extremely difficult. Fishermen had a highly individualistic lifestyle, worked only 100 days in the year, and were reluctant to change their way of life. They poached lobsters out of season, and showed no interest in earning money from unused resources. Irish moss, thrown up along the island's coast, could have been marketed, but the fishermen neglected to take advantage of the opportunity. They took only the best parts of the cod they caught, and discarded the liver and other internal organs. Croteau turned to the provincial government to finance a way to recover oil from cod livers, which was another product in demand.

If the fishermen were reluctant to cooperate to make better use of local resources, other communities were enthusiastic. One built a cannery through cooperative efforts: 'The mistake here was that they did not grow anything to put into the cans' (Croteau 1951:43). Croteau knew that local merchants were at the mercy of forces over which they had no control. He saw the roots of the Maritimes' ills in 'the monopolistic and absentee control of finance and manufacturing, so prevalent in Canada' (Croteau 1951:23). Croteau also recognized that government had to play a role in local development and take vigorous action to stimulate and support residents to act on their own behalf.

The Antigonish Movement

While Croteau was organizing study groups, credit unions, cooperatives, and libraries on Prince Edward Island, similar moves were afoot in eastern Nova Scotia. The spiritual father of what came to be known as the Antigonish Movement was a small, zealous Catholic priest, Father Jimmy Tompkins. Born in a rural community in Cape Breton in 1870 and trained in Rome, he began to teach at St Francis Xavier University in 1902. As economic conditions in the region deteriorated and young people left the land to work in cities and factories, Father Jimmy pressured the university to engage in adult education. His involvement in what today would be called community development occurred as the Catholic Church struggled with new world forces. Industrialization, urbanization, secularization, nationalism, bureaucratic expansion, and the emergence of mass society and mass communications changed the way people in Europe saw themselves and their societies. On 15 May 1891 Pope Leo XIII issued his encyclical *Rerum Novarum*, asserting the rights of the family and of private property against the encroachments of the state. The pope stressed that 'labour is not a commodity' and that workers should receive their just rewards. He also approved of legislation that encouraged the formation of trade unions and cooperative ventures.

This encyclical gave Catholics a mandate for action. Eastern Nova Scotia had been settled by Scottish Catholics, and their leaders and priests began to pressure St Francis Xavier University to meet their needs. An old economy slowly vanished as subsistence living gave way to a market-driven society. Farmers found themselves working too hard for too little. Many left the land for wage employment in the coal mines, steel mills, and factories in Pictou County, industrial Cape Breton, and elsewhere. Activist priests, such as 'Little Doc' Hugh MacPherson, organized buying clubs and other collective ventures through which farmers bought what they needed and sold what they produced. Through collective action, they saved money and increased their incomes.

These and similar initiatives were scattered, individualistic ones with limited impact. Father Tompkins had a vision of the university as an engine of change in the region, putting its resources at the disposal of small communities, not merely educating the fortunate few. In 1921 he wrote a pamphlet, 'Knowledge for the People', which surveyed the state of adult education in North America and Britain, and called on St Francis Xavier University to develop a cadre of enablers, facilitators, and animators to link the university's resources with community needs. In the same year, the university made a small beginning in doing this, inviting fishermen and farmers to the campus for courses at the People's School. Father Tompkins strongly supported the amalgamation of universities in the Maritimes, a cause that made him unpopular with the academic and clerical hierarchy. The Carnegie Corporation offered to fund a scheme whereby the small, religiously based colleges would send students to Dalhousie University in Halifax. Opposition came from those who thought the tender minds of the young would be endangered by life in the big city and a secular institution. Because of his promotion of amalgamation, Father Tompkins was sent into exile to the village of Canso as a parish priest.

In Canso Father Tompkins promoted adult education as a way of giving poor and dependent fishermen control over their lives. If they understood the roots of their problems, then they could start solving them. For four and a half years, Father Tompkins pushed and prodded everyone with whom he spoke into doing something to alleviate the abysmal conditions under which the fishermen lived. On 1 July 1927 fishermen at Canso came ashore, complaining that they had little to celebrate on the sixtieth anniversary of Confederation. Favourable weather conditions in the previous winter had resulted in the landing of large quantities of fish, glutting the markets and lowering prices. Large steam trawlers competed for the catch with the small inshore fishermen. The Canso fishermen organized a meeting. Father Tompkins generated media coverage of his parish's plight, and priests elsewhere pressured the federal government to act. The government responded by establishing the Royal Commission on the Fisheries of the Maritime Provinces and the Magdalen Islands (the MacLean Commission) on 7 October 1927. The commission reported on 4 May 1928, painting a grim picture of empty harbours, idle boats, and inshore fishermen barely earning a living at a hard trade while beam trawlers overfished the Atlantic waters.

As McKay has pointed out, only slightly more than 8 per cent of the full- and part-time waged workforce in the 1920s was employed in the fishing industry: 'The typical Nova Scotian adult was more likely to be a coal miner or an urban wage earner than one of the fisherfolk' (McKay 1994:242). However, the plight of the fishermen and their families generated a social movement that became internationally famous.

The Antigonish Movement came to fruition as a result of the work of Father Moses Michael Coady, its charismatic leader and cousin of Father Tompkins. In 1928 St Francis Xavier University established an extension department under Coady's direction. The MacLean Commission had recommended cooperatives as a way for fishermen to gain more control over their economic destiny. The federal government asked Coady to organize them. An impressive speaker, with the knack of making complex issues understandable to ordinary listeners, the priest emphasized one constant theme: adult education through economic cooperation. The genius of the Antigonish Movement was in how its leaders combined adult education methods with the formation of credit unions and cooperatives. On 26 June 1930 Coady brought together 208 representatives of fishermen's groups to create the United Maritime Fishermen, an industry cooperative.

At the extension department, he gathered a remarkable group to help people in rural communities set up study clubs as the first step in establishing credit unions and cooperatives. Among them were many gifted women and a number of able and dedicated parish priests. They formed a network to encourage action in eastern Nova Scotia, using the university as a base. By the end of 1931, 173 study clubs had been established, most of them in rural Scottish Catholic parishes. By the time Coady's book, *Masters of Their Own Destiny*, was published in 1939, the movement had established 342 credit unions and 162 other forms of cooperative organization. The Antigonish Movement's approach was summarized in four imperatives: Listen! Study! Discuss! Act!

The Antigonish Movement reached its peak just as the Second World War broke out, with 19,600 people studying self-help in 2,265 groups in the Maritimes. The war stripped away the movement's leadership. In the years of affluence after 1945, cooperatives and credit unions grew larger and increasingly bureaucratized. They became more and more businesslike, losing the fire and enthusiasm of the early days. Adult education ceased to be an integral part of cooperative and credit union activity.

The Rediscovery of Community Development

In the postwar world, governments encouraged community development. In 1952 the Saskatchewan government launched the Royal Commission on Agriculture, which reported in 1956. In the following year, the commission director, William Baker, became director of the Centre for Community Studies at the University of Saskatchewan. The centre received provincial government funding and had a threefold mandate: to study the development of Saskatchewan communities, to serve organizations interested in community development, and to offer in-service training for professionals in the field. The centre suffered from a built-in organizational tension between its research activities and its outreach program to stimulate community action. Nevertheless, it performed valuable work in the early years on problems in rural municipalities and villages.

But the centre's style of action research disturbed the university. In 1964 when the government changed, it lost its provincial subsidy and survived for a while on federal contracts. It moved off the university campus in 1965, and slowly faded out of existence. As one commentator put it, the concept of community development had become a euphemism for 'doing little things in little places' (Davis 1968:63). Significant social change involves lasting changes in economic, social, and political structures, and in the role patterns and relationships between and within them. Community development looks attractive to governments because it costs little and seems like an effective way of stimulating self-help in tackling local problems: 'It was difficult for the Institute's community developers to face up to the fact that substantial local development would mean a large scale investment—inevitably from outside sources—either in the area's underdeveloped resources, or else in the relocation and rehabilitation of underemployed local populations' (Davis 1968:63).

Around the same time, Manitoba's program of community development had begun to run out of steam after a promising beginning. In March 1956 the Manitoba legislature asked the Department of Agriculture and Immigration to carry out a study of the Indian and Métis peoples in the province. Members of the legislature expressed anxiety, regret, and guilt about their plight. The three-volume report that appeared in 1959 detailed the extent of poverty and despair among Native peoples, and gave examples of racism and discrimination against them.

The report recommended a community development program 'to help people of Indian ancestry to solve their own problems', adding that it 'might be judged too idealistic were it not that there are already such programs operating successfully in different parts of the world' (Department of Agriculture and Immigration 1959:109). Community development workers would win the confidence of local people, help them identify their needs, prepare them for action, assist them in using local resources, coordinate the work of other government services, identify the people's readiness for action, and serve as bridges between Native and White community members.

The Manitoba government set up the Community Development Branch in the Department of Welfare. Jean Lagassé, a Métis social worker who had headed the study of Indian and Métis peoples in the province, became director of the branch. His concept of community development encompassed these beliefs:

1.   That all people, no matter how unambitious they may appear, have a desire to better themselves.
2.   The difficulties preventing the fulfilment of people's needs are too great for the resources which they have.
3.   All groups can do something to help themselves when given an opportunity to do so on their own terms.
4.   In order to achieve lasting change it is necessary to influence simultaneously various aspects of human behaviour (Lagassé 1961–2:234).

Lagassé saw community development workers as facilitators, enablers, organizers, animators, first-aid technicians, and mediators who would help residents identify problems, plan ways of solving them, and carry out the solutions. He recognized that many communities were divided, with expatriates and transient Whites holding power and Native peoples living in misery and powerlessness. The community development workers would encourage cooperation between all residents. The program attracted an exceptional group of young, idealistic, and enthusiastic university graduates and people experienced in working with individuals and groups. One who arrived on a reserve was asked what he would do for its residents. He replied, 'I'm here to find out what you can do for yourselves.'

The program owed much of its credibility to its director, who was equally at home on Native reserves and in the corridors of power. When Lagassé left this position in 1963, the program began to founder. Too much depended on the abilities and personal characteristics of scattered individuals seeking gradual change in isolated communities.

When first established, the Community Development Branch had a high degree of autonomy and strong support from the deputy minister of the Department of Welfare, but the workers were slowly absorbed into the bureaucracy. They had to report to regional directors of welfare instead of to the director of community development. In an attempt to spread the philosophy of community development throughout the Department of Welfare, the director and his staff became The Consulting Group. They had 'no authority to hire or fire, or even to visit community-development workers without . . . first [securing permission from] the regional welfare director' (Deveau and Deveau 1971:95). By 1968 the program had faded away and lost committed and skilled people. In 1970 The Consulting Group was disbanded.

Lessons Learned

In studying the various ventures in adult education, community development, and community action that took place in Canada from the 1920s to the 1960s, it is apparent that most followed the usual trajectory of social movements. They began with high hopes and much enthusiasm about generating social change and improving the lives of marginalized people and communities. Led by competent and charismatic people, these initiatives attracted a band of faithful followers who worked hard at encouraging self-help and local enterprise. Slowly but surely, the processes of bureaucratization crept in as the initial successes led to more and more demands on the community development staff.

The vagueness of the concept of community development encouraged a wide variety of personal styles of action, some of which became threatening to the established political and bureaucratic structures. Community development programs in government were absorbed, marginalized, or abolished. After all, if communities could solve their own problems, why did they need civil servants and politicians to attend to their needs? And governments are mainly concerned with encouraging stability in society, whereas community development questions the existing structures of power and works to make them more open, accessible, and accountable. To some people, involvement in community development is part of their lifelong learning process. To others, it is an obsession. For example, community development workers in Manitoba tried to involve First Nations peoples in tackling local problems. Is it mere coincidence that the Natives in Manitoba are the first group to negotiate self-government with Ottawa as they were doing in 1995? Did the early start in community development influence this move?

Community development has too often been seen simply as a process or an approach for dealing with the problems of marginalized and disadvantaged groups and people. Seldom is it recognized as a way of coping with the central government's failure to understand ordinary people's needs and aspirations and institute the structural changes required to meet them. In the past, the problems of disadvantaged people were seen as being 'out there', among 'others', not in the policies devised in centres of power, based on a limited understanding of how people outside them live and work. Community development is about changing relationships between the governors and the governed, national ideals and local realities, technology and humanity. It takes diverse forms in different places and depends on inspired leadership, a factor not susceptible to policy prescriptions.

Many of the successful community development ventures in the past were distinguished by charismatic leaders. At the University of Alberta, Ottewell had a missionary vision of how people's lives could be changed through adult education. Corbett followed the path he blazed, then handed over his responsibilities to Haynes, who had special knowledge, skills, and experience in theatre. She provided the detailed direction necessary for drama groups to improve their performances. The University of Alberta's trinity of community innovators all came from outside the province, and focused on culture as a way of helping people to cope with change and uncertainty.

The three leaders of the Antigonish Movement were all Nova Scotians. Tompkins offered people a vision of a better life through learning and collective action. Coady's charismatic presence swayed audiences and convinced people of the rightness of the cooperative way. A.B. MacDonald, Coady's right-hand man, did the hard, detailed work of establishing credit unions and cooperatives. These leaders put organization and economic matters at the top of their priorities. Cultural development would come later when communities had a stable economic base and their residents a steady income and control over their own destinies. 'Beans before Brahms' and 'Spinach before Spinoza', counselled Coady.

It is extremely difficult to analyse and identify all the forces and factors that make for success in community development. The depression of the 1930s resulted in men and women in eastern Nova Scotia and Prince Edward Island staying home rather than seeking jobs elsewhere. Thus the organizers of credit unions and cooperatives had a pool of talented people on which to draw. In turn, these new ventures offered jobs, career opportunities, and economic and social structures through which able people could earn a living and use their abilities for their own benefit and that of their communities. The Antigonish Movement encouraged local people to seek the source of their discontents by understanding how their world was changing. Participants learned to think globally and act locally, but none of these social movements in the 1920s involved large numbers of people, nor did they do much to change the prevailing political cultures. The depression spawned two radical movements, on the left and the right, in the Canadian west. The Co-operative Commonwealth Federation and Social Credit parties sought to bring about large-scale and lasting change in very different ways. One criticism levelled at community development ventures is that they merely placate people and divert them from pressuring the government and the private sector to act more effectively in creating a good society.

Community development is about redistributing power and resources. It is a political process, not simply a tool or technique for calming people or rubbing raw the sores of discontent. The pioneers in the field did not have to cope with the excesses of the media, whose members are eternally on the prowl for indications of radical change and social discontent. The concept of 'liminality' proposed by Turner (1966) can be useful in understanding community development. The process becomes popular when crises affect individuals, communities, and governments who find the existing ways of dealing with them no longer effective. Governments dealing with marginalized people, communities facing outside intervention, and people who have lost their jobs enter a liminal state. They reach certain limits (the root word is the Latin *līměs*) and seek frantically for new ways to solve their problems and resolve their dilemmas.

Turner points out that all societies contain elements of 'structure' and 'antistructure'. Structure holds people together through laws, organizations, customs, and rituals, rewarding those who conform and punishing those who do not. 'Antistructure' operates informally, bringing people together in common quests, striving to resolve opposites and contradictions in society. It is spontaneous, seemingly unorganized, cutting across established boundaries to link together very diverse people in new (if sometimes ephemeral) quests and communities. Between structure and antistructure lies liminal space where the sacred and the secular, the rational and the intuitive, common sense and the mystical meet and mingle, sometimes in conflict as opposites, at other times generating new symbioses. Thus the community development process can encourage the revitalization of existing structures, or assist in the creation of new ones more suited to the needs of those involved and of the larger society. In its paradoxical way, community development strives to stabilize society and encourage innovation and change in human relationships. The process is fraught with ambiguity as it seeks to avoid the perils of bureaucracy and anarchy to develop structures and organizational forms that help communities to understand the problems they face and to deal with them effectively. As the Antigonish Movement demonstrated, it is possible to devise ways of encouraging individual, organizational, and community development in marginal areas through the involvement of skilled leaders, who place their services at the disposal of those seeking a better life.

The ethical and moral dimensions of community development are often overlooked in the search for quick answers to complex problems. Sim wrote one of the few papers on the ethics of intervention, which lies at the root of the community development process:

> Intervention that is defensible on ethical grounds must always be paradoxical. One acts for others only to the point of initiating a symbolic gesture of genuine concern and respect. This is the first overture. There is further action if, and only if the other responds positively. The response is much more than consent as we usually think of consent. After this accepting response, a spiral of action, reaction and interaction can result between the two. In the final act of love, who is to say who [is] the helper and who the helped? Then the notion of help is finally irrelevant (Sim 1969:14).

Despite our divisions, Canada remains a community of memory, of shared dreams and achievements. We are bound together by a common concern for creating a better, more open, more democratic society than can be found elsewhere. There is idealism aplenty in Canada, but it has to be linked to the harsh realities of a vast nation seeking to break the various colonialisms and paternalism that afflict Canadians.

Recovering the authentic history of community development in this country takes on added urgency as forces from outside our boundaries and new ideas on solving our problems affect the way we view ourselves and our collective future. This country has had a large number of community development programs and projects that worked well, as well as others that failed for a variety of reasons. By examining and understanding them, we can perhaps map ways into the future that strengthen the sense of national, regional, and local integrity, identity, and pride that the community development process seeks to encourage.

References

Central Office of Information.
    1966. *Community Development*. London: COI.

Coady, M.M.
    1939. *Masters of Their Own Destiny: The Story of the Antigonish Movement of Adult Education through Economic Cooperation*. New York and London: Harper and Brothers.

Croteau, J.T.
    1951. *Cradled in the Waves*. Toronto: Ryerson Press.

Davis, A.
    1968. 'A Prairie Dust Devil: The Rise and Decline of a Research Institution'. *Human Organization* 27, no. 1:56–63.

Department of Agriculture and Immigration.
    1959. *A Study of the Population of Indian Ancestry Living in Manitoba*. Winnipeg: Department of Agriculture and Immigration.

Deveau, B., and K. Deveau.
    1971. 'The Enemies within Community Development'. In *Citizen Participation: Canada*, edited by J. Draper, 93–105. Toronto: New Press.

Lagassé, J.
    1961–2. 'Community Development in Manitoba'. *Human Organization* 20, no. 4: 232–7.

McKay, I.
    1994. *The Quest of the Folk: Antimodernism and Cultural Selection in Nova Scotia*. Montreal and Kingston: McGill-Queen's University Press.

MacPherson, I.
    1979. *Each for All: A History of the Co-operative Movement in English Canada, 1900–1945*. Toronto: The Macmillan Company.

Sim, R.A.
    1969. 'Intervention: The Ethics of Helping Others' (mimeo). Ottawa: Special Planning Secretariat of the Privy Council.

Turner, V.W.
    1966. *The Ritual Process: Structure and Anti-Structure*. Chicago: Aldine.

United Nations.
    1955. *Social Progress through Community Development*. New York: United Nations.

Chapter Three

The History of Community Development in Quebec

Jean Panet-Raymond and Robert Mayer

Introduction

This brief history of community development is intimately linked to the political, economic, social, and cultural history, and is an integral part of Quebec's evolution. It is therefore important to understand Quebec's history in order to understand the evolution of community development. Though this chapter deals with the last thirty years, it is important to emphasize that community development existed before the 1960s. It did not receive much recognition, nor has it been sufficiently documented, but it is closely intertwined with the history of the Church, political parties, labour unions, the women's movement, and the local development of rural communities since the 1930s. Beyond the progressive ideologies that inspired community development, there are also organizational lessons to be learned from the strategies and tactics used in bringing about social and political change based on values of social justice, democracy, and community.

This chapter deals with the recent history from the early 1960s up to the present. We divide this history into a number of 'natural' or relevant periods that are defined by significant events or social changes. The selection of such events is based on our judgement call. The first period is the decade from 1960 to 1968, which corresponds to the beginnings of the Quiet Revolution[1] in Quebec. The year 1968 was one of questioning directions, not only in community development but also in postsecondary education when demonstrations, occupations, and bombs marked the end of the Quiet Revolution. Another key year in Quebec's history was 1970, which was marked by bombings, kidnappings, the War Measures Act, and Canadian troops' occupation of Quebec during the October Crisis. From a community development perspective, the 1980s started in 1983 and signalled a change from radical and very militant (Marxist-Leninist) organizing to the beginning of consensual, local community development and partnership between community groups and the state. Finally, the last period began in 1991 with the implementation of the Health and Social Services Act, which defines community organizations and recognizes them as partners of the state.

If we were to label these different periods with the terms used at that time, we could say that the 1960s saw the birth of 'social animation' and citizens' committees, while the 1970s were marked by some radical community organizing. The 1980s saw the emergence of service-oriented community development and community groups. The 1990s mark economic and social community development with community and voluntary organizations searching for a holistic and concerted partnership that links individuals and communities, private and public interests. Through this historical background, we identify the evolution of practice, strategies, approaches, and the people involved while outlining the issues and lessons that mark each period.

Social Animation and Citizens' Committees in the 1960s

Community development as we know it today appeared in the midst of a broad transformation of Quebec society. The Quiet Revolution (1960–6) saw the emergence of a modern Quebec and with it a certain democratization of political institutions and services, such as education, health, social services, and housing, which were supported by federal funding and policies. The state began to increase its influence in economic, social, and cultural spheres. Urban renewal and demolition of old buildings brought about citizens' committees demanding decent housing and the right to be consulted on the construction of public low-income housing in urban cores. Health became an issue when reports revealed that a large segment of the population did not have access to adequate services, or that existing services were too expensive (Boucher 1961; Conseil du bien-être du Québec 1965). Demands for parks and recreation centres came from urban neighbourhoods where children had nowhere to play. Some consumer advocacy groups (Association coopérative d'économie familiale/Cooperative Family Budget Association) developed with the help of labour unions to fight credit companies and loan sharks that weakened union members during strikes for better working conditions. Thus unions got involved in the 'second front' (the term first appeared in a report from the president of the Confederation of National Trade Unions) for improved living conditions in order to complement the 'first front' for better working conditions (Pépin 1968).

The Union générale des étudiants du Québec, created after a split within the Canadian Union of Students in 1964, developed the Travailleurs étudiants du Québec, which was inspired by the Company of Young Canadians (CYC), while the Chantiers étudiants was inspired by the French Abbé Pierre. The creation of a new, well-educated petit bourgeois in the social services and a growing desire for citizen participation led to the development of private agencies funded by the Church and the United Way, supporting community development initiatives. The first experiences of community development, called social animation, started in urban inner cities and rural areas in this context.

A new definition of social practitioners appeared: *animateur social* or social animator. Various authors (Blondin 1965; Doray 1967; Doré 1992; Robert 1971) have tried to define social animation and the roles of social animators. They generally agree that social animation aims to bring order and purpose to community action, and that the social animator's role is to inform, stimulate participation, and provide a rational planning approach. An animator helps a group to arrive at a coherent and autonomous decision concerning the issues to address.

At this point, it is useful to understand the various influences that made and defined social animation in the mid-1960s. There was a strong influence of a progressive socialist Christian streak from France (notably from Abbé Pierre, who worked and still works with the homeless) and Latin America (best exemplified by Paulo Freire and the conscientization approach). There was also a certain influence from the civil rights movement in the United States and the tactics of Saul Alinsky (Doucet and Favreau 1991). (The work of Freire and Alinsky is briefly described in Chapter 1.)

Social Animation in Inner Cities

Social animation is associated mostly with the old urban cores of Montreal and Quebec City, though it also developed in small towns and rural areas such as the Gaspé Peninsula. The cities underwent major transformations and speculation: urban renewal, construction of low-income public housing, private offices, residential towers, and the development of new institutional and commercial sectors in old industrial neighbourhoods in Montreal and in the *basse ville* of Quebec City. These changes resulted in a migration of the working class and the deterioration of social networks, and thereby provided a fertile ground for organizing. It explains why social animation developed in these neighbourhoods and involved women and unemployed men in living conditions and the loss of work. With the help of social animators and financial assistance from the Church and the United Way, tenants, consumers, and the unemployed organized themselves into committees. They advocated for rights to housing, work, health, leisure, and recreational facilities, especially for children and families. Their demands were founded on a concept of community development rooted in a sense of democracy and equal opportunity for all marginalized people. It was therefore supported, to a certain extent, by church and state in a modern democratic society where pressure groups are accepted within certain legal and political boundaries.

The first organizing took place in the St-Henri area of Montreal, an old, deteriorating working-class neighbourhood. It was initiated in 1963 by the Conseil des oeuvres de Montréal (COM), funded by what was to become Centraide (United Way). COM created parents' associations and demanded a school, trees in parks, children's play groups, and an inventory of sports and recreation facilities in the area, etc. It wanted to become a training ground for leaders and to be recognized as the people's representative in dealing with the city. It soon ran into differences with the city's Department of Recreation and concentrated on organizing children's play groups in parks. The city never really recognized the legitimacy of the COM as the people's representative, nor its ability to organize activities in municipal parks.

Probably the best example of action in 1965 was centred on the issue of urban renewal. COM declared that it wanted to be involved in decisions concerning its neighbourhood. It organized information meetings with government officials and local residents, and pressured local authorities to involve COM in decisions regarding areas targeted for renewal, proposed housing, recreation facilities, and the rent scale, which to this day is still an issue.

These committees inspired others in the neighbouring Pointe St-Charles to advocate for schools, parks, and better housing. This type of organizing was accompanied by support for a new leadership from the grassroots to confront the traditional élites. The social animators were instrumental in bringing this new leadership to the fore and nurturing it.

With the renewal program came expropriations and evictions, and the mood became more and more confrontational as residents felt they were the victims of a vast clean-up when Montreal hosted Expo 67. Local newspapers were created, and the problems were made public in order to put more pressure on the city. Demonstrations were organized in front of city hall (Lesemann and Thiénot 1972).

In the meantime, a similar movement was happening elsewhere in old working-class areas of the city, in other towns around Montreal and in the *basse ville* of Quebec City. The issues were mostly the same: schools, parks, housing, and lack of services for the poor. One noteworthy project was the Urban Social Redevelopment Project (1964–9), created by the University Settlement in the downtown area, referred to as the *Centre ville de Montréal*.

The Settlement activity is significant by virtue of the fact that it is the first English agency that has attempted to do organizing in an Alinsky oriented way and therefore has moved away from the Community Development style, characteristic of the COM. . . . The French groups were organized along parish lines. English groups, working out of the Settlement became welfare rights groups, allying with . . . the Greater Montreal Anti-Poverty Coordinating Committee, a food co-op and the Milton Park and anti-Concordia group (Benello 1972:474–5).

Soon a number of groups sprang up in these parishes and regrouped into neighbourhood federations and even larger bodies. They also started to address the lack of health services.

Five years of widespread organizing culminated in a meeting of more than 200 representatives from twenty-two groups from all over Quebec, but mostly from Montreal. The representatives' conclusion at the end of the 19 May 1968 meeting was emphatic: 'We feel that the time has come to change the system of government that we have. . . . We all face the same fundamental problems; we must overcome isolation and localism; government must become our government; we have no choice but to enter political action' (Quiron 1975:68). We will address the issues and models discussed at that historic meeting after describing what happened in more rural areas.

Social Animation in Rural Areas

There were a number of experiences in rural areas ranging from opposition to mine closures and demands for more government involvement in economic development in areas of high unemployment, but the most noteworthy development was in the Gaspé Peninsula, a rural and isolated area of Quebec. Following an agreement in 1963 between the federal and provincial governments, the Bureau d'aménagement de l'est du Québec (BAEQ) was created. The objective was to raise the standard of living. Developed by technocrats and researchers, the plan was to modernize socio-economic structures while increasing people's skills with training. This was to be supported by a massive effort in popular education and social and cultural animation to involve the local population in the planning process. The plan called for citizen participation in transforming a backward rural culture into a modern urban world. Planning and participation were identified as the path to economic growth and development, but in reality the plan meant closing small parishes and villages and relocating people to medium-size cities along the shores of the St Lawrence. In many ways, it resembled urban renewal in some inner-city neighbourhoods.

Citizens took part in gathering information on resources, skills, traditions, etc., with the help of researchers and social animators. The consultation process included many meetings in parish halls and schools. Finally, citizens participated in the decision-making process concerning objectives and the means of development (Quiron 1975:63–4).

For the technocrats designing the project, the first goal of organizing is promoting dialogue and cooperation for development, planning, and administration. A second goal is to gather objective data on a social problem with the assistance of a group. The professional animator is not personally involved as an activist in the process, and questions existing values, attitudes, and collective conscience (Quiron 1975:65). Social animation was deemed a tool of integration or co-optation in a citizen participation process in which the 'dice' were loaded and where the experts took over (Lesemann and Thiénot 1972). It was a most striking example of a top-down planning process disguised as a bottom-up process (Morency 1966).

Issues and Models

Rothman's framework (introduced in Chapter 1) inspired a number of authors and was taught at the School of Social Work at the Université de Montréal in the early 1970s (Quiron 1972). However, some analysts (Lesemann 1975) did not agree with Rothman and defined the early citizens' committees as traditional pressure groups, while the role of social animators was to integrate these groups into an accepted form of activity in a democratic and liberal society.

Various models of animation were identified (Robert 1971): adaptation animation, pressure animation, and conflict animation. Depending on the model chosen, a social animator might become more an agent of political change, helping people build democratic organizations, than an agent of social integration, helping to improve community resources. The former role could be associated with the work of the 'the New Left' in the US, while the latter would correspond to social planning. Using this continuum, one could place the tenants' associations of St-Henri at the conflict end and the BAEQ at the adaptation end. Even though both approaches emphasize education and collective changes, it is obvious that there is a difference in their nature and scope, which stems from the difference in constituencies. The professionals of the BAEQ tried to organize all residents and encouraged cooperation between citizens' groups and élites, whereas the animators focused on the grassroots, the poor, and the working class, and criticized the local élite for failing to address and resolve the issues of housing, education, and unemployment.

Quiron refers to the BAEQ as an integrative and consensual approach and the urban citizens' committees as integrative and conflictual (Quiron 1975:62).

Another influential author in Quebec (Médard 1969) identified two approaches (consensual and conflictual) as ways to understand citizens' committees. Consensual organization was based on three principles: (1) the community was the primary field for action, (2) emphasis was on participation and self-help, (3) and all interventions are initiated by needs. Of course the premise was that those who experience social problems are the best ones to talk about these problems and find appropriate solutions. According to the consensual approach, participation should develop cooperation rather than conflict, which is considered a waste of energy. By the end of the 1960s many others, such as Alinsky (1971), criticized the consensual approach as co-opting oppressed people. The consensus approach does not consider the unequal distribution of resources and power in society (Deshaies and Simard 1971). The conflict approach was based on three fundamental principles: (1) self-interest is the main motivation for people to act, (2) there is power in numbers and organization, and, finally, (3) conflict promotes ideas and innovations.

Citizens' committees in Quebec were based on both approaches, emphasizing conflict at some times and cooperation at other times, often when pressure tactics and mobilization were necessary. Certain critics (Collin and Godbout 1977; McGraw 1978) argue that social animators converted citizens' committees to their own class self-interests by using methods that favoured integration and acceptable forms of conflict (petitions, letters, and rallies) rather than more violent forms (bombs, fires, and kidnappings), such as those used by the Front de libération du Québec. However, these critics agree that the citizens' committees of the 1960s represented a philosophy based on local participatory democracy, a redefinition of social problems with a collective perspective that criticized the casework approach. These committees also redefined the rapport between state and civil society by organizing disenfranchised people. They developed a conflictual rapport that was quite different from the social and labour movements inspired by the Catholic Church in the 1930s and 1940s. New forms of organizations and community work emerged from that dynamic. This also contributed to the definition of the welfare state that was to develop in the 1970s.

From Radicalization to Demobilization (1969–1982)

As noted earlier, the meeting held in Montreal in 1968 concluded that community development should be more political. This partially explains why a social democratic party like the Parti Québécois, elected in 1976, got little support from popular groups (as citizens' committees came to be known) and unions who had adopted a socialist ideology. The year 1976 marked the election of the PQ as well as the stronger presence of Marxist-Leninist groups, such as In Struggle (founded in 1973) and the Communist League (founded in 1975), which became the Workers Communist Party in 1978. These groups were founded by former social animators and progressive militants who had experienced the limits of pressure group tactics and corporate unionism. The strong military intervention and arrest of more than 500 militants without warrants during the October Crisis in 1970 contributed to the perception of the state as a repressive class apparatus. The Marxist-Leninist groups were also influenced by the writings of Lenin, Mao Zedong, and Third World liberation movements.

This radicalization was accompanied by political unrest in 1970 and an expansion of Quebec's welfare state through the establishment of health insurance and the Ministry of Social Affairs. The Commission of Inquiry on Health and Social Services (1967–71), headed by Claude Castonguay, recommended vast changes in the organization of services and the nature of professional practice. The commission created the modern health care and social services that are now being dismantled in the 1990s. It advocated a public system that was to be decentralized and involve service users on the boards of hospitals, nursing homes, social service centres, and the new Centres locaux de services communautaires (local community service centres or CLSCs). The CLSCs are health and social service centres established throughout Quebec and serve populations of about 20,000 to 70,000, depending on the urban or rural setting. Their mandate includes prevention and community development. By 1995 over 350 community development workers were employed in CLSCs.

These organizations had a major impact on community development in Quebec and still do (Hurtubise 1989). In 1970 and 1971 massive investment through provincial and federal agreements resulted in jobs (Local Initiatives Program) that helped develop a number of popular groups, many of which did not last beyond government subsidies. The provincial government gave in to many demands from the labour and social movements, which resulted in the Consumer Protection Act in 1972, a public network of legal aid centres in 1973, a rental board, construction of low-income housing, and of course CLSCs, which were inspired by the popular health clinics and community centres set up in the late 1960s and early 1970s. Do these accomplishments represent victories or co-optation to quell social unrest? Critics (Collin and Godbout 1977; Lesemann 1979; McGraw 1978) charge that the emphasis on community participation legitimizes the power of a new élite.

Citizens' committees focused on the working class and the poor rather than a geographic area, and continued to grow in numbers and in a variety of new fields: women's rights, gay rights, print and electronic community media, food cooperatives, and public housing. They also continued to criticize the reforms and public services they helped to create. Community organizers working out of CLSCs were instrumental in developing these new groups. Of course, the public services network, through its participatory structure, did not result in the kind of democratic citizen participation that had been originally demanded. Criticism came especially from working-class citizens elected to CLSC boards that had a bureaucratic style of management.

With the arrival of the PQ in 1976, the extent of state intervention grew, as did the radicalization of certain groups. Conflicts arose within many organizations in the search for a progressive society based on real participatory democracy, including citizen control of services and government. Many splits occurred at a local and provincial level within organizations in the second half of the 1970s. Marxist-Leninists took over control of many popular groups and local unions in the pursuit of their political goals, which caused many groups to shut down or to isolate themselves in a very populist and localist perspective. The end of this period was marked by internal debates in the search for the correct political line.

The 1980 referendum on the sovereignty of Quebec increased the ideological divisions in popular groups. Marxist-Leninists espoused the unity of the working class within Canada, but did not recognize the possibility of a socialist nationalism that many militants proposed.

A terrible recession occurred in 1982. The provincial government took a hard line in its negotiations with public sector employees, including health and social service workers and teachers. The demise of Marxist-Leninist organizations marked the end of the radicalization of popular groups. The dogmatism and lack of sensitivity towards the progressive nationalism of the working class was a major factor in the demise of these organizations. Neoconservatism led to a questioning of the role and place of government, and even a social democratic PQ was not immune to it. Quebec's social movement was changing.

From Social Animation to Political Action

The various activities of social animation evolved through much soul-searching into a radicalization of rhetoric and objectives. In 1968 an evaluation of groups from Montreal and rural areas revealed dissatisfaction with the lack of success and the slow pace of change. Two approaches emerged from those evaluations: (1) the need to create the people's own social services that would emphasize self-help, and (2) the need to politicize social animation into political pressure groups and eventually to create a political party at the municipal level.

People's health clinics, food cooperatives, housing cooperatives, cooperative businesses (building), day care centres, community social service centres, and other services were established to resolve social problems. These services were set up in poor and working-class neighbourhoods where some organizing occurred. They were run by very democratic boards and structures in which professionals and users were considered on the same level. Some were modelled after worker co-ops. The funding continued to come from churches, the United Way, private foundations, unions, and technical support came from militant university faculty members and students doing field placements. The health and legal clinics were the services most supported by universities. These community clinics were to become the local community service centres through the health and social services reform implemented in 1973 (Lesemann and Thiénot 1972).

Among the numerous organizations that took a community development approach, one in particular illustrates the bilingual character of Montreal and Pointe St-Charles. Parallel Institute was created in 1967 by a small group of anglophones 'with the general objectives of improving the conditions of community and promoting self-help organizations and doing research in these areas' (Benello 1972:485). Actually, the main objective was to create a community development corporation (CDC) modelled on the American CDCs. It hoped to develop a plan to attract businesses for the whole neighbourhood of Pointe St-Charles. It also hoped to set up a furniture-refinishing workshop and a housing renovation co-op with the help of federal funds and another local organization called Projet d'organisation populaire d'information et de regroupement, which we will describe later. Its goal of setting up a conseil de quartier based on the concept of community control was hindered by internal squabbles.

The other approach to community development resulted in the creation of single-issue advocacy groups for welfare recipients, tenants, the unemployed, and consumers. They advocated for rights and new legislation, and evolved rapidly from strictly local groups to Quebec-based organizations, such as the Association pour la défense des droits sociaux du Montréal métropolitain (ADDSMM) and its English-speaking counterpart, the Greater Montreal Anti-Poverty Coordinating Committee (GMAPCC). These organizations were inspired by the welfare rights movement in the US and combined individual case advocacy and collective mobilizations for welfare reform.

After 1970 the two organizations evolved differently. GMAPCC used Local Initiative Program projects and other federally funded programs and, as a result, 'drifted in the direction of service delivery and case by case advocacy rather than direct political action' (Shragge 1994:27). ADDSMM was funded more by United Way and unions and was able to pursue its political pressure on welfare offices and governments while doing individual case advocacy.

At the same time, some multi-issue organizations developed in the early 1970s, integrating a political analysis into advocacy. The Projet d'organisation populaire d'information et de regroupement (POPIR) of St-Henri was created in 1970 by the Conseil des oeuvres, with funding from the Catholic Archdiocese of Montreal. Its objectives were to promote a new local leadership, create a permanent organization by developing a coalition of the whole southwest area of Montreal, and develop an understanding of the root causes of their problems (Lesemann and Thiénot 1972:343). POPIR worked on several fronts, using pressure tactics and development (as Parallel Institute did to fund a renovation business) to advocate for housing, health, work, consumer rights, and popular education 'in order to develop a critical consciousness of the élites' perspective and to make their own choices' (Lesemann and Thiénot 1972:329). POPIR was involved in many issues regarding welfare rights and played a major role in training *avocats populaires* (popular advocates). It also contributed to the broader political struggle in trying to develop a municipal party. POPIR still exists today with the same focus on housing and welfare, and heads a coalition against cuts in social programs.

This community development approach, which emphasized both individual and collective empowerment through advocacy and grassroots organizing, led to the political action committees that formed the Front d'action politique (FRAP, or the Political Action Front), which became a formal political party for the 1970 elections in Montreal. FRAP involved both popular groups and union members and benefited from the organizational skills of social animators and CYC volunteers. The purpose of FRAP was to encourage coherent political thinking, a clear orientation for citizens' committees' struggles and demands, and to become a regional structure for mobilization. There was more consensus over the need for political power and a party than on actual strategies. Internal strife followed the November 1970 electoral defeat in Montreal, in the midst of the October Crisis, and the party was disbanded in 1973.

Radicalization, Diversification, and Professionalization

As the radicalization of citizens' committees continued into the 1970s, a critical analysis of the state forced groups to choose between co-optation with a service orientation within the state apparatus or radicalization of demands and conflict strategies. Radicalization took the form of advocacy groups espousing agitation and mobilization to create a source of political power for the masses. The Marxist literature influenced practice as did Paulo Freire's conscientization methods (Deslauriers 1985).

This radicalization was accompanied by diversification in education, day care, seniors' rights, community television, the environment, employment, and working conditions. Alliances were forged between groups advocating for rights to better living conditions and labour unions advocating for better working conditions (Groulx 1975a). Many employee strikes were actively supported by popular groups. Welfare recipients were seen as a reserve army of cheap labour to keep workers in poor working conditions. The links between the economy and social problems were well articulated by community and labour leaders as the labour movement supported many community groups (McGraw 1978).

Community development was also initiated by community organizers in CLSCs. Labelled as troubleshooters and agitators in the first CLSCs established in militant working-class neighbourhoods in the first half of the 1970s, professional community organizers were forced to become promoters and supporters of government programs rather than agents of change (Groulx 1977). While the governing structures of CLSCs involved citizens, this represented only token citizen participation and did not lead to real community empowerment (Godbout 1983). This created divisions in community development that were initiated by the public sector (Doré 1992). However, many community organizers in CLSCs managed to bridge some of these gaps by taking a militant stance and pushing the limits of institutional tolerance. Some organizers lost their jobs in the process, resulting in a crack-down on militant practice in an agency (Larivière 1978). Militancy in a public organization had a price!

Political action at the municipal level continued after the FRAP's ill-fated experience in 1970. An alliance between the labour movement and popular groups led to a new municipal party in Montreal called the Montreal Citizens' Movement (MCM), which had a progressive ideology but one that was not as radical as that of FRAP. The MCM had relative success in the 1974 election with a mayoral candidate who was a priest and came from the first generation of social animators. He later became the minister of immigration in the PQ government between 1976 and 1981. The MCM became the official opposition in Montreal during the 1970s. A similar party, the Ralliement Populaire, which also had strong neighbourhood grassroots, was founded in Quebec City in 1977.

Models and Issues

In such a period of change and turmoil, many questions were raised about the strategies for guiding community development, particularly about the roles of the practitioners. There was also the question of partisan political action and its links to community development (Groulx 1977). On this latter issue, many embraced the position of Marxist-Leninists, advocating direct links between a proletarian party (the political arm), the labour movement, and popular groups (the social arm). The social arm was to influence the masses regarding problems of concern to the party. Many embraced this approach, but it also caused many others to abandon community development and militant work altogether. The dogmatism of the approach and its lack of sensitivity to nationalism and women brought about its demise in the early 1980s. However, its emphasis on critical analysis and education left a strong imprint in community development practice.

In trying to define a framework for community development in the 1970s, most critics did not keep Rothman's framework and took a different stance. The 1977 Community Organizers Manifesto defined three main strategies of community development in an attempt to regroup both professional and militant organizers in CLSCs and popular groups (Doré and Larose 1979). The first radical liberal strategy defined its constituency as socially and economically underprivileged and had the objective of organizing pressure groups (single-issue advocacy). A second strategy focused on community development of services and businesses to give communities an economic base and enable them to become as autonomous as possible. A third strategy centred on organizing workers to get political power to build a socialist society at the municipal and national levels.

A similar framework outlined three approaches and corresponding roles for practitioners (Tilman 1979). A Marxist approach tends to give the organizer a leadership role as a 'professional revolutionary' for political change (Deslauriers 1985). The reformist approach, which is associated with the development of pressure groups, focuses on demands to the state. In this approach, the organizer's role is to give expertise in changing recriminations into negotiable demands. In the third approach, the workers cooperatives (inspired by Yugoslavia under Tito and French labour unions) tended to pursue objectives of creating businesses and services run by users themselves. In this approach, organizers put their knowledge at the members' disposal without assuming leadership.

These approaches exclude community development as practised in CLSCs as a form of social integration and co-optation of popular demands: '. . . it is better to give jobs and services to a population than to take a strong military stance in quelling their demands'. A close analysis of speeches by various ministers of the provincial government would easily come to that conclusion (Lesemann 1979).

New Beginnings (1983-1991)

The beginning of the 1980s was marked by a collective depression following the referendum in 1980, the repatriation of the Canadian Constitution without Quebec in 1982, and the lack of workable solutions from both Marxist-Leninists and the PQ government. This was followed by an economic crisis that forced the provincial government to make deep cuts in public spending, especially in social and health programs. Community development had to look to new horizons. Many groups and individuals were scared by dogmatic internal struggles involving a lot of energy and broken promises for a better future. The welfare state was in a financial and political crisis. Neoliberalism was dawning upon the Western world. Thatcherism and Reaganism were starting to influence Canadian politics as Mulroney's Conservatives came to power in Ottawa and Robert Bourassa's Liberal Party was elected in Quebec in 1985. The perspective moved from social to economic. Economists and business people were regarded as having credibility and leadership. In this difficult context, community development grew tremendously and took on a new perspective.

From Politics to Economics

Popular groups and political organizations realized that radical political action had not produced the results expected, and that militants and ordinary people had been disillusioned by their experience. Radical groups gave way to a plethora of community groups, which became much more service oriented and less apt to organize large demonstrations. Certain critics (René and Panet-Raymond 1984) were asking if they should burn the placards. Many would have answered yes in the 1980s even though living and working conditions worsened for the poor while a few speculators and entrepreneurs got rich with the help of the state in what has been called 'Quebec Inc.'

In fact, there were a few large demonstrations regarding language in 1989 and the Meech Lake Agreement in 1990. Apart from that, only the struggle against a new welfare law introducing workfare and 'learnfare' in 1989 produced a large coalition and a few big rallies. In the 1980s community groups recognized that strong, well-planned lobbying could bring about changes as well as political action (Panet-Raymond 1985). This signalled a change in attitude for activists and community organizers. Changing from strictly defensive actions and criticisms of policies, community development then took on the challenge of economic and social community development. Coalitions evolved into partnerships that involved labour, business, government, and community to create new local social services and businesses. As groups received more funding in the 1970s from a still-progressive PQ government, they were integrated into government programs (Doucet and Favreau 1991). This continued in the 1980s, producing some groups that were created mostly because there was funding than because there was a clearly expressed need in the population. Home care for the elderly grew tremendously, especially within the mandate of CLSCs. The provincial budget allocated to community groups involved in home care grew from a few hundred thousand dollars to more than $10 million from 1979 to 1989 (Panet-Raymond 1989; Panet-Raymond and Bourque 1991). This was certainly not true of all fields of service, and many groups (such as local community newspapers, tenants' associations, and consumer rights groups) barely survived or disappeared because of lack of public funding and community support.

Advocacy groups generally had a hard time getting funding and surviving (Hamel 1983). In this context the grassroots and class-based popular groups became neighbourhood multiclass community groups and organizations with a definite service orientation, even though many kept a very critical analysis of public policies while pursuing various campaigns for social reform. It is also important to point out that a strong advocacy movement has continued to pressure governments. The Quebec organization Front d'action populaire et de réaménagement urbain (Urban Renewal Popular Action Front), created in 1979, has a large following of local tenants' associations, combining individual advocacy services and mobilization across Quebec. It has campaigned mostly for public housing and urban renewal. It still organizes marches, demonstrations against city halls, and occupations of ministers' offices.

Another example of the continuity of this sociopolitical action is the welfare rights movement, which has survived through the 1980s and pursued its attacks on the welfare system with the inception of workfare. The Front commun des personnes assistées sociales (Welfare Rights Coalition) has not had great success in changing the spirit of the welfare reform of 1989, which introduced a form of 'learnfare', but some of the local groups still mobilize people.

There were also some areas of development, such as the women's movement, which evolved from a radical feminism to a more pragmatic, service-oriented feminism. This is exemplified by the plethora of women's centres all over Quebec. Though diversified in their specific activities, these centres focused on services, information and referral, education, collective action, and research. Whereas health clinics and crisis shelters for battered women often evolved in isolation from the community movement, the women's centres are an integral part of it. They have also influenced the community movement and put women's issues on the public agenda of community groups, unions, governments, and even business (Fournier and Gagnon 1991). Women's centres number more than 120 and have been federated in a provincial organization since 1984.

Another example of this mushrooming of groups is the development of youth groups. The Regroupement des maisons de jeunes was created in 1980 and the number of these drop-in centres has increased even though funding has been very limited. Their aim is to help youths ages twelve to eighteen take control of their lives and their environment by organizing sociocultural activities and sports while emphasizing a democratic, non-sexist, and non-racist perspective (René 1991). In a way they resemble the YMCA on a smaller scale, but encourage a more participatory approach. Another movement that increased its membership considerably in the 1980s is the Regroupement des maisons d'hébergement jeunesse (for homeless youths ages twelve to thirty). These shelters offer individual social services and advocate collective rights for those who have dropped out of the system. Another organization for youths eighteen to thirty was created in 1983 to pressure for equal treatment of welfare recipients under thirty, who received about one-third of the money for single adults. The organization, Regroupement autonome des jeunes (RAJ), was created partially as a result of a disagreement within the welfare rights movement whose membership was composed mostly of single mothers. The younger adults did not feel comfortable with a highly politicized advocacy approach based on consciousness raising. RAJ eventually became a very splintered and loosely knit coalition of small and very militant groups. It organized some marches, bivouacs in public parks, spontaneous demonstrations in public political meetings involving ministers, and occupations of ministerial offices, etc.

Community organizers in CLSCs contributed greatly to the rapid growth of community organizations for targeted populations. After these agents of change were redefined as agents of integration, they supported and initiated many local initiatives to create community services for female victims of violence, day care, home care for seniors and the disabled, youths, drug users, etc. (Hurtubise 1989). Community groups became partners, although unequal and dependent, with the state as it opted out of services it could no longer afford. This became formally recognized in the Health and Social Services Act in 1991, which defines guidelines for funding and partnerships with community groups based on a population and epidemiological perspective. The health side was supported by the Healthy Communities movement, which initiated many health promotion projects involving community organizations through various coalitions. This meant that community groups had to take a much more focused and specialized approach to problems and populations in order to comply with public policies and funding. In certain cases, community groups even adapted their activities to fit funding criteria, but all had to diversify their funding sources and use much more creativity in fundraising. As applying for funding became more and more time-consuming and difficult, staff and members had to learn about community development and management.

Professionalization of community development followed specialization and bureaucratization. The emphasis moved from political to technical preoccupations (Panet-Raymond 1985, 1989) as more public institutions became involved in community projects. Community organizers had to become more resourceful and less openly political to obtain funding and recognition in a much more competitive environment. The critical, dogmatic stance of the 1970s had given way to a pragmatic, almost subservient attitude in the 1980s.

Community Development and Voluntary Action

Another change in the 1980s was the culture of voluntary work, which became the focus of government and community groups. As political leaders recognized voluntary work as essential to compensate for the dwindling role of the state, many service-oriented groups developed with the support of volunteers, especially in the area of home care. Traditional volunteer work had always existed in institutions and communities and were often frowned upon by labour and social movements, but now community groups evolved from a militant membership to a volunteer membership. The two cultures, charitable and militant, started to build bridges (Panet-Raymond and Bourque 1991) and work in concerted efforts. A new culture of voluntary action replaced the culture of militant political action. There are still certain differences depending on the areas of community development: tenants' associations and welfare rights organizations do not recruit volunteers, nor do advocacy groups for the unemployed initiated by labour unions. However, seniors' groups and women's groups that might have been open only to fairly militant members have recruited volunteers.

Models and Issues

Major issues confronting community development are the loss of its autonomy and its recognition as a credible agent of change that combines creativity and competence. A third issue is funding. These issues were constantly brought up in negotiations with the provincial government as it developed its social policies and reforms in health, social services, education, and manpower training. Community groups were regarded as a cheaper option to public services, but were not recognized nor funded for their alternative ways of doing things. While defined as partners, they are treated as subcontractors for public institutions offering services. The issues of recognition, funding, and respect for autonomy are all linked. Community groups felt they were used as a cheap option for service delivery, especially in home care, youth homes, drop-in centres for drug users, battered women's shelters, etc. Community organizations accused governments of dumping their responsibilities on them. The state imposed very strict conditions that limited groups in their action and, in particular, hindered their consciousness raising and mobilization against injustice and advocacy for preventive programs. The emphasis was thus on offering quality services and support for self-help groups rather than on political debates and change. Groups found themselves doing things that were not related to their original missions, expertise, and resources in order to answer needs defined by subcontracts. Funding therefore became a time-consuming straitjacket that forced groups to comply with government priorities and programs. This change was draped in government rhetoric on partnership, self-help, and volunteer work in the community (Panet-Raymond 1989). Hence autonomy of community groups became a key issue in the 1980s.

Based on these issues, new models of practice were identified, although sometimes they were not even relevant to original definitions of community development. One model was identified as a community approach and made popular by the Federation of CLSCs. It used this approach to give itself a broad framework to identify personal and environmental factors in defining intervention with individuals, small groups, and communities (Gingras 1991b). It also called for a more equal relationship between professionals and clients, in order to support self-help and the use of natural networks. It based this approach on the assumption that communities and individuals have potential and resources, so the emphasis should be on strengths rather than weaknesses. This approach challenged and frustrated professional community organizers who were pressured to do more and more group work and help set up self-help groups rather than organize for change (Hurtubise 1989; Panet-Raymond 1988).

Two conceptual frameworks were used mainly in the 1980s to define the various strategies of community development. Doré (1985) identified four broad models in community organization. The first favoured integration of communities involving local leaders and projects by using the local power structure (élites). A second model favoured pressure groups by creating a new source of power based on the interests of the exploited and dominated classes of a community. A third model aimed to build businesses and economic projects controlled by those who use the services or consume the goods produced. A fourth model uses political action to transform existing political structures. These four models correspond to others that were defined in the 1960s and 1970s, defining a continuum from integration to political action and from a defensive pressure strategy to a more offensive type of development involving user control.

At the end of the 1980s some analysts (Doucet and Favreau 1991; Panet-Raymond and Mayer 1991) started bringing back the Rothman framework. They associated the traditional advocacy work and mobilization (welfare rights, unemployed, tenants, etc.) with social action. Social planning corresponded to the CLSCs' organizing for community resources, such as home care, women's shelters, youth shelters, etc. Locality development was associated with the resurgence of community economic development and the many concerted actions in communities involving business, unions, community groups, and local governments for such issues as safety on the streets, the homeless, gang warfare, the environment, job creation, etc.

There was a less conflictual approach to community development in the 1980s even though social and economic conditions hit the poor very hard. Class discrepancies grew, but there was no radicalization of social movements. On the contrary, neoliberal policies created a form of moral pressure that isolated radical models of development. This favoured the more cooperative or consensual approach to community development.

Partnership Becomes the Model (1991–Present)

In Quebec in the 1990s, another hard recession hit mostly the poor and revealed that public finances were inadequate. The great mobilizations of the past decades have slowed down. The trends of the 1980s—neoliberal ideology, difficult economic recessions, and government cutbacks—have continued and increased. The recession is deeper, the cutbacks are larger, and the neoliberal ideology is more widespread, even in social democratic governments. Other trends have gathered more momentum: volunteer work as a value, decentralization, individualism, self-help as a value and a means to solutions, and community as an important factor in economic and social policy. The apparent contradictions between certain trends, such as individualism and communitarianism, have actually reinforced neoliberalism and the government's declining role in favour of community and private and individual solutions. Simultaneously the words justice, equality, solidarity, and democracy are heard in community and labour union rhetoric as never before. Even some members of the business community are talking about the need for these values in hard times. These words come up again and again at the Forum pour l'emploi, which is a broad coalition of community groups, unions, and business leaders. The very existence of such a coalition is a phenomenon of the 1990s.

Partnerships and Concerted Action

In this decade social policies are confirming the importance of communities and individual initiatives, so community development is being recognized as a viable solution to social problems. Governments have continued to opt out of responsibilities in favour of community alternatives. These policies are pragmatic, based on budgetary analysis and not necessarily based on values favouring participatory democracy and community control. The provincial government formally recognized the existence of community groups as partners because they have become a cheaper alternative to government intervention. Many community organizations had demanded that recognition for the last ten years, but in recognizing their contribution, the government is also jeopardizing the groups' autonomy and creativity because they will have to fit into the public policies and priorities and be evaluated on that basis. The dilemma facing community development in the 1990s is how to become a viable partner while not losing its original mission (Panet-Raymond and Bourque 1991).

The other perspective that has defined practice in the 1990s is the trend for concerted action. The number of joint committees, round tables, and coalitions is increasing at local, regional, and national levels. They relate to single issues (such as employment, welfare reform, and gay rights) or to broad objectives related to social policies. They coordinate sectorial groups: Regroupement des centres de femmes du Québec, Fédération des femmes du Québec (which organized the June 1995 march 'For Bread and Roses'), Association québécoise pour la défense des droits des retraités et préretraités (seniors' rights advocacy), Front commun des personnes assistées sociales (welfare rights advocacy), Collectif de défense des droits en santé mentale (mental health advocacy), or very diverse organizations. Such is the case of Solidarité populaire Québec, which is a broad alliance of local, regional, and national groups and labour unions. Its objectives started as an opposition to cuts in social programs in 1987, but it has since developed the Charter for a People's Quebec (La charte d'un Québec populaire, 1994), which constitutes a non-partisan, progressive political platform. It took over three years for this Charter to be accepted and involved more than 1,500 groups and unions and thousands of people in a vast consultation that was very educational for all concerned. Solidarité populaire Québec has also been a leader in coordinating a broad, concerted reaction to the Axworthy reform in 1994. The federal government's attempt to cut deeply into social security programs and to redesign such programs as the Canada Assistance Plan and unemployment insurance infuriated community organizations and unions all across Quebec. It was also an opportunity for a critical view of present policies and their shortcomings. Very few organizations were innovative in their analysis of the policies or dared to be more proactive in suggesting major changes using a community development approach. However, during the various forums and debates, there were many references to creating jobs and supporting decentralization at a regional and local level to promote social and economic community development.

The trend to concerted action among community groups has also been spurred on by government programs and structures, as in health and social services. The 1991 Health and Social Services Act created regional boards that called for the election of board members from community groups. Government consultations and joint committees in various fields such as justice, education, and manpower have also favoured the creation of such coalitions, but these coalitions and round tables are not always focused on action. They also serve as forums for discussion and exchange of information. Some would argue that they are often an excuse for lack of direct action and spend a lot of time going around in circles discussing broad issues. Many of these coalitions, particularly at a local level, involve public servants and municipal officials, which has influenced their agenda and strategies. These coalitions tend to lobby government officials rather than mobilize people around issues and demands for change.

Models and Issues

The 1990s have confirmed the trends of the 1980s (Panet-Raymond 1989) towards more consensual and cooperative work. Community care has developed considerably as organizations are recognized as offering services that correspond to government priorities. Social action is still alive and certainly relevant in view of the social security reform and budgetary cuts in public spending. Social planning is growing as CLSCs have initiated a number of actions within public policies, mostly to create service resources (shelters for women, addicts, and homeless youths) and also to establish health promotion campaigns (Favreau and Hurtubise 1993). However, locality development, as exemplified mostly by social and economic community development, has almost become *the* primary model of development. It is important to note that the Rothman framework should be used cautiously as groups tend to mix models, depending on the issues and the circumstances. (This is well illustrated by Le Chic Resto Pop in White's chapter.)

As the obsession for job creation preoccupies everyone, the objective of community economic development (CED) can integrate almost all models.

There are two main types of community-based, local development organizations in Québec which have adopted a CED framework: the 'corporation de développement économique communautaire' (CDÉC) and the 'corporation de développement communautaire' (CDC). Both have emanated from the communitarian movement and share strong ties to such progressive values as feminism and women's issues, more liberal employment policies and labour relations, the integration of persons with disabilities, etc., as well with organizations that support such values (Ninacs and Favreau 1993:8).

A CDÉC has a board made up of individuals, community organizations, labour unions, local businesses, city officials, and often CLSCs. It usually focuses on business development and job readiness training (Ninacs and Favreau 1993).

The oldest and probably the best example is Regroupement pour la relance économique et sociale du Sud-Ouest de Montréal (RÉSO), which was created in 1984 in Pointe St-Charles and has been active in the southwestern area of Montreal (Perry and Lewis 1994; Shragge 1993). It has developed a number of programs, such as a job-support centre, job search and placement assistance, occupational training, promotion of local cooperative businesses, business technical assistance, etc.

In addition to these programs, RÉSO has been a leader in pressuring governments at all levels to support CED as a viable option for economic development. CDÉCs have developed mostly in Montreal and other cities, while other organizations (Sociétés d'aide au développement des collectivités) have promoted similar goals and strategies in rural areas. Provincial and municipal governments are enthusiastic about this model because they see it as a means of producing cheap services and as a new labour market for people on welfare. It entails low-paying jobs that do not require expensive training. There is growing criticism from community organizations concerned that CED will become just a panacea to rationalize workfare policies and create ghettos of dead-end jobs. They argue that CED must be based on community initiatives and values, such as justice, solidarity, and equity, and should not be imposed by political leaders as a quick fix to alleviate some economic and social problems (Bélanger and Lévesque 1992; Fontan and Shragge 1996).

CDCs, on the other hand, are a small-town phenomenon. They are basically a network of community organizations whose purpose is to recognize and support each other by combining technical resources, such as offices, printing, and even staff. CDCs try to initiate community projects and contribute to social and economic development without the financial backing of the CDÉCs. In certain towns CDCs are trying to become CDÉCs (Ninacs and Favreau 1993). Both CDCs and CDÉCs target poverty and the breakdown of the social fabric of local communities.

More and more links are being made between social and economic issues, individual and collective development, and empowerment. This is very compatible with the trend towards self-help in the 1980s, which has continued through the 1990s both for individuals and communities. The 1970s concept of empowerment is also making a comeback as an objective of casework, group work, and community organization (Lévesque and Panet-Raymond 1995; Ninacs 1995). It is almost ironic that empowerment is an objective recognized even by public CLSCs in their definition of a community approach (Fédération des CLSC du Québec 1994), but of course it is devoid of any political meaning. Empowerment is espoused by progressive organizers in community development as an objective to build a democratic and more just society. Public proponents of empowerment see it as a way to develop self-help and less dependence on public services.

The 1990s seem to be a mixture of contradictory models and concepts. Some of the words used are the same, but do not necessarily have the same meaning for individuals and groups coming from different political perspectives. Community groups have taken on a strategy of critical cooperation or cooperative conflict (Lamoureux 1995; Panet-Raymond and Bourque 1991) in their partnership with the public sector. This strategy relies on the use of conflict only if necessary, and, of course, it has been necessary in order to reaffirm principles and opposition to certain policies, such as workfare and cuts in public services.

Conclusion

Community development in Quebec is clearly rooted in its social, economic, cultural, and political fabric. It has been influenced by history, but it has also contributed to society: social policies and institutions that are the result of pressures from community groups: health and legal clinics, CLSCs, women's shelters, employment and manpower training programs, youth programs, labour laws, family laws, etc.

This impact on public policy and the broad recognition of its contribution through the years is the result of a long-standing partnership between the state and the social movement. The Quiet Revolution led the state and labour unions to recognize civil servants' right to collective bargaining. Some of the first social animators became union leaders and political leaders in the PQ governments and municipal parties in Montreal and Quebec. In that way, one might say that the social involvement inspired a social contract that was agreed upon between the state and the civil society.

But the argument does not hold if one considers the very hard battles fought between the state and social movements over major social, economic, and political policies. The 1970s had many conflicts that were based on political, economic, and cultural factors. However, one must recognize the many personal relationships between politicians, senior civil servants, and community leaders. Quebec is small and the university-trained organizers are apt to know colleagues who went into politics. This is especially true of the petit bourgeois from the baby boom generation. The first university-trained organizers considered the state as a major tool of development in the 1960s when the Church's influence waned.

The overall trend through the years is one of opposition between values, strategies, and means. The struggle over the welfare reform in 1987–8 is a case in point. Even the partnership the state has promoted recently is a very conflictual one that is not espoused wholeheartedly by many in the community movement. Therefore, another explanation for community development's impact on Quebec society and public policy will have to come from within the strength of the movement, albeit with the support of many politicians and civil servants over the years. Support for the movement has also come from the progressive wing of the Catholic Church and many members of religious orders who have been involved in grassroots organizing, as well as from some critical, thought-producing, and influential magazines. The Church was officially replaced by the state, but many of its members have continued supporting the struggle against poverty. They are still very much a part of the welfare rights movement, the refugee rights movement, and the fight against hunger through coalitions and parish and community groups. Some priests and bishops have even come out publicly against workfare policies in their Sunday sermons. Is this a remnant of the Church's past involvement in education and family policies? Possibly. It might explain the vast support and influence the community movement has had on a Quebec society. In addition, the movement is much more structured and unified regionally and provincially than in other provinces, and its links with unions (although difficult) have always been stronger than elsewhere in Canada. Community development is really a social movement in Quebec, which explains its impact. Finally, in the 1980s many community groups developed services that have been seen as a cheaper and more viable alternative to the bureaucratic and costly welfare state. Some (Bélanger and Lévesque 1992) would argue that the search for a new social contract between the state and civil society has resulted in the community movement as a legitimate actor in this contract, however small its role. Of course there is also a downside to this recognition.

Recognition, funding, and the risk of institutionalization are still difficult issues to reconcile with autonomy and community development. An interventionist state, even in a neoliberal context, tends to create strict guidelines in its subcontracting to private or community organizations. If community groups are to play the game, they have to make concessions while not relinquishing the basic values they stand for. That is going to be the issue in the future. Will community development integrate neoliberal values in working with public and business partners? That debate is still open. Some groups are becoming involved in policy making, while others are avoiding any joint ventures. The balance between a critical viewpoint and concerted action is still necessary if community development is to influence policies and societal values. The long tradition of social action is still alive, well, and respected within the social movement. It has not isolated itself in dogmatic rhetoric, but, more important, it has been able to mobilize people and get media attention. These radical advocacy groups are also involved in many coalitions and round tables. In a way they are keeping the more institutionalized and service-oriented groups honest! In any negotiation with governments, it is important for the leaders involved to feel the pressure from their constituencies and to blend consensual and conflictual strategies. The future will tell if the blend of strategies was a good choice.

Note

[1] The Quiet Revolution refers to the period of 1960–6 under the Liberal Party. It hailed the

development of a modern state involved in all aspects of society. During that period, major reforms in education, social security, and work relations increased public spending by 21 per cent annually. The Catholic Church's formal role in these areas dwindled to a few institutions as people stopped going to church almost completely. Finally, the Quiet Revolution saw the rise of the labour movement, notably in the fast-growing public sector (54 per cent annual increase), the student movement advocating free tuition in universities and colleges, and, of course, the community development movement.

References

Alinsky, S.
1971. *Rules for Radicals*. New York: Random House.

Bélanger, P.R., and B. Lévesque.
1988. 'Une forme mouvementée de gestion du social: les CLSC'. *Revue internationale d'action communautaire* 19, no. 59:49–64.

_____, and B. Lévesque.
1990. 'Le système de santé et de services sociaux au Québec: crise des relations de travail et du mode de consommation'. *Sociologie du travail* 2, no. 90:231–44.

_____, and B. Lévesque.
1992. 'Le mouvement populaire et communautaire: de la revendication au partenariat (1963–1992)'. In *Le Québec en jeu: comprendre les grands défis*, edited by G. Daigle and R. Rocher, 713–48. Montreal: Presses de l'Université de Montréal.

Bélanger, P.R., et al.
1987. *Animation et culture en mouvement*. Ste-Foy: Presses universitaires du Québec.

Benello, G.
1972. 'Social Animation among Anglophone Groups'. In *Animations sociales au Québec*, edited by F. Lesemann and M. Thiénot, 435–93. Montreal: Université de Montréal.

Blondin, M.
1965. 'L'animation sociale en milieu urbain: Une solution'. *Recherches sociographiques* 6, no. 3:283–403.

_____.
1968. 'Vie urbaine et animation sociale'. *Recherches sociographiques* 6, no. 1–2:111–23.

Boivin, R.
1988. *Histoire de la clinique des citoyens de Saint-Jacques (1968–1988): Des comités de citoyens au CLCS du plateau Mont-Royal*. Montreal: Victor Lévy-Beaulieu.

Boucher, E.
1961. *Rapport du comité d'étude sur l'assistance publique*. Quebec City: Gouvernement du Québec.

Bourque, D.
1985. 'L'approche communautaire en centre local de services communautaires: les enjeux en cause et les conditions requises'. *Service social* 34, no. 2–3:328–40.

———.
1986. 'Le renouvellement des pratiques sociales qu Québec: le projet des acteurs dominants'. *Canadian Review of Social Work*, 208–18.

———.
1989. 'Conceptions et orientations de l'approche communautaire dans les CLSC'. Master's dissertation in social work, Université de Montréal, Montreal.

Bozzini, L.
1989. 'Les centres locaux de services communautaires (CLSC): évaluation et perspective'. *Intervention* 83:4–16.

Cloutier, C., and P. Hamel.
1991. 'Les services urbains: le défi du partenariat pour le milieu communautaire'. *Cahiers de géographie du Québec* 35, no. 95:257–83.

Collin, J.P., and J. Godbout.
1977. *Les organismes populaires en milieu urbain: contre-pouvoir ou nouvelle pratique professionnelle?* Montreal: INRS-Urbanisation.

Conseil des affaires sociales.
1992a. *Le Québec solidaire: rapport sur le développement*. Boucherville: Gaétan Morin éditeur/Publications du Québec.

———.
1992b. *Agir ensemble: rapport sur le développement*. Boucherville: Gaétan Morin éditeur/Publications du Québec.

———.
1992c. *Deux Québec dans un: rapport sur le développement, social et démographique*. Boucherville: Gaétan Morin éditeur/Publications du Quebec.

Conseil du bien-être du Québec.
1965. *Les inégalités socio-économiques et la pauvreté au Québec*. Montreal: Conseil du bien-être conference proceedings.

Côté, C., and Y. Harnois.
1978. *L'animation sociale au Québec: sources, apports et limites*. Montreal: Editions Saint-Martin.

Couillaird, R., and R. Mayer.
1980. 'La pratique d'organisation communautaire à la maison de quartier de Pointe St-Charles (1973–1978)'. *Revue internationale d'action communautaire* 4, no. 44:110–20.

Deshaies, A., and P. Simard.
1971. 'M. Ross: l'ancienne droite déguisée ou le drame d'une pensée ossifiée'. *Intervention* no. 34:4–9.

Deslauriers, J.P.
1985. 'De l'animation à la révolution'. *Service social* 2, no. 3:269–89.

_____, and H. Pouliot.
1982. *Les groupes populaires à Sherbrooke: pratique, financement et structure.* Sherbrooke: Département de service social, Université de Sherbrooke.

Désy, M., et al.
1980. *La conjoncture au Québec au début des années '80: Les enjeux pour le mouvement ouvrier et populaire.* Rimouski: La libraire socialiste de l'Est du Québec.

Doray, M.
1967. 'Méthodes et techniques d'animation'. *Les cahiers de l'Institut Canadien d'Education des Adultes* no. 4–5:23–39.

Doré, G.
1985. 'L'organisation communautaire: définition et paradigme'. *Service social* 34, no. 2–3: 210–31.

_____.
1992. 'L'organisation communautaire et les mutations dans les services sociaux au Québec, 1961–1991'. *Service social* 41, no. 2:131–62.

_____, and C. Larose.
1979. 'L'organisation communautaire: pratique salariée d'animation des collectivités au Québec'. *Service social* 28, no. 2–3:69–96.

_____, and D. Plamondon.
1980. 'Les pratiques urbaines d'opposition à Québec'. *Revue internationale d'action communautaire* 4, no. 44:120–9.

Doucet, L., and L. Favreau.
1991. *Théorie et pratiques en organisation communautaire.* Ste-Foy: Presses de l'Université du Québec.

Favreau, L.
1989. *Mouvement populaire et intervention communautaire (1960–1988): continuitées et ruptures.* Montreal: Éditions du Fleuve/Centre de formation populaire.

_____.
1990. 'L'action communautaire au Québec: les transformations en cours'. *Revue canadienne de service social* 7, no. 2:159–68.

_____, and Y. Hurtubise.
1993. *CLSC et communautés locales: la contribution de l'organisation communautaire.* Ste-Foy: Presses de l'Université du Québec.

_____, R. Lachapelle, and L. Chagnon.
1994. *Pratiques d'action communautaire en CLSC: acquis et défis d'aujourd'hui.* Ste-Foy: Presses de l'Université du Québec.

_____, and W. Ninacs.
1992. 'Le développement économique local communautaire au Québec'. *Coopératives et développement* 23, no. 2:115–23.

Féderation des CLSC du Québec.
1994. *Pratiques d'action communautaire en CLSC*. Montreal: Fédération des CLSC du Québec.

Fontan, J.-M., and E. Shragge.
1996. 'L'économie sociale: une économie pour les pauvres?' *La Presse* (30 April):B33.

Fournier, D., and L. Gagnon.
1991. 'L'organisation communautaire avec des femmes'. In *Théorie et pratiques en organisation communautaire*, edited by L. Doucet and L. Favreau, 293–306. Ste Foy: Presses de l'Université du Québec.

Gareau, J.M.
1990. *La percée du développement économique communautaire dans le Sud-Ouest de Montréal: Le programme économique de Pointe Saint-Charles*. Montreal: Institut de formation en développement économique communautaire.

Gingras, P.
1991a. 'L'approche communautaire'. *Théorie et pratiques en organisation communautaire*, edited by L. Doucet and L. Favreau, 187–200. Ste Foy: Presses de l'Université du Québec.

_____.
1991b. *Le traitement en première ligne des demandes individuelles d'aide en CLSC (selon une approche communautaire)*. Montreal: Fédération des centres locaux de services communautaires du Québec/Governement du Québec.

Godbout, J.
1983. *La participation contre la démocratie*. Montreal: Éditions Saint-Martin.

_____, and J. Guay.
1988. *Le communautaire public: le cas d'un CLSC*. Montreal: INRS-Urbanisation.

_____, and N.V. Martin.
1974. *Participation et innovation*. Montreal: INRS-Urbanisation.

Groulx, L.
1975a. 'L'action communautaire comme diversité et ambiguïté'. *Revue canadienne de science politique* 8, no. 4:510–19.

_____.
1975b. 'L'animation urbaine: politisation pédagogique'. *International Review of Community Development* 33, no. 34:207–20.

_____.
1977. 'Les critiques du modèle professionnel en service social'. *Service social dans le monde* 42, no. 2:17–30.

Guay, J., and Y. Lapointe.
  1985. *Document d'initiation aux types d'intervention communautaire*. Quebec City: Centre de recherche sur les services communautaires, Université Laval.

Guay, L.
  1991. 'Le choc des cultures: bilan de l'expérience de participation des ressources alternatives à l'élaboration des plans régionaux d'organisation de services en santé mentale'. *Nouvelles pratiques sociales* 4, no. 2:43–58.

Hamel, P.
  1983. 'Crise de la redistribution étatique et financement des organismes populaires'. *Revue internationale d'action communautaire* 10, no. 50:63–76.

———, and J.L. Klein.
  1991. 'Partenariat et territoire: vers une nouvelle géographicité du social?' *Cahiers de géographie du Québec* 35, no. 95:233–6.

———, and J.F. Léonard.
  1978. 'Les groupes populaires dans la dynamique socio-politique québecoise'. *Politique aujourd'hui* 7, no. 8:155–64.

———, and J.F. Léonard.
  1981. *Les organisations populaires: l'État et la démocratie*. Montreal: Nouvelle Optique.

———, J.F. Léonard, and R. Mayer.
  1982. *Les mobilisations populaires urbaines*. Montreal: Nouvelle Optique.

Houle, G.
  1972. 'L'animation sociale en milieu urbain: une idéologie pédagogique'. *Recherches sociographiques* 13, no. 2:231–52.

Hurtubise, Y.
  1989. 'L'action communautaire en CLSC: problèmes et enjeux'. *Intervention* 83:51–7.

———, and P. Paré.
  1989. *Pratiques d'action communautaire en CLSC*. Quebec City: Centre de recherches sur les services communautaires, Université Laval.

Huston, L.
  1978. 'La petite-bourgeoisie et les groupes (pas très) populaires: un conte de fées pour militant averti'. *Possibles* 3, no. 40:147–53.

Jacob, A.
  1985. 'Des enjeux pour l'action militante des anneés '80'. *Service social* 2, no. 3:353–69.

Lamarche, F.
  1968. 'Les comités de citoyens, un nouveau phénomène de contestation'. *Socialisme* 68 15:105–15.

Lamoureux, H., R. Mayer, and J. Panet-Raymond.
  1989. *Community Action*. Montreal: Black Rose Books.

Lamoureux, J.
1995. *Le partenariat à l'épreuve*. Montreal: Éditions Saint-Martin.

Larivière, C.
1978. 'L'intervention en milieu urbain: Du professionalisme au militantisme'. *International Review of Community Development* no. 39–40:37–48.

_____.
1989. 'Les intervenants sociaux des CLSC'. *Intervention* 83:32–40.

Lesemann, F.
1975. 'A propos de la formation à l'intervention collective'. *Revue canadienne d'éducation en service social* 2, no. 2:13–27.

_____.
1979. 'De la communauté locale à la communauté multinationale: l'État des monopoles et ses politiques communautaires dans la gestion de la santé et des services sociaux'. *International Review of Community Development* 25, no. 39–40:49–98.

_____, and M. Thiénot.
1972. *Animations sociales au Québec*. Montreal: Université de Montréal.

Lévesque, J., and J. Panet-Raymond.
1995. 'L'évolution de la pertinence de l'approche structurelle dans le contexte social actuel'. *Service social* 43, no. 3:23–40.

McGraw, D.
1978. *Le développement des groupes populaires à Montréal*. Montreal: St Martin.

Mathieu, R.
1987. 'Approche communautaire ou intervention communautaire?' *Revue canadienne de politique sociale* 18:112–13.

Mayer, R.
1994. 'Évolution des pratiques communautaires au Québec (1960–1990)'. *Canadian Social Work Review* 11, no. 2:238–60.

_____, and J. Panet-Raymond.
1991. 'L'action communautaire de défense des droits sociaux'. In *Théorie et pratiques en organisation communautaire*, edited by L. Doucet and L. Favreau, 97–118. Ste-Foy: Presses de l'Université du Québec.

Médard, J.F.
1969. *Communauté locale et organisation communautaire aux Etats-Unis*. Paris: A. Colin.

Morency, M.A.
1966. 'Animation sociale: quelques éléments historiques de l'expérience du BAEQ. *Annexe technique au plan de développement* no. 20.

Ninacs, W.
1991. 'L'organisation communautaire en milieu semi-urbain, semi-rural'. In *Théorie et*

pratiques en organisation communautaire, edited by L. Doucet and L. Favreau, 257–72. Ste-Foy: Presses de l'Université du Québec.

_____. 1995. 'Entraide économique, création d'entreprise, politiques sociales et empowerment'. *Nouvelles pratiques sociales* 8, no. 1:97–119.

_____, and L. Favreau. 1993. 'CED in Quebec: New Features in the Early 1990s'. *Making Waves* 4, no. 4:8–12.

Panet-Raymond, J. 1985. 'Nouvelles pratiques des organisations populaires ... Du militantisme au bénévolat au service de l'état'. *Service Social* 34, no. 2–3:340–53.

_____. 1988. 'Le "patchwork": illusion ou réalité pour les CLSC?' *Intervention* 79:12–20.

_____. 1989. 'The Future of Community Groups in Quebec: The Difficult Balance between Autonomy and Partnership with the State'. *Canadian Social Work Review* 6, no. 1:126–35.

_____. 1990. 'Le service et la mobilisation: une apparente contradiction'. In *Méthodologie de l'intervention*, edited by J. Lévesque, M. Moreau, and J. Panet-Raymond, 231–8. Montreal: Librarie de l'Université de Montréal.

_____, and D. Bourque. 1991. *Partenariat ou pater-nariat? (La collaboration entre établissements publics et organismes communautaires oeuvrant auprès des personne âgées à domicile)*. Montreal: Université de Montréal.

_____, and R. Mayer. 1991. *Trois modèles en intervention communautaire*. Montreal: Ecole de service social, Université de Montréal.

Pépin, M. 1968. *Le deuxième front: Pour une société bâtie pour l'homme*. Montreal: Confédération des syndicats nationaux.

Perry, S., and M. Lewis. 1994. *Reinventing the Local Economy*. Vernon, BC: Centre for Community Enterprise.

Quiron, H. 1972. 'Community Organization and Political Action in Montreal'. *Social Work* 17, no. 5:8–90.

_____. 1975. 'Social Mobilization and Institutional Resistance'. Doctoral thesis, University of California, Berkeley.

René, J.-F.
1991. 'L'organisation communautaire avec des jeunes'. In *Théories et pratiques en organisation communautaire*, edited by L. Doucet and L. Favreau, 275–92. Ste-Foy: Presses de l'Université du Québec.

_____, and J. Panet-Raymond.
1984. *Faut-il brûler les pancartes?* Montreal: ACEF du Centre de Montréal.

Robert, L.
1971. 'Le comité de citoyens de Hochelaga-Maisonneuve'. Master's thesis, Department of Sociology, Université Laval.

Roy, M.
1987. *Les CLSC: Ce qu'il faut savoir*. Montreal: Éditions Saint-Martin.

Shragge, E.
1993. *Community Economic Development: In Search of Empowerment and Alternatives*. Montreal: Black Rose Books.

_____.
1994. 'Anti-Poverty Movements: Strategies and Approaches'. *City Magazine* 15, no. 2–3:27–9.

_____, and T. Letourneau.
1987. *Community-Initiated Health and Social Services*. Quebec: Commission d'enquête sur les services de santé et les services sociaux.

Tilman, F.
1979. 'Le GRAIN: Groupe de recherche et d'action pédagogiques'. *Revue internationale d'action communautaire* 2, no. 42:25–30.

Chapter Four

Contradictory Participation: Reflections on Community Action in Quebec

Deena White

The analysis of community action presents an increasingly subtle challenge in the 1990s. While we used to be able to differentiate between interest and community groups, bottom-up and top-down organizing, confrontational and cooperative approaches, such analytic distinctions are less and less meaningful. Community action is now most likely to be kindled by the convergence of grassroots and government strategies, in spite of their different objectives. Confrontation and cooperation are no longer separate tactics to be used according to need or inclination, but are integrated in new, holistic strategies that have required the invention of terms such as 'cooperative conflict' (Dommergues 1988; Doré 1990; Lévesque and Mager 1992), 'contradictory participation' (Klein and Gagnon 1991; Maclouf 1985), 'critical cooperation' (Lamoureux 1994a; Panet-Raymond and Bourque 1991), and 'parallel agency' (Lustiger-Thaler and Shragge 1993). These are the lessons drawn from the recent experiences of the community movement in Quebec.

In the previous chapter, Jean Panet-Raymond and Robert Mayer provided an astute appraisal of the evolution of community development, organization, and action in Quebec. They have explained how (despite a long, militant, and highly politicized history) the recessions of the 1980s took their toll on the adversarial energy of the community movement. Weary of the political factionalism that occupied the movement during the 1970s, and faced with both soaring unemployment and government cutbacks in health and social services, activists turned their attention towards responding directly to communities' urgent and intensifying needs. The socio-economic climate of the 1980s depoliticized community action to some extent, but it also stimulated a remarkable proliferation of self-help groups and non-profit organizations, cautiously open to partnerships with government agencies. In the 1990s community action in Quebec has become completely bound up with government policy. This chapter will focus on the recent evolution of that relationship and raise questions about its eventual consequences.

The thesis of the chapter is as follows. By the mid-1990s, community action is virtually institutionalized in Quebec. It is coming to be seen by outsiders, and by many insiders as well, as an established and legitimate category of social organizations and relations—an institutional 'sector'—rather than a local form of resistance, advocacy, or protest movement. This development might mean two things. On the one hand, the values, behaviours, and relationships associated with community action may be permeating the general society to such an extent that they are now accepted as legitimate alternatives to the standard welfare-capitalist ethic. On the other hand, the positions taken by the community movement may have become diluted to the point that they are now easily integrated into the mainstream. We can observe both these tendencies unfolding simultaneously in Quebec, but the power to transform social values is hardly as compelling as the drive towards the 'domestication' of community action. Only the emergence of militant provincial associations of community groups has made it possible to maintain some level of political tension in the seemingly irresistible move towards partnership with the state.

I will illustrate these developments by focusing on one domain of community action that has been at the leading edge of the institutionalization process during the 1990s: the domain of mental health. First, I describe the proliferation of community resources in mental health during the 1980s, and demonstrate how community action and government action combined to develop a politically neutral community *sector*. That decade concluded with the adoption of Quebec's first official mental health policy, the content of which was influenced primarily by the discourse of the community movement.

The second issue is the partnership component of that policy, and the responses of the community movement. Paradoxically, partnerships in regional service planning created the climate for community groups' increasing militancy at the political level. Finally, I discuss new trends in the financing of community groups, trends that go beyond the significant 'contracting' controversies of previous decades. Here the investigation carries us into domains that are rapidly taking over as the major determining forces of community action in Quebec. Community economic development is one of these,[1] but I will focus instead on the impact of Quebec's modified 'workfare' system, since it has been accorded little attention in the literature. Yet more than any other development, it has the potential to transform significantly the underlying ethic of community action in our society.

The Solidarity Ethic

The word 'community' is an emotionally powerful one, for it signifies, on the one hand, a sense of belonging and, on the other, the local, immediate, and familiar social environment. Even political philosophers are lately turning in droves towards communitarian concepts to analyse the nature of 'being together' in society (Corlett 1989; Nancy 1986; Taylor 1989). Governments and other authorities build their rhetoric around the term community to legitimate policies and mobilize the population, whether towards conservative or progressive ends. The symbolism of community has infiltrated the collective imagination and is widely used to validate a vast array of interventions that may have little in common, as Panet-Raymond and Mayer (in this book) mention with respect to community organization and the 'community approach' in CLSCs.[2] Despite its conceptual promiscuity (White 1993a), and the vagueness of the term, community groups seem to have maintained an identifiable ethic that they practise, whether or not they articulate it. This is why the relative depoliticization of the community movement in the 1980s has not entirely wiped out its role as challenger of the status quo. Newer forms of community action may not centre around political activity, but the form and content of their interventions are none the less political in the following sense: they both demonstrate and implicitly call for a more generalized social ethic significantly different from that which distinguishes the private or public sectors (Godbout 1992).

As Panet-Raymond and Mayer have shown, the community movement's challenge to the status quo in Quebec has come to be expressed less and less through direct political action—aimed at challenging the powers that be—and more and more through providing social support resources for those who fall through the state's safety net, or offering alternatives to failing or inefficient public services and programs. Alternative mental health resources have been the most conspicuous in Quebec, since activists succeeded in initiating comprehensive reforms, but women's shelters, centres for homeless youths, and others have played similar roles. In all cases, the principal difference between these projects and those programs implemented by, for example, public ('community') health professionals lies in the significance attached to 'la vie associative': conviviality, or ways of 'being together', are the very essence of the 'intervention'. This seems to be true not only of those organizations initiated by activists but also of less politically conscious, local self-help projects, such as collective kitchens and thrift shops. The 'community' in this form of action is often embodied in the organization itself, consisting of both workers and users for whom the organization *becomes* their community.

In contrast to the solidarity ethic around which community action is structured, private services are structured around the ethic of *exchange*: you get what you pay for. Public services, on the other hand, are structured around an ethic of *mandate*: governments hand responsibilities down to institutions and, in their discharge of these responsibilities, the institutions are accountable to those who conferred the mandate, not to their clients. Both the exchange and mandate ethics are rejected by the very nature of community action. Community groups, including those with no specifically political objectives, are typically born of a feeling of solidarity or shared experience, and the conviction that through collective action ordinary people can make significant change. Potential sources of hierarchical difference, such as 'expertise' versus 'dependence' or 'vulnerability', are downplayed while members (whether workers or users, to the extent that these are distinguishable) both give and seek what they can from the group. The solidarity ethic is embodied, first, in the widespread voluntarism and self-help that characterize community groups; second, on intervention that relies on competence (of both the helper and the person helped) rather than on professional qualifications; and, third, on the mutual gratification of the 'gift relation' (Godbout 1992) rather than on contractual obligation.

But the ethic of solidarity also accounts for other structural characteristics of community organizations, characteristics that make them particularly attractive to the faltering welfare state. First, the relative lack of distance between worker and user can encourage more sensitive and flexible forms of intervention, as well as faster recognition of new or unmet needs. Governments see that community groups may respond more efficiently than traditional bureaucracies to both old and new social problems. Second, and perhaps more importantly, community groups value voluntarism and semi-voluntarism in all its forms. These groups eschew profit, and not only are workers willing to accept absurdly low salaries compared to what their credentials or responsibilities would earn them in the private or public sectors, but also they are not likely to push for unionization since this would drive an 'unnatural' wedge between workers and users. For all these reasons, community organizations come to represent a cost-effective alternative to public services, and shifting from a service system that relies on bureaucratic institutions to one that relies on community groups is a highly attractive proposition for governments (Panet-Raymond 1987; White 1994).

This lies at the root of the Quebec government's efforts to institutionalize the participation of community groups in service planning and delivery. It is not the first time Quebec has made such an effort: community participation was a major theme in the massive health and social service reforms of the Quiet Revolution (Panet-Raymond and Mayer in this book; White 1993c), but lessons were learned from that experience. For example, Quebec's community activists are suspicious of policies that go no further than offering citizens the right to participate on the boards of public establishments. In the past, such policies have ended in powerless participation and ultimately withdrawal or apathetic non-participation (Godbout 1983, 1987). In the 1990s, community participation seems to be taking a *collective* form. The current government seems prepared to recognize a role for organized community interests rather than only for independent citizens. The most recent and definitive evidence of this new track is the Secrétariat à l'action communautaire, inaugurated in April 1995 by former premier, Jacques Parizeau, and affiliated directly with his office. (The current premier, Lucien Bouchard, has gone a step further by committing his government to developing a 'social economy, or non-profit sector'. The first report of the committee set up to examine the practical application of such a policy had not yet been released at the time of this book's publication.) The mandate of the *secrétariat* is to facilitate community groups' access to government resources. According to the government communiqué announcing this move,

> . . . Quebec occupies a privileged position, being amongst those Western nations able to count upon a highly developed community sector. [Parizeau] reminded members of the National Assembly that community action is autonomous action, and that therein lies its strength. But curiously, despite the fact that it is highly regarded and enjoys much respect in those areas where it is practised, community action receives all in all very little support from the state . . . M. Parizeau also mentioned that in his inaugural speech, he had announced his government's desire to recognize community action and to support its development . . . (Communiqué, Cabinet du premier ministre, 27 April 1995; author's translation).

The establishment of this *secrétariat* was a decisive move to institutionalize community action in Quebec: to give it an identifiable and manageable shape and form and to draw it into the 'family' of national institutions recognized and supported by the state. Yet the ambiguity expressed in the communiqué is remarkable: on the one hand, it says the strength of community action lies in its autonomy; on the other hand, it ought to benefit from greater government involvement. However, this ambiguity is echoed within the community movement itself, and has been since the Quiet Revolution. Autonomy has been hailed as the only means for maintaining the ethic that distinguishes community action from behaviour characteristic of the private economy or of public bureaucracies. But in Quebec as elsewhere, sources of funding, such as Centraide (United Way), are highly inadequate. Historically community groups have therefore turned to the government for financing, while simultaneously struggling to maintain their autonomy. The high level of institutionalization reached in Quebec provides a testing ground for this tension: can relatively depoliticized community service groups be drawn into the social mainstream without losing the solidarity ethic that distinguishes them and sets them up as a challenge to traditional ways of operating?

From Community Movement to Community Sector[3]

In Chapter 3, Panet-Raymond and Mayer have described the important shift away from politically oriented community groups towards service-oriented organizations during the 1980s. Among the first generation of service-oriented organizations were those in mental health, responding to the growing needs in the community created by poorly conceived deinstitutionalization and non-institutionalization policies. Initiated by ex-patients or their families, with the help of disillusioned and ideologically driven professionals, many of these early groups were short-lived, folding for lack of funds and other forms of support. However, the momentum was not lost: persistent and pressing needs continued to elicit collective responses, and new groups constantly appeared on the scene.

These community groups could not be easily identified in terms of the services they offered, since these were infinitely diverse and did not lend themselves to any sort of traditional classification (Chaume 1988). They ranged from advocacy and drop-in centres to therapeutic communities and group psychosocial programs, including crisis intervention, housing, etc., sometimes all in the same organization. In some cases, they relied exclusively on self-help rather than the help of 'paraprofessionals'. Their philosophical and political roots were the only consistent characteristics of these alternative resources. On the one hand, they were inspired by the antipsychiatry movement generated in the 1960s by the sociological critique of psychiatry as a form of social control, and of mental illness as a social construct (Cooper 1967; Foucault 1961; Goffman 1961; Szasz 1961). On the other hand, their roots were firmly planted in the community action movement of the 1960s and early 1970s, which stressed localism, participatory democracy, user control, and non-bureaucratic, non-hierarchic organization. They shared as well a common, overarching objective: to remove mental health from the exclusive domain of medical practice, to transform the way that society defined and dealt with mental health problems, and to promote policies of inclusion. Issues such as poverty, housing, and work were seen as central to understanding mental health problems. Interventions focused not on the control of individuals' symptoms but rather on acceptance, flexibility, and collaboration with the users, employing their own perceptions, values, and social relations.

By 1982, about forty of these alternative community organizations banded together to form the Regroupement des ressources alternatives en santé mentale du Québec. The principal objectives of the *regroupement* were to defend the survival of alternative mental health resources, and to apply political and social pressure for the demedicalization of the mental health domain. In fact, it was highly effective. It quickly seized the imagination of the new director of mental health services in the Ministry of Health and Social Services, herself a sympathizer of the community movement, as were many civil servants in the Parti Québécois government of the time.[4] She catapulted the *regroupement* to legitimacy by agreeing to provide funding and by including it in various government-sponsored activities in the field of mental health. From this time on, the *regroupement* was to play a highly influential role in pressing for and shaping mental health reform.

But its members, local-level grassroots organizations, had to scramble for survival. Some found the occasional ally in their Regional Health and Social Service Council, much as the *regroupement* had found an ally within the ministry. The councils did not control any significant funding, but once in a while, an enterprising civil servant could find a few thousand dollars to get a group started, or provide useful information or technical advice. In some cases, reform of the mental health domain became an independent objective of a regional council, and where no grassroots organizations existed, civil servants themselves took on the function of community organizing. Some were able to use funds they received from the ministry for such projects as taking pressure off hospital emergency wards, or funds garnered from hospital cutbacks, to advance the development of community organizations. The participation of some regional councils in this development was not without controversy. Even the most progressive civil servants rarely shared the ideological convictions of grassroots activists. While the councils often supported psychiatric hospitals that wanted to create support structures in the community for their deinstitutionalized patients, the activists ultimately wanted to *remove* the psychiatric establishment and *eliminate* narrow medical treatment. Many refused to provide what they called 'complementary' services (services that supported rather than supplanted medical interventions) or to sign contracts with hospitals.

The upshot of this ambivalent relation between some regional councils and alternative organizations was, first, the rapid multiplication of community groups in mental health, and, second, the ideological diversification of these organizations. For while the antipsychiatry ethos still animated a fair number, many created through support of the councils were less committed to the radical demedicalization of the field. They wanted to see psychiatry's dominant position curtailed, but were primarily interested in elaborating their own forms of intervention. These generally included an antibureaucratic and antivictimization stance, put in practice by working with people in their own neighbourhoods, by cultivating meaningful relations with resource users, and by involving them actively in developing their own autonomy and support networks. Although uninterested in the political dimensions of community action, these groups none the less put the community ethic into practice. The diversification of community organizations in mental health certainly diluted the ideological and political position represented by the original groups that had formed the *regroupement*. But had the community movement ever really represented a close-knit family of ideologically unified groups?

The diversification of actors and the watering down of ideology were inevitable counterpoints to the rapid proliferation of community organizations in mental health. The result was something unknown in Quebec since pre-Quiet Revolution days: the emergence of a 'community sector' that had virtually disappeared with the collapse of church- and lay community-controlled services during the 1960s. The state had taken over with its elaborate system of public services, all couched in community rhetoric. Now when *ad hoc* groups sought funding to provide a service, they had to constitute themselves as some form of legitimate organization with recognizable means for administering funds. The non-profit organization eventually became the official form taken by the service-oriented community action groups of the 1980s, as well as by those groups resulting from top-down community organization by the regional councils. Thus was born a new community sector in Quebec.

The 1990s ushered in a whole host of new possibilities for the cash-strapped state with respect to the provision of social services and the management of increasing socio-economic marginality. The commitment to solutions in the community spread from mental health to other social problems, such as violence to women, youth unemployment, homelessness, the rehabilitation of offenders, and so on. The community sector would come to the rescue, but is it correct to see this development in terms of appropriation and manipulation on the part of government? In fact, by the 1990s the alternative community resources in mental health had won much of what they had been fighting for during the 1980s: more stable funding without enforced contracting or loss of autonomy; the adoption by government of an official, community-oriented mental health policy; a shift of government allegiance away from the psychiatric establishment; and, as we will see in the following section, the collective empowerment of community organizations in the regional planning process. The transformation of a radical community movement into a non-partisan community sector comprised of non-profit, service-oriented organizations was effectively initiated by the demands of the original movement and promoted by a convergence of bottom-up and top-down strategies.

Partnership and the Organization of Organizations

The two most innovative and consequential aspects of Quebec's mental health policy were decentralization and the restructuring of power relations between the major actors in the field of mental health. Each had a significant impact on community development in Quebec, particularly as they piloted a more widespread reform of the entire health and social service domain in the province (White 1992, 1993c). While the community movement tended to have greater faith in local than in central power, the Quebec experience suggested that this was misplaced faith. Throughout the 1980s, community groups had been able to multiply thanks to the relatively generous *marge de manoeuvre* enjoyed by all those authorities at some distance from the central ministry. Thus a wide variety of government departments and agencies were able to justify the funding of community organizations in mental health, and regional councils could often find ways to divert dollars to the cause. But decentralization actually blocked such *ad hoc* strategies.

The mental health policy decentralized planning, coordination, and budgeting for all mental health services to the regional councils, soon to be renamed regional authorities, or *régies*.[5] Community groups would no longer be able to negotiate funding from various bodies within the ministry but would have to work through the new *régies*. The *régies*, on the other hand, having been granted a degree of autonomy from the ministry, concentrated regional administrative authority in their own hands. Furthermore, not only public institutions but also community organizations now fell under their 'jurisdiction'. Such new responsibilities were incompatible with the former role of some as the secret allies of community groups. Thus decentralization actually meant the centralization of authority at the regional level. Furthermore, the policy called for the *régies* to develop five-year plans for the reorientation of mental health services in their territories. Ongoing development of community resources came to a standstill for at least one year while the planning process unfolded. Once the plans were completed, the organizations realized that they would now be called upon to play an official role in dispensing services, but only in so far as they filled specific service slots identified in the regional plans. Community organization had been transformed into an administrative exercise under the decentralized authority of the *régies* (White et al. 1994).

The saving grace was the way that the regional planning process was structured. The policy required the *régies* to constitute tripartite advisory committees made up of equal representation from the psychiatric establishment (including psychiatrists, social workers, and other professionals), community organizations in mental health, and the community at large. For the first time, traditional professionals found themselves forced to debate and negotiate, face to face, with an equal number of 'radicals' who did not share, first, their definition of mental illness and its treatment, and, second, their definition of the proper means and basis for discussion and planning. The exchange of pithy data and executive decision making were foreign to the community representatives, who were more at ease with debates on fundamental issues and decision making by hard-won consensus. Community actors experienced the confrontation of these two universes under the auspices of the technocratic *régies* as a painful 'culture shock' (Guay 1992).

Despite the structural arrangements whereby each social sector was equally represented, the partnership in planning was hardly an equal one. Not only did representatives of community groups have difficulty understanding and using the scientific-bureaucratic language familiar to professionals and technocrats, but they also lacked their sophisticated organizational backup and administrative experience. The representatives of the 'community at large' did not generally come to their aid: the delegates from municipalities, police forces, school commissions, and other public institutions were relatively uninformed and disengaged from the process. Furthermore, they had little understanding of the stakes involved for community groups. In most regions, the *régies*, which were ultimately responsible for the planning process, bulldozed their way through the advisory committees, burying them in barren documents that they had too little time to read, all in an effort to meet the government's deadline for submitting the plans, by hook or by crook. The psychiatric establishment had the wind taken out of its sails, but the community groups were not the winners. Administrative power came out on top.

Paradoxically, both decentralization and the restructuring of power relations had the potential to overthrow the gains that the community movement had made by the end of the 1980s. The community sector would become, in the eyes of the *régies*, simply another set of organizations to integrate into their service delivery system and consultation processes. They had their quirks, but so did the medical types. This prospect was averted, however, by the concerted efforts of the Regroupement des ressources alternatives en santé mentale. Representatives to the regional tripartite committees had typically been local community workers, far more concerned with helping people than with political manoeuvring. The *regroupement* toured the province at the end of the first year of planning and collected information on their jarring experiences. On the basis of this information, they prepared and circulated an evaluation of the process from the perspective of the community groups (Guay 1992) and opened up debate on whether the groups should continue their partnership in regional planning or go back to the instability and insecurity of the old days. Many groups indeed withdrew from the planning partnerships, but the *regroupement* took the position that with the proper backup to provide information and advice to regional and local representatives, and a provincial association active at the political level, there was more to gain than lose.

Indeed, the *regroupement*, working in concert with similar provincial associations in other domains, made considerable gains in their negotiations with the government.[6] For example, although the ministry was supposed to have abandoned all direct funding of community groups as decentralization progressed, it ultimately dropped this plan. Now organizations that do not fit into a regional service plan can still apply for support from the ministry, with the help of the new *secrétariat*. Also, the ministry agreed to a moratorium on the controversial requirement that all community groups receiving government funding be regularly evaluated. A special joint committee of community activists and government representatives could not agree on an evaluation formula nor on who would finance the evaluations. They did agree, however, that since only 1 per cent of the health and social service budget goes to community groups, there was no great loss to the government in dropping the matter. Finally, with the help of the provincial *regroupement*, regional and local umbrella associations of community organizations mushroomed to deal with the new conditions of fundraising and participation. Through their membership in these associations, almost all community groups are now aware of the political issues that affect them. Only a minority are truly militant, and they tend to act as relays between associations in smaller localities, in the regions, and at the centre, but such developments have helped these non-partisan organizations of the community sector to gain or maintain a sense of their distinct identity and role in society.

Formal partnerships between public agencies and community groups were clearly initiated by the government in an attempt to integrate these groups into the service system in a respectful manner, but integration inevitably also means 'normalization', the setting up of rules and procedures regarding the partners' roles, rights, and obligations. Such a preoccupation with administrative concerns resulted in the empowerment of the *régies* rather than of communities. This outcome might have dealt a serious blow to the community movement in Quebec. Instead, by delegating time-consuming political negotiation to provincial, regional, and local umbrella associations, the community movement has actually become repoliticized. The existence of a single, corporate community voice has allowed positions to be formulated and even hardened. There may be a price to pay for repoliticization, however. In a strange parallel to the state of community action in Quebec at the end of 1970s (Panet-Raymond and Mayer in this book) politicization may polarize the community movement. The highly politicized stance taken by militant activists risks alienating grassroots groups that simply want to provide services.

Community Sector or Potential Ghetto?

Struggles over the development and implementation of the mental health policy ushered Quebec's community movement into the 1990s. The process of taming the movement was well underway, first through its redefinition as a legitimate institutional sector and, second, through the initiation of partnerships with the private and public sectors. The trend was to be compounded, however, by reforms in the welfare domain that touched on the community sector in an equally profound but far more subtle fashion.

Since community action began to take the form of meeting communities' needs, financing has always been the crucial determinant of its endurance. The dangers of contracting with government agencies or public institutions has been well documented in the literature (Gutch 1992; Ng 1990; Rekart 1993). In particular, it may interfere with groups' own objectives and ways of working by imposing bureaucratic and professional norms, such as worker-client ratios and limits to client autonomy, or it can lead to external regulation of community groups, for example, through evaluations using criteria such as quotas or other extraneous outcome measures. The threat of the sponsor withdrawing funding and closing the organization down is a potent control mechanism. While developments in the mental health domain suggest that partnerships can be nourished even while contracting is avoided, a more serious and subtle threat lies in the flooding of the community sector with the coerced and unpaid labour of disadvantaged people dependent on the state.

In 1989 Quebec's Ministry of Income Security officially embraced its own version of workfare.[7] Able-bodied welfare recipients receive their full benefit only while participating in formally designated job-search programs, employability development measures, or work experience opportunities. Two types of work experience are offered: one, called EXTRA, simply offers welfare recipients the chance to gain up to one year's work experience, for which they are paid an extra $25 a week over their welfare benefit; the other, called PAIE, consists of a six-month wage subsidy paid to employers, who agree to retain the former welfare-recipient in regular employment at the end of the subsidized period. While on PAIE, the worker exits welfare and is officially employed for the period of the job subsidy and afterwards if the employer agrees to pay his or her salary. In contrast, workers on EXTRA are still officially welfare recipients, are subject to the controls and stigma that accompany that status, and are not protected by the labour code. These workfare programs, and EXTRA in particular, must take much of the credit for the spectacular growth of Quebec's community sector in the 1990s.

Community groups in Quebec have eagerly embraced the EXTRA program. It provides them with a labour pool never before dreamed of. In January 1995 there were over 16,000 welfare recipients working on EXTRA, almost all of them in the community sector (Ministère de la sécurité du revenu 1995).[8] Many see this program as a means for welfare recipients to maximize their monthly income while participating in community work of benefit to society as a whole, and gaining work experience that might eventually help them re-enter the labour force. In some cases, people on welfare who would be volunteering in such groups anyway (occasionally as militant activists) now receive $25 a week for doing so. In the majority of cases, however, people are initially led to community work by the desire to increase their welfare benefits. Both paths are seen as perfectly legitimate by the community groups that 'hire' welfare recipients. Why deprive these people of the chance to effect some small improvement in their situation? In the meantime, new community groups spring up every day on the sole basis of the EXTRA program. This represents an interesting distortion of the concept and ethic of collective and voluntary community action.

Now, not all elements of the community movement approve of taking advantage of the nearly free labour that EXTRA provides. Indeed, the Front commun des personnes assistées du Québec (the chief umbrella association of welfare rights groups) officially opposes EXTRA and counsels members not to use it. It has two principal arguments. First, if people are working, they should be paid and otherwise treated according to the labour code with respect to wages and working conditions. Second, EXTRA actively contributes to the deterioration of the labour market by taking over where the state previously provided the same services at real wages. Some of the most notorious examples are the widespread use of EXTRA or PAIE labour for the provision of basic home care services by CLSCs,[9] and as crossing guards by school commissions, two low-skill areas in which 'normal' jobs have by now been almost eliminated in Quebec. Because such arguments are usually couched in structural and partisan terms, they seem to have little impact on the majority of community groups that are more concerned with helping people than advancing a political agenda. Even groups with a high level of political awareness and a strong political conscience have great difficulty pretending that EXTRA does not exist. If they themselves do not avail themselves of EXTRA labour, they may none the less steer people towards those organizations that do.

The PAIE program raises similar political issues as EXTRA. For example, although these subsidized jobs do conform to the labour code, they are accused of reducing the creation of permanent jobs in private enterprises; for despite the official objective that workers be retained at the employers' cost at the end of the subsidized period, many employers instead avail themselves of repeated subsidies, replacing one PAIE worker with another every six months—and this is often done with impunity since employers are not monitored (White 1995). The pattern has been particularly evident in the case of community organizations that do not have the funds to maintain workers after the PAIE subsidy runs out. Many welfare recipients find themselves caught in a vicious circle leading from welfare to a subsidized minimum wage job in the community sector, to federal unemployment insurance and back to welfare, with all the instability and anxiety that such status changes entail. Indeed, since community groups are clearly less able than private enterprise to accommodate workers after the subsidy, the ministry has decided to limit their use of PAIE as much as possible. It has, however, made a significant exception by inventing a new kind of community organization called the *corporation intermédiaire du travail*.

The *corporation intermédiaire* is a non-profit enterprise involved in the production of goods or services for either the private or public sector, with a primary mandate of employing welfare recipients in subsidized, PAIE positions. This mandate is twofold: first, to offer welfare recipients work experience and training in specific skills to prepare them for participation in the labour market and, second, to become self-financing enterprises within a given number of years. Most sell services to the private sector, such as office cleaning or recycling, and are expected to become self-financing within five years. Those offering public services—for example, home care—enjoy an exceptional status in which eventual autonomy from government subsidy is not expected. Unlike the private and community organizations participating in the standard PAIE program, the new *corporations intermédiaires* are not expected to offer their workers permanent jobs at the end of the subsidy. Instead, they are expected to find placement for them in the private sector labour force at the end of the six-month subsidy. Few are successful in this goal, some reporting success rates of only 5 to 10 per cent.

Their promoters hail the *corporations intermédiaires* as the first step in the development of a 'social economy'—*économie sociale*—a concept of European inspiration claimed to be a strategy to favour social solidarity: the state supports and develops a vibrant non-profit sector to meet social needs by subsidizing jobs for the unemployed (Defourny and Monson Campos 1992; Eme 1990; Laville 1992; Lipietz 1989, 1992). The difference between the development of a 'social economy' and the development of Quebec's *corporations intermédiaires* is this: in a true social economy, subsidies are long term as a means of maintaining people in employment and maintaining the viability of the non-profit sector in certain areas of social importance. For example, in Belgium many local community health clinics (*maisons de santé*) are permanently staffed by professionals, who are paid at subsidy wages but who would otherwise be unemployed. In Quebec, however, the *corporations intermédiaires* serve as a mill through which low-skilled welfare recipients continue in a vicious circle from welfare to PAIE to unemployment insurance and back to welfare.

The story of one highly politicized community group, Le Chic Resto Pop, reveals the dilemma created for community groups by the new workfare programs. Le Chic Resto Pop, as a self-initiated, self-help enterprise for people on welfare, began in a Montreal community with an unemployment-welfare rate of almost 40 per cent. Their plan was to collect donations of surplus foodstuffs from local grocery stores and restaurants, and set up a kitchen-cum-dining room in which they would prepare and serve low-cost meals for other welfare recipients. The objectives were to boost self-respect by running a successful enterprise, and to enhance employability by gaining training and experience in the various skills associated with commercial food preparation and service. Resto Pop has grown considerably, and has become a fixture in the community, a local meal-time meeting place for the jobless. It now 'employs' about ninety welfare recipients in various jobs, for which they receive training and which they are expected to carry out with the same level of discipline required in the labour market. The level of 'forgiveness' for transgressions, such as not showing up for work, is somewhat greater than in the private sector, but not unlimited. While a very few former welfare recipients are now supported in permanent positions through Resto Pop's earnings, most of the workers are welfare recipients on EXTRA, and can stay for up to one year. At the end of the year, almost none of them manage to get jobs in the private service sector. They remain on welfare, losing the $25 weekly supplement they had received while they worked at Resto Pop.

Resto Pop has been embroiled in an ideological war with the major welfare rights umbrella association, the *front commun*. Although it is hardly alone in this practice, Le Chic Resto Pop has expanded through the unpaid work of welfare recipients to the extent that it can no longer be considered a self-help group but is now a medium-size non-profit enterprise. It has come this far, however, without losing its political conscience or its solidarity ethic. Aside from its productive activities, it also organizes its members in direct action, publicly denouncing the welfare system and EXTRA in particular. On the one hand, it defends its massive use of EXTRA by arguing that it is helping welfare recipients obtain the highest possible benefit. On the other hand, it lobbies for its 'employees' to be recognized as 'workers' rather than welfare recipients, since they are indeed carrying out real work that clearly meets the needs of people living in the community. It is inconsistent that they should have to bear the stigma, loss of civil rights, and pitiful income that accompany welfare status. Such recognition would require the state to agree to subsidize Resto Pop and other similar community enterprises at a level where they could pay and otherwise treat their workers according to labour code standards.

Recently the ministry has offered Resto Pop what it has apparently always wanted: subsidies to take their workers off welfare and employ them at minimum wage. The means, however, is through the PAIE program, and would entail Resto Pop accepting the mandate of a *corporation intermédiaire*. In fact, Resto Pop might have been taken as the prototype for the *corporations intermédiaires*, since it does precisely what they are supposed to do—provide workers with the social and vocational skills needed for participation in the labour force—but Resto Pop is refusing to accept such a mandate. It argues that since PAIE does not provide long-term employment, it is no better than EXTRA. Indeed, perhaps it is worse, as there is more instability and uncertainty in leaving welfare for the vicious circle of a short-term subsidized job than in remaining on welfare and participating in EXTRA. Resto Pop and the Front commun des personnes assistées du Québec are in agreement: both are cynical about the *corporation intermédiaire* concept as conceived in Quebec.

The impact of the *corporation intermédiaire* and other welfare programs such as EXTRA on the integrity of the community sector itself is not well recognized, however. For in the 1990s, that sector is fast becoming triply harnessed to postwelfare state policies: first, through its dependence on government financing; second, through its exploitation of a government-packaged labour pool; and finally, in cases such as the *corporations intermédiaires*, through an externally imposed, government-devised mandate. The community sector is being defined as a bridge between the public (welfare) and private (labour market) sectors. It is coming to be identified as a residual employment sector for hard times into which the state can temporarily route its dependants—the deinstitutionalized, the unemployed, welfare recipients, visible minorities, homeless youths, and others. However, as an employment sector, it offers short-term, unstable, low-paid, or unpaid work, work that sometimes need not even meet the terms of the labour code. Exploitative and externally determined relationships are now rapidly infiltrating community organizations. The abundance of non-voluntary labour, the constant turnover, and the remuneration inequities created by workfare programs are endangering the solidarity ethic that has characterized the community sector up to the 1990s.

Perhaps the biggest threat comes from the growth of community organizations themselves as they absorb more and more marginalized workers— including professionals—who find themselves shunted into the sector through coercion rather than conviction. The 'common cause' that bound workers and users in community groups is paradoxically jeopardized by the influx of reluctant 'volunteers' complying with the imperatives of the welfare system. It was to meet the needs of these very people that, in the face of the recessions of the 1980s, the community movement had stridently demanded a political commitment to the steady, stable development of a 'third way', a set of social institutions to meet growing needs, based on local solidarity rather than exchange or administrative control. The current Quebec government has rhetorically embraced this third way, backing it up with policy and even financial commitment, but clearly there is some danger in having wishes granted. Both exchange (increased welfare benefits for community work) and mandates (for example, the *corporations intermédiaires*[10]) are becoming commonplace in the rapidly expanding community sector.

Cautious Optimism

Community and partnership are the dominant slogans of political discourse in Quebec today as elsewhere. They have superseded those of the 1980s: privatization and deregulation. While it was relatively easy to formulate arguments against privatization and deregulation, community and partnership are concepts that appeal to all shades of the political spectrum. They evoke not only consensus and cooperation but also the sharing of power, and thus insidiously disguise the socio-economic schisms that are in fact widening and intensifying in our societies. The depth of poverty is increasing as welfare policies are declared bankrupt, and the number and types of people being moved out of the economy altogether (or to the margins of the economy in part-time, temporary, contractual, non-unionized jobs) are steadily expanding. Can the expansion of the community sector deal effectively with this trend, or is it invoked only as a palliative, a means of countering feelings of powerlessness and exclusion, while local, regional, and even national levels of action become increasingly powerless to take effective control of global economic determinants (White 1994)?

Quebecers tend to be optimistic. Issues relating to the community sector's autonomy, to the risks of state appropriation of community action, or of state exploitation of community groups have been abundantly and critically addressed (e.g., Doré 1990, 1992; Hamel 1993; Lamoureux 1994a; Lévesque and Mager 1992; Lustiger-Thaler and Shragge 1993; Maclouf 1985; Panet-Raymond 1987; Panet-Raymond and Bourque 1991; White 1994). Entire journal issues (*Cahiers de recherche sociologique*, 1994; *Nouvelles pratiques sociales*, 1995) and collections (e.g., Gagnon and Klein 1992; Klein and Gagnon 1991) have been dedicated to these questions. But more often than not, a partnership with the state and the multiplication of local community organizations are ultimately seen as the only means of overcoming the crushing consequences of global economic restructuring. The government is the major supporter of this new consensus. The value for the state of promoting a consensual discourse under current socio-economic conditions is evident, but its political strategy goes further than that. It is apparently prepared to shift public investment into community action. In the health and social service field alone, the funding for community organizations in Quebec has increased more than fivefold in the last decade (Caron 1995), and is the fastest-growing sector of the province's socio-health budget. In the area of income security, the minister argues for 'solidarity with the poor' and 'a new form of social organization':

> Some [community initiatives and practices] are extraordinarily innovative and illustrate particularly well the new logic of poverty as well as new forms of action. Led by community organizations, these new practices are centred on new fields of activity, in response to newly emerging needs; they are founded on novel partnerships with local collectivities. Their originality lies in their basing themselves on the daily practices of the population and on the relations that constitute the fabric of local life . . . It is therefore essential that the state provide them all the support they need (Blackburn 1995:169; author's translation).

The Quebec government may be depending upon community development to deal with the repercussions of globally operative economic practices and strategies, but can community action carry such a responsibility, even with state support? Some community organizers seem to believe so. They find the trend towards the 'communitarization' of social policy both necessary, given contemporary socio-economic conditions, and highly encouraging (Bergeron 1993; Favreau 1995; Gagnon and Klein 1991;Vigeoz 1995). One, writing from a relatively traditional perspective, confidently claims that not global restructuring but 'defeatism' is the principal enemy, and characterizes the current dynamic as heralding: (1) a new relation between the social and economic domains; (2) local empowerment; (3) novel partnerships between the public, private, and community sectors; (4) a holistic, multidimensional approach to social problems; and finally, (5) innovative strategic planning (Favreau 1995). The advancement of partnership policies is generally seen as good for government and for the community sector (Davies and Shragge 1989; Mendell 1991). Both sides recognize that prudence is required to ensure that community action not lose its 'soul', but the prevailing feeling seems to be that the community ethic has at last permeated Quebec's political culture.

How are community activists responding to this overwhelming optimism? We have already seen that those involved in the 'organization of organizations' seem prepared to move towards partnership, but from a position of 'cooperative conflict', implementing strategies of oppositional participation. Collective representation of the community sector, in a quasi-corporatist vein, seems, to them, to hold promise for sustained political clout and maintenance of the sector's distinct identity. But this perspective may prove to be too narrowly corporatist, according to some observers, and may risk alienating the collectivity or grassroots. Rodrigue (1995), for example, warns of a tendency towards sectorial propriety, in which community action is taken to be embodied in the community organizations of the 'third sector'. Communitarization, for him, represents a 'vector of change' rather than the empowerment of a particular set of institutions, and includes a nebulous but ubiquitous shift towards community-based and community-oriented solutions of diverse types. In short, it refers to the emergence of a new relation between civil society and the state. He calls for the radical extension of democratic citizen participation at the individual level as an antidote to the dangers of corporatism, which, from his perspective, weakens the democratic process (Godbout 1983; Rodrigue 1995). Yet he, too, optimistically believes that a new 'political reflex' is emerging in Quebec, in which social change is being initiated at the bottom and is gradually influencing the entire social architecture. In the Quebec of the 1990s, cynicism with respect to this trend is clearly not a fashionable stance.

New Wave or New Struggle?

Has the community movement really permeated Quebec's political culture, or is it perhaps more accurate to say that the current political climate has per-meated the community movement? The community sector today represents an institutionalized version of Quebec's historically vibrant community movement (Lamoureux 1994b). The Quebec government, through its efforts to integrate community-level collective action into its social policies, has made considerable headway in transforming radical politics into interest-group politics, grassroots unrest into services by and for vulnerable social groups, and confrontation into apparent consensus. Nowhere is this success-ful push towards institutionalization more evident than in the recent creation of the Secrétariat à l'action communautaire:

> Madame Lapointe [special advisor to the premier on community action] envisaged that the creation of the Secretariat would provide more direct access by the community sector to government, and also respond to the government's need to be better informed on the concerns and needs of community organizations.... Amongst the mandates of the secretariat [are] ... *to elaborate a global policy of government support for community action* in a spirit of decentralisation, to favour concerted action between the ministries and the organizations concerned with community affairs, and to support inno-vative projects ... [The government] wants to create a light structure but one whose *official character* will give real credibility to this sector at the gov-ernmental level (Leclerc 1995:26; author's translation, italics added).

Clearly the government of Quebec is harnessing community action to its own cause, but the independent voice of community action has never completely disappeared. In Quebec's community movement, cooperation and participa-tion have always been accompanied by opposition and conflict, and vice versa. The current strong tendencies towards service provision, partnership with both government agencies and private enterprise,[11] and rapid, state-supported growth have all engendered ambivalence in even the least politically astute organizations, and regardless of some observers' and organizers' optimism, internal dissent at the grassroots level is becoming more pronounced.

Ambivalence and discord are good things, but they may not be enough. Unopposed state investment could ultimately have the unintended conse-quence of turning the community sector into a peripheral, impoverished, exploitative, non-profit ghetto for the marginalized and excluded (White 1994). The state is routing its traditional target groups into the community sector: the deinstitutionalized, welfare recipients, battered women, visible minorities, and even its own former employees who have lost their jobs in the streamlined public service sector. To survive as a positive social movement rather than as a residual institutional sector, community action must be seen to stand for a coherent and viable alternative to current sociopolitical and economic tendencies. The question remains: Are localism and partnership viable alternatives to current socio-economic tendencies, or are they merely palliative and perhaps even self-defeating strategies in the face of the restructuring of the welfare state? Must such questions be dismissed as 'defeatism', or might they open the door to a new, critical consideration of the place and role of community development in contemporary societies?[12]

Quebec observers, for the most part, approve of the route that is being taken precisely because it appears to conjoin the traditional categories of community development identified, for example, by Rothman (1970): the territorial basis associated with 'locality development', the grassroots initiative associated with 'social action', the strategic dimension associated with 'social planning', and the governmental support associated with 'social reform' and 'community care'. But there is more than simply an amalgamation of approaches represented in the contradictory participation of Quebec community groups today. Rather, this contradictory participation represents the *confrontation* of traditional approaches. On the one hand, we find a convergence of those forms of community action identified by Miller, Rein, and Levitt (1990): grassroots organizing around consumption, based on self-help and advocacy, and couched in terms of social identity, claiming a place in society for the marginal and the excluded. On the other hand, we find the community movement thoroughly embroiled, at the national level, in the most significant of current political issues: the restructuring of the relation between the state and civil society. At this level, where 'the organization of organizations' plays its more important role, the analysis allowed by traditional models of community development may be inadequate.[13]

The institutionalization of the community movement entails, as Quebec shows, a restructuring of the community movement and the emergence of highly influential provincial umbrella associations. It entails the legitimization of the community voice and the creation of avenues of communication to the highest levels of government. These conditions can easily swamp the community movement in sterile bureaucratic exercises, and reduce it utterly to the status of an institutional sector for managing the least fortunate members of society. On the other hand, these same conditions can make way for renewed and more powerful, institutionalized political action to promote an alternative vision of the future of society. While community organizations do their work in the field, the provincial umbrella associations in Quebec are now in a better position than ever to translate that work into a coherent political voice for those being herded into the community sector as both workers and users. The principal danger lies in their becoming a corporate voice for the organizational interests of the community sector rather than a communal voice for the disadvantaged, the marginal, and the excluded.

It would be accurate to say that in the 1990s the community movement has made significant inroads into the mainstream society in Quebec. Its struggle against centralized, bureaucratized, professionalized, and standardized services has been embraced by the state. The value it has placed on local, independent social action and self-help is now recognized and increasingly supported. Indeed, Quebec's society is turning to community action to carry it through a massive, global socio-economic restructuring that has disastrous consequences for local communities. The institutionalization of the community movement in Quebec means that independent community institutions—identified as the community sector—may one day work hand in hand with the private and public sectors in decision-making circles at the highest levels. This is no time to sound the bells of doom. It is important, however, to maintain a firm grip on the alternative nature of the community ethic throughout this period of rapid development and transformation. What distinguishes community action from public and private action is not simply local participation, non-profit organizations, and independently defined objectives. Reduced to these bare characteristics, we have seen that it can still exploit and be exploited.

We will know if the movement has truly influenced political culture, or if it has been a victim of that culture—that is, drawn into its service—when we see that the ethic of solidarity translates into more than the sloughing off of society's most pressing problems onto communities. Doubts will have to be raised if, for example, popular clinics and alternative health organizations are supported by government while it ravages the Medicare system, if community-based employability development services and job-search clubs are supported by government while it dismembers the social safety net, or if community economic development is supported by government while it demolishes local economies through its industrial and trade policies. Community action must roll with the times, but it must also face them down.

Notes

[1]Community economic development has been the subject of a considerable number of Quebec studies, including, Lévesque, Chouinard, and Joyal (1989), Fontan (1991), Shragge (1991), Gagnon and Klein (1992), Lévesque and Malo (1992), and Morin et al. (1995).

[2]CLSCs (*Centres locaux de services communautaires*, or local community service centres) are small,

public, primary health and social service establishments. The network of approximately 160 CLSCs extends throughout the entire province, and receives its mandate (and budget) from the Ministry of Health and Social Services.

[3]This section and the next are based on research carried out by the author and colleagues between 1991 and 1994, under a grant from the National Health and Research Development Program, Health and Welfare Canada, entitled 'The Development of Community Resources in Mental Health: A Study of Reform Processes'. See White and Mercier (1991a and 1991b), White (1993a and 1993b), and White et al. (1994).

[4]The PQ attracted many social democratic intellectuals, including many former community activists, into government positions between 1976 and 1986.

[5]For a view of the impact of the wider health and social service reform on community groups, see Panet-Raymond (1994).

[6]Panet-Raymond and Mayer, in this book, discuss the more militant actions in which numerous associations have cooperated to pressure government on particular issues and to present a coherent, alternative political vision.

[7]This section is based on research carried out by the author and colleagues between 1993 and 1995, supported by the National Welfare Grants, Health and Welfare Canada, entitled 'Welfare as a Site of Social Action'. See McAll et al. (1996).

[8]There are also roughly 3,000 people working in community groups on the PAIE program. These represent a different issue than EXTRA and will be discussed separately.

[9]CLSCs offer a variety of health and social services in line with local priorities. One of their basic mandates is to coordinate home care for the frail elderly, the disabled, and the convalescent. This includes not only skilled nursing services but also relatively unskilled, essential housework and personal care services.

[10]Intermediary structures such as the *corporations intermédiaires*, exist in other domains as well, including the mental health domain. Here they take the form of non-profit organizations established in the community by psychiatric institutions, with a mandate to provide community-based services for the deinstitutionalized patients of that institution alone. Users and workers operate under the authority of the institution. See Guertin and Lecomte (1983); White and Mercier (1989, 1991a, and 1991b).

[11]In the case of community economic development, partnerships are typically formed between municipal agencies, the private sector, and community groups.

[12]These very questions are at the centre of debates around community development the world over, as suggested by the recent international collection edited by G. Craig and M. Mayo (1995), *Community Empowerment: A Reader in Participation and Development*.

[13]At Quebec's 1996 socio-economic summit, organized by the provincial government, the community movement was officially represented along with the union and business sectors. This suggests the need for a more political analysis of the role of community development in the broader context of national socio-economic development.

References

Bergeron, L.
   1993. 'Le rapport partenariat-bénévole: Incompatibilité ou moyen de sortie de crise?'
   Unpublished, Department of Sociology, Université de Montréal.

Blackburn, J.
   1995. 'Nouvelles pratiques et nouvelles perspectives face à la pauvretée des individus et des
   collectivités: L'action du gouvernement québécois'. *Nouvelles pratiques sociales* 8, no. 1:161–71.

Caron, S.
   1995. 'Les enjeux de l'arrimage entre le communautaire et le secteur public vus de la
   fenêtre d'un haut fonctionnaire du Ministère de la santé et des services sociaux'.
   Nouvelles pratiques sociales 8, no. 1:245–52.

Chaume, C.
   1988. 'Les pratiques alternatives en santé mentale au Québec: Un portrait de notre
   différence'. Unpublished, Regroupement des ressources alternatives en santé mentale du
   Québec, Montréal.

Commission d'enquête sur les services de santé et les services sociaux.
   1988. 'Rapport de la Commission d'enquête sur les services de santé et les services
   sociaux' (Rochon Report). Québec: Les publications du Québec.

Cooper, D.G.
   1967. *Psychiatry and Anti-Psychiatry*. Toronto: Tavistock Publishers.

Corlett, W.
   1989. *Community without Unity*. Durham: Duke University Press.

Craig, G., and M. Mayo.
   1995. *Community Empowerment: A Reader in Participation and Development*. London:
   Zed Books.

Davies, L., and E. Shragge, eds.
   1989. *Bureaucracy and Community*. Montreal: Black Rose Books.

Defourny, J., and L. Monson Campos.
   1992. *Économie sociale, entre économie capitaliste et économie publique/The Third Sector:
   Cooperative, Mutual and Nonprofit Organisations*. Brussels: De Boeck University.

Dommergues, P. 1988. *La société du partenariat*. Paris: Anthropos.

Doré, G.
   1990. 'L'enjeu de la "coopération conflictuelle" pour les groupes communautaires'.
   Paper presented at the conference on 'Politiques économiques et politiques sociales: 18
   mois après le libre-échange', Université de Montréal.

————.
1992. 'Les groupes communautaires et le partenariat social au Québec: Une question de stratégie'. Unpublished, School of Social Work, Université de Montréal.

Eme, B.
1990. 'Développement local et pratiques d'insertion'. *Économie et humanisme* no. 315:28–37.

Favreau, L.
1995. 'Quand l'économique interpelle le social: Les nouveaux enjeux de l'intersectorialité dans le champ de la santé et des services sociaux. *Nouvelles pratiques sociales* 8, no. 1:235–44.

Fontan, J.-M.
1991. 'Les corporations de développement économique communautaire montréalaises: Du développement économique communautaire au développement local de l'économie'. Doctoral thesis, Department of Sociology, Université de Montréal.

Foucault, M.
1961. *Histoire de la folie à l'âge classique*. Paris: Plon.

Gagnon, C., and J.L. Klein.
1991. 'Le partenariat dans le développement local: Tendances actuelles et perspective de changement social'. *Cahiers de géographie du Québec* 35, no. 95: 239–58.

————, and J.L. Klein.
1992. *Les partenaires du développement face au défi du local*. Chicoutimi, Quebec: Groupe de recherche et d'intervention régionale, Université du Québec à Chicoutimi.

Godbout, J.
1983. *La participation contre la démocratie*. Montreal: Saint-Martin.

————.
1987. *La démocratie des usagers*. Montreal: Boréal.

————.
1992. *L'esprit du don*. Paris: Éditions la découverte.

Goffman, E.
1961. *Asylums: Essays on the Social Situation of Mental Patients and Other Inmates*. Harmondsworth: Penguin.

Guay, L.
1992. 'Le choc des cultures: Bilan de l'expérience de participation des ressources alternatives à l'élaboration des plans régionaux d'organisation de services en santé mentale'. *Nouvelles pratiques sociales* 4, no. 2:43–58.

Guertin, M., and Y. Lecomte.
1983. 'Éditorial: Structures intermédiares ou alternatives'. *Santé mentale au Québec* 8, no. 1:3–6.

Gutch, R.

1992. *Contracting Out: Lessons from the US*. London: National Council for Voluntary Organisations.

Hamel, P.

1993. 'Contrôle ou changement social à l'heure du partenariat'. *Sociologie et societés* *XXV*, no. 1:173–88.

_____.

1995. 'La question du partenariat: De la crise institutionelle à la redéfinition des rapports entre sphère publique et sphère privée'. *Cahiers de recherche sociologique* 24:87–106.

Klein, J.-L., and C. Gagnon, eds.

1991. *Les partenaires du développement face au défi du local*. Chicoutimi, Quebec: Université du Québec à Chicoutimi.

Lamoureux, J., ed.

1991. *Le choc des cultures, bilan synthèse de la participation aux comités tripartites*. Montreal: Regroupement des ressources alternatives en santé mentale au Québec.

_____.

1994a. 'L'articulation des dynamiques institutionnelle et communautaires: une expérience paradoxale dans le domaine de la santé'. Doctoral thesis, School of Social Work, Université de Montréal.

_____.

1994b. *Le partenariat à l'épreuve*. Montreal: Éditions St-Martin.

Laville, J.-L.

1992. *Les services de proximité en Europe*. Paris: Syros Alternatives.

Leclerc, Y.

1995. 'Là où l'initiative locale est stimultée, le Québec grandit'. *Nouvelles pratiques sociales* 8, no. 1:13–27.

Lévesque, B., O. Chouinard, and A. Joyal.

1989. *L'autre économie, une économie alternative?* Ste-Foy: Presses de l'Université du Québec.

_____, and L. Mager.

1992. 'Vers un nouveau contrat social? Élements de problématique pour l'étude du régional et du local'. In *Les partenaires du développement face au défi du local*, edited by J.-L. Klein and C. Gagnon. Chicoutimi, Quebec: Université du Québec à Chicoutimi.

_____, and M.-C. Malo.

1992. 'L'économie sociale au Québec'. In *Économie sociale, entre économie capitaliste et économie publique / The Third Sector: Cooperative, Mutual and Non-profit Organisations*, edited by J. Defourny and L. Monson Campos. Brussels: De Boeck University.

Lipietz, A.

1989. *Choisir l'audace, une alternative pour le XXIe siècle*. Paris: La Découverte.

———.

1992. 'Bases pour une alternative démocratique'. In *Les formes modernes de la démocratie*, edited by G. Boismenu, P. Hamel, and G. Labica, 275–95. Montreal: Les Presses de l'Université de Montréal.

Lustiger-Thaler, H., and E. Shragge.

1993. 'Social Movements and Social Welfare: The Political Problem of Needs'. In *Welfare Theory*, edited by G. Drover and Patrick Kerans, 161–76. Brookfield, Vermont: Edward Elgar.

McAll, C., et al.

1996. 'Le cheminement des personnes assistées à travers le système d'aide sociale du Québec'. Research report, Équipe de recherche sur la pauvreté et l'insertion au travail, Department of Sociology, Université de Montréal.

Maclouf, P.

1985. 'Les restructurations économiques et l'ancrage territorial de la crise de l'État-providence'. *Revue internationale d'action communautaire* 13, no. 53.

Mendell, M.

1991. *New Social Partnerships*. Unpublished. Montreal: Karl Polanyi Institute of Political Economy, Concordia University.

———.

1993. *New Social Partnerships: Crisis Management or a New Social Contract?* Montreal: Karl Polanyi Institute of Political Economy, Concordia University/Éditions du Seuil.

Miller, S.M., M. Rein, and P. Levitt.

1990. 'Community Action in the United States'. *Community Development Journal* 25, no. 4:356–68.

Ministère de la sécurité du revenu.

1995. *Rapport statistique mensuel: Programmes de la sécurité du revenu, janvier 1995*. Quebec City: Gouvernement du Québec.

Morin, R., et al.

1995. 'Les corporations de développement économique communautaire en milieu urbain: L'expérience montréalaise'. Montreal: Département d'études urbaines et touristiques, Université du Québec à Montréal.

Nancy, J.-L.

1986. *La communauté désoeuvrée*. Paris: Christian Bourgois.

Ng, R.

1990. 'State Funding to a Community Employment Centre: Implications for Working with Immigrant Women'. In *Community Organisation and the Canadian State*, edited by R. Ng, G. Walker, and J. Muller, 165–83. Toronto: Garamond Press.

Panet-Raymond, J.

1987. 'Community Groups in Quebec: From Radical Action to Voluntarism for the State?' *Community Development Journal* 22, no. 4:281–6.

──────.

1994. 'Les nouveaux rapports entre l'État et les organismes communautaires à l'ombre de la loi 120'. *Nouvelles pratiques sociales* 7, no. 1:79–93.

──────, and D. Bourque.

1991. Partenariat ou pater-nariat? (La collaboration entre établissements publics et organismes communautaires oeuvrant auprès des personnes âgées à domicile). Unpublished. Montreal: School of Social Work, Université de Montréal.

Rekart, J.

1993. *Public Funds, Private Provision: The Role of the Voluntary Sector.* Vancouver: University of BC Press.

Rodrigue, N.

1995. 'La communautarisation: Vecteur de changement sociale'. *Nouvelles pratiques sociales* 7, no. 1:229–34.

Rothman, J.

1970. 'Three Models of Community Organization Practice'. In *Strategies of Community Organization: A Book of Readings*, edited by F. Cox et al. Itaska, Illinois: Peacock Publishers.

Shragge, E.

1991. *Community Economic Development in Montreal: Some Political Questions.* Montreal: School of Social Work, McGill University.

Szasz, T.

1961. *The Myth of Mental Illness.* New York: Hoeber-Harper.

Taylor, C.

1989. 'Cross-purposes: The Liberal-Communitarian Debate'. In *Liberalism and the Moral Life*, edited by N. Rosenblum. Cambridge: Harvard University Press.

Vigeoz, M.

1995. 'Les enjeux de l'arrimage entre le communautaire et le secteur public vus de la fenêtre d'une directrice générale de CLSC'. *Nouvelles pratiques sociales* 7, no. 1:221–7.

White, D.

1992. 'La santé et les services sociaux: Réforme et remise en question'. In *Québec en jeu*, edited by G. Daigle, 225–47. Montreal: Les Presses de l'Université du Québec à Montréal.

──────.

1993a. 'The Community-Based Mental Health System: What Does It Mean?' *Canadian Review of Social Policy* 31:31–61.

————.

1993b. 'Les processus de réforme et la structuration locale des systèmes: Le cas de la réforme dans le domaine de la santé mentale au Québec'. *Sociologie et sociétés* 25, no. 1:77–97.

————.

1993c. 'The Rationalization of Health and Social-Service Delivery in Quebec'. In *Health, Illness and Health Care in Canada*, 2nd ed., edited by B. Singh Bolaria and H.D. Dickinson, 83–105. Toronto: Harcourt Brace Canada.

————. 1994. 'La gestion communautaire de l'exclusion'. *Lien social et politiques: Revue internationale d'action communautaire* 32:37–51.

————.

1995. 'Québec's Employability Development Programs: A View from the Inside'. *Policy Options* 16, no. 4:25–8.

————, and C. Mercier.

1989. 'Ressources alternatives et structures intermédiaires dans le contexte québécois'. *Santé mentale au Québec* 14, no. 1:69–80.

————, and C. Mercier.

1991a. 'Coordinating Community and Public-Institutional Mental Health Services: Some Unintended Consequences'. *Social Science and Medicine* 33, no. 6:729–39.

————, and C. Mercier.

1991b. 'Reorienting Mental Health Systems: The Dynamics of Policy and Planning'. *International Journal of Mental Health* 19, no. 4:3–24.

————, et al.

1994. 'The Development of Community Resources in Mental Health: A Study of Reform Processes'. Montreal: Groupe de recherche sur les aspects sociaux de la santé et de la prévention, Université de Montréal.

Chapter Five

Thirty Turbulent Years: Community Development and the Organization of Health and Social Services in British Columbia

Michael Clague

This chapter attempts to capture the essence of community work in this province through almost four decades, from the 1960s to the 1990s. It does so primarily through the perspective of the human care services, particularly health and social services. In the 1960s and 1970s these two sectors experienced more challenge and turbulence than any other, and community development was intimately connected with much of it through government and independent citizen advocacy. While the health and social services story is woven throughout the chapter, it is set in the context of the political and economic conditions of each decade and of the other community development activity that emerged in response to these conditions.

1960s and 1970s: Turbulence and Change

Since the mid-1960s there have been significant attempts to integrate community development into the health and social services of the province. Beginning in the 1960s and extending through to the mid-1970s were several imaginative and comprehensive developments that, as at present, were initiated by the provincial government. These were in addition to the major federal programs of the period described elsewhere in this book.

The story really begins in Vancouver, for the provincial initiatives were preceded (albeit with provincial support through the Canada Assistance Plan) by important experimentation within the city. The innovative work during this period had significant influence on government initiatives that were soon to follow throughout British Columbia, particularly in social services.

The City of Vancouver and the United Way (then United Community Services), with financial support from the two senior governments, established the Local Area Approach in 1964. Local citizen area councils were established in city neighbourhoods. They were matched by local area services teams made up of front-line workers from voluntary and public social, recreation, education, and health agencies. Together the two groups worked to ensure that services addressed local needs and priorities. Each area council had a community development worker chosen from the community development staff of the Neighbourhood Services Association and funded by the United Way and the City, with the Canada Assistance Plan (CAP) matching dollars. Each area services team had a social planner assigned by the city's Social Planning/Community Development Department.

At city hall, a Social Development Committee of Council, chaired by a councillor, was composed of the elected heads of the school and parks boards and the chairperson of the library board. As at the local level with the area services teams, a City Joint Technical Committee was composed of the directors of the school board, parks and library boards, and United Community Services (United Way) and was chaired by the director of Social Planning/ Community Development.

The Local Area Approach itself was the outcome of an early 1960s experiment, known as the Area Development Project, in the Little Mountain area of Vancouver. This project focused on coordinating the multiplicity of social services to poor people in public housing, and involving them in developing new approaches to social support.

In the late 1960s and early 1970s community development activities in health and social services further accelerated in British Columbia. They were fuelled in part by important initiatives elsewhere. The national report of the Commission on Emotional and Learning Disorders in Children (CELDIC) was a landmark statement in the planning and provision of human care services (CELDIC 1970). It went far beyond its immediate constituency and mandate in arguing that services needed to be decentralized to neighbourhoods, coordinated and integrated through the community services centre model, and held locally accountable through community management of these centres. The Castonguay-Nepvu Commission in Quebec applied similar principles to the organization of health and social services in that province, and the new system that resulted was quite unlike anything else in North America. It was followed by the federally funded report on community health centres by John Hastings, of the University of Toronto.

No doubt another influence was the 1960s War on Poverty in the United States. It, too, advocated greater community and consumer input in human care services. One of its expressions was the neighbourhood services centre, a place for advocacy, for supporting neighbourhood groups, and for coordinating and providing services.

In Vancouver's downtown east side, First United Church had an advocacy ministry. Its staff and volunteers challenged the social and environmental conditions that degraded life for people in the city's poorest neighbourhood. The church also helped launch the Inner City Services Project. Inner City, operating out of a former church, hosted a variety of student social action projects. The founder of Inner City's community law office would become the province's second New Democratic premier. Inner City sponsored The Plunge. Social work students and others working as advocates for social justice were given $5 and had to survive for two nights and three days on the streets of the inner city.

In Strathcona, the predominately Chinese community in the inner city, young people and their parents teamed up to oppose the construction of a freeway and the destruction of their homes for urban renewal projects. Their organization, the Strathcona Property Owners' and Tenants' Association, gained national recognition for imaginative preservation of their historic neighbourhoods. They also cooperated with the activist youth organization in the neighbouring Grandview-Woodlands area (Association to Tackle Adverse Conditions) and the Grandview-Woodlands Area Council to defeat the planned freeway. In this same period, the Militant Mothers of Raymur, in a large public housing project in the east side, staged a sit-down on a railroad track to protest the danger it posed for their children *en route* to school. An overpass was built.

On Commercial Drive, in Grandview-Woodlands, the REACH Community Health Centre brought University of BC medical students, local doctors, nurses, nurse practitioners, dentists, and nutritionists together to provide a community-based health program. The Community Information Centre on Commercial Drive was also a centre for community organizing and advocacy, sponsored by the area council, one of a half-dozen such centres supported by United Way and city funds in local areas of the city. Later, in the mid-1970s, the large Britannia Community Services Centre would be located just off Commercial Drive.

The Britannia Community Services Centre epitomized the CELDIC report, occupying nine buildings on a 17-acre (7-ha) site. The centre offered educational, social, recreational, and library services, including an elementary and secondary school, a pool, and a rink. Britannia had its own community-managed board, funded by the city, coordinating the planning and provision of the services of public and private agencies, with its own administrative staff. Britannia pioneered the fullest expression of decentralization of services to the community, coordinating and integrating them, and having them locally accountable. It was very much a part of the temper of the time: to rejuvenate communities and neighbourhoods by giving authority and responsibility to the people who live there.

Outside Vancouver, in the Fraser Valley community of Abbotsford, a rural variant of the community services centre model was launched. Matsqui-Abbotsford Community Services (MACS, now Abbotsford Community Services), funded by National Welfare Grants and sponsored by the Social Planning and Review Council of BC (now Research Council), was a direct application of the CELDIC report to British Columbia. MACS gathered in under a single society a number of services that were functioning under federal and provincial grants and contracts. This agency has continued to grow and prosper, and is now a singularly successful organization.

The confluence of people and events of this period was a mixture of serendipity, optimism for what might be possible, and a climate filled with the winds of change. Some of the actors were younger, coming out of the student activism of the 1960s. Others had long chafed in the human care systems in which they worked. Poor people, too, were, for the first time since the Great Depression (but in a very different economic climate), organizing and making themselves known, laying claim to the same prosperity that the majority of citizens were enjoying. Public housing tenants' associations, antipoverty groups, and single parents on social assistance were particularly prominent. This feisty turbulence produced some creative outcomes, occasionally from rather unusual parentage. One such example was the Vancouver Opportunities Program (VOP).

The VOP was a publicly funded program managed by women on social assistance. Member of Parliament Grace McInnis and community organizer (and later Member of Parliament) Margaret Mitchell assisted the women in creating their organization. It included mutual support and self-help groups, life skills and pre-employment training, volunteer placements in community organizations and citizen advocacy groups, and job development. VOP members were entitled to receive an additional $50 per month (if single) or $100 (if a parent) on top of their social assistance allowance. By 1975 the VOP members were administering a budget of $1.85 million from the Department of Human Resources for approximately 1,500 active volunteers (Mitchell and Goldney 1975:46).

The VOP secured the support of the conservative city council and administration of the day and of the long-reigning and decidedly conservative and populist Social Credit government. The VOP is a classic example of change as a product of the environment, people, the circumstances of the moment, and resources. With respect to the latter, the introduction of the Canada Assistance Plan in 1965 proved to be invaluable for projects like the VOP. The CAP provided 50 per cent in matching federal funds for community development work with poor people, making it easier for local and provincial governments to support such work.

There was increasing recognition in the late 1960s that the postwar prosperity had left some groups behind and that the existing policies and programs were inadequate to building genuine inclusion for poor people. Too often there were traps. The civil rights movement in the United States had raised the profile for social justice in many Western countries. There were people inside and outside the conservative structures of the day who saw the need for change.

1970s: Provincial Government Experiments

The arrival of the first new government in more than fifteen years in British Columbia unleashed a backlog of change and reform. That it happened to be a New Democratic government meant that particular attention was paid to human care services. The changes here shared similar themes: make services more responsive and more accountable; promote citizen participation; encourage rationalization and decentralization, coordination and integration. The departments of the attorney-general, education, health, human resources, and the Alcohol and Drug Commission all initiated changes within their respective systems, which tested these themes as instruments for the implementation of policies (Clague et al. 1984:27–8).

The attorney-general's department launched three pilot Unified Family Court experiments. Community panels were established with these courts. Two citizens would sit with the judge in hearing child protection cases, and advise the judge in arriving at the dispensations or findings. A family court counsellor could help families with a new approach (mediation), which could mean going to court with an agreement rather than seeking judicial settlement of family disputes. The counsellor could provide referral to other services and coordinate families through the two or three levels of court if necessary.

Another innovation from the attorney-general's department was the introduction of community justice councils. Composed of local volunteers, the councils provided an opportunity for citizen input into the justice system. They could look at whatever issues might interest them (youths, alcohol and drugs, legal aid) and pass on their views and recommendations to the department. Regional justice council coordinators acted as community development workers in bringing citizens together.

The most far-reaching reforms were proposed and attempted in health care and social services. Community human resources and health centres were to be the harbinger of a complete reorganization of health care in BC, part of Dr Richard Foulke's *Health Security Program for British Columbians* blueprint, commissioned by the provincial government.

Community resources boards were the inspiration of Norman Levi, the new minister of human resources. Norm Levi had worked in the John Howard Society and was committed to a major overhaul of social services. He took to heart the message of reports such as CELDIC, that we defined children by their problem and that our response was characterized by fragmentation, gaps, and duplication, and that neither the client nor the community had a significant voice in this process. Levi was a founder of the 'Action Slate', a group of social and community workers who ran candidates for the board of the United Way, independent of the slate proposed by the board's nominating committee. Their aim was to break what they saw as the establishment domination of the United Way: a closed shop of business, professional, and institutional interests more concerned with doing things 'to' poor and marginalized people than in helping them gain control of their lives (though, paradoxically, the United Way was also a major partner in funding community development in the city). Levi and his colleagues also led union-organizing drives in the established non-profit agencies with the aim of improving wages and working conditions.

The community resources boards (CRBs) were to become the most fully developed of the changes launched by the government during this period. Local residents were elected to boards through the municipal electoral system (though the elections were not always held to coincide with the regular municipal balloting, a factor that contributed to low turnout for the CRB polls). Their responsibility outside the City of Vancouver was to coordinate the setting of community priorities for non-statutory social services, and to recommend to the minister the allocation of funds to community organizations for this purpose. This process of community grants would evolve into today's contract for service practice, with both non-profit agencies and private social service firms as the primary vehicles for service provision in the province.

In Vancouver the CRB model was carried further. The Vancouver Resources Board (VRB), established under provincial statute, was responsible for statutory and non-statutory social services. It took over the work of the Catholic and non-sectarian Children's Aid Societies and the City Welfare Department, plus additional responsibilities stipulated by the provincial government (including grants to non-profit community organizations to fund locally developed, non-statutory services in response to provincial priorities, usually of a preventive and remedial nature). The VRB's governing board was composed of representatives of neighbourhood CRBs (who formed the majority) and appointments from the city, the school board, and the minister. Each of the CRBs had its own locally elected board of directors and management staff. The CRBs coordinated social services planning in their neighbourhoods and made recommendations to the VRB for the allocation of grant monies to community groups.

Six community human resources and health centres were established. The James Bay community in Victoria was the only urban centre. The remainder were in remote and semiremote areas of BC; the Queen Charlotte Islands, Houston, Granisle, and Grand Forks. Each had a package of provincially mandated core services: public health, medical (staff doctors), and social services. To these the centres could use their operating budget to add other human care services. Locally elected boards were supported by their own management staff. The nursing and social services staffs were seconded from the ministries of health and human resources. The centre hired the doctors under contracts negotiated provincially by the Ministry of Health and the BC Medical Association.

However, the life span of these experiments was brief. A return to a Social Credit government in 1975 heralded their demise. First to go was the community resources board system, replaced by the provincial Ministry of Human Resources, directly operating statutory and non-statutory social programs through its management regions in the province. The experiment in citizen participation in governance ended. Ministry managers and officials in Victoria managed the grants and contracts for service with no formal community participation. Interestingly, many of the non-metropolitan CRBs (and those CRBs waiting to be officially designated) continued as community resources societies in their communities. They became active in providing provincial services under contract and were to evolve into the multiservice agencies operating around the province today.

The community human resources and health centres did not expire so quickly. They were providing badly needed services in remote areas and, in the case of James Bay, had strong community support, and were sheltered by sympathetic officials in government. Two still continue to function, one in James Bay and the other in the Queen Charlotte Islands (Haida Gwaii). However, they lost their legislated status long ago and function as private health care societies. The Ministry of Human Resources ended its commitment to providing social services staff many years ago (though local arrangements mean that ministry social workers still work closely with the centres).

In so many ways the community resources boards and the community human resources and health centres represented the full realization of the pioneering ideas and experiments of the 1960s: decentralizing services to the community; coordinating, integrating, and rationalizing them; and creating a local political accountability for human care services to the *whole* community where none had existed before (or since).

These major public policy initiatives in the 1960s and 1970s seemed at the time to demonstrate that the lessons of countless years in community work and social services could at last be transmitted to and transform public sector institutions and bureaucracies. Although elements of these changes have continued, their distinguishing essential characteristics vanished quickly. What remain, whether the Britannia Community Services Centre or the community human resources and health centres, are but mismatched appendages, aberrations to larger systems with whom they have little in common.

What were the reasons for the failure of the grand CRB experiment? In their book on the subject, Clague et al. (1984) suggest several. The community resources boards were seen variously as a nuisance and a threat by local governments and by some in the social agency establishment. The bureaucracy in the Department of Human Resources was uncomfortable with this new community-based system, which was of the department, yet not part of it. Nor, within the government, was there informed, solid support behind the necessary display of public unity. Some government members of the legislature felt uncomfortable with the boards. Their role in the allocation of provincial funds for community priorities challenged the traditional influence of MLAs.

The CRB elections brought the most negative publicity to the experiment. Indeed, the experiment might well have survived if the Community Resources Act had not called for public elections of citizen boards. Advisory boards, appointed by government, are much less threatening, but then they are a far cry from community governance.

Public support for the community resources boards idea never gelled. It was evident in the low voter turnout for elections. The major media were openly hostile. While those elected to serve on boards and other volunteers associated with them became well informed and generally keen supporters (regardless of political orientation), lack of public understanding about the role and place of social services in the community contributed to the lack of interest or support for this experiment.

Issues of power and accountability were the two main reasons for the demise of the community resources boards. They threatened the power of established interests. These same interests inevitably exploited the vulnerability of the boards on the matter of accountability. Though popularly elected, the boards were influencing and determining the expenditure of provincial dollars, not dollars they were responsible for raising locally. Critics suggested this was an incompatible situation (Clague et al. 1984:195–212), yet the legacy of the community resources boards suggests that while this is an important issue, it is possible to form partnerships between senior and local governments that ensure accountability to both senior government and local community priorities. The Britannia Community Services Centre in Vancouver, Abbotsford Community Services, and the James Bay Project are three notable examples that are functioning well more than twenty years since their establishment. So, too, are multiservice agencies in communities like Terrace, Parksville, Kelowna, Golden, and Nelson, the origins of which are in the community resources societies and boards of the 1970s.

1980s: The Arrival of Neoconservatism in British Columbia

On 27 July 1983 twenty-seven bills were introduced in the provincial legislature. They cut like a knife through government programs and services. At once a number of government agencies were terminated, from the Motor Vehicle Testing Service to the Human Rights Commission. Renters' protection was reduced. School district finances were taken over by the province. When the Vancouver School Board refused to comply, the elected trustees were replaced by a provincially appointed administrator. The salaries of senior municipal administrators were frozen. Fines or jail sentences could be imposed on any municipal council that disobeyed. In social services, provincial child abuse teams were abandoned. A number of other services in social services and corrections departments were terminated and put out to contract.

The major trigger for the public mobilization that followed, however, was Bill 33, which authorized lay-offs in the public service without regard to seniority. In the highly unionized provincial workforce of the period, this was seen as a deliberate provocation of organized labour. Ten thousand civil servant positions were to be abolished without any established process.

These events happened shortly after the re-election of the Social Credit government (the second since the fall of the NDP in 1975). They were unexpected. In its previous mandate, this same administration had abolished the community resources boards of the NDP, but had in other ways maintained and expanded social programs. Indeed, its consolidation of all public, private, and non-profit care programs for the elderly into a new long-term care program was generally seen as a progressive and far-reaching improvement.

A dramatic fall in government revenues from natural resources was the official reason for the dramatic actions in 1983. However, it was evident that these changes also had a new ideological bent. According to the minister of finance, 'where possible government . . . [intended] to give the private sector the opportunity to take over functions and activities not appropriate to government' (Rekart 1993:33). This was the new ('neo') conservatism.

Downsizing was occurring, not just because of government financial problems but because of a belief that the government's role in a postwar welfare state had to be changed. The private sector, the community, and the family had to assume much more responsibility for the well-being of society and themselves. In the process, the language of community acquired new meanings. Those in community development and those on the new right ('neoconservatives') used many of the same words, but they held quite different meanings.

Whereas community development focused on social justice and collective social responsibility through both the community and the state, the new right focused on individual initiative and responsibility in place of the state, and by default to the community. Whereas community development argued for the state to redress the imbalance of power between rich and poor and to empower more equitable, democratic communities, the new right argued for the market as the primary means for generating and distributing wealth and opportunity in the community and society. Community development challenged the state to practise fully the democratic ideals that it professed. The new right challenged the state to step aside: 'conservatives must actively work for the welfare state to whither [sic] away as personal prosperity and independent provision takes its place' (Clague 1984:45).

For community development, 'community' means deliberately strengthening the formal and informal obligations and systems of governance that people have to support and care for one another, assisted by the state to ensure equity. To the new right, these obligations may be important, but they are a matter of individual choice, a place in which the state has little or no part. People will act voluntarily in community to collaborate on social concerns if they so wish.

Regarding this point, the familiar conservative, liberal, and democratic socialist parties in postwar Western governments had held the common belief that government had a public, social responsibility for its citizens' welfare. Where they differed was on the means (more or less direct government), not on the fact that government had such a responsibility. Now the provincial government, committed to a different ideology, took the position that the family and the community were responsible for social welfare.

The government's dramatic actions in the summer of 1983 immediately gave rise to widespread public protests and wildcat strikes. Two major movements were born. Operation Solidarity brought public sector and private sector unions together to oppose the labour legislation. The Solidarity Coalition, also organized by labour, brought community organizations, social justice advocacy groups (antipoverty and equity groups), and labour together. Large marches and demonstrations were held in Victoria and Vancouver. Public transit shut down, and teachers stayed away from work for a day. There was the remarkable sight of the International Woodworkers of America providing parade marshals and security for thousands of people of all ages marching through the streets. In the process of planning these actions, an eclectic variety of people learned to work together: gays and lesbians, people with disabilities, students, racial minorities, and the public and private sector unions were all learning how to work together—a remarkable and unlikely alliance.

All the partners in the solidarity movement had agreed to similar goals: halt the lay-offs and restore the programs and agencies that furthered social equity in the province. For the unions, however, the major issue was the threat to the fundamental principle of seniority in collective agreements. On the verge of a provincewide general strike, the premier met with the acting leader of Operation Solidarity. The premier agreed to reinstate seniority and to hold further discussions on the other issues. The strike was called off. The government was to make no other changes or concessions.

Operation Solidarity wound down in the subsequent two years. The Solidarity Coalition organized a large program of public forums around the province, producing a 'people's report' to offer a clear alternative to government's neoconservative agenda. The coalition gradually dissolved, and the government and its agenda remained in place. Power in the provincial government was more centralized than it had been for a long time. There were no initiatives to strengthen partnerships with communities in health care and social services, or to foster community development.

However, there was no escape from the need for change in the organization and provision of human care services in the province. During the 1980s there were two developments, one by the government and one outside government. The first illustrates the weakness of any change initiative if it lacks conceptual vision and commitment to systemic reform. The second epitomizes an abandonment of belief in government, urging consumers to take matters into their own hands.

During the 1980s in BC, there was an effort to improve interministerial collaboration through the Inter-Ministerial Child and Youth Committees regionally and locally. These were replaced in the early 1990s by Child and Youth Committees, supported by the Child and Youth Secretariat in Victoria. The secretariat, as of this writing, has just been disbanded. A new Ministry for

Children and Families has been established. This ministry is consolidating almost all services for families and children that were previously provided through half a dozen other ministries, with the exception of education.

The experiments with the Inter-Ministerial Child and Youth Committees and the Child and Youth Committees had inherent weaknesses. There was a lack of political will to make them work. They were concerned with overcoming obstacles in the existing ministerial systems rather than with making systemic change. They lacked accountability to consumers and the community. The new ministry is an attempt at systemic change.

While the above examples have focused on attempts to make existing government policies and practices work better, the self-help/mutual-help empowerment movements have eschewed government (though, paradoxically, government itself has been a promoter of this philosophy, notably in health care). In British Columbia this movement has two primary components. One is that of client empowerment, particularly in mental health and for the mentally challenged. The other is more diffuse—an invitation for those who share common problems or difficulties to come together in groups and networks for mutual support and help.

The BC Association for Community Living (BCACL) is an especially noteworthy example of client empowerment for people with mental challenges and their relatives. The association has drawn on the work and advice of John McKnight, an American academic and community worker. McKnight is a severe critic of social services as a self-serving, need-creating industry. He argues for less governmental, bureaucratic, and professional intrusion in clients' lives. The money saved, he proposes, should be given directly to the clients themselves.

McKnight is a powerful influence among those who have been dependent on government and the 'system'. His advocacy of an assets rather than a needs approach is an affirming message for people who have been dependent and disenfranchised. His advice and support, linked to the BCACL as one of the most effective advocacy networks in the province, have in many ways revolutionized for the better the respect and treatment accorded people who are mentally challenged. Equally important, it has changed the nature of volunteering among their friends and supporters. It becomes a mutual learning opportunity based on shared interests and managed as much as possible by the mentally challenged themselves.

The BCACL story is a good example of a successful community development strategy in the human care services that was initiated outside of government in the 1980s, and that affected major public policy and organizational change for the better. This has meant giving authority and resources to the parents of mentally challenged people and to the mentally challenged themselves. In place of large, passive, state-run institutions, there are now parent-, client- and community-managed non-profit group homes. Mentally challenged people sit on the boards of these organizations. They are supported in making independent and collective decisions to the full extent of their capacities. They are encouraged and assisted in participating in work and community life. They have access to 'client advocates', and a new Adult Guardianship Act (not yet promulgated) helps ensure they are treated as human beings with respect, dignity, and security of person. BCACL achieved these changes through dramatic advocacy (sit-ins when a major institution was being closed with no assurances for the future of its residents), through cultivating public opinion and the media, and through astute negotiations with politicians and bureaucrats. System change did result.

The other self-help/mutual-help component is broader and more diffuse in its origins and philosophy. It is, however, omnipresent throughout the human care services and virtually every other facet of organized living. Its premise is simple: people who share common problems, conditions, and interests come together for mutual emotional and practical support. Through such associations and networks, its members are helped in managing their own lives and contributing to the well-being of others in similar circumstances.

Self-help/mutual-help/empowerment movements have contributed significantly to changing thought and practice in human care services. In the case of BCACL, they have generated changes in the system. However, systems have short memories. They fail to take the lessons learned from one experience (e.g., BCACL) and apply them to their responsibilities elsewhere. And even where there is success, it is necessary to be vigilant about encroaching bureaucratization and disempowerment.

In their disenchantment with the system, the self-help/mutual-help/empowerment movements have begged the question about changing the forms and practices of governance and administration that created the dependency model. They may be frustrated by it, they may take large swipes at it, but they have not developed thorough and compelling alternatives for how public policies, public administration, public funding, and governance can best support the values and practices these movements represent. Without such new arrangements, the system itself will remain out of step and an obstacle to their realization.

At the conclusion of the 1980s community development in health and social services was limited to the self-help/mutual-help/empowerment movements. The provincial government had, however, spawned and supported a whole new relationship with the voluntary sector—that of the 'purchase of service' contract. The downsizing of government, particularly in social services, had produced a huge 'upsizing' in the number and size of non-profit social agencies and businesses providing services with public funds that might in former times have been done by government. Despite its rhetoric, government had not abandoned its role to support a diverse range of social services (Rekart 1993:74). It did so, however, through surrogate agencies, and community development was not an active presence in the contracting process.

By the end of the decade there was another sector, that of community economic development, in which community development had taken root and was showing promise. The tough economic times in the first half of the 1980s encouraged groups that were hardest hit to take an interest in taking charge of their own economies. Community economic development emphasized the development of local human and financial resources. Federal programs, like Community Futures and Innovations, were major catalysts. Advocacy and community development organizations, like the Social Planning and Research Council of BC, Westcoast Development, and Womenfutures, conducted workshops and training around the province. Non-profit community agencies, like Abbotsford Community Services, incorporated profit-generating enterprises to supplement their budgets and provide training and employment opportunities for clients.

The 1980s brought to an end the buoyant optimism of social progress and economic growth that had characterized postwar British Columbia. A sharp economic depression and then an economic upturn incorporating jobless growth, the loss of high-paying jobs in the resource industries (notably forestry), and growth in lower-paying service sector employment were all evidence of an economy in transition—one harnessed to global trends in trade, technology, and international finance.

The future was filled with much economic, social, and psychological uncertainty. The rise of the community food bank is perhaps the most telling legacy of the decade. Not since the 1930s had there been such a large non-sectarian response to hunger among British Columbians. The public social safety net could not cope with the basic food and shelter needs of the poor, whose numbers were being swelled by the newly unemployed and by the employed whose income was inadequate.

Food banks posed a conundrum to community workers. Some saw the issue in very straightforward terms: the mobilization of resources to feed hungry people. Others resisted involvement, convinced that supporting food banks was letting government off the hook for meeting its social obligations. Some, such as the Vancouver Food Bank, attempted both: to serve the poor and mobilize public opinion to pressure government. Its strong advocacy work was not well received either by government or by the public.

The food bank is emblematic of the failure of postwar governments' belief that the problems of poverty would be solved through continuously expanding economic growth. Tackling public deficit and debt became the new all-dominating theme at the end of the decade. Antipoverty organizations were further abandoned as the interest in combating poverty through public policy waned. There were no public dollars for community workers to work with poor people's organizations. This they did for themselves, at poor people's wages.

1990s: The Rediscovery of Community

The idea of community has emerged as one of the compelling rediscoveries of the 1990s. There are two reasons. One is that of default by government. Governments believe they no longer have the resources to maintain their existing responsibilities, therefore these fall by default to the community. Nor have governments, particularly senior governments, demonstrated that they have the adaptability and flexibility to respond in a timely and appropriate fashion to the unique problems that people now experience in their community and personal lives. These problems are multifaceted, crossing established boundaries, jurisdictions, and disciplines. They can simultaneously include social, economic, and environmental issues. They frequently have both local and global dimensions. They compete on the public agenda for urgency. The shrinking margin for error in making the wrong decision is intimidating. There is the immensely complicated task of trying to anticipate the secondary consequences of a particular decision or course of action; solving one problem may create an even greater problem elsewhere. These problems are experienced first-hand in communities, and governments are defaulting because they don't know how to respond.

The idea of community is being rediscovered and reinterpreted in this environment, with myriad voices all attempting to articulate a vision that gives meaning and purpose in a very confused world. Two of the most prominent voices are those of neoconservatism and what Rekart has identified in the literature as welfare pluralism (Rekart 1993:21). Neoconservatism and its less strident relative, fiscal conservatism, percolate throughout the policies and practices of governments in the 1990s. The one energetically advocates the market-place community in place of government. The other infuses the policies of more liberal and social democratic governments—and there are consequently fewer resources for community.

Welfare pluralism's advocates would retain the central role for government in ensuring the equitable distribution of resources, articulating overall social policies, and maintaining standards. They believe, however, that the responsibilities for many of the services of government, along with their resources, can be decentralized politically and administratively to community through voluntary associations and other intermediary bodies (Rekart 1993: 25). Political decentralization, in their view, increases citizen participation and the capacity to respond to local priorities in forms that are both appropriate and timely.

The election of a second New Democratic government in British Columbia in 1991 triggered a new round of interest in community by public officials. The government vigorously launched a number of initiatives that extended beyond the human care services.

The Commission on Resources and Environment (CORE) brought stakeholder groups together in key regions of the province to work together and arrive at land-use conclusions acceptable to loggers, miners, foresters, environmentalists, recreational interests, and the communities that would be affected by the Commission on Resources and Environment's recommendations.

Community resources boards have resurfaced, only this time they are concerned with management of the forests. The Ministry of Education, Skills, and Training, along with Human Resources Development Canada (Canada Employment), are establishing locally managed community skills centres around the province, linking training, work experience, as well as employment.

Unhappy with the previous government's approach to child welfare, the government instituted a provincewide review. Two community panels visited communities around the province and held discussions with key individuals in child welfare. In its report, the panel's Aboriginal Committee argued 'the paramountcy of Aboriginal law' and the establishment, on a timetable determined by Aboriginal peoples, of Aboriginal control and self-government with respect to laws, programs, and services affecting Native children and families (Community Panel, Family and Children's Services Legislation Review in British Columbia 1992:Appendix 1). The main panel described a comprehensive package of change relating to protective, preventive, organizational, and legislative measures. It proposed that direct services to families and children of several ministries be provided through integrated neighbourhood service centres with community-based mechanisms that ensure the centre is responding to the needs of the community. It made recommendations for the government to support community development activities that assist families and communities and for an interministerial commission (with a majority representation by community groups) 'to create a work plan leading to a new community development focus within government' (Community Panel, Family and Children's Services Legislation Review in British Columbia 1992:29).

Though it struck a committee of assistant deputy ministers on community development, the government has not to date developed an overall community development focus. However, the Ministry of Social Services launched a community development initiative in 1993. Twenty-two community development positions have been created in the administrative regions of the Ministry of Social Services (MSS). There is a provincial adviser on community development, an experienced community work practitioner.

The community development workers are to assist clients in organizing mutual support, self-help, and advocacy projects, and to be a resource to line staff in taking a community development approach to their work. The community development initiative 'is seen as a step toward expanding the role for child welfare workers as mandated by the new Child, Family and Community Services Act.' Section 93 of the act gives responsibility to local offices and child welfare staff for 'establishing services to assist communities to strengthen their ability to care for and protect children' and 'to promote and encourage the participation of communities in the planning, development and delivery of these services' (Swets et al. 1995). An evaluation at the eighteen-month point has established a number of important substantive and process outcomes within local communities and in front-line MSS worker practice. Significantly there has been a mutual empowerment of both clients and workers.

The Ministry of Health's New Directions program has incorporated an intense and comprehensive process of citizen participation in the planning of the new health care system. The new system is to emphasize citizen participation and governance in its operation at the community and regional levels through community health councils and regional boards (the former to eventually have a majority of popularly elected citizens). Health services are to emphasize the health promotion principles of mutual help and well-being and to incorporate wider determinants of health, such as social and economic factors. The community health centre is to be the focal point for the provision of primary care programs in the community (including medical care where necessary).

The New Directions program involves the transfer of $3.2 billion (out of a $6.5 billion budget), thousands of personnel, and hundreds of programs and services to regional health boards and community health councils. For the past three years the boards and councils have been getting established, hiring their management staff, working on community health plans, and preparing to assume administrative responsibilities for institutional and non-institutional health care in British Columbia.

Not surprisingly, a change process of this size has had problems and many critics, but the drive to regionalization appears certain. What is less certain, again (not surprisingly), is the durability of the community development and citizen participation principles that are at the core of the New Directions approach. The ministry launched the New Directions program somewhat ahead of itself. The rhetoric of citizen participation and community development preceded the ground rules and framework within which citizens would participate in building the new system. Consequently, the ministry found itself issuing correctives and clarifications as work progressed. Inevitably these reflected a reining in of the process that had been let loose. Community development and participation were being learned on the run. In Chapter 14, Joan Wharf Higgins documents the problems with this approach in the Victoria experience with New Directions: 'a top-down provincial directive to reorganize the health care system from the bottom-up'. There was the challenge to build a truly inclusive process. Now a newly elected NDP government has announced that the entire New Directions program is under review. Regionalization and the transition to regional boards and community health councils have been put on hold.

The BC government's current initiatives in community development appear to be an eclectic stew of fiscal conservatism, welfare pluralism, and unfocused belief that community participation is a good thing. It has mixed community consultation with community development, the one seeking advice about policies and programs, the other giving greater control and power to the community. There is much weariness with consultation and considerable confusion about community development.

Amidst all of this, it is becoming evident that a transition in governance is taking place in this province, from senior governments to municipal governments, and from governments in general to people and their communities. Whether the result will be greater democratic participation in new forms of community governance remains to be seen. An ever-present danger is the devolution of administrative responsibility to community while political control becomes even more centralized in the provincial government.

Beyond the vagaries of government interest in the subject, community development continues through countless community initiatives throughout British Columbia. In this extra environmentally conscious province, it exists in the land-use confrontations between environmentalists and loggers, where both parties utilize parallel strategies to win the hearts and minds of the public. It exists in the negotiations and direct actions of Aboriginal communities regarding land title and self-government. It is exemplified in the inner city by the work of the Downtown Eastside Residents Association, notably in its unending campaign to preserve and improve the housing stock in Vancouver's poorest community.

Though its profile is lower, community development is also at work through countless community planning exercises, whether initiated by the Healthy Communities movement or the city of Nanaimo's Imagine Nanaimo campaign. The Healthy Communities movement has been especially active and effective in both metropolitan and non-metropolitan areas, bringing people together to identify social, economic, and environmental factors that affect community well-being and mobilize action. The movement has served to prepare the ground for New Directions, and if the latter does indeed come to be truly community managed and reflect community priorities, it will be due in no small part to the pioneering work of the Healthy Communities movement.

Community development, through community social planning, is present in the network of voluntary social planning councils and municipal social planners in BC. Their numbers have grown, and many have an influence beyond their modest resources. Social planning has been given a boost by the provincial government with the passage of Bill 25 in 1994. It is enabling legislation for local governments to incorporate social planning into their official community plans. Leadership for the bill came from the Social Planning Round Table, an informal consortium of community social planners initiated by the Social Planning and Research Council of BC (SPARC). (The minister of municipal affairs at that time was a former social planner and SPARC board member.) Still, there is no provincial funding program for social planning or community development, either locally or for provincial organizations. Properly supported, local community development and social planning initiatives can provide the informed and skilled citizen infrastructure for managing the community decentralization initiatives being taken by the provincial government.

The development of skills is very much a priority of SPARC. Working with another coalition of community development organizations, it has established the provincial Community Development Institute, an annual one-week program of courses, workshops, and celebration for practitioners, both volunteer and paid.

Conclusion: Can Community Development Serve Government Reform?

The history of the reform of human care services in British Columbia over the past thirty years is a story of bold initiatives that fell upon political misfortune and half-measures that never fully developed. What is striking is that when one initiative falls out of favour, the next inevitably takes one or all of the same organizing premises: decentralization, coordination/integration, and local accountability/citizen empowerment. It is now evident that these can only be achieved through changes to our overall system of governance in British Columbia.

These changes require as their starting-point the community and the development of new forms of community governance within broad new policy, resource, and regulatory frameworks of senior governments. It is increasingly recognized that senior governments do not have the ability to directly serve the particular requirements of each community efficiently and effectively. Their instruments are too blunt and remote. Working through the design and implementation of these new forms of local governance is an assignment eminently suited to community development.

Community and community development are once again being rediscovered. However, the legacy of the past thirty years is only absentmindedly informing the present. The analysis, critiques, and recommendations from the Commission on Emotional and Learning Disorders in Children (CELDIC 1970), from the Foulkes Report of 1973, and from the experiments of the community resources boards (Clague et al. 1984) are being relearned rather than built upon. The continued absence of a community development framework in the provincial government means that the community initiatives of various ministries are taken in isolation. There is no common vision and no coordination across ministries (the previously mentioned committee of assistant deputy ministers is now moribund).

Community development has been the enabling means for system change in the health and social services examples described here. It was the chosen instrument of government in 1972–5 and is so once again. However, it fell out of favour in the 1970s when the full import of the changes that had been launched became clear. Will this happen again?

Community development is a reluctant servant for government reforms. It has to be treated more like a partner than a servant. It has its own vision, values, requirements, and practices if reforms are to be truly owned and managed by the communities and peoples affected. This is its continuing challenge to the legislative and administrative mandates of our governments.

This chapter concludes at the midpoint of the decade. Perhaps it is fitting to return to that social indicator so emblematic of the 1980s, the food bank. In the 1990s food banks have become institutionalized parts of the patchwork of public and voluntary human care services in British Columbia. We no longer question them. Government neither provides financial support nor, despite many reviews and studies of poverty and employment, implements comprehensive policies that would eliminate them. Unlike health or social services, there is no partnership between government and community development that would blend enlightened public income support, training, and employment policies with strengthening the capacity of poor people to take charge of their own lives. In British Columbia the elements for several of these are in place, but they founder on the twin problems of low social assistance rates and restrictive regulations and too few jobs. There is much community development to be done in arguing and advocating for the necessary policies and programs.

References

Aboriginal Committee, Community Panel, Family and Children's Services Legislation Review in British Columbia.
1972. *Liberating Our Children: Liberating Our Nations.* Victoria: Community Panel, Family and Children's Services Legislation Review in British Columbia.

British Columbia Royal Commission on Health Care and Costs.
1991. *Closer to Home,* Vol. 1. Victoria: British Columbia Royal Commission on Health Care and Costs.

CELDIC (Commission on Emotional and Learning Disorders in Children).
1970. *One Million Children.* Toronto: Commission on Emotional and Learning Disorders in Children.

Clague, M.
1984. 'Britain: The Buoyant Conundrum of Growth and Rising Unemployment'. *Perception* 7, no. 5:45–6.

_____, et al.
1984. *Reforming Human Services: The Experience of the Community Resources Boards in BC.* Vancouver: University of BC Press.

Community Panel, Family and Children's Services Legislation Review in British Columbia.
1992. *Making Changes: A Place to Start.* Victoria: Community Panel, Family and Children's Services Legislation Review in British Columbia.

Foulkes, R.
1973. *Health Security Program for British Columbians.* Victoria: Health Security Program Project.

McKnight, J.
1994. *Community and Its Counterfeits.* Toronto: CBC (Ideas) Radio Works.

Mitchell, M., and C. Goldney.

1975. *Don't Rest in Peace—Organize: A Community Development Scrap Book.* Vancouver: Neighbourhood Services Association of Greater Vancouver.

New Directions.

1993. *A Guide for Developing Community Health Councils and Regional Health Boards.* Victoria: British Columbia Ministry of Health and Ministry Responsible for Seniors.

Rekart, J.

1993. *Public Funds, Private Provision: The Role of the Voluntary Sector.* Vancouver: University of BC Press.

Swets, R., et al.

1995. *The Community Development Initiative in the Ministry of Social Services.* Victoria: School of Social Work, University of Victoria.

Thomson, D.

1995. 'New Directions or Misdirection? Lost in the Labyrinth of the Health Bureaucracy'. *SPARC News* 12, no. 2:6–8.

Chapter Six

Meaningful Work and Community Betterment: The Case of Opportunities for Youth and Local Initiatives Program, 1971–1973

Jennifer Keck and Wayne Fulks

During the early 1970s the federal government introduced a series of community-based job-creation programs that incorporated principles related to community development and participation. In the spring of 1971 the prime minister announced the introduction of Opportunities for Youth (OFY), as part of a package of programs to provide jobs for students during the summer months. In the fall of 1971 the government introduced the Local Initiatives Program (LIP) as part of a special employment plan to address the problem of high levels of unemployment during the winter months.

Both of these programs marked an important departure from the previous practice of funding cost-shared public works projects with the provinces. The design of OFY and LIP can be traced to a number of programs that were introduced under the first term of the Trudeau administration to promote citizen participation (Loney 1977). Promoting citizen participation was a different way to administer government funds to community groups for 'managing their own solutions' to problems affecting their communities (Ng 1988). Under OFY and LIP, federal funds went directly to community organizations, Indian bands, and municipalities to sponsor projects and create jobs. The program criteria stressed themes related to participation, community betterment, and the development of new and innovative services.

This chapter examines the factors that influenced the design and implementation of both programs. While the focus is on state intervention, a review of the first three years of OFY and LIP provides us with important insights as to the relationship between the federal government and community organizations. In this period OFY and LIP were attempts to mediate broad political tensions related to rising unemployment and the demands of a new generation of social activists. The policy context shifted dramatically in the period after 1973. A number of changes were introduced to minimize the political impact of the more organized LIP sponsor base and return OFY and LIP to their original mandate of job creation. These changes resulted in a sharp reduction of the political opportunity for progressive forces to influence policy.

Opportunities for Youth Program

Early discussions of the need for a youth program that would provide jobs and activities for young people can be traced to 1970. Social tensions related to youth alienation, unemployment, and unrest escalated during the spring and summer. To offset the problem, the Secretary of State and Minister of Youth Gérard Pelletier introduced a $28 million summer student employment assistance package that included funding for a travel and exchange program, hostels, and public service employment. Despite these measures, the summer of 1970 was a difficult one. Unemployment for young people soared. There was near riot in Regina, and in Vancouver a demonstration to legalize marijuana broke into a riot. In October a real crisis emerged with the kidnapping of James Cross, senior British trade commissioner in Montreal, and the killing of Quebec Minister of Labour Pierre Laporte by members of the Front de libération du Québec (Huston 1973; Loney 1977; Verzuh 1989).

The impact of the 1970 October Crisis, together with the prospect of a summer of discontent, helped set the stage for the planning of OFY in the fall. Gérard Pelletier received a draft copy of *It's Your Turn*, the report of the federal Committee on Youth, the same day the War Measures Act was declared (Gwyn 1972). The report predicted that high levels of unemployment among young people were likely to continue for the rest of the decade. It also confirmed widespread alienation among youths who were sceptical of their opportunities to find meaningful work. The government needed to channel the energies of young people into useful and viable work. Young people wanted to work, but they were interested in meaningful work, not just any employment. Community development, social animation, and participation were recurring themes in the text (Committee on Youth 1972).

In November the federal government established two committees of deputy ministers and senior officials to study the youth problem and develop imaginative proposals for a federal youth program for the following summer. According to the Treasury Board representative on the committee, cost was not a significant factor (Green 1973). Most of the proposals outlined plans to expand public service employment during the summer months. A notable exception was a proposal submitted by two young civil servants from National Health and Welfare, Cam Mackie and Stewart Goodings. Both had worked directly with the Company of Young Canadians and had drafted an earlier proposal for a youth employment program that had been rejected in 1968. Mackie had also developed a summer project at National Health and Welfare that hired students to develop and manage pilot projects that were alternative social services (C. Mackie, personal communication, 6 February 1993).

The 1970 proposal for the Youth Opportunities Program built on what Mackie and Goodings felt were the successful element of the Company of Young Canadians and National Health and Welfare youth summer program. Dollars would go directly to young people and more established organizations to develop new and innovative projects. To be effective, the program should be built on community development principles and involve the participation of young people in the planning and management of projects. The program was expected to build on the organizing work that was already taking place at the grassroots level. The proposed cost was $12 million: $10 million allocated to traditional service agencies (such as the YMCA, Canadian Mental Health Association, and Red Cross Society) and $2 million for student-initiated projects (Green 1973; National Council of Welfare 1970).

The proposal to turn over federal funds directly to young people was greeted with considerable scepticism by the civil servants on the committee. Key members of the Liberal Cabinet Social Policy Committee, including Gérard Pelletier, John Munro, and Otto Lang, proved more receptive. At their request, the proposal was brought back to the senior officials' committee, which allocated a total of $5 million. That amount was raised again to $14.7 million after several weeks of negotiations between members of cabinet and the bureaucracy. The politicians considered $5 million too low to make a significant dent in unemployment or have a political impact on the public consciousness (Gwyn 1972).

Trudeau announced OFY in the House of Commons on 16 March (House of Commons 1971). He issued a challenge to young people: '. . . we believe they are well motivated in their concern for the disadvantaged . . . we have confidence in their value system . . . we are saying that we intend to challenge them and see if they have the stamina and self-discipline to follow through on their criticism and advice' (House of Commons 1971:4288). The response to the call for application exceeded all expectations. By the end of April over 8,600 applications were received (National Archives of Canada RG 6 ACC 86-87/319 Vol. 148 File 19-1 part 1). Cabinet approved an additional $10 million for the 1971 summer program in May. This brought the total to $24.7 million (Green 1973).

OFY: The Hip Bureaucracy

Once OFY received cabinet approval, Mackie was seconded from National Health and Welfare to act as coordinator and implement the program at Secretary of State. Mackie's background for the position included a Master of Social Work degree from the University of Manitoba and experience as a street community worker in Winnipeg. The thirty-two-year-old Mackie was part of a new breed of young civil servants recruited to work in the federal bureaucracy in the late 1960s and early 1970s.

National headquarters for OFY was set up one floor below the minister's suite. A Secretary of State publication described the OFY office as a 'wide open space, open to new ideas, quick action and sharing of ideas' (National Archives of Canada RG 6 ACC 86-87/319 Vol. 148 File 19-1 part 1). Most of the people hired to work on the program were between the ages of twenty-three and forty, and had completed some level of postsecondary education. Community work experience was an asset for the job, especially experience with the Company of Young Canadians or the student movement (National Archives of Canada RG 6 ACC 86-87/319 Vol. 149 File 19-3 part 1).

The project evaluation criteria set out by cabinet stressed that 'young people would have to be involved in the planning, management and evaluation of projects' (National Archives of Canada RG 6 ACC 86-87/319 Vol. 148 File 19-0 part 1). Projects would be assessed on precision, viability, and the potential for achievement. A higher ranking would be given to those projects involving new services, ideas, and programs. All projects were approved by the end of June. Project activities ranged from the coordination of recreational programs for children and senior citizens to the publication of underground newspapers and the establishment of day care centres, tenants' associations, and welfare rights groups. Approximately 30 per cent of OFY projects fell into the category of community services and activities, 19 per cent involved creating 'a new cultural awareness to strengthen the Canadian community', 28 per cent were community research projects, and approximately 6 per cent provided various educational services (Secretary of State 1972).

It was not long before the program became the subject of considerable controversy. The main complaint was that the program had been conceived too hastily. The result was chaotic administration: some projects had still not received their cheques in July. There was considerable media coverage, including 2,587 stories in the print media. The program was both attacked and praised with headlines ranging from 'The Future: It Works' to 'Larceny Perpetrated with Canadian Tax Collars' (Gwyn 1972). The program was also the subject of debate in the House of Commons. Opposition MPs complained about the funding of so-called counterculture projects. Regional opposition was particularly vehement in Ontario, BC, and Quebec. In British Columbia there was local opposition to the funding of communes, American draft-dodgers, and 'long-hairs'. MPs from Quebec were concerned that federal dollars were being used to fund projects sponsored by separatists. The *Toronto Sun* charged that some government money was going to so-called 'radical' groups, and pointed to projects sponsored by Rochdale College, a Satanist cult, and 'other Marxists' (Best 1974; National Archives of Canada RG 6 ACC 86-87/319 Vol. 149 File 19-3 part 1).

Pelletier defended OFY in an eloquent speech to the House of Commons on 18 June 1971: '. . . today there is a lot of talk about participatory democracy, community solutions, grass roots participation . . . but there appears to be considerable uneasiness about giving these forces a chance to operate' (National Archives of Canada RG 6 ACC 86-87/319 Vol. 148 File 19-0 part 1). While the minister defended the program publicly, the supervision and monitoring of the program remained an ongoing source of concern (National Archives of Canada RG 6 ACC 86-87/319 Vol. 148 File 19-1 part 1). A policy regarding project termination was developed in response to the cancellation of two projects involving underground newspapers (National Archives of Canada RG 6 ACC 86-87/319 Vol. 148 File 19-1 part 1). On 15 June the government cancelled a $15,000 grant to the *Georgia Strait*, an alternative newspaper in Vancouver (Verzuh 1989). In Regina, *Prairie Fire*, another alternative newspaper, had its grant withdrawn after it ran a story on 11 June about Liberal gerrymandering in the Saskatchewan provincial election. The Liberal leader, Ross Thatcher, was livid and publicly accused the federal Liberals of funding a paper that reflected the views of:

> . . . militant minority socialists, Maoists and left-wingers . . . Secretary of State Pelletier announced a grant of $7,000 to this bunch of kooks to put out a newspaper. I sometimes wonder if Pelletier and his impractical schemes are more of a menace to Saskatchewan Liberals than the NDP (*Regina Leader-Post* 1971).

Despite a stormy beginning, OFY was considered a qualified success by officials at the Citizenship Branch and the Department of Secretary of State at the end of the first summer. Media coverage improved as projects demonstrating community service were given a higher profile (Green 1973). Plans were in place in September to begin a review of the program and make recommendations for a possible repeat of the program the following year (National Archives of Canada RG 6 ACC 86-87/319 Vol. 148 File 19-0 part 1).

Two formal evaluations were conducted. The mandate of the first Evaluation Task Force (ETF) was to evaluate OFY in the context of the government's youth policy and criteria set out by the Treasury Board. The ETF's final report criticized the overall mandate of the program and the Interdepartmental Committee's original definition of the problem facing youth: 'At no stage did the Committee consider the promotion of social change as an objective nor did they attempt to place the sources of the problems of young people in the wider context of the economic and political structures of the society as a whole' (Cohen et al. 1972). The committee was concerned with the question of unemployment and the 'distinct possibility that a combination of unemployment and inactivity' would lead to social unrest (Cohen et al. 1972).

There were several other concerns. Wages were much too low to provide students with enough money to enable them to return to school. There were too few jobs to meet the needs of students looking for work. The emphasis on students meant that a large group of youths were still left unemployed.

When it became clear that the Evaluation Task Force was going to issue a negative report, a second evaluation team was hired in the fall. The tone of this report was much more sympathetic to the program and the government. It praised the program as an 'endorsement of community' that provided 'one amongst many' initiatives to solve student unemployment. The success of the program was attributed to the fact that unemployed youths had been engaged in 'socially useful' work. The three objectives—employment, meaningful work, and satisfying tasks—were seen as part of the larger participation 'vision' anticipated by Pelletier and Trudeau (Systems Research Group Incorporated 1971). The second, more favourable, report was tabled in the House of Commons in December.

Rethinking Participation: Changing the Rules

There were few developments over the fall months. In January the minister announced that the $34 million OFY program for 1972 would have a new set of criteria. The changes were designed to minimize the political controversy attached to the program. Based on the experience with the *Georgia Strait* and *Prairie Fire*, the program would not fund 'publications whose chief purpose was commentary and confrontation rather than information'. The refusal to fund newspapers that espoused partisan views was intended to reduce direct attacks on the Liberal Party at the provincial or federal level. A second provision required prospective applicants to include letters of support from more established organizations in their community. There would also be a political check on the program that allowed MPs to review projects in their constituency. This change was a direct response to concerns raised by members of the federal Liberal caucus in December 1971. New constituency advisory groups were established to advise on the selection of projects (National Archives of Canada RG 118 ACC 85-86/071 Vol. 234 File 3972-1-1972 part 1).

Pelletier defended the tighter regulations in a revealing interview with the media shortly after the program was announced in January. When reporters questioned the 'frivolous' aspects of an OFY-funded film on the art of spaghetti-making, Pelletier argued that OFY had a mandate to support creativity, particularly in cultural projects. An important distinction was made between these fringe artistic projects and periodicals that indulged in political partisanship or systematic confrontation. The latter would not receive funding under the second round of OFY. It was important to protect the ability of groups to complete projects that were 'innovative and non-traditional'. Projects that promoted 'alternative' services and culture would continue to be eligible for the program. Projects that criticized the government or the Liberal Party could expect to be turned down (National Archives of Canada RG 118 ACC 85-86/071 Vol. 234 File 3972-1-1972 part 1).

The second year of the program was relatively uneventful. In late April 1972, 3,041 projects were selected, providing 30,080 jobs. Fifty-eight per cent of the projects were devoted to rural projects, and 45 per cent of the participants were female. The administration was vastly improved. Over 125 project officers were hired to provide field support in the regions. An experimental private sector branch was set up to solicit funds from industry and for good projects that required more money. There was still public debate over the value of a four-month program. Some complained that the projects were 'too repetitive', others that the program was still too 'middle class' (Best 1974). By 1973 there were over 140 OFY project officers located across the country (Best 1974). That same year, the program was transferred to the Department of Manpower and Immigration as part of a larger project to rationalize federal job-creation programs.

Although there was a narrowing of the scope of OFY projects as the government evaluated reactions to the first group of projects, there were possibilities that had not existed before, or perhaps since. The more progressive members of the government and the bureaucracy could use OFY (and later LIP) to prod the more traditional parts of the bureaucracy and to force the provinces to look at the issues raised by OFY projects.

Local Initiatives Program 1971-1973

A second community-based job-creation program was introduced by the Department of Manpower and Immigration in October 1971. Modelled after OFY, the $100 million Local Initiatives Program (LIP) was part of a $438-million special employment plan announced by the minister of finance to deal with unemployment. The proposal for LIP stemmed from discussions that had taken place between Rod Bryden, the executive assistant, to Minister of Manpower and Immigration Otto Lang and Cam Mackie in early September. LIP represented an important departure from the more traditional, cost-shared public works initiatives that were already included in plans for the October announcement. The emphasis was on projects that promoted community betterment and the development of new and innovative services. Federal funds would be made available directly to municipalities, community organizations, and Indian bands. While the program was expected to build on the 'innovative' aspects of OFY, it was primarily a jobs program during periods of high unemployment in the winter months.

Several themes were associated with LIP: projects would have to make a contribution to the community and the needs of the people served, participation in the program would offer satisfaction to the persons involved over and above the income earned, and the program would encourage widespread participation. Early documents were careful to distinguish LIP from 'normal make-work or leaf-raking' schemes. There was only one cautionary note. The government would have to guard against the potential for creating dependency in the development of new services (National Archives of Canada RG 118 ACC 86-87/319 Vol. 25 File 1-20-9).

Cabinet approved additional criteria on 21 October. Work on the projects would have to take place between November 1971 and May 1972. Projects had to include activities that promoted community betterment. Wages would reflect the prevailing rate up to a maximum of $100 per week. Eligible participants would have to be considered active members of the labour force. Special provisions ensured that Natives living on reserves and potential day care workers would be included (National Archives of Canada RG 118 ACC 85-86/071 Vol. 25 File 1-20-9).

Two important principles were described in a briefing paper for Manpower and Immigration officials: (1) the unemployed should be directly involved in the development and management of projects, and (2) the government should limit its role to the provision of resources and information in such a way as 'to achieve the most benefit for and the highest potential of individuals through support to local groups and communities' (National Archives of Canada RG 118 ACC 85-86/071 Vol. 112 File 3440-1). The introduction of LIP was an experiment 'to test whether state intervention can take the form of supporting groups of unemployed or sub-employed individuals to seek solutions to their problems through the creation of projects, programs and enterprises in the public sector' (National Archives of Canada RG 118 ACC 85-86/071 Vol. 112 File 3440-1). The government would fund LIP projects, but the relationship between the government and LIP sponsors would be arm's-length: '. . . we cannot consider these to be our projects, we do not have a supervisory role in the sense that we control them' (National Archives of Canada RG 118 ACC 85-86/071 Vol. 112 File 3440-1). The description of participation bore a strong resemblance to the legacy of OFY, but the emphasis on employment and the creation of jobs marked an important shift in direction.

Applications were quickly drawn up in November and distributed through 400 Canada Manpower Centres and mailed directly to groups using the mailing lists that had been put together at Secretary of State for OFY. The application forms stressed the role that individual and collective initiative were expected to play in the development of projects. Eligible projects included services for children, the elderly, and the handicapped; pollution and the environment; day care programs in their initial stages; and storefront services that needed to be expanded or improved. Only two types of project were explicitly excluded: newspapers and projects that promoted social animation (National Archives of Canada RG 118 ACC 85-86/071 Vol. 112 File 3440-1).

From the outset it was clear that the program would fund alternative services. Minister of Manpower and Immigration Otto Lang was consulted directly as to whether or not the program should fund three types of services: day care centres, legal aid clinics, and programs to First Nations communities. All three involved potential jurisdictional issues with the provinces and/or other federal departments. Lang agreed to proceed with all three types of projects. After consulting the ministers for national health and welfare and justice, Lang agreed to use LIP to prod the provinces to support legal clinics and day care centres. Lang also agreed to allocate one-third of LIP dollars to projects directly administered by First Nations. This was intended to bypass the approval process at the Department of Indian and Northern Affairs (C. Mackie, personal communication, 6 February 1993).

The response to the call for LIP applications exceeded the expectations of program officials. Applications arrived in January at a rate of 150 per day. On 11 January 1972 Lang announced that the program would be allocated another $50 million for non-profit projects. By the end of the month, many applications was competing for the last dollars. The last approvals were announced on 31 January. Out of a total of 13,766 applications (estimated worth $483 million), 5,600 were approved, providing 92,000 jobs (National Archives of Canada RG 118 ACC 85-86/071 Vol. 112 File 3440-1).

Demos and Demons

Early media reports were mixed. Government MPs were embarrassed by the unexpected disclosure that a Toronto religious group, The Satanists, received a grant of $25,900 from LIP. Later it was revealed that Pierre Vallières, a prominent member of the Front de libération du Québec, was discovered working on a LIP project in Mont Laurent. In a particularly acrimonious debate in the House of Commons over the throne speech, Robert Stanfield, the leader of the opposition, accused the prime minister of hiring his 'FLQ friends' on LIP projects (Stevens and Saywell 1974).

In March the *Toronto Sun* launched a full-scale attack on the program. The paper quoted 'a senior official' with LIP as having confirmed that preference was being given to groups that were committed to political and social change. Mackie denied the allegation. The department's response was to release a list of the more established organizations that had received LIP funds, including the East City YMCA, the Metropolitan Toronto Social Planning Council, Central Neighbourhood House, and the Ontario Association for the Mentally Retarded (National Archives of Canada RG 118 ACC 85-86/071 Vol. 112 File 3440-1).

Otto Lang met with the first large delegation of community groups in January. The Front Uni of Montreal organized 160 people to meet with the minister at the Conference Centre in Ottawa. The group complained about the assessment process and the types of projects that were being excluded. Of particular concern was the fact that a number of legal clinics in low-income areas had been rejected. Lang denied that political pressure had been involved in the rejection of any LIP projects. The purpose of LIP was to create jobs, not to fund social services (National Archives of Canada RG 118 ACC 85-86/071 Vol. 114 File 3440-8-1 part 1). At an executive board meeting in January, officials expressed concern that community groups would begin to think that they could 'get the rules changed by the use of protest pressure' (National Archives of Canada RG 118 ACC 85-86/071 Vol. 114 File 3440-8-2 part 1).

As the program came to a close in May, another series of demonstrations erupted in most of the larger urban centres across the country. In Toronto, LIP employees organized and held meetings. Over 2,000 letters and telegrams were sent to Ottawa. Plans to fight for the extension began in the offices of The Storefront, a LIP project sponsored by the Metropolitan Toronto Social Planning

Council. The project was mandated to look into sources of additional funding for Toronto LIP projects. A spokesperson for the organization described the tenacity of the group: 'In a poor community people are used to losing, but LIP people are really different. These people are for the most part middle class and aggressive. They are not hampered by the idea that things can't change' (Rowan 1973). Complaints that the government was abandoning LIP projects and services received widespread coverage across the country. In response, the minister announced that an additional $40 million would be allocated to the program. This meant that some projects would be continued until 30 November 1972. The extension would allow the government time to review the program and make a decision about its future the following year (Rowan 1973).

LIP's high political profile was not lost on cabinet members and the Liberal caucus. A new list of eligibility criteria were included in the 1972–3 program to deal with their concerns. There were four major changes. First, project sponsors would now be expected to hire persons receiving unemployment insurance and social assistance. This measure reflected concerns related to the debate over unemployment insurance amendments introduced in 1971, and the view that programs such as OFY and LIP encouraged new labour market entrants (Muszynski 1985; Pal 1993). Second, to eliminate the number of controversial projects, sponsoring groups would have to solicit community support before making an application. The third change was designed to appease the provinces. Projects with activities that were expected to continue after 31 May would have to demonstrate that they had concluded arrangements for continued financial support from alternative sources (National Archives of Canada RG 118 ACC 85-86/071 Vol. 114 File 3440-8-2-1).

A fourth provision ensured that politically sensitive projects would be reviewed by an executive board made up of senior civil servants. Projects that would be referred to the executive board would have:

1. political implications such that the project was designed in a way to enhance or attack a political party, group, or level of government

2. social implications, including projects that were considered socially unacceptable to the general public, or projects that had emotional overtones; this included 'any project which could trigger widespread public reaction'

This definition made more explicit the practice that had already developed under the 1971–2 program (National Archives of Canada RG 118 ACC 85-86/071 Vol. 114 File 3440-8-2-1).

Just as with OFY, as the government ministers and departmental officials digested the reactions to the initial projects, the scope of what was possible started to narrow to more closely reflect government goals.

More Controversy and Extensions

The fall election had a major impact on the Liberal government's policy agenda. Issues related to the state of the economy, unemployment, and inflation dominated the campaign. On 30 October the Liberals lost their majority. In the wake of the election, the balance of power swung to the NDP. The Liberal losses were attributed to a number of factors. Public opinion studies conducted during the campaign revealed that unemployment, inflation, and the economy were important issues for the electorate. Programs like unemployment insurance, OFY, and LIP were included in the list of social programs that had a negative impact on the Liberal campaign (Meisel 1975). Unemployment and job creation maintained a high profile in the wake of the election, but many Liberal Party activists advocated a more pragmatic approach to politics during Trudeau's second term (McCall-Newman 1990). An immediate fall-out from the election was the resignation of Bryce Mackasey from the Manpower and immigration portfolio. The new minister was Robert Andras, the MP for Thunder Bay.

It was not long before LIP was in the news again. In November provincial welfare ministers attending a conference in Victoria accused the federal government of initiating special social service programs and then abandoning them to the provinces (*Victoria Times* 1972a). The government faced another round of demonstrations and attacks in the media over the potential demise of LIP-funded services. At the base of this conflict was the *ad hoc* nature of LIP. Speaking to a group of volunteer agency workers, the new national director, Larry Davies, admitted that LIP had 'created monsters . . . good projects that had grown'. LIP was still essentially an employment program. The federal government was not willing to accept permanent responsibility for the 'social needs uncovered by LIP' (*Hamilton Spectator* 1972).

Attacks on the government for its handling of unemployment continued throughout most of December. On 2 December Trudeau announced plans to combine an extension of LIP with an intensification of the traditional manpower programs associated with the standard pump-priming of the economy (*Winnipeg Tribune* 1972). Andras announced a number of additional changes that were planned for the 1972–3 LIP program. A special $10 million fund was allocated for a pilot program to allow the private sector to sponsor non-profit activities. The money was given to businesses as grants to subsidize the costs of wages for laid-off workers. There were also plans to develop an entrepreneurial program under LIP that would allow non-profit projects to produce goods and services and become more self-sustaining. Plans were underway to fund the Local Employment Assistance Program, which would provide three-year funding for projects to employ the chronically unemployed and disadvantaged (*Ottawa Citizen* 1972; *Victoria Times* 1972b).

Pressure to expand LIP increased in the spring as project sponsors began to lobby for extensions. At the end of April Otto Lang announced that there would be a limited extension of LIP to fund 1,400 projects located in high-unemployment regions. The seasonally adjusted unemployment rate had declined for the fourth month in a row (Townson 1973). Officials at Manpower were hard-pressed to get additional money for projects in the larger urban areas where unemployment was relatively low. The program was allocated $40 million for a maximum of six months. The additional funds would bring the total allocated to LIP to over $195 million. The extension would apply only to communities with unemployment rates over the national average of 6.8 per cent. This resulted in the extension of approximately 3,000 projects. There were three exceptions to this rule: (1) educational projects that are eligible for continued funding up to the end of June, (2) projects involving Native peoples, and (3) projects that had the potential of becoming self-sustaining businesses (*Toronto Star* 1973a).

Increased targeting produced its own set of political dilemmas. The change in eligibility criteria meant that the larger urban centres would be excluded. Toronto and Montreal were the hardest hit. The situation was only slightly better in Vancouver. In metropolitan Toronto the rate of unemployment was 4.8 per cent. This meant that approximately 90 per cent of LIP projects in Toronto would be excluded from the spring extension. The changed criteria were expected to have a similar impact in Montreal. With an unemployment rate of approximately 6.7 per cent, it was estimated that as many as 3,600 people could lose their jobs on LIP projects. LIP project members organized across the island. One coalition, representing about seventy representatives from eleven LIP projects, was organized under the auspices of the Federation of Catholic Community Services. In Manitoba the provincial government was directly involved in lobbying for more funds (*Globe and Mail* 1973a; *Toronto Star* 1973a).

LIP officials defended the tighter criteria for project extensions. Each project had been notified about the decision to end on 31 May. That rationale offered little solace to LIP sponsors. There were more demonstrations between 5 and 18 May. The Metro Toronto Working Group spearheaded the protest in Toronto with 100 demonstrators representing more than half of Metro's 250 workers. The government's cancellations were arbitrary: 'The federal government moved into the provincial jurisdiction of social welfare by instituting LIP projects and now they want out. . . . provincial government cannot support entirely. We would like to find money from city, province and outside agencies' (*Globe and Mail* 1973b). In Pointe St-Charles organizers promised global action following the demonstrations in Montreal, Toronto, and Winnipeg. Protesters pointed to Pointe St-Charles as a good example of a neighbourhood within a larger urban setting that had a consistently high rate of unemployment and low income (*Montreal Star* 1973).

Andras announced a second allocation of $30 million to fund approximately 800 of the total 5,800 LIP projects to continue on 19 May. Projects were sent notices of approval or rejection within ten days of the announcement. Liberal back-benchers from Montreal and Toronto lobbied heavily in favour of broadening the criteria for extensions (National Archives of Canada RG 118 ACC 85-86/071 Vol. 120 File 3440-22). In a media interview Andras conceded that he had changed his mind largely because of the 'very considerable representations by members of my own party' (Demarino 1973). The groups affected by the extension in Toronto tended to be the more organized and vocal, including Rochdale Free Clinic, Hassle-Free Clinic, Ward Seven News, and Toronto Free Theatre. Projects that were not renewed included the Boy Scouts of Canada and the Canadian National Institute for the Blind (MacDonald 1973).

This last extension increased the total LIP allocation for 1972–3 to $235 million. This was the federal government's largest annual allocation to a job-creation program. In two years LIP had been renewed and/or extended eight times. There was four announcements in 1971–2, and another four in 1972–3. The impact of this last extension was not lost on the minister. LIP was supposed to be a short-term program to provide jobs during the winter months. It was fast becoming a year-round program. In a media interview, Andras described LIP as 'a bit of a monster' that was beginning to require 'colossal investments'. The government was now 'facing the crunch' of whether to continue with LIP and in what form (Demarino 1973).

While the federal government remained under attack, the provinces were also under increased pressure. The tensions were particularly strong in Quebec and Ontario. Grassroots organizations joined with more traditional agencies and elected officials to lobby the provinces to cover the costs of the new LIP services (National Archives of Canada RG 118 ACC 85-86/071 Vol. 114 File 3440-8-1 part 2). In Metro Toronto a group of eighty agencies, including the United Way, the Metro Toronto Labour Council, and the United Church, voted at a public meeting to spend the next six months pressuring Ontario to take over financial responsibility for LIP projects. Martin Novick from the Metropolitan Toronto Social Planning Council described the sentiment behind this new organizing effort: 'LIP helped to show that there are a lot of services that are not being provided by the traditional agencies. . . . there is a strong feeling in the social welfare community that LIP had been a good program and Ontario has not lived up to its responsibilities' (Rowan 1973). On 14 June the provincial minister of community and social services told 100 demonstrators that the provincial government was willing to review existing LIP projects (*Toronto Sun* 1973). In Winnipeg a coalition of LIP projects lobbied the provincial government to establish a review committee to assess eighty-eight LIP projects that were set up in that province over the past year (*Winnipeg Free Press* 1973).

There was no additional money announced in June, but the demonstrators had already won this round. LIP had $70 million in additional funds. The stipulation that only high-unemployment areas would receive funds was defeated. The political lessons of the spring were not lost on Liberal politicians or the senior officials at Manpower. If LIP was going to continue, something would have to be done to weaken the political impact of LIP sponsors and pressure groups. The dilemmas were outlined in an article that appeared in the *Ottawa Citizen* in May: '. . . every time the government tries to let LIP funded projects die a natural death those directly employed in projects and those directly served within the community have raised such a fuss that the government has had to arrange extensions' (Demarino 1973).

Job Creation under Review

By the spring of 1973 federal officials were committed to ending the political turmoil surrounding LIP. The program's future had been hotly debated since the Liberal losses in October 1972. Many Liberal Party activists blamed programs such as OFY and LIP for the image of the party as big spenders on social policy (Desbarats 1973; Meisel 1975). There were two other concerns. First, the program was creating a demand for social service projects and the provinces were vehemently opposed to these efforts. LIP's intrusion into provincial jurisdiction was not consistent with the move to greater federal-provincial cooperation in the area of social services or social policy (*Globe and Mail* 1973a). The second concern related to a more general critique of the program and its impact on unemployment. The view was still prevalent that OFY and LIP 'brought people into the labour market' and therefore increased unemployment when the projects ended. Anthony Westall, *Toronto Star* commentator, made this argument in an article in January. Government programs to ease unemployment 'made matters worse'. The programs 'lured people, mainly women and young people into the labour force and helped to swell the ranks of the unemployed' (Westall 1972).

Andras advised reporters in July that he was favourably disposed to another round of LIP for 1973–4. LIP was a job-creation program with a strong social development objective. The problem was trying to balance these concerns against the priorities of the program. Part of the problem was trying to justify expenditures of $200 million for LIP when unemployment had declined slightly in mid-1973 and the government was trying to find funds to increase family allowances. The government 'needed the courage to switch off funding if necessary' (*Montreal Gazette* 1973). It would be difficult to cancel LIP entirely. There were too many groups with vested interests in the program. Said Andras, 'I don't blame LIP people for raising hell. . . . They're telling me they don't give a damn where the money comes from just as long as they can continue' (*Montreal Gazette* 1973).

LIP and OFY were still two of the best and most innovative federal programs. The programs took 'a very restless energy and channelled it into more social change than sporadic demonstrations could have accomplished' (*Montreal Gazette* 1973).

In August 1973 cabinet approved an allocation of $83 million for LIP for 1973–4 (Malling 1973). There were a number of changes designed to minimize the impact of political activity by the LIP sponsor base. There would be no extensions of LIP in the spring of 1974. There would be a new system of Constituency Advisory Groups. More local participation in the assessment process was expected to help reduce political comment and criticism. Part of the rationale was to decrease the number of 'wild applications' and ensure a broader base of support for the program. Staggered end dates were also introduced to help minimize the political impact of having all LIP projects end in the same month. New groups and new projects would be preferred, and any projects after 31 March would have to prove that they had alternative sources of funds. In a major concession to the provinces, all applicants would have to comply with provincial regulations and demonstrate evidence of provincial support. The Liberal caucus also won a change that allowed for constituency allocations. MPs would also be involved in the selection of members for the new constituency advisory groups. A final change involved the establishment of a permanent administrative structure to oversee the administration of the program and ensure that the LIP was more clearly viewed as a job-creation program.

The changes to the 1973–4 LIP criteria marked an important turning-point in the administration of the federal government's job-creation strategy.

Up until now the activities of the organized LIP sponsors had wielded considerable influence in terms of funding and program criteria. The changes for the 1973–4 program were designed to minimize the political impact of these groups and return LIP to its original mandate: job creation during the winter months. The new Job Creation Branch was set up in September. In December OFY was transferred to this branch as part of a larger plan to rationalize job-creation programs at the federal level and reduce the funding for student unemployment. There was a growing perception that OFY was a political liability. The student unemployment rate was considerably lower in 1973 than it had been in previous years. Applications to the program declined significantly. The political conditions had also changed: university students no longer alarmed politicians (Gwyn 1973).

There would be few changes to the programs over the next two years. There were demonstrations in the larger cities lamenting the loss of LIP services in the spring of 1974, but the government held fast in its decision to terminate projects. The impact of the worldwide recession began to take hold by the last quarter of 1974, but there were no major increases in funds available for OFY or LIP. In December 1975 OFY was cancelled together with the CYC. In the same speech, Minister of Finance Jean Chrétien announced that the 1975–6 LIP was cut back from $150 million to $100 million. These cuts were part of the austerity program associated with the government's anti-inflation program (Lazar 1976). Both programs would re-emerge as Canada Works and Young Canada Works in the federal government's announcement of an employment strategy in 1976. In his speech to the House of Commons, Minister of Manpower and Immigration Bud Cullen stressed that the emphasis would be on funding established organizations with projects that promoted real work (House of Commons 1976).

Conclusion

In the early 1970s a number of competing interests came together to support OFY and LIP: a generation of social activists intent on developing alternative services, a number of young civil servants interested in forging new relationships between the federal government and the new social movements, and politicians with money to spend worried about the potential for unrest and interested in the opportunity to court a number of new political constituencies. This confluence of interests increased the budget for OFY from $14.7 million to $24.7 million by the end of its first year. Funding for OFY helped increase the budget fivefold for the Citizenship Branch in the period from

1970–3. LIP increased from an initial allocation of $85 million to $235 million in 1972–3. Healthy federal revenues, an expanding welfare state, and the prospect of an upcoming election created conditions that were conducive to these developments.

A number of factors contributed to the breakdown of this consensus after 1973: the view that OFY and LIP had cost the Liberals votes in the 1972 election, concerns about the political visibility of the sponsor base, and the shift in political tide in favour of the provinces (which strongly opposed the infringement of their jurisdiction). There were also internal pressures built into the programs. The duality of job creation and social development was never fully resolved. The stopgap nature of the program meant that it did neither effectively. Deteriorating economic conditions and the shift to a more conservative economic paradigm in the period after 1974 merely served to reinforce changes that had been introduced in 1973 (Gwyn 1976; Ostry 1978; Pal 1993).

There were important elements of social control in the initial design of the programs. This was particularly true of the attempt in OFY to channel the political energies of youths. Changes to the criteria of both programs over the next few years were specifically designed to minimize controversy and limit the types of activities that were considered legitimate. While the political activities of the organized service projects made the headlines, this group represented a small percentage of the projects sponsored by LIP. Approximately one-third of the LIP funds for 1972–3 went to municipalities for projects to install sidewalks, new roads, streetlights, and water-pipes during the slack winter months. For the second year in a row, 70 per cent of the participants lived in households that fell below the poverty line (*Ottawa Citizen* 1973).

At the same time, state action both shaped and was shaped by a new constituency of sponsors. If there were limits to the dissent that would be tolerated, there were also a number of key bureaucrats and politicians willing to challenge the social welfare and cultural establishments at all levels. The funding of social service projects was a deliberate attempt to force the provinces to finance alternative programs. When they were first introduced, OFY and LIP represented a different way of administering federal funds to groups representing the new social movements and First Nations. That enthusiasm for change and innovation waned considerably over the next few years.

It is much more difficult to assess the lasting legacy of OFY and LIP. There was a dramatic increase in the funds available to community organizations. A survey of 304 non-government agencies in thirteen Canadian cities, conducted by the Canadian Council on Social Development, found that government funding rose from $9,578,115 in 1962 to $51,467,044 in 1972. LIP and OFY funds represented a significant percentage of this increase (Carter 1974). The funding of new and innovative services had a major impact on the design of a number of key services. LIP money, for example, made it possible for groups advocating parent-based cooperatives to provide child care. The current structure of child care in Quebec reflects this legacy (Rose 1990). LIP and OFY subsidized a wide range of experimental projects, such as women's centres, transition houses, legal clinics, birth-control services, and storefront welfare rights organizations. Many of these projects were able to successfully lobby provincial governments to continue funding after LIP (*Montreal Gazette* 1974; *Toronto Sun* 1973; *Winnipeg Free Press* 1973). LIP and OFY also formed the basis for a number of community-based job-creation programs that followed, such as the Local Employment Assistance Program and entrepreneurial LIP. These programs funded a number of projects, such as The Women's Press, Hassle-Free Clinic in Toronto, and First Nations trading cooperatives, which are still in existence (Keck 1995).

Despite this legacy, the programs were not particularly effective as job-creation mechanisms or for the financing of new services. OFY was never intended to have a major impact on student or youth unemployment. This was the harshest criticism of the program in the Evaluation Task Force's report released in 1972. In June 1971 56 per cent of Canada's 568,000 unemployed were under the age of twenty-five. OFY employed 27,000 people in 1971 and 29,000 people in 1972 (National Archives of Canada RG 118 ACC 85-86/071 Vol. 234 File 3972-1-1972). In response to a question about the labour market impact of the program in January 1972, Pelletier made it clear that it would not be possible to have a program large enough to meet the needs of all unemployed students. There were similar problems with LIP. In the absence of a wider commitment to full employment, LIP was unable to make a serious dent in the unemployment rate. As unemployment increased over the rest of the decade, the total allocation to job-creation programs (in constant dollars) tended to decrease (Muszynski 1985; Smith 1984).

There is still the question of whether programs such as OFY and LIP promoted community development. The example of OFY and LIP illustrate how the terms associated with community work are themselves part of a contested terrain (Mayo 1994). Ostensibly designed to promote participation and change at the community level, there was never an attempt to analyse power or challenge the existing social or economic structures that contributed to unemployment or other forms of inequality, nor was there an attempt to promote a broader vision of community economic development. There were contradictions inherent in looking to community solutions for a problem that was both national and global in scope. The short-term nature of the program made it difficult to promote any type of longer-term community economic development. Part of the problem was the liberal definition of participation implicit in the design of both programs. Promoting participation and local involvement was endorsed as an ideal, but there was no corresponding analysis or commitment to challenging the overall distribution of power. In the absence of such a vision, key elements of the program design were intended to legitimize some organizing at the expense of others.

Acknowledgements

This paper is based on research for Jennifer Keck's doctoral dissertation, 'Making Work: Federal Job Creation Policy in the 1970s'. Research on this project was made possible with the financial support of a doctoral fellowship from the Department of National Health and Welfare and assistance from the Dean of Professional Schools, Laurentian University. Dr David Wolfe deserves special credit for his support and comments during work on the dissertation.

References

Best, R.
   1974. 'Youth Policy'. In *Issues in Canadian Public Policy*, edited by B. Doern and V. Wilson, 137–65. Toronto: Macmillan.

Carter, N.
   1974. *Trends in Voluntary Support for Non-government Social Service Agencies*. Ottawa: Canadian Council on Social Development.

Cohen, A., et al.
   1972. 'Report of the Evaluation Task Force to the Secretary of State: OFY 1971'. Ottawa: Department of Secretary of State.

Committee on Youth.
   1970. *The Socio-Economic Aspects of Canadian Youth Unemployment*. Ottawa: Department of Secretary of State.

————.
   1972. *It's Your Turn*. Ottawa: Department of Secretary of State.

Daly, M.
   1970. *The Revolution Game*. Toronto: New Press.

Demarino, G.
   1973. 'LIP Get Another $30 Million'. *Ottawa Citizen* (19 May).

Desbarets, P.
1973. 'Unfolding But Upside Down'. *Vancouver Sun* (4 May).

Globe and Mail.
1973a. 'Future of LIP Projects Clouded as Andras, Staff Debate Merits' (23 February).

————.
1973b. '100 Protest LIP Project Cancellations' (5 May).

————.
1974. '70 Protest Loss of LIP Grants; Want Made an Election Issue' (18 May).

Green, H.
1973. 'Decision-making, Sociology and Policy Analysis: A Case Study of the Canadian Government's Opportunities for Youth Program, 1971'. Master's thesis, Carleton University.

Gwyn, R.
1973. 'The Death Knell Has Sounded for OFY'. *Toronto Star* (24 November).

Gwyn, S.
1972. 'The Great Canadian Grant Boom (and How It Grew)'. *Saturday Night* 87:22–4.

————.
1976. 'Lost Passions: A Requiem for the 1960s'. *Maclean's* (January):14–15.

Hamilton Spectator.
1972. 'Group Claims LIP Creates Unemployment' (30 November).

House of Commons.
1965–76. *Debates.* Ottawa: House of Commons.

Huston, L.
1973. 'Flowers of Power: OFY and LIP Programmes'. *Our Generation* 8, no. 4:52–61.

Keck, J.
1995. 'Making Work: Federal Job Creation Policy in the 1970s'. Unpublished doctoral dissertation, University of Toronto.

Kostash, M.
1980. *Long Way from Home: The Story of the Sixties Generation in Canada.* Toronto: Lorimer.

Lalonde, M.
1973. 'Working Paper on Social Security in Canada'. Ottawa: Health and Welfare Canada.

Lazar, F.
1976. 'The National Economy'. *Canadian Annual Review of Politics and Public Affairs 1975.* Toronto: University of Toronto Press.

Lethbridge Herald.
1972. 'LIP Starts for Winter Employment' (2 December).

Levitt, C.
1984. *Children of Privilege: Student Revolt in the Sixties.* Toronto: University of Toronto Press.

Loney, M.
1977. 'The Politics of Citizen Participation'. In *The Canadian State: Political Economy and Political Power,* edited by L. Panitch, 446–72. Toronto: University of Toronto Press.

McCall-Newman, C.
1990. *Grits.* Toronto: McClelland and Stewart.

MacDonald, R.
1973. 'Toronto Alderman, Rochdale to Get LIP, OFY Grants' (31 May).

Malling, E.
1973. 'Ottawa Warning: Learn to Live with Unemployment'. *Toronto Star* (24 August).

Manpower and Immigration.
1974. *Final Report of the Interdepartmental Task Force on Direct Job Creation: Policy Alternatives Group.* Ottawa: Department of Manpower and Immigration.

Mayo, M.
1994. *Communities and Caring: The Mixed Economy of Welfare.* London: St Martin's Press.

Meisel, J.
1975. *Working Papers on Canadian Politics,* enlarged ed. Montreal and Kingston: McGill-Queen's University Press.

Montreal Gazette.
1972a. 'Chaos as Day Care Grants Lifted: 200 Staff at 20 Centres Out of Work' (6 December).

———.
1972b. 'Province to Meet Day Care Workers: Four Hour Montreal Sit-in Gets Results' (12 December).

———.
1973. 'With 5 New Lives, LIP Shows Signs of Mortality' (12 July).

———.
1974. 'Quebec Agrees to Shoulder Day Care Load' (14 June).

Montreal Star.
1973. 'Coalition Protests LIP Funds Cut-Off' (26 May).

Muszynski, L.
1985. 'The Politics of Labour Market Policy'. In *The Politics of Economic Policy,* edited by G.B. Doern, 251–305. Toronto: University of Toronto Press.

National Archives of Canada.
1966–76. RG 118 archival records. Department of Manpower and Immigration.

————. 1970–3. NAC RG 6 archival records. Department of Secretary of State.

National Council of Welfare.
1970. *Student Summer Employment Proposals*. Ottawa: National Health and Welfare.

————. 1973. *Incomes and Opportunities*. Ottawa: National Council of Welfare.

Ng, R.
1988. *The Politics of Community Services: Immigrant Women, Class and State*. Toronto: Garamond Press.

Ostry, B.
1978. *The Cultural Revolution*. Toronto: McClelland and Stewart.

Ottawa Citizen.
1972. 'LIP Enlists Business' (7 December).

————. 1973. 'Largest Portion of LIP Funds Used for Municipal Buildings' (22 February).

Pal, L.A.
1993. *Interests of State: The Politics of Language, Multiculturalism and Feminism in Canada*. Montreal: McGill-Queen's University Press.

Paris, E.
1972. 'Are There Really Any Opportunities for Youth?' *Maclean's* (October): 34–7, 54–5, 59.

Regina Leader-Post.
1971. 'Thatcher Raps Pelletier for Nutty Project Support' (12 June).

Rose, D.
1990. 'Collective Consumption Revisited'. *Political Geography Quarterly* 9, no. 4:353–80.

Rowan, M.K.
1973. 'Save LIP, Urge Metro Social Agencies'. *Toronto Star* (2 June).

Secretary of State.
1970. *Report of the Department of the Secretary of State for the Year Ending March 31, 1970*. Ottawa: Department of Secretary of State.

————. 1972. *A Canadian Experiment: Catalogue of Projects Funded in 1971 under the Federal Government Opportunities for Youth Program of the Department of the Secretary of State*. Ottawa: Department of Secretary of State.

Smith, D.
1984. 'The Development of Employment and Training Programs'. In *How Ottawa Spends 1984*, edited by A. Maslove. Toronto: Methuen.

Stevens, P., and J. Saywell.

    1974. 'Parliament and Politics'. *Canadian Annual Review of Politics and Public Affairs 1972*, 3–128. Toronto: University of Toronto Press.

Systems Research Group Incorporated.

    1971. 'Evaluation of the Opportunities for Youth Program, 1971. Ottawa: Department of Secretary of State.

Toronto Star.

    1972. 'Centre for Italians May Have to Close' (7 December).

———.

    1973a. 'MPPs Urge Extension of Grants for Projects' (16 May).

———.

    1973b. 'Save LIP, Urge Metro Social Services' (2 June).

Toronto Sun.

    1973. 'Now Queen's Park Will Consider Aid for LIP Projects' (14 June).

Townson, M.

    1973. 'The Changing Job Picture'. *Financial Times* (18 June).

Vancouver Sun.

    1972. 'Trying to Save a Centre' (2 December).

Verzuh, R.

    1989. *Underground Times: Canada's Flower Child Revolutionaries.* Toronto: Denecum.

Victoria Times.

    1972a. 'Provincial Ministers Attack Abandoning by Ottawa' (29 November).

———.

    1972b. '$325 Million for Winter Jobs' (6 December).

Westall, A.

    1972. 'Hiding Umemployment Lessens Strain'. *Lethbridge Herald* (5 January).

Winnipeg Free Press.

    1973. 'Provincial Funds Sought for LIP' (7 June).

Winnipeg Tribune.

    1972. 'PM Pledges Major Winter Job Program' (2 December).

Chapter Seven

The Company of Young Canadians

Dal Brodhead, Stewart Goodings, and Mary Brodhead

Introduction

The Company of Young Canadians (CYC) was launched in the mid-1960s, and its spirit and legacy are still very much alive in Canada. Its birth marked the beginning of a nationwide, grassroots approach to community development for disadvantaged groups and underdeveloped areas. Internally, the organization reflected the turbulence, optimism, and innovation characteristic of that period. Its parentage is a matter of some dispute between politicians and community activists. Officially, it was an initiative of the federal government, a product of an organizing committee established within the Privy Council Office in 1965. It had roots reaching back into the Federal War on Poverty Office of the early 1960s. It was also an outgrowth of student and community activism and the desire for change evident across Canada at that time. The CYC's Canadian predecessor by several years, the Canadian University Service Overseas (CUSO) had been created as a non-government organization (NGO) to capitalize on the interest of Canadian youths in overseas development. A further influence came from south of the border; the American government had set up the Peace Corps to send volunteers to work overseas in developing countries, and it had internally established Volunteers in Service to America. The CYC was, however, a unique vehicle for change, started by government but shaped by both officials and activists in Canada. Its structure was designed to be participatory and the strategy it embraced was aggressively change-oriented.

Early government press releases described the CYC as an organization dedicated to putting youths to work in communities across Canada. In the April 1965 speech from the throne, the Liberal Pearson administration spoke of harnessing the energies of youths to improve the quality of community life and channelling their idealism into constructive community service. The organization became much more than its founders had intended; it went beyond assigning young volunteers to help communities. In a very short time, it took on the task of transforming Canadian society, at first naively, then flamboyantly, and finally more strategically. It became a development organization, at times confrontational and almost always committed to the grass-roots, to the disadvantaged, and to the marginalized in the community.

The CYC's initial mandate was broad and permissive. Its interpretation and implementation proved be the source of a fundamental disagreement. At first the battle was within the organization itself, between radical activists and those board members, staff, and volunteers interested in less aggressive change. Later the government and the organization came into conflict over many of the same issues. It was the approach, the process of improving communities—whether to contribute to marginal improvements or to foster significant change in the status quo—that was the focus of debate.

Activist youths in the early 1960s, those likely to be attracted by the CYC, were not willing to be harnessed, but were motivated towards effecting more fundamental change. In contrast to traditional top-down approaches to change and development, other more grassroots-based models had begun to emerge. In Canada, the Student Union for Peace Action (SUPA) was one example—a ban-the-bomb organization with a grassroots community organizing zeal. In the summer of 1965, it sent groups of students and youths into a variety of urban and rural 'disadvantaged' communities across Canada. Their approach was to live in communities, to learn from local people, and to avoid imposing solutions. SUPA differed from the CYC in that it was entirely supported and operated by students with no government involvement.

At almost the same time, some provincial government rural development practitioners were abandoning more traditional government-led strategies and embracing a community development approach. In the prairie provinces, community development workers assigned to Aboriginal communities were increasingly coming into conflict with their public servant superiors as they opted to support local people opposed to past government policies. In Manitoba and Ontario, for example, provincial community development workers had sided with Aboriginal peoples in conflict with the provincial governments and had been fired for their efforts. The federal Department of Indian Affairs had acted in a similar manner and had disciplined staff in similar circumstances. These conflicts also represented a reaction by community development workers to top-down approaches imposed from outside the Aboriginal communities.

The organizational innovation integral to the design of the CYC was a powerful motivator that attracted youths to its activities. Incorporated into the act of Parliament creating the CYC was the concept of a participatory democracy in which the field force—the volunteers—would eventually become the elected majority on the board. The act creating the CYC contained a number of unique provisions that made it quite different from other voluntary organizations. It enshrined the concept of participation within the structure of the CYC in several ways by providing for the election of volunteers to the board with majority representation after a period of time. It redefined the concept of volunteerism by requiring a full-time commitment for a set period of time (two years initially) with a stipend to pay for room and board, travel, as well as a small lump-sum payment upon successful termination. The challenge proved irresistible to hundreds of young idealistic applicants and to scores of communities that requested assistance in the form of young volunteers.

The Start-Up

In the spring of 1967, two pilot projects were launched, one in Cape Breton, Nova Scotia, and the other in Alert Bay, British Columbia. Both involved work in Aboriginal communities. There was no set development approach but a confidence that the communities would establish the tasks for the volunteers based upon an overall project description approved by the CYC. The actual work of the volunteers was left to be defined in practice, not theory, but it was understood that the approach would be participatory and community based.

Within a year, several hundred volunteers were at work in every province and territory. The variety of tasks was as great as the diversity of the people and places involved. Community organizing to bring together the disadvantaged to protect their rights was underway in urban renewal areas, such as in downtown Calgary, in the Pointe St-Charles district of Montreal, and in central Vancouver. In the struggling rural areas of Cape Breton, northeastern New Brunswick, and northwestern Ontario, local antipoverty efforts were launched or supported. Food cooperatives were begun, and welfare rights groups were assisted. Alienated youths were also a priority, and alternative schools, drop-in centres, and outreach projects to deal with drugs and violence were established. A significant emphasis was placed on Aboriginal communities: Métis, status, non-status, and the Inuit. Those with mental and physical disabilities were supported in organizing themselves into self-help groups to obtain adequate and accessible housing or other services that enabled them to become more self-reliant. They frequently had to establish their right to equitable and honourable treatment as people, not objects of pity.

A common denominator in the approach to development emerged during the start-up period in most of the CYC projects. The disadvantaged were not to be treated as clients, as recipients of largesse. They were people with a potential to help themselves. The CYC volunteers were expected to be facilitators, animators, organizers, and motivators in support of community initiatives and those advocating positive community change. They were not to take advantage of situations to manipulate the disadvantaged, nor was it ever acceptable to promote violent change.

The Experience

The CYC began as an instrument of government policy aimed primarily at involving youths, but it rapidly defined itself through its actions as a development and change organization. It has seldom been understood in these terms for its critics and the media concentrated on its more sensational and later its weaker points. We took an active part in the early launching of the CYC, and our collective involvement took us through its start-up, its controversial period, its reorganization, consolidation, and two years before its demise in 1976. Our various roles included those of volunteer, board member, senior management staff, and assistant director, as well as executive director. This account is thus based on direct knowledge and is biased, but not blind. The essence of the CYC's contribution, however, was at the community level and in the accumulated experience of its volunteers and staff. To date, the importance of the CYC is only partially documented and not well understood, especially in terms of its development policy impacts.

In its early years, from 1966–70, the CYC responded to hundreds of requests from communities across Canada for help in dealing with their community issues and problems. Poverty, discrimination, inequity, urban renewal, youth alienation, and rural underdevelopment—the communities and the CYC volunteers faced all these issues and more. Many of these problems had remained unresolved in the face of earlier, often well-intended, traditional, top-down development approaches and government policies. The Department of Indian Affairs had tried to improve the conditions of Aboriginal communities, voluntary organizations had provided services to the disabled, and welfare departments had subsidized the disadvantaged. The approach to these problems had often perpetuated the situations and encouraged dependency. The CYC and its young volunteers, who had high expectations and commitment, were thus faced with difficult, often intractable issues, as well as with pent-up local anger and frustration. It was not surprising that the work became controversial. What is disappointing is that few observers and commentators saw the CYC as an innovative development instrument for needed change. Nevertheless in its early years, the federal government continued to see it as a useful vehicle to channel youthful energies and not as a threat to the status quo. A few of its supporters within and outside government were open to its innovative potential and stood by it.

Two books, now long out of print, tell the story of the early years of the CYC. *The Children's Crusade*, by former CYC information director Ian Hamilton, and the *Revolution Game*, by journalist Margaret Daly, both describe the evolution of the organization up to mid-1970. Both accounts were limited in their perspective and tended to focus either on the sensational events or the internal dissension within the CYC, not its community development and training contributions.

The Learning

It was not long before those of us who were volunteers in the field realized (as others had before us) that effective community organizing and development was hard slogging. It was seldom spectacular, often agonizing, frequently discouraging, and occasionally confrontional. Above all, it took time and energy to wait for communities to act (and sometimes to avoid acting), to take charge, and to change. All the while, the volunteers and their community colleagues accumulated development experience, but much of this learning was overlooked by other less involved observers of the CYC.

The collisions with the status quo and the establishment captured the limelight. In the Petite Bourgogne and Pointe St-Charles areas in Montreal, urban renewal (often described in the 1960s as slum clearance) was threatening to destroy long-established and admittedly poor communities. Local people assisted by CYC volunteers fought back to retain their community identity and improve their housing conditions. They challenged the prevailing urban development policies and the governments that supported them. Similarly, in downtown Calgary, the Stampede organization sought to expand its land holdings and, in order to do so, advocated the demolition of some so-called decaying communities. They were stopped by community organizations to which CYC volunteers had been assigned. A new Calgary-wide political leadership emerged, and new policies were designed that did not simply bulldoze neighbourhoods.

It was the work with alienated youths that attracted much of the media attention. In the Yorkville area of Toronto, the press reported the work of the CYC with so-called hippies, who dressed unconventionally, frightened the authorities, and demanded fair treatment from the police. Transient youths flooded urban centres, and dropping out of school was widespread. In response, CYC volunteers worked with local groups to establish alternative schools, such as those in Vancouver and Everdale in Toronto, as well as other youth outreach projects, which attempted to involve disaffected youths. These initiatives also questioned the (educational) status quo.

Elsewhere, CYC volunteers worked alongside Aboriginal peoples: the Nimpkish in Alert Bay, BC, the Innu in Labrador, and the Inuit and Dene in the Northwest Territories. They helped establish local and regional Aboriginal organizations to promote their rights and obtain access to services. Communications societies and cultural groups were launched to revitalize cultural and linguistic traditions. In northwestern Ontario, an Aboriginal radio network was begun, along with a local Aboriginal-run newspaper. These were the forerunners of the present-day Aboriginal media organizations, which communicate by radio and television, as well as in print.

Paternalistic government policies and officials were often the target of grassroots organizations and the CYC volunteers working with them. Inevitably, a few sensational incidents widely reported by the press coloured the public's perception of what the CYC and its volunteers were doing. It should be remembered that demonstrations and protests to promote change were not as commonly accepted then as they are now. These strategies made some politicians and officials with a stake in the status quo very uncomfortable, so they started to look for the CYC's Achilles' heel, its weak spots. Rather than dealing with the fundamental issues constructively by looking for new development approaches, some sought to stamp out the symptoms (the activists and the protests). The CYC was the lightning-rod for much of the criticism, and was seen as an obstacle.

The very nature of the CYC as an innovation and an experiment was not always successful. Its internal structure was intended to be participatory, as was its development approach. It was in its administration that it gave its critics opportunity to question its credibility. While its volunteers were tackling community issues, its Provisional (government-appointed) Council and newly hired staff were wrestling with the CYC's philosophy, creating its structure and testing so-called avant-garde training techniques. As a new organization, it took time to establish effective administrative systems, financial accountability, and staff performance measures while supporting a growing field force of volunteers and community partners. Its organization chart evolved rapidly and, after considerable pressure, the federal government agreed to appoint some CYC volunteers, who had been elected by the volunteers at work in communities across Canada, to the CYC Provisional Council.

Initially, the greatest conflict took place within and between the staff group and the Provisional Council. The critical issues concerned the implementation of the concept of participatory democracy within the CYC itself.

In addition, its activist community organizing and development approach in the field created difficulties. Differing interpretations of the CYC's mandate (gradual versus more immediate and fundamental change) were at issue, as well as the style of volunteerism (activist versus passive or service oriented). With CYC volunteers agitating (in the field and subsequently as board members) for organizational innovation and responsiveness to their needs, the divisions became even more complex. Add to this the presence of some charismatic and sometimes disruptive and inexperienced individuals, and the organization appeared to the outside world as chaotic, aimless, and divided.

Balancing the desire for participation and the need for accountability to the government for funds and to the community for actions were nearly impossible tasks. Include the scepticism of 'experts' and 'the establishment' (outlined in the CYC's 1966 *Aims and Principles* document), which ran throughout the organization from its inception, and one can see some of the forces at play when the CYC began its work. Unlike more traditional organizations, there was also a naive belief in the need for complete transparency and openness. Thus much of the drama was played out in the public domain before a public and politicians not accustomed to such debate.

Inevitably, the organization made some mistakes that its critics and the media jumped on. One glaring example was the purchase of a number of Volvos for certain CYC projects—the public perception of volunteers and staff working with the disadvantaged and driving good cars was not helpful. Overlooked in all the hubbub was the cost-effectiveness of the initial federal government budget allocation for the CYC, which was $1-2 million annually between 1966 and 1970. Even in the mid-1960s, the CYC budget was minuscule when compared with the tens of millions of dollars spent on regional development, urban renewal, and education. Its volunteers were paid a monthly allowance of between $150–$200 for room and board, plus a small amount for local project travel. On successful completion of the maximum two-year term, a lump-sum payment was made to assist the volunteers in getting into school or a job. The CYC also provided training and staff support, as well as the headquarters infrastructure required by a national Crown corporation accountable to the federal government. It also functioned as a bilingual national organization well before government policy required it; its volunteers and staff needed to communicate effectively and to learn from each other. In its later years, the CYC was able to field more than 400 volunteers and sixty staff and operate nationally for less than $3 million, which was, in our view, a cost-effective instrument for national development and education.

The culmination of the confrontations with governments and officials, coupled with the reaction to some successful community organizing, unsettled certain political interests. In addition, the internal divisions within the CYC and some of its bureaucratic mistakes were enough to cause the government to intervene early in 1970 to impose a trusteeship. In the background, it must be remembered, were the events leading up to the October Crisis of 1970. The strains being felt in Quebec and elsewhere in Canada were mirrored within the CYC, for with its desire to promote change, this national organization was a microcosm of the country. It contained elements of many of the upcoming forces for change apparent in the nation: western alienation, separatism, youth alienation, bilingualism, women's rights, Aboriginal sovereignty, access for the disabled, etc. What was so exciting and positive was the challenge presented to the CYC volunteers: go and help bring about positive change with the direct involvement of those most concerned, especially those communities with limited resources.

The Reorganization

The Company of Young Canadians was perceived by many activists and all of its chroniclers to have perished with its ideals in 1970 when the federal government imposed a trustee and undertook to revise the CYC charter. Certainly many of the organizational innovations (i.e., its internal participatory democracy) were dropped. Much greater bureaucratic and programmatic accountability was demanded. However, where it counted in the communities, volunteers continued to do important community organizing and development work that did not stop challenging the status quo. By early 1970, the numbers were fewer, down to approximately 100 volunteers in dozens of communities. Expenditures had shrunk to $1.4 million from a high of nearly $2 million in its heyday. The CYC was down but not out, different but not irrelevant, and certainly still working with the disadvantaged, the unorganized, and the powerless in every province and territory in Canada.

In October 1970 Dal Brodhead became the new national executive director, having been one of the original volunteers in 1966. He found a demoralized and dispirited group of volunteers and staff, as well as an intimidated and angry project staff in Quebec. Many were being held in jail as a result of the arbitrary arrests effected under the War Measures Act during the October Crisis. But he also found among volunteers and staff a continuing commitment to pursuing the important community-based project work— the *raison d'être* of the CYC. Some 100 volunteers were still at work. In addition, communities in need hadn't disappeared, nor had their demands for assistance from the CYC, so it was back to work again with less media attention, more accountable administrative systems, the same mandate, and a continued commitment to community involvement and change.

Consolidation

It was not the same CYC after 1970. Certainly its participatory structure was no more, but it had also gained some new assets. It had acquired five years of invaluable hands-on development experience without being excessively limited by traditional development baggage. Its remaining staff and community partners had built up a considerable intellectual capital through successes and failures in every region of Canada, which was part of an important legacy.

The content of the work did not change significantly. What did evolve were the style, techniques, and focus. Given the early controversies and excessive media exposure, public confrontations were less frequent and, when needed, became more strategic and community directed. The community organizing became more planned and the organizing techniques more subtle and more community driven. The focus of the development became more local, project-oriented, and directed by community project committees. The CYC volunteers were more apt to be recruited from within the same milieu or community where the project was located. For example, Aboriginal peoples were working for their own communities, and the disabled with their own constituency, not always, but more and more often. The community became more directly accountable for the work of the volunteers and played a larger part in their hiring, support, and dismissal.

In content the work changed as well. Where previously the creation and exercise of rights were characteristic of much of the work, once they were established it became evident that the effective implementation of these new rights by the disadvantaged often required additional power. Legal rights and power needed to be bolstered by legislation and economic clout if underdeveloped communities were to change situations effectively, develop greater self-reliance, and obtain more control over their future and their sovereignty. In mid-1972 the CYC commissioned an internal working paper on community economic development, and by 1974 over half of the CYC's projects contained an important economic component. Community control of area resources, community-owned development corporations, and cooperative development, to cite a few examples, became part of the CYC's vocabulary and work.

Yet the nature of the people and communities where the CYC projects were located remained remarkably similar. They were mostly disadvantaged, voiceless, and underdeveloped. In the period between 1971 and 1974, the

CYC grew from approximately 100 volunteers in the field to over 400 located in hundreds of communities across Canada. Its federal government allocation expanded from $1.2 million to over $3 million in the same period, and it repeatedly received a clean bill of health from the auditor-general for its administrative and financial practices.

The federal government appointed the last executive director of the CYC in November 1974, and the organization persisted in its efforts to effect community change. The CYC struggled to respond to the continuing community demand for its volunteers while trying to implement a governmentwide budget-cutting exercise, which hit the CYC in late 1974. A year later, during the next federal budgetary exercise, the government announced the immediate closure of the CYC and Information Canada. It is our opinion that the politicians and bureaucrats, whose status quos had been disturbed years earlier, finally obtained their revenge. They convinced the then minister of finance, now prime minister, to approve the budget cuts, which resulted in the demise of the CYC ten years after its inception.

Conclusions

The CYC is still very much alive in many communities across Canada. Its effects and legacy are visible, but its impacts have not yet been formally evaluated. In the 1970s, as a result of community initiatives supported by the CYC, positive changes were evident in many communities. Rights had been created, urban renewal areas had retained their identities, the legitimacy of organizing locally to effect change had been established, Aboriginal communities had taken charge of their school systems, disabled people had come together, cultural values had been affirmed, and some behaviours had been changed. Above all, the status quo had been challenged, sometimes successfully, and the establishment had been put on notice. Naturally all of these changes cannot be attributed to the CYC, but some can. The most visible evidence can be found in some of the people who experienced the CYC: the past grand chief of the Assembly of First Nations, the current mayor of the City of Toronto, a teacher-adviser in racism and multiculturalism in an urban school system, many federal and provincial public servants (including a former assistant under-secretary of state), countless Aboriginal managers and leaders, as well as many teachers, social workers, consultants, community development workers, a number of civil rights lawyers, and business people.

Some CYC projects or their successors are still functioning, and others' roots can be traced back to the CYC. An innovative community health centre in Ottawa–Carleton; cultural education centres in Yellowknife and Alert Bay; a municipal bus system in Whitehorse; a regional Aboriginal organization in Labrador; an Aboriginal communications society in Sioux Lookout, Ontario; community associations in downtown Vancouver, northeastern New Brunswick, Toronto, southwestern Montreal, and in many other places, all have one thing in common. These projects were all associated with the CYC and were supported by CYC volunteers at one stage or another.

Many lessons can be learned from the CYC experience in terms of development policy, voluntarism, youth policy, and in other areas as well. They include a confirmation that, if supported, communities can and will help themselves to become more self-reliant. It is also clear that even the most disadvantaged communities have some capital to invest—the human resource potential and the will that goes with it. Furthermore, the CYC demonstrated that youths can play a positive role if a constructive framework is created to support the work. The development implications of the CYC approach are numerous and argue forcefully for a participatory approach at the community level and an investment in innovative strategies—economic as well as social and cultural. In addition, the CYC demonstrated that governments should invest in the initiative of local people while letting them design, develop, and operate their own projects. This long-term perspective reinforces the idea that development from within the community is more effective and lasts longer than paying outside companies huge incentives to relocate, sometimes called 'smokestack chasing'.

The training potential of institutions such as the CYC must not be overlooked. The CYC trained hundreds of young people and community groups. The absence of similar training opportunities for young people today points out the lack of understanding of the value of informal education of the type provided by organizations such as the CYC, CUSO, and others. If there is a disappointment now, it is that so much work remains to be done and that there are fewer avenues for youths and others of all ages to be able to afford to volunteer time for the benefit of their communities. Some new bridges will be needed—different from the CYC in form, but perhaps not in intent—to assist the less advantaged communities to bring about more fundamental change whenever and wherever possible.

The CYC also provided evidence that people from very diverse and distant places in Canada can find common ground building on community experience to communicate and cooperate across linguistic, cultural, and other barriers. The CYC, as a microcosm of the nation, was dynamic, difficult, and even divided at times, but nevertheless its volunteers and community groups tackled similar problems, exchanged common strategies, and found some workable solutions to community situations. As a structure, the CYC was unique as well as being an innovative development model. It evolved continually to adjust to new demands and to the reality of its regions. In the end, it was a very decentralized organization with its key field coordinators and its national executive, made up of a small core staff. Its board of directors, although government appointees, sought significant field input before proceeding, and projects were approved as part of overall priorities approved nationally. The CYC made its greatest investment in the field, where its projects were designed, developed, and delivered in response to community initiatives and accountable to community groups.

In 1991, twenty-five years after the passage of the CYC act, some fifty former volunteers and friends of the CYC turned up at an impromptu reunion in Ottawa. Most were still active in one way or another in social and economic causes, whether or not they were employed in the field of development. Some had maintained contact with the communities in which they had worked: Alert Bay, Sydney, Victoria Park, Pointe St-Charles, Goose Bay, Halifax, Lesser Slave Lake, Sioux Lookout, Yellowknife, Little Mountain, and many others. Participants believed that there was a need once again for positive, inventive political leadership in Canada of the sort that produced the CYC. It seems to us that another generation of political leaders is currently needed at the national level. A more modern leadership is required in Canada, perhaps one drawn from among those community activists and volunteers who could build on the legacy of the CYC and other similar national and international development experiences.

References

Daly, M.
    1970. *The Short Unhappy Life of the Company of Young Canadians.* Toronto: New Press.

Hamilton, I.
    1970. *The Children's Crusade.* Toronto: B. Martin Associates.

Chapter Eight

Assessing the Gap between Community Development Practice and Regional Development Policy

Teresa MacNeil

Introduction

This chapter addresses the relationship between community development and regional development. Some regional development programs of the past thirty years are examined to determine the extent to which community development was included as a component of regional development policy. Community development is regarded throughout as a vehicle for learning: a way to build competencies within the community to govern its social and economic health. Because of the reciprocal relationship between community strength and economic well-being, one would expect that as experience is gained and success is realized through community development, its dimensions would be increasingly built into economic development measures. Although community strength might not be a sufficient predictor of regional prosperity, it should at least be one of the important supports for improved economic activity.

As a basis for drawing conclusions about the connection between community development and regional economic policy, the chapter includes some introductory references to the purpose and forms of Canada's regional development programs, it mentions characteristics of community development that one might expect to find associated with regional development efforts, it presents evidence of community development characteristics from a selection of regional development programs, and it outlines some of the skills and capacities that community development helps people to acquire. Finally, suggestions are offered that would allow community development to become an integral part of regional development policy and programs.

Regional Development in Canada

Regional development policy usually refers to public policy, which is explicitly designed to reduce economic disparities between and within Canada's regions. Constitutional responsibility for economic development is not assigned to either provincial or federal governments. Each naturally promotes the well-being of its own jurisdiction and searches for ways to develop the potential of their respective wealth-producing resources. Economic prosperity serves everybody's interests. While federal and provincial governments cooperate on programs, federal leadership is required to equalize economic well-being across the nation's regions. This has been true especially since the latter part of the 1950s when the federal government established a fiscal equalization program. Savoie (1986) describes the program as Ottawa's way 'to ensure that all provinces would have the revenues sufficient to offer an acceptable level of public services'. Important as this was, Savoie notes that it did not necessarily help the poorer provinces gain equality as generators of economic activity. Further support is needed to achieve higher levels of economic activity, but the pivotal question for regional development policy is what kind of additional support would be needed.

Two characteristics have dominated Canada's regional development policy over the past thirty years: it has been centrally determined and has focused on economic development initiatives, yet Ottawa also provides social development programs. Why, one might ask, have these not become part of regional development efforts? Why limit regional development to economic policy measures when so many other factors influence regional well-being? Organization and jurisdiction provide two possible answers.

Organizationally, it would take amazing rearrangement and coordination of government departments to achieve a comprehensive approach to development. The sheer size and complexity of the social programs that currently comprise Human Resources Development Canada (HRDC) illustrate this difficulty. On the economic side, the Department of Regional Economic Expansion (DREE) brought together a collection of economic-oriented programs twenty-five years ago and has held to that economic emphasis through its subsequent reorganizations. The mandates of these major departments are so distinct that it becomes extremely difficult to connect social and economic programming. From a jurisdictional point of view, the inability to sort out the appropriate responsibilities of the respective levels of government limits the prospect of achieving a comprehensive approach to regional development, hence despite the need for integrated economic and social development programs, some very pragmatic factors interfere.

There is, however, one good example of a national effort to assist economic growth in less-developed areas. The Agriculture Rehabilitation and Development Act (ARDA) of 1961 was directed towards the reduction of rural poverty through efforts to increase small-farm income and find more productive uses for marginalized lands. ARDA will be the subject of further discussion later in this chapter, but the ARDA precedent was not repeated in subsequent, even more specialized, programs designed to assist specific, low-income areas. For example, the Fund for Rural Economic Development was designated to apply to certain localities in Manitoba, Quebec, New Brunswick, and Prince Edward Island. And, exclusive to the Atlantic region, the Atlantic Development Board was formed in 1962 to promote economic growth through the development of such infrastructure as highways, water and sewer systems, and industrial parks.

As the 1960s came to a close, a multitude of regional development initiatives were assembled within the new Department of Regional Economic Expansion. For approximately fifteen years after its beginning in 1968, numerous variations occurred in the way the federal government related to the provinces through DREE. By allowing specialized attention to provincial circumstances, the department gradually altered the form of the federal-provincial agreement, in that program variations between provinces meant diminished program control by the federal government.

Its successor, the Department of Regional and Industrial Expansion included the business, industry, and tourism divisions of the Department of Industry, Trade, and Commerce, but remained essentially a decentralized agency working closely with the provinces. Further, in the mid-1980s, regional development agencies were established in Atlantic Canada, northern Ontario, and western Canada, each with its own board and policies, and reporting to a minister whose electoral constituency was in the respective region. These agencies continue, and allow for programs and funding that respond to particular circumstances of the respective region. Consequently, they differ considerably from each other.

At the same time and parallel to economic development programs, human resource development measures were initiated through agreements designed to improve the occupational skills of residents in areas of high unemployment. Through the years, as the federal Department of Manpower and Immigration changed its name to Employment and Immigration Canada (and later to Human Resources Development Canada), its programs included such community-based training initiatives as the New Start Corporations, the Local Economic Development Agency, the Local Employment Assistance Program, Community Futures, and the Atlantic Groundfish Strategy.

Despite large injections of dollars and effort to develop both entrepreneurial skills and economic activity, these programs were and are largely social development measures. They were designed to engage communities in the process of creating local economic development to counter unemployment. They were rooted in a learning process through which citizens gained knowledge and skills as they determined what to do about economic development. Officially, the objective was always economic, but the route was through social change measures, and progress was often judged in terms of human and social development. Apparently this was an acceptable route for agencies whose mandate was manpower development, but not for those whose mandate was regional economic development. As noted earlier, it is puzzling why officially declared regional development programming stayed so exclusively with economic instruments. Is it the community development dimension that causes policy makers to exclude social instruments? Does it imply a form of amateurism (i.e., unsystematic, community-led activity) that threatens economic success? I return to these questions in a later section of the chapter and suggest how community development might become more closely associated with regional development strategy.

This brief review of programs leaves out numerous, relatively smaller regional development measures. Not least among them is the long-term program directed specifically at Cape Breton Island through the Cape Breton Development Corporation, the Crown corporation established in 1967. Again, it is an economic development measure. Further, and as mentioned earlier, the overall system of direct transfer payments from federal to provincial governments is itself a form of regional development, although it is not usually categorized as such.

Characteristics of Community Development

Community is a collective measure that engages community members in problem solving through planning, organization, and action. In the process, communities improve their immediate circumstances and gain strength and power to engage in further challenges. For the purpose of this chapter, community development falls within the two traditions of social learning and social mobilization.

As social learning, community development engages people whose lives are negatively affected by circumstances that were previously beyond their understanding and control. They learn through group activity to define the problems affecting them, to decide upon a solution, and to act to achieve the solution. As they progress, they gain new knowledge and skills. It is a deliberate, systematic process that is either organized by the group itself or by a leader who assists the group to become consciously engaged in it.

As social mobilization, community development has quite radical implications. Its objective is structural transformation realized through action at the community level involving people who, in Friedmann's (1987) words, take hold of their lives, recognizing that 'society is their own handiwork and not that of the state'. As was true with social learning, the decision to act is taken by the people who experience the need to realize a changed state of affairs. It is action 'from below' to overcome circumstances that might be rooted well outside the community.

Social learning can be part of the social mobilization process. Both involve conscious, deliberate attention to the need for change. In each, the choice about what form change should take is made by those who will do the work to achieve it. Social learning stops short of social mobilization in the sense that it does not imply structural change. Each requires long-term and continuous commitments of time, energy, and interest. Social mobilization might necessarily go further and include confrontation with established sources of power as a way to achieve desired shifts. Funding is undoubtedly an enabling factor for each, but it is not the primary requirement for success. More vital resources include skilful activity, determination, and commitment on the part of the majority of participants. In either case, these two traditions of community development permit those for whom change is required to be the major force in choosing and achieving it. Either way, the participants themselves are changed by the process. In a later section mention is made of some of the tasks that engage people when citizens pay conscious, deliberate attention to change through a community development process.

When regional development is limited to economic improvement, it usually excludes opportunity for local citizens to initiate and realize change. It excludes complex community conditions, including cultural considerations. It fails to take into account the knowledge and disposition of the population. To take a more comprehensive, community-oriented approach, regional development would include at least three characteristics. One is the need for those who reside in less-advantaged regions to have the opportunity to realize their potential as productive citizens. This represents equality of opportunity, which goes beyond the production and marketing of goods. It extends to qualitative measures, such as better housing, better opportunities for cultural development, and attention to strengthening local community resources.

A second characteristic of a community-based approach is that residents must be able to analyse the range of development options available in order to deal with the challenges posed by those options. By virtue of being long-time residents of the area, they already know a great deal about their circumstances, about the features that serve them well and those that do not.

A third characteristic of a community-based approach to regional development is continuous learning. It is not a matter of following a given formula to add certain numbers of dollars to certain types of enterprise for highly desirable outcomes. Rather it is an approach in which there is no firm or static description of the desired results, and where a shared vision of what is possible is continuously debated. Despite its evolving nature, there is still the need to plan. The planning process enables those who have a critical stake in the outcome to learn what is involved in selecting and realizing it. Citizens have to turn the disadvantage of their milieu to advantage, learning to use their unique knowledge of the region to achieve outcomes that they deem to be highly desirable. It is a purposeful problem-solving process from start to finish.

Evidence of Community Development in Regional Development Programs

Economic development implies a shift from a state of underdevelopment. As such, and as noted previously, one might expect community development to be a significant component of regional economic development measures. Without question, economic development must result in business ventures that bring in more money than they cost. This being so, people who live in economically underdeveloped communities have to learn how to achieve successful business ventures. With the goal of improving their own situation, they have to determine what is possible, they have to plan to achieve it, and they have to act. It is about learning and, because of barriers to their entry into new areas of social participation, in all likelihood it is also about social mobilization.

No matter what financial formulae or other infrastructure are available to stimulate economic development, if people who have limited entrepreneurial experience are expected to become either successful business persons or supporters of successful business, they have to learn how to overcome the barriers. The other alternatives are either to import business ventures or to fail. Importation implies government provision of financial and other incentives to attract enterprises to areas that heretofore were unattractive for various reasons. If the businesses prosper, the local economy improves. If they fail, there is essentially no net benefit. This approach leaves out the idea of investing in the development of people who would learn to build their own economy. Allowing for human development means that if a business fails, it at least results in some lessons in the community as a result of government's investment in development.

As noted throughout this chapter, Canada's regional development approach has not included attention to the development of human capital, nor, correspondingly, has community development been part of regional programs. Since ARDA is an exception, it is useful to look at features of that program in order to determine whether community development is compatible with regional development. Terms of reference relating to ARDA are explicit about including the following community development principles: the economic and social problems of the area first had to be identified, a comprehensive development plan then had to be elaborated, and the whole planning process had to involve citizens from start to end.

The descriptions of the ARDA experience in New Brunswick and Quebec (Allain and Coté 1983), and in Prince Edward Island (Crossley 1990), point to common features of community development approaches. However, these are individual examples that give no reason to claim that comparable ARDA experience might be found across Canada.

In New Brunswick, regional development councils were organized in keeping with ARDA guidelines. Allain and Coté say that the initial committees were made up mainly of members of the 'traditional elites'. The authors' opinion is that this was the very kind of citizen participation that ARDA encouraged: 'a form of controlled citizen participation, basically in agreement with governmental objectives'. They added that it was 'out of this joining together of traditional local and regional forces and technocratic government objectives that the development of the regions was to occur'. As it turned out, increasing numbers of 'ordinary people' joined the councils over time and actively opposed the proposed technocratic measures they felt would negatively alter their lives. Leaving one's community to live elsewhere is an example of such a measure. Gradually, people of low socio–economic status became the majority seat-holders on council boards as a result of declining interest from influential community members. Fieldworkers sympathetic to the interests of the less-advantaged citizens often took positions in their favour. On occasion these positions ran counter to provincial government objectives, despite the fact that fieldworkers' salaries were paid by the program.

In New Brunswick, examples of the social mobilization tradition of community development included public demonstrations to oppose such government measures as land expropriation for park development. Eventually the very funding for regional councils was a subject for dispute between the New Brunswick government and opposition politicians. As support for the governing Liberals waned, a provincial election resulted in a new government, which, while not always enthusiastic about the councils, nevertheless supported them until 1980, when the Hatfield government abandoned them, rationalizing that they had outlived and overstepped their mandate. The councils were replaced by other structures whose members were, once again in the words of Allain and Coté, 'the local and regional conservative elites'.

In Prince Edward Island, the Rural Development Council (RDC) was initiated in 1966, independently of ARDA and of the province. Crossley credits rural clergy for its initiation and describes their approach as one through which a community development process would enable whole communities to create better social and economic conditions. The province's ARDA agreement provided *ad hoc* financial support for the RDC to employ rural development officers, thereby implying that the council's definition of community development was compatible with ARDA's development goals. As Crossley describes the gradual involvement of the RDC in the province's ARDA-related comprehensive development plan, the original notion of community development slipped significantly to take on 'the view of an agent of the state, not a promoter of "economic democracy" and "community leadership"'. As for how the state viewed community development, Crossley provides a quotation that says it meant '"raising incomes and living standards and creating employment in rural areas"'.

Over time, Crossley contends, field staff of the RDC were neither agents of the state nor were they working as the RDC originally intended. They organized public meetings and were seen by provincial officials as using these events to undermine public policy rather than to reflect the will of the population. By 1975 the relationship between the RDC and the provincial government was such that 'the provincial cabinet decided to end the hostility by terminating the contract between the Department of Development and the RDC.'

These few examples from the ARDA experience underscore the earlier suggestion of incompatibility between regional and community development. Such seeming incompatibility is not inherent. It takes time to enable populations within less-developed areas to gain strength through learning and social mobilization. It also requires attention to reconciling the divergent interests of program administrators, community development agents, and sponsoring governments. The necessary time, skill, and understanding might be greater than program administrators will allow due to pressures on them to achieve tangible economic development results. One wonders whether these are the principal deterrents, or whether there are more fundamental problems. For example, allowing opportunity for citizens to select the direction for development implies that program administrators are willing to believe in the effectiveness of such direction. If they do not acknowledge social development as an integral part of economic development, they are unlikely to see the value of engaging in a relatively inefficient change process. Long after ARDA, administrators of regional development programs can find ample evidence of the value of merging social and economic goals. For example, they might look to the analysis of ten cases of community economic development initiatives and note the following central finding:

> The multi-functional approach makes the CED [community economic development] organization more effective for *merging economic and social goals* and for stressing the *empowerment* of disadvantaged populations and communities, especially in terms of their participation in the governance of the organization and in terms of human resource development, generally speaking (Perry and Lewis 1994:194).

Although ARDA is the principal example of an approach to regional economic development that incorporated community development, two other examples of national programming merit mention. Rooted in social development policy, the New Start Corporations (from 1967) and Community Futures (from 1986) incorporated economic development efforts in their respective programs.

The New Start Corporations were created to generate research and development activity in the field of adult education and training. Situated in the federal Department of Manpower and Immigration, their principal focus was human resource development for people who lived in areas of high unemployment. Although the program was not adopted by all provinces, each of the corporations formed had a five-year mandate to research and develop innovative ways to return adults to continuing and rewarding employment. In several instances (e.g., Nova Scotia, New Brunswick, and Prince Edward Island) New Start Corporations initiated community economic development projects to serve as test-tubes for experimentation with various approaches to motivating and training citizens in selected communities to manage their own economic, personal, and social development.

At the end of their respective funding periods the corporations produced far more than reports to bequeath to the newly created Department of Regional and Economic Expansion. Work done, particularly through Saskatchewan New Start, on curriculum development and social animation training resulted in the widely adopted DACUM (Developing a Curriculum) Process and Life Skills Program. As well, methods were developed for community animation and planning, entrepreneurial development, and citizen participation training. These are viable products that were not subsequently built into regional development policy.

Community Futures, a program of Employment and Immigration Canada, was created in the late 1980s under the Unemployment Insurance

Act. Its mandate was to 'assist selected communities in the assessment of their economic problems and in the development of employment opportunities through small business development, entrepreneurial support, training and relocation assistance' (Gallup Canada, Inc. 1990). It is another example of a program rooted in a social development base that utilized economic development procedures to achieve its purpose. Community Futures committees, established in more than 220 areas of high unemployment across the country, learned to analyse economic opportunities, plan approaches to development, and communicate with their respective communities. Often they received formal training, using materials prepared especially for them. There is no evaluation report that assesses the human development impact of the community development approach followed by Community Futures. During 1995, the program's departmental home (HRDC) decided to transfer the program to the respective regional development agencies. This could be viewed very positively as evidence that, finally, community development is acknowledged as integral to regional economic transformation. Or, it might be interpreted as another separation of social from economic programming, with HRDC limiting its role to training for employability in a more restricted sense than is implied within community development processes. It remains to be seen whether the regional development agencies will incorporate Community Futures' distinctive community development procedures in their economic development programming. If they do, it will signal commitment to social learning, and perhaps even to social mobilization, as necessary features of regional economic development.

Incorporating the Human Development Dimension

From time to time, there are short-term examples that attend to the need for citizens to learn to be successful agents for economic improvement. These are more likely to be the product of dynamic local leadership than the result of public policy. Nevertheless, there is ample ground for research in those communities where measures deliberately attend to competency development of local people in the process of generating economic activity. Such research would yield firm guidelines to govern the way community development can be incorporated as a critical component of regional development policy. Although there is no major body of systematic research on which to base reliable developmental approaches, there are identifiable competencies inherent in a social learning approach to community development. The following outline of four stages represents one approach to building economic development competencies of inexperienced people as part of the process of realizing comprehensive local development. It illustrates how social development might be incorporated into regional development programs. Each of the four stages includes brief mention of a set of related tasks. The principal feature of this model is its emphasis on being very clear about what has to be done and thereby capturing the interest and involvement of citizens in the development process while assisting them to be the principal performers of the required work.

Stage One: Determining the community's readiness to initiate development action.
Associated with this stage are the tasks of: (a) assessing the extent to which the community is politicized (the assumption is that a less politicized community is more open to devising its own solutions); (b) determining the extent to which the community is facing reality about its social and economic condition; (c) determining the extent to which community groups are initiating measures to improve their own social and economic prospects.

Stage Two: Selecting the appropriate local mechanisms for change.
Necessary tasks within this stage include: (a) negotiating with organization(s) already at work on projects intended to realize community economic and social change; (b) establishing and adopting a blueprint for a system of community development, including statement of mission, objectives, development processes, training, role of manager and staff, and mode of relating to development agencies; (c) assigning organization responsibility to a manager, preferably on a paid, full-time basis; (d) ensuring the presence of a steering committee that is able to distinguish consistently between decisions relating to policy and those relating to procedure, while recognizing that its role has to do with policy; (e) determining what form of organization will most effectively serve the community's purposes; (f) ensuring that local government and the various development agencies of federal and provincial governments are involved in the development effort.

Stage Three: Activating the development process.
Tasks within this stage include: (a) preparing job descriptions for those positions in the organization requiring paid employees; (b) employing full-time staff to serve as chairpersons of various task groups and as support staff; (c) training staff to perform their respective roles competently; (d) engaging voluntary task groups and, where necessary, the assistance of a professional planner and representatives of selected development agencies to prepare a set of development scenarios.

Stage Four: Implementing concrete plans.

This stage includes seven tasks: (a) establishing ways to find viable ideas for enterprise development; (b) establishing systems for new product development; (c) locating and securing financial support for enterprise development; (d) training local workers to meet new workforce requirements; (e) establishing production capacities through appropriate equipment and facilities; (f) establishing a range of available marketing resources; (g) establishing a system for monitoring new enterprise developments for a minimum of three years.

The Influence of Community Development on Regional Development Policy

With these rather specific tasks in mind, and with the above description of federal programs, one concludes that community development has had virtually no influence on regional economic development policy. Admittedly, the program examples are limited and come primarily from eastern Canadian experience. However, they are rooted in national policies. In cases where attention was given to community learning and mobilization (e.g., through ARDA, New Start Corporations, and Community Futures), there is no evidence that those approaches carried over as positive influences on subsequent programs. It is too early to assess the extent to which the Community Futures transfer will affect regional development agencies.

The current regional development landscape is not entirely without the influence of community development. There is at least one example in Canada of an economic development policy base that incorporates a strong community development component. The 1995 task force report on community economic development in Newfoundland and Labrador is a joint effort between that province and the federal government. The report gives primary attention to establishing economic zones that would integrate 'private, public, and community-based organizations, working in tandem with provincial, national and international agencies and firms'.

If one views the province of Newfoundland and Labrador as a region, then this example of development policy is quite distinct from what has come out of Ottawa in the years since ARDA. It builds on the notion of community development, which it defines as 'a process with a focus on wealth creation, job creation, value-added activities, business and co-operative development, and enhanced viability for the community, the region and the province'. Treating the province in this case as the 'region', the report calls upon all parties, including politicians and government officials, to 'buy into the community-based approach'. The report acknowledges that regional economic development cannot take the same shape in all areas, and presumes that the framework it presents can be used by the respective zones to fit their own circumstances, while acknowledging that this will not happen easily.

It is noteworthy that the above definition of community development makes no reference to features that might be interpreted either as community learning or community mobilization. Rather, it centres on enhancing economic viability. However, the organization structure for each zone emphasizes local decision making and allows for variable circumstances. This is surely a positive move away from the usual one-size-fits-all approach of federally initiated regional development measures, which tend to proceed without reference to the readiness levels of localities within the region. It allows for local differences, but is silent about the importance of community development as a route to economic transformation.

Conclusion

There is an essential and positive connection between building people in community, and building the economy of disadvantaged regions. That the connection has not generally been fostered through regional development policy is more a fact of the past than an inevitability. It points to work to be done. Ideally, there should be no such gap. The question of how to close it calls into play the concepts of citizen learning, process modelling, program evaluation, and institutional flexibility.

Learning is a major consideration. The Community Futures and New Start Corporations programs (which were not part of regional economic development policy) are examples of deliberate attention to helping citizens learn their development role. One challenge for change is for community development advocates to reference clear, systematic procedures that will say what it means to do what the ARDA principle suggested: 'implicate citizen participation from start to end'. It must not be left to the judgement of politicians who fear the risk of sharing power. A claim for the importance of learning carries the additional challenge of generating evidence that developmental outcomes do in fact emerge from a deliberate and successful learning process. Evidence can and should be provided to demonstrate that the time and trouble required for systematic social development produces important social and economic results.

Much the same is true for process modelling. As the abovementioned stages illustrate, there are explicit operations involved in a community development process that enable communities to build their economy successfully. These cannot be left to chance nor couched in such soft words as empowerment and self-realization. There is room within the community development field itself for practitioners to be precise about the development process and systematically demonstrate how it functions. In that way they will remove the mystery and, what is more, assert that there are concrete steps involved.

Only against a base of rigorous evaluation of community development efforts can policy makers reliably conclude that community development is a necessary component of regional development policy. Evaluation research is required if they are to know what economic benefits to expect when citizens take responsibility for achieving economic development.

Finally, community development is a very comprehensive process. For example, the notion of learning can refer to literacy skills, sophisticated long-term planning, and a host of other outcomes. Or, the notion of planning can refer to an operation within municipal government, a personal development exercise, or any number of planning operations. It is difficult for public policy to encompass such a range of considerations, but it is possible for policy to allow for such breadth even if it might not, or cannot, be implemented through a single agency. The objective to achieve certain outcomes will at least set an agenda to find ways to achieve them.

Economic and social development are far from being incompatible measures. They must necessarily operate together when the goal is to build and sustain society, especially where there is long-term social and economic disadvantage. The challenge in Canada is to close that gap through deliberate effort to provide support beyond the economic to achieve improved levels of economic activity.

References

Allain, G., and S. Coté.
    1983. 'The State of Regional Development Organizations: A Comparative Analysis of
    Citizen Participation in Quebec and New Brunswick (1960–1980)'. Unpublished paper
    presented at the Annual Meeting of the Canadian Sociology and Anthropology
    Association, Vancouver.

Crossley, J.
    1990. 'Community Development, Administrative Rationality, and Politics: The Rural
    Development Council and the Canada-PEI Comprehensive Development Plan'.
    Unpublished paper presented at the Annual Meeting of the Atlantic Provinces Political
    Studies Association, St John's.

Friedmann, J.
1987. *Planning in the Public Domain: From Knowledge to Action*, Part 2. Princeton: Princeton University Press.

Gallup Canada, Inc.
1990. 'Evaluation of Community Futures: Survey of Clients, Participants, Facilitators and Managers'. Ottawa: Gallup Canada, Inc.

Perry, S.E., and M. Lewis.
1994. *Reinventing the Local Economy.* Vernon, BC: Centre for Community Enterprise.

Savoie, D.J.
1986. *Regional Economic Development: Canada's Search for Solutions.* Toronto: University of Toronto Press.

Task Force on Community Economic Development in Newfoundland and Labrador.
1995. 'Community Matters: The New Regional Economic Development'. St John's: Task Force on Community Economic Development in Newfoundland and Labrador.

Chapter Nine

Community Economic Development: Making the Link between Economic Development and Social Equity

Michael Lewis

The story of community development in Canada goes back to economic self-help strategies born out of the collective misery of the depression. In the absence of effective public or private action to address that decade's social and economic convulsion, local action became the well-spring of survival-driven innovation. Most prominent was the creative and energetic movement to create producer, consumer, and financial cooperatives. The idea of locally controlled, democratic institutions that met social goals through business means took root.

Interestingly, the concept of economic development and its emergence as a deliberate practice did not emerge until after the Second World War. The postwar reconstruction of Europe and the newly independent states in the Third World were the locus out of which the idea of deliberate action to develop economies became internationally recognized (Perry and Lewis 1994). However, the action organized under the rubric of economic development was certainly not community based. Targets included major physical infrastructure projects (e.g., hydroelectric dams), monetary reforms, and major export-oriented projects.

The language of community-based economic development did not emerge until much later. Moreover, it was in the US during the 1960s, not in Canada, that the use of the term came into prominent usage. In Canada the key words in the development lexicon of the time did not include community economic development. Community development in its various forms did emerge and take form in such agencies as the Company of Young Canadians. However, mainstream development concepts were dominated by the language of regional development, a set of concepts and programs that were the creature of our federal state searching for a means to even out the distribution of benefits from industrial development among Canada's disparate regions.

The US was a very different situation. The broadly based organizing and political action of the American civil rights movement created a mass movement among poor Blacks. In addition, President Johnson's War on Poverty extended the breadth and depth of local action to fight poverty. It was in this context that community economic development evolved as a distinct field.

Much of the organizing energy throughout the 1960s was focused on what I refer to as 'rights fights': actions aimed at establishing and/or enhancing publicly sanctioned entitlement. Civil rights and rights to basic health and social security were a major focus of activists intent on pressuring the state to entrench basic benefits for economically and socially disenfranchised populations. While the primary targets of such actions were governments, there is also evidence of actions related to jobs for minorities in major corporations and rights for migrant workers. The emphasis was oriented to social action and social reform (Rothman and Tropman 1987), although the methods of locality development and social planning remained discernible.

Community economic development (CED) grew out of a recognition that there were real limits to what could be yielded by a strategy concerned solely with rights advocacy. Many leaders within these movements began to see that while they were out on the hustings organizing around rights, economic decisions that had critical implications for poor people's interests were being made completely outside the public realm. Economic action came to be seen as a necessary front, and this translated into organizing community-controlled institutions that could contend in the murky halls of economic power. This strategic conclusion—that gaining public rights was not enough and that economic action was a pressing necessity if real change was to be sustained—is the root of CED as a strategy of empowerment that links social and economic goals.

The Definitions Debate: What Is Community Economic Development?

The evolution of CED as a distinct field has led to a burgeoning literature, part of which is devoted to a debate over definition. Just what is CED? This question is not the sterile domain of academics. The principles and actions that we decide CED is to include (and exclude) will have a real impact on policy makers and on people making things happen 'on the ground'. Moreover, as will become apparent, how one defines CED is vitally important to its application as a strategy to fight poverty. The debate turns on a matter of emphasis. Is CED primarily a way in which local people realize substantial economic growth in their community, or is it a means of empowering the poor and disadvantaged?

The first school of thought describes a development process 'in which local governments or community-based organizations . . . stimulate or maintain business activity and/or employment' (Blakely 1994). The principal goal of this activity is to develop jobs that improve the community's use of local human, natural, and institutional resources.

In Canada, the basic thrust of this definition was encompassed by the federal government's Community Futures program. It has been intended to increase communities' economic adaptability and create jobs, particularly by encouraging and supporting entrepreneurship. Community Futures understood the process of community-based economic development in terms of people at the local level coming together and innovating in order to combat unemployment (Employment and Immigration Canada 1990) (It should also be noted that Community Futures did evolve in its understanding over time as well. Nothing stands still.)

In contrast, the second school of thought asserts that community-based economic development specifically addresses the problems of the poor and the powerless. Rather than merely alleviating living conditions, this 'unique strategy . . . seeks to change the structure of the community'. It builds institutions that embody the active control of community resources by residents, and that can interact with institutions external to the community (Swack and Mason 1994).

Unlike the aforementioned Community Futures program, this approach makes social goals the central priority of community-based economic development. In particular, it places the creation of greater local control and accountability at the very heart of CED.

Research and practice suggests these two orientations are not mutually exclusive. Indeed, in the context of the revitalization of poor communities or populations, it would appear that empowerment and local economic development must go together if success is to be realized over the long term. The following definition, derived from our review of the literature and the results of best practice, demonstrates that synthesis of viewpoints:

Community economic development is a comprehensive, multi-faceted strategy for the revitalization of community economies, with a special relevance to communities under economic and social stress. Through the development of organizations and institutions, resources and alliances are put in place that are democratically controlled by the community. They mobilize local resources (people, finances, technical expertise, and real property) in partnership with resources from outside the community for the purpose of empowering community members to create and manage new and expanded businesses, specialized institutions and organizations (Perry, Lewis, and Fontan 1992).

Or, in the concise terms expressed by one leading Canadian practitioner, CED is a strategy by which people meet social goals through business means.

Linking CED to Sustainable Development Concepts

A critical debate to emerge in the 1980s concerned the significance of sustainable development in the practice of CED. To round out the discussion of CED's evolution, it is important to make some comments about this relationship.

Translating our definition of CED into the tridimensional parlance of 'sustainable development'—economic, social, and ecological—emphasizes the centrality of people as social actors. 'Sustainability must be socially constructed, that is, arrangements of a social and economic nature must be made purposively' (Cernea 1993).

Getting organized remains the key. It means the social actors themselves must be involved. This is not an empty slogan about 'beneficiary participation'. Rather, it is a clear recognition that without local participation through existing or new institutions, enduring benefits cannot be generated and more sustainable approaches to development cannot be fostered.

The World Bank confirmed these basic facts once again in a recent study. Twenty-five projects that the World Bank financed in Africa, Asia, and Latin America were examined to assess their sustainability:

> Disappointingly, the study found that over half of them (13 projects) had left no lasting developmental impact 6–10 years after completion and had failed to produce the expected flow of benefits. Among the basic causes of non-sustainability were the neglect of sociological factors in project design and the lack of supportive institutions and grassroots participation. In sum, the 'social scaffolding' of sustainability was missing. Conversely, all the projects that proved to be sustainable undertook from the outset purposive institution building (Cernea 1993).

This notion of building the 'social scaffolding' is important to all aspects of sustainable development. On the environmental side, governments have developed a wide array of environmental laws and regulations, but meeting goals of environmental protection and restoration over the long term requires local/bio-regional cooperation, participation, and action. Local stakeholders are an important part of the equation. In many cases new institutions must be developed to appropriately mandate and structure the local stakeholder's role.

This reordering of relationships is one part of the social dimension of sustainable development. Equally important is to find the means by which to include the growing numbers of people on the margins of the economic and social life of the country. For the poor, this clearly implies empowerment to participate meaningfully as individuals and groups, particularly through community-level organizations in which they are a significant stakeholder.

Lastly, it is obvious that the economic dimension of sustainable development is critical to the process of transforming the way we do business. CED's best practice takes some small steps to redesign business goals from a community perspective, particularly in the context of issues relating to poverty and quality of life. Best practice has demonstrated that the integration of social and economic action by appropriately supported community organizations is cost effective and creates durable results. It therefore seems appropriate to think of CED as one important area of inquiry when looking for strategies that move our communities and our country onto a more sustainable footing.

CED's Best Practice: Building the Foundations to Make a Difference

A tremendous amount has been learned since 1975, when Canada's first community development corporation was formed in one of our most depleted regions (New Dawn Enterprises in Cape Breton). A wide range of local leadership and dedicated activists have built organizations that are producing long-term results. A variety of models and approaches have emerged. While only a few can be cited within the limits of this chapter, they make their point: CED's best practice has laid a foundation of knowledge, skills, and tools that can make a real contribution to building more inclusive, creative, and sustainable communities.

It is also important to note that 'best practice' did not emerge without many false starts and numerous 'failures'. Of these there have been plenty, and for plenty of different reasons: lack of a supportive policy context, unavailability of experienced technical assistance, too large an effort put into single projects and not enough into building development organizations, and inadequate financial resource are but a few of the factors that have contributed to failures.

However, it is equally important to recognize that this new field was, during its first ten years, primarily focused on local communities, which is where it stayed. Distress and crisis, characteristics of many of CED's birthplaces, did not leave a lot of time for research or broader organizing. There was no national antipoverty program and civil rights movements to jump-start the movement as in the US. There were no national and regional intermediaries organized to promote CED and provide technical and financial support. Indeed, as of 1996, there is still no national organization, although the Centre for Community Enterprise has helped a national network to evolve.

Yes, there have been failures, which created opportunities for learning. Learning from failure is embodied in various best practice organizations across Canada and many more that are emerging. Indeed, it could be argued that the following case, Nisga'a Economic Enterprises, demonstrates just how much learning has taken place in the last ten to fifteen years regarding how to build CED organizations that empower communities to act in the economic sphere. Much of the knowledge and methods applied to building Nisga'a Economic Enterprises did not exist fifteen years ago, or if they did, they were not generally accessible in Canada.

Reclaiming Their Homeland:
The Case of Nisga'a Economic Enterprises Inc.

Nestled in British Columbia's northwest is the spectacular Nass River Valley, homeland to the Nisga'a people. For decades the four Nisga'a villages scattered along the Nass River have been relegated to the economic sidelines, virtually ignored by the governments and companies exploiting the valley's wealth. Other than a few jobs, few durable benefits have been left behind. What the communities have are high unemployment, high dependence on transfer payments, a myriad of social problems, and a smoldering anger that comes from being cut out of the economic equation.

Throughout the late 1980s the communities and the Nisga'a Tribal Council tried to find ways to capture some of the benefits of development. Five years of effort yielded some significant learning, but not much by way of concrete results. In 1990 Mat Moore, the tribal council's talented economic development officer, approached Westcoast Centre for Development Management (a subsidiary of the Centre for Community Enterprise) to help them build an effective development organization.

Each of the four First Nations had already created its own community corporation. They had also established a legal entity named Nisga'a Economic Enterprises Inc. (NEEI) and appointed a board, but very little was happening apart from some limited action at the community level. Neither the community corporations nor NEEI had the knowledge or level of organization needed to translate opportunities into economic and social benefits.

With Westcoast's assistance, a training and technical assistance program was designed that would support the planning, decision making, and policy development required to get an effective development operation up and running. It was a blueprint for a substantial investment in Nisga'a 'organizational capacity', to use the jargon of CED. Leadership and staff undertook training to acquire knowledge and skills, which they immediately applied. The result was a development program and organizational structure that aimed to establish NEEI as a business owner in every key sector of the regional economy (Lewis 1994).

After fourteen months of hard work, NEEI was organized and equipped to target and capture business opportunities, a key plank in their economic development strategy. Joint ventures with private companies were to be among their major strategies, with an initial emphasis on the forest sector. Since then, NEEI has begun to transform the economic and social base of their communities. By 1996, just four years after the initial training/planning process, NEEI has:

- Created five businesses and more than 150 jobs in logging, stevedoring, fish processing, and a fishing-related tourism lodge (the latter two are wholly owned by NEEI).

- Become self-sufficient, paying its own operating costs (approximately $275,000 per year).

- Accumulated enough profits to have in hand a $4.3 million investment fund.

- Established a $150,000 loan guarantee fund to help Nisga'a entrepreneurs to obtain credit.

- Provided a $100,000 grant to establish the Nisga'a House of Learning and endowed it with $250,000 to develop and operate the Nisga'a Language, Culture, and Training Institute. Similar endowments are planned for resource management and the area of business and economic development.

- Jump-started a non-profit subsidiary (Nisga'a Economic Development Services) with $150,000 over two years. Its mandate is to create and implement a human resource development strategy to strengthen the Nisga'a labour force and entrepreneurial capacity. NEEI knows that getting people ready, willing, and able to take advantage of new opportunities is central to meeting their economic and social goals.

- Increased both the competency of the board and the level of understanding and support of its owners, the four First Nations councils, as well as Nisga'a citizens and the central political institution, the Nisga'a Tribal Council.

Taken together, the achievements of this community development corporation represents significant progress. The central mission of NEEI, to build an economic base for the Nisga'a people, has a solid beginning. In the 1980s there were opportunities, but little organized capacity to take advantage of them. The investment of time and resources in the early 1990s to get organized, equipped, and strategic is beginning to pay economic and social dividends.

From Dependence to Dignity: Halifax's HRDA

The Human Resource Development Association (HRDA) was formed in 1978 as an experiment in reducing welfare costs by creating real jobs. The idea was to build businesses that would provide employment opportunities and a ladder out of poverty. Three things were needed: leadership, capital, and a core organization given enough support to become self-reliant.

The Social Planning Department of the City of Halifax was headed by a social entrepreneur. One of the originators of the HRDA vision, he also had the political acumen, tenacity, and basic development skills to get things moving. He appointed a board of community members with a variety of skills. He convinced the city to provide the core financial support required for the HRDA administration. Lastly, on the capital side, he convinced the city and the province to take $275,000 directly out of the welfare budget to use as the equity stake that HRDA Enterprises (the subsidiary of HRDA) required to get its first businesses up and running.

Armed with these basic resources, HRDA Enterprises, after eighteen years of struggle and strain, has become the owner of several businesses. The range of enterprises it has launched extends from manufacturing to the service sector. One is a joint venture company that runs the Halifax–Dartmouth recycling plant. By these means in the last ten years, over 1,400 people have moved off welfare and into employment. HRDA's training systems have involved another 1,000 people, the majority of whom have gone on to either further education or to private-sector jobs. This combined strategy of building assets through business development, as well as a creating a solid training system, has yielded the public treasury $1.83 for every $1 invested in HRDA (Bay State Skills Corporation 1993).

Profits have been part of the means for financing new business development. Another important source has been a fee for service that HRDA receives from the municipal welfare budget. For every person it removes from social assistance, 50 per cent of that person's wages and benefits is paid monthly to HRDA for up to a year. Interestingly, Halifax's traditional private sector is also eligible for this incentive, but has shown little interest. Changes in the way social assistance is administered in Nova Scotia have, in 1996, removed the municipal role and this incentive. At the time of writing, it was not clear whether the province would reinstate it. In addition, federal and provincial training programs used by HRDA to prepare people for employment are changing due to public sector budget cutting.

Through HRDA's slow but steady increase in capacity since its inception in 1978, the association is facing interesting challenges. It is positioned as a self-sufficient, independent CED organization. In the 1995 fiscal year, its businesses (currently employing 135 people) generated a $500,000 net profit for their holding company. On the one hand, it has the capital for reinvestment and the experience to continue the mission of helping people climb out of poverty. On the other hand, reduced access to training dollars and the prospect of no payment for getting people off social assistance could create pressures that, over time, will reduce its capacity to link business creation to the development goal of increasing social equity and individual dignity. It will be instructive to observe how HRDA adapts in the years ahead.

Revitalization of Neighbourhood Economies: Fighting Back in Montreal

The Regroupement pour la relance économique et social du Sud-Ouest de Montréal (RÉSO) has a mandate for the economic and social renewal of southwest Montreal, an area that has suffered continuous industrial decline over the last twenty years. In some neighbourhoods, 50 per cent of the population is on social assistance, and unemployment reaches 35 per cent.

RÉSO is a broadly based community development corporation that emerged from the persistance of a community movement. In 1984 organizations in the Pointe St-Charles neighbourhood began organizing on the economic front. Pressures to 'condo-ize' the Lachine Canal, plus persistent job loss, convinced community actors that they had to organize. In 1989 these efforts culminated in the formation of RÉSO, a unique partnership focused on the renewal of five poor neighbourhoods in that part of town (Gareau 1991).

RÉSO is a membership-based organization. In 1995 the organization made a major push to increase its individual membership from neighbourhood residents to 1,000. Its board is structured on what is almost an electoral college system. Each of the key sectors elects its representative from among its constituents. There are four representatives of the community movement, two from trade unions in the area, one from big business, two from small business, and one from the banking sector. One important result of this membership and board structure is the political influence RÉSO has achieved. Another is the accountability. RÉSO can draw 500 people to an annual meeting. It can also mobilize hundreds of people onto the streets to protest, which it has done more than once when the neighbourhood's economic interests were being threatened.

RÉSO has been implementing a multifaceted strategy. Intervention occurs through two main avenues: employability services and business services. Owing to the comprehensive nature of its mandate, the organization is also involved in issues related to land use, development of infrastructure, and promotion of the area. RÉSO even plays a role in the representation, consultation, and promotion relating to community economic development in the whole Montreal region. In addition, it experiments with innovative approaches to reaching those who are hardest to reach, e.g., chronically unemployed youths. One result of this effort has been Formetal, a successful training business in the metallurgical field.

On the employment side, RÉSO is involved (directly or by brokering to other community-based organizations) in training between 700 and 800 people per year. Training investments are continuously becoming more effectively linked to the local labour market, in large part because of the unique relationship RÉSO has fostered with businesses in the southwest.

Between 1993 and 1995 RÉSO provided technical assistance to over 200 businesses. This outreach has been facilitated, in part, by an early warning system. When trade unions see a firm threatened by succession (a business owner retiring with no buyer), financial difficulties, and so on, they notify RÉSO. It then works with management and others to address problems related to product development, marketing, financial restructuring, etc.

The information gained from its involvement with so many large and small businesses has provided RÉSO with a detailed understanding of the local labour market: emerging roles, job training needs, and so on. This enables RÉSO to tailor its training investments to real demand. Competency-based curricula directly derived from profiling business and labour market needs are now being developed and delivered. Through this integrated approach, RÉSO is building effective bridges between the needs of the poor and the needs of the business community.

There is evidence that the partnership RÉSO represents is having other dramatic effects. For example, the largest manufacturer in southwest Montreal (whose president was on the RÉSO board) now sees CED as a vital component of its business plan. He is beginning to link systematically the company's $70 million annual procurement budget to suppliers in the southwest. This has already led to a Spanish firm opening a business in Montreal in order to keep the $5–6 million supply contract it has enjoyed for several years. The result is another forty or more jobs for neighbourhood people.

Recent statistics (released in 1994) revealed the success of this wide range of integrated interventions. At the height of a recession, southwest Montreal had halted, at least for two years, the twenty-year decline in its manufacturing base.

RÉSO is now in the early stages of adding direct business ownership as an element of its strategy. Building an economic base that will reduce its vulnerability to government funding is an important goal for the corporation. An important breakthrough to securing the means to pursue this goal was made in 1995. RÉSO negotiated from private and public sources a $5 million investment fund that will serve as its source of equity. It would appear that RÉSO is well positioned to invest in and strengthen its community as an owner in the local economy.

Lessons and Implications

The NEEI, HRDA, and RÉSO are among a growing number of organizations that are building economic bases from which to reach out to impoverished people and communities and give priority to their interests.[1] Creating such an economic base involves five key functions: (1) creating equity for reinvestment, (2) improving access to credit, (3) developing people, (4) good planning and research, and (5) an ability to broker and create partnerships inside and outside of the community. Each of the organizations cited are paying attention to these key functions. If they are not performing them directly, they are taking action to make sure related institutions do. In short, they are building a network of resources and organizations that link social and economic development. In the process they are creating hope, strengthening community, and continuously building organizational capacity, all prominent themes in CED's most effective organizations. Moreover, they are building for the long term.

Given these and many other examples of CED's best practice in Canada and the US, it is evident that dramatically impressive models can be found for a variety of intervention strategies. Collectively they represent a new paradigm in development thinking (Perry and Lewis 1994). These models:

- serve as vehicles of empowerment; they demonstrate how responsibility for performance can be devolved to community organizations and their beneficiaries while creating a sense of dignity and discipline and a high expectation for performance

- link the alleviation of poverty directly to broader goals, rather than viewing it as an end in itself

- pursue market-based strategies, often geographically and sectorally specific, that exploit market niches for beneficiaries

- seek to become sustainable components of the local economy, often through the creation of profitable enterprises

These efforts stretch beyond the boundaries of 'programs'. They have evolved into 'development systems' for the unemployed and the poor. This feature is borne out by other research into CED organizations:

- Most successful CED organizations embody a multifunctional approach, or are closely connected to other groups with the necessary supplementary functions. They provide or facilitate equity investment; lending (accompanied by technical assistance for borrowers); human resource development; and research, planning, advisory, and advocacy services. These multiple functions make up the requisite elements of a 'development system'.

- This multifunctional approach is critical to the merging of economic and social goals and tends to stress the empowerment of marginalized populations and communities, especially in terms of organizational and human resource development.

- Through strategic planning or similar efforts, successful projects become specific about what they are trying to do, even though they use many means to achieve their objectives.

- Successful CED organizations generate enough funds for longevity and accelerated growth through effective use of public and non-government financing and through asset building, particularly in housing, real property, and business development. Their larger scale of operation is thus one component of their success.

- Most successful programs arise from local initiatives rather than top-down strategies, and develop through independent (usually non-profit) entities. They are also led by 'social entrepreneurs': local leaders (usually) who combine social vision, organizing and management skills, and political acumen with the tenacity to perform in a very difficult arena in trying times. These professionals, also known as 'development managers' are in short supply.

Expanding Best Practice in Canada

If CED is so effective, why is it not more widely discussed and practised? Two factors work to keep CED in the shadows. First, it has been and continues to be characterized by innovation. CED's practitioners (as the preceding discussion indicates) are driven to meet the needs of marginalized people, neighbourhoods, and communities. Essentially, this debate centres on a single question: What works? What really enables communities to become more creative, inclusive, and sustainable? That focus on the practical, regardless of received wisdom or traditional ideology, has made innovation, not self-promotion, the outstanding feature of the field. As a result, research has begun only recently to catch up with practice. Many policy makers do not understand what CED is and why it should be taken seriously. It remains to be seen if CED practitioners and researchers can lead in a broader public discussion of the importance of CED. Hitherto the pressing needs and challenges of community practice—to which innovation remains central—have commanded their attention.

The second factor is the inverse of the first. Just as no one has been 'selling' CED, it is not the sort of thing most people are eager to 'buy' in the marketplace of ideas. A related problem is that when the idea is 'bought', as it was by the NDP government in Ontario, there have been some spectacular failures that have had the nomenclature of CED attached to them. A careful analysis of the policy and program design at the heart of the Ontario NDP's approach reveals just how important it is to learn from what is working. One of the key factors in the general failure of the Ontario experiment was a failure to invest in organizational capacity building, relying instead on project-focused financing. The political need for quick results backfired. CED got a bad rap in the process (Perry and Lewis 1994).

CED offers no quick fix to economic distress. Successful initiatives usually take several years to have significant impact and to reduce their need for grants or other support. CED is complicated. The whole process involves a gradual accumulation of skills, practices, and assets of local folk with their neighbours' knowledge and agreement. There are a good many more actors than most people are used to seeing on the economic stage. It takes rigorous planning, research, and consultation to accomplish.

CED defies classification according to political and economic conventions. Meeting the criteria of neither capitalism nor socialism, left nor right, it has been generally eschewed by those who rely on the old typologies to understand experience. In short, CED is neither the sort of response to economic distress that political parties want to explain to electors, nor is it what the public wants to hear. Retreads of old notions of government intervention, or untrammelled free enterprise, or workfare programs are still seen as more effective means to garner and maintain political power. That being said, it must also be observed that there may never have been a more advantageous time for CED to make its bid for recognition. The ideas, analysis, and experience exchanged by practitioners is giving them and their work a greater sense of identity and concreteness. Conventional politics and economics have alienated (and marginalized) so many of Canada's citizens that real alternatives have a substantial audience with the patience and determination to listen.

If now is the time, a long-term, sustained effort to expand the practice of CED will require action on a number of levels. A national strategy must combine the resources of the public, private, and philanthropic sectors. Assistance given to expand and strengthen the support base nationally must be decentralized in structure and responsive to local situations and institutions. At the same time, there must be a strong, proactive element to the following:

- Accelerate dissemination and learning based on best practice. This will avoid reinventing the wheel in hundreds of localities. It will also broadly promote the market- and sector-based planning and intervention strategies that are proving successful.

- Support the appropriate replication of methodologies from model initiatives, including exchanges and interchanges with leading practitioners.

- Support continued innovation and learning in less accomplished approaches to employment and enterprise development, e.g., microenterprise development and training enterprises.

- Integrate financial support for local institutions with training and technical assistance, especially for the small and/or recent programs undertaken in distressed communities and regions. This must include leadership training and training in development management.

The federal and provincial governments have a critical role to play in this. Unlike former eras, however, they might best act as the catalysts and facilitators for a long-term employment and enterprise development strategy for disadvantaged citizens, not as the ones to implement the strategy. The governments are best positioned to place the issue of poverty alleviation squarely within our economic priorities, to establish goals and coordinate strategies, to gain legislative and public support, and to provide seed capital to mobilize action. Given our currently diminished capacity to promote broadly state-of-the-art interventions, initial outlays should be modest, with a high concentration on capacity building. Investments should increase over time as absorptive capacity grows.

In meeting all these concerns, the most appropriate strategy may be to decentralize decision making, planning, and finance to organizations in which governments are partners around a larger table. This could involve creating regional entities (institutes perhaps) governed by key stakeholders. An arm's-length approach from government would avoid bureaucratic tendencies to focus on a delimited number of centrally driven strategies and would instead allow more flexibility and innovation in developing and supporting local- and region-specific approaches to alleviate poverty.

More detailed discussion of policy and program design is beyond the scope of this chapter. Let it suffice to say that some important work has been done to enable the federal and provincial governments to strengthen their resolve and capacity to assume a role supportive of the types of initiatives and directions outlined in this chapter.

Conclusion

People and institutions are responsible for creating the economic, social, and environmental crises we face today. Obviously, it is people who must build organizations and institutions with the capacity to mobilize resources and relationships that move us away from crises and towards durable solutions.

CED's best practice makes an important contribution to building the kinds of locally accountable organizations necessary for such a transition. By linking economic development directly to increasing social equity, particularly poverty alleviation, CED is directly contributing to part of the solution. Increasingly CED organizations are deliberately integrating the concept of sustainability into their vision, plans, and practice. Environmental restoration and protection and business development are becoming an important focus for several CED organizations.

By building on CED's best practice, governments have a real opportunity to facilitate a modest but systematic expansion of CED as a strategy for poverty alleviation. The organizational and institutional innovation that a public sector commitment would foster, while not a short-term solution to unemployment, does create the basis for durable results that are cost effective and efficient. Just as important, organizations like HRDA, RÉSO, and NEEI are essential initiators and partners in the nitty gritty—that is, getting real things done to create, promote, and implement sustainable strategies of local and regional economic development.

By investing in local capacity building and supporting community own-ership of assets, governments as well as the private and philanthropic sectors can begin to make real, on a national scale, the greater self-reliance being achieved by some Canadian communities. The linkage between the goals of alleviating poverty, economic development, and environmental sustainability can and should be acted upon in a balanced, managed way.

Note

[1] The recent work of S.E. Perry and M. Lewis, *Reinventing the Local Economy*, supplies informa-tion about several examples of Canadian community economic development. In addition to chapters on HRDA and RÉSO, the authors assess the record of the following:

A-Way Express, a downtown Toronto courier service that employed many former psy-chiatric patients; Cape Breton Labourers Development Company, an approach to financing and building community housing; West End Community Ventures, building a business system in a locality defined by low-income high-rises; Saskatchewan Community Bonds, a provincial initiative to create local pools of capital to support business development; Homes First Society, a community-based housing and venture development among Toronto's homeless; ACEM, a pri-vately capitalized loan fund for small businesses in Montreal; and VanCity, a major financial institution that tries to define a community economic development agenda without a unified constituent base.

References

Bay State Skills Corporation.
 1993. HRDA *Alternative Welfare Model*. Boston: Bay State Skills Corporation.

Blakely, E.J.
 1994. *Planning Local Economic Development: Theory and Practice*, 2nd ed. Thousand Oaks, CA: Sage.

Cernea, M.
 1993. 'A Sociologist's Approach to Sustainable Development in Finance and Development'. *Quarterly of the International Monetary Fund and the World Bank* (December):11–13.

Employment and Immigration Canada.
 1990. 'Community Futures Program'. Ottawa: Employment and Immigration Canada.

Gareau, J.-M.
 1991. PEP, *the Pointe St-Charles Economic Program: The Rise of Community Economic Development in Montréal 1983–89*. Port Alberni, BC: Westcoast Development Group.

Lewis, M.

1991. 'Integration of CED Training & Planning in BC's Nass River Valley'. *Making Waves: A Newsletter for CED Practitioners in Canada* (October):4–7.

———.

1994. 'Nisga'a Economic Enterprises: Investments Building Durable Community Results'. *Making Waves: Canada's Community Economic Development Quarterly* (Summer):1–4.

Perry, S.E., M. Lewis, and J.-M. Fontan.

1992. 'Revitalizing Canada's Neighbourhoods: A Research Report on Urban Community Economic Development'. Vernon, BC: Centre for Community Enterprise.

———, and M. Lewis.

1994. *Reinventing the Local Economy: What 10 Canadian Initiatives Can Teach Us About Building Creative, Inclusive, and Sustainable Communities.* Vernon, BC: Centre for Community Enterprise.

Rothman, J., and J.E. Tropman.

1987. 'Models of Community Organization and Macro Practice Perspective: Their Mixing and Phasing'. In *Strategies of Community Organization: Macro Practice*, edited by F.M. Cox et al., 3–26. Itasca, Illinois: F.E. Peacock.

Swack, M., and D. Mason.

1994. 'Issues of Capital Needs and Co-operative Development: A Report Prepared by the Institute for Co-operative Community Development for Co-op Atlantic'. Moncton: Coop Atlantic.

Chapter Ten

Feminist Community Organizing in Canada: Postcards from the Edge

Marilyn Callahan

Introduction

Feminist thinking was not evident in community work during my social work education and early practice in the 1960s. In fact, quite the opposite circumstances prevailed. Male social work students, then almost half the class, were heavily enrolled in the specialities of community organization and social welfare administration. In these courses almost all theorists and historians were male, including powerful and illustrious writers like Rothman, Alinsky, and Ross. We did not study the organizing work of Canadian suffragettes, farm women organizers, and settlement house workers. After graduation, my male classmates soon occupied most of the leadership positions in community work: as local developers of area councils to mobilize citizens, as planners in the fledgling municipal social planning efforts, as managers in the federal government community development efforts (such as the Company of Young Canadians) and as activists in the development of public service unions and Vietnam draft-dodgers services. While women also worked in these agencies, community work itself was conceived of as a gender-neutral activity concerned with giving voice to local citizens.

My first job after graduation was at the YWCA outreach program in downtown Vancouver, an unusual community agency wholly devoted to the needs of women and children and managed by women. I soon found myself immersed in the issues of inner city poverty and racism, which were often exacerbated by urban development initiatives, such as the large concrete high-rises located across from the 'Y'. Although I had been assigned to develop groups for school-aged Chinese-Canadian girls, it was impossible to ignore the lives of their mothers. Most of these women could not speak English, remained close to home, and seemed uncomfortable even in the neighbourhood 'Y' where they came to collect their daughters. My early struggles to begin language classes for them were unsuccessful because, as I eventually learned, they did not wish to learn another language. Their children were bilingual, they themselves did not work outside the home, and they had a large, close circle of friends and family, none of whom spoke English. While there were likely other reasons for their disinterest, I learned a fundamental lesson: that successful community developers begin by listening to the needs of others and moving at their pace, in their directions, using their methods. I also learned that outsiders, particularly those from dominant cultures, often do not understand the realities of women of colour who cope daily with gender and race both within and outside their culture.

Many social workers and activists gained feminist understanding of community work not through our education, our paid work, or our knowledge about the contributions of our foremothers but through tough experiences in the second-wave women's movement, which had gained momentum by the end of the 1960s. In these years, women's organizing consisted of a blend of consciousness-raising groups, education programs about our past and present inequality, and direct actions, including rallies and protests. The boldness of some of these actions startled and exhilarated many women who were first venturing into women's organizations. The occupation of some abandoned houses in downtown London, England, and New South Wales, Australia, by groups of women who had been mistreated by their mates left a lasting impression. Anne Summers describes the Australian experience:

> We explained that we intended to break into the house we had found, change the locks and thereby establish legal tenancy, and then try to shame the Church of England into letting us remain there rent-free until we could approach the federal government for funds to run the refuge. . . . It was accomplished with utter ease. Once we had taken possession of the two houses, we rang all the television networks and announced to the world that Australia's first women's refuge was now open for business (as quoted in Gilmore and Weeks 1995:77).

These events captured a great deal of international media attention, and for the first time the issue of wife assault was articulated and debated. A group of women in Victoria and in other cities across Canada were inspired to develop transition houses of their own and to insist upon government support for their operation. My own commitment to feminist work began here in the development of transition house and sexual assault services. It has since spanned work within government and in the community and includes grassroots organizing, social planning, and social action, all of which are included in my use of the umbrella term feminist community organizing.

Defining Feminist Community Organizing

In the first chapter of this book, the authors cite the work of Lena Dominelli (1990) and her six-category formulation of community work: (1) community care, (2) community organization, (3) community development, (4) class-based community action, (5) feminist community action, and (6) community action from a Black perspective. While this schema is helpful in the sense that it identifies clearly the main activities of community work (care, coordination, development, and action) and the unique features of groups organizing on the basis of class, gender, and race, it is also puzzling. It implies (although likely not intended) that only the 'action' activity differs on the basis of class, race, and gender and that class, race, and gender organizing does not include care, coordination, and development.

In my view, feminist community organizing includes all of the traditional activities of community development (care, community organization, community development, and social action). What distinguishes feminist community organizing from other approaches is its insistence that all activities must be informed by an analysis of gender (and race and class) and modified on the basis of this analysis. It is also characterized by its commitment to a social movement and by its attempts to connect local efforts to those taking place in other jurisdictions and at other levels. It differs from feminist organizing in general because of its concern with place, with helping women in a geographical space define their needs and aspirations and begin to work on these. It enriches the feminist movement by grounding it in the realities of local women and local solutions.

Although feminist community organizing shares common features with community development, it has remained on the periphery of community development theory and practice for several reasons. First, it raises questions about the contradictory nature of communities and the gendered nature of much community work. This is a disconcerting analysis for those who believe deeply in the power of community development to heal anomie and create egalitarian relationships. Second, there are few women academics in social work and related disciplines who write about feminist community organizing in the mainstream community development literature, most likely because, as my experience illustrates, it has been regarded as a male domain. A content analysis of eighteen years of the *Journal of the Community Development Society* indicates that female authors ranged from 6.8 per cent (1970–3), peaking at 22 per cent (1982–5), and falling again to 17 per cent (1986–9) (Donnermeyer and Passewitz 1991). Female theorists and activists are more likely to write books on their own or in feminist and social movements literature where they expect a better reception (Cunningham et al. 1988; Dominelli 1990; Kuyek 1990; Ng, Walker, and Muller 1990; Wine and Ristock 1991). Further, women organizers have had their hands full with struggling community services, increasing needs, and diminishing funds, and simply have had little time to put their pens to paper.

Another reason, an outcome of the first two, seems central to me. In spite of the long legacy of women's organizing at the community level, this history is scarcely known or appreciated. Two prevailing images of women's community work persist: 'worthy work', in which women labour together to provide services for communities, and 'radical organizing', where women assemble to change unfair laws and policies, using flamboyant, confrontational tactics. Women occupying each of these so-called domains are stereotyped in different ways. The worthy workers are devoted volunteers who believe that home and community is their proper domain and seek to strengthen it. The radical organizers are unladylike activists, 'bra burners', who chafe at the confines of womanhood. The two poles of women's community work have been constructed as follows:

Devoted Volunteers	*Radical Organizers*
• short-term, small-scale changes	• long-term, large-scale changes
• care	• cause
• victims	• actors
• collaboration	• confrontation
• volunteer	• demand pay
• all women	• only feminists

The intent of this chapter is to challenge these stereotypes, which were fuelled during the 1960s and 1970s by both media images and the debates within the feminist movement. It is my contention that these stereotypes have weakened women's community work, pitting some women against others, and burying the real accomplishments and challenges of feminist community organizing.

Creating Stereotypes:

Stereotyping disadvantaged groups is a powerful mechanism to ensure their ongoing oppression. Not only do stereotypes provide justification for those in power to maintain it, they are absorbed by members of the oppressed group who, in turn through their behaviour and manner, confirm the stereotypes of them and the cycle continues. Feminist theorists have unravelled the process of stereotyping, which is embedded in the binary thinking so common in Western epistemologies. Pairs such as public/private, active/passive, hard/soft, and rational/emotional are oppositions that reflect the 'original' and 'natural' couple, man/woman. Invariably the first side of the pair, which describes male qualities, is privileged over the other, the female side. The original stereotype for male and female behaviour is established through this deeply ingrained way of thinking.

Women who try to escape their roles and venture into male domains are ridiculed for having masculine qualities (Callahan 1994; Garlick et al. 1992), yet if they remain within their female realm and its characteristics (for example, private, soft, passive, emotional), they are diminished and deemed ineffective. Thus women cannot win. The two stereotypes of women in community work fit this pattern exactly. The devoted volunteers are womanly but harmless. The behaviour of radical organizers reflect masculine qualities, inappropriate for women. They are ridiculed as antifeminine, against the values of home and hearth, and their organizing efforts are similarly dismissed.

While the process of stereotyping is much more complex than can be tackled in this chapter, feminist theorists have contributed immensely to its understanding beginning with the challenge to dualism: 'Binary divisions, such as health/ill, normal/abnormal or, . . . rich/poor, which are like steamrollers of the mind; they level a multiform world, completely flattening anything which does not fit' (Sachs 1992:9). Instead, feminists suggest that contained within most issues are ironies and contradictions. Resisting the tendency to fall into either/or thinking is to resist patriarchal epistemology and to begin to create another understanding of the world based upon new maps and new words. While this chapter attempts to unravel the binary divisions separating women in community work, these divisions also prevail in other areas of community organizing: for instance, economic/social or outcomes/process. The challenge to binary thinking is useful to all community organizers.

Stereotyping Feminist Community Organizing

I was reminded of the ongoing process of misconstruing feminist community organizing when I read a recent newspaper article of a project in the Victoria community. Beneath a picture of a group of women of different ages and races dressed in work clothes, the story unfolds:

They're Building a Future: Twenty Women Pull Themselves Out
of Poverty and Learn How to Turn a Downtown House
into a Shelter for Their Sisters

Dressed in brand-new work boots and leather carpenter's aprons, the 20
women from the Downtown Women's Construction Project are ready for
renovation.

'We call this our golden opportunity,' single mother Janet Kettlewell
said Tuesday. With $636,000 in B.C. 21 funding, the women will begin ren-
ovating a house on the corner of Blanshard and Burdett streets in mid-April
after four months in the classroom. Once completed, the house will be an
emergency shelter and drop-in centre for women on the streets.

All of those involved in the project were on income assistance before
being chosen. Their backgrounds encompass abuse, drug and alcohol addiction, living on the streets. Many have raised children in poverty with no job
prospects.

And the need for a downtown shelter is giving the women an extra
impetus in their work.

'I have lived on the streets all my life. I used to panhandle so I know
what it's like,' said construction worker Deneze Lujanen.

Karen Tuey, a recovering drug addict and alcoholic, said she 'got a
lump in my throat' when they were talking about this being for women.
'Something like this I could have used', said Tuey as she looked around the
former bed-and-breakfast that will become a 15 bed shelter. 'It's hard to
describe what a difference this has made in my life. I have a purpose now.'

The women were chosen from 50 applicants, said project co-ordinator,
Jannit Rabinovitch.

The design is uniquely flexible, Rabinovitch said. 'For example, the
young women on the street said, "If I can't bring my dog, I can't stay there,"
so now we've added dog kennels.'

Kennel construction will be one of the first practical parts of the project, said Meg Herweier, carpentry instructor and training team leader.

'They'll be made like miniature houses, so we'll do framing and roofing.'

Herweier, who owns a home improvement company, has high hopes
for her team despite women's ongoing problems in finding trades work.

'But I think it is changing. There's no reason a woman can't do this sort
of work—you don't need a thick neck, you just have to work smart.'

Counsellor Jean Willow is rooting for the group, too. But the onus is
also on contractors and other employers, she said.

'Give the women an opportunity to prove they do have skills. These women will give themselves 100 per cent of the job because they know they have to prove themselves.'

The house, bought by the province for $450,000 is leased to the Greater Victoria Women's Shelter Society and opens in October.

Women's Equality Minister, Penny Priddy toured the building Tuesday.

'If we are going to make a difference in the lives of women, one of the most important areas is economic security and independence,' said Priddy. 'And we won't make any progress towards economic security without training, skills and then jobs' (Judith Lavoie, *Victoria Times Colonist*, 25 January 1995:B1. Reprinted courtesy of the *Victoria Times Colonist*.).

On the surface at least, this story is an account of 'worthy' women's work. It describes a small-scale venture in which women help themselves. Leadership is provided by experienced professional women, who appear to volunteer their time and, while funding is provided by government, there are plans for women to be self-sufficient in the long haul. Differences in age, socio-economic status, race, and experience seem not to matter to these women as they work together in a spirit of mutual collaboration. Even the elected politician and the minister of women's equality affirm the possibilities of projects such as this to advance the economic security of women. Women's profound concerns are muted in this account.

This press coverage is markedly different from that which is usually accorded the 'Take back the night' event or abortion rallies. Here women are often portrayed as young, wildly dressed, unreasonable, shrill, and behaving provocatively. It could be argued that all controversial social movements suffer from exaggerated media images and that the public wisely discounts most of it. In the case of women's organizing, I am not sure. I regularly discuss women's struggle for reform with graduate students, mostly women who are deeply committed to social change. Those who shy away from identifying themselves as feminists do so because of the abrasiveness of the movement. When asked, most have obtained these images from the media rather than their own participation. Wolfe (1993) has a further analysis. Her research indicates that women resist identifying themselves as feminists because such a label comes with a checklist of ideological positions about which they may not agree: abortion, pornography, heterosexuality, and so forth. This 'ideological overloading'

. . . closed the word 'feminism' off to enormous numbers of people: women who are not sure about, or who actively oppose, abortion; women who are terrified of being tarred with the brush of homophobia; some who strongly resist identifying themselves as victims; women who are uneasy with what they see as man bashing and blaming; conservative women; and men themselves (Wolfe 1993:61).

She maintains that the sharply drawn stereotype of the 'feminist' portrayed in the media is effective in distancing many women from the movement because it seems like dogma rather than a movement that provides room for individual differences and dialogue among differences. Thus confronting the stereotypes about what feminists believe and how they act is an important task. In the next section of the chapter, I will examine each of the components of the stereotypes and compare these to women's actual work in communities. Emerging from this examination will be some of the central issues occupying feminist community organizers, issues not reflected in the stereotypes of them and their work.

Short-Term, Small-Scale versus Long-Term, Large-Scale?

The two stereotypes of feminist community organizers present contrasting views of the goals of feminist organizing: short-term 'band-aid' type service provided in worthy work or long-term reform, the aim of radical organizers. For instance, the Downtown Women's Construction Project is described as a particular project meeting the needs of a small group of local women and creating short-term, small-scale change. Although such resources are undoubtedly needed, it has been argued that projects like this hide the very reasons why women must bear these conditions. Patriarchal attitudes and institutions responsible for their lack of safety and resources will actually prosper by the presence of a safe house that diminishes the embarrassing presence of such women on the downtown streets.

Feminist community organizers would claim that debating the short-term/long-term dichotomy has not been productive and takes attention away from the *connection* between short- and long-term, and the intractability of patriarchal institutions. Feminist analysis directs attention to different ways of viewing the world: 'the universe in a grain of sand' and 'eternity in an hour'. Patriarchy can be exposed within everyday interactions and some long-term changes result. Women struggle to live as well as they can in the present world and, at the same time, maintain their hopes for the future. Janice Raymond calls this 'two-sight' seeing:

> Every meaning of vision . . . is possessed of a certain tension. This tension is linguistically present in the dual dictionary definition, but it is also experienced in any attempt to live out a vision. At one and the same time, vision is 'the exercise of the ordinary faculty of sight' and 'something which is apparently seen otherwise than by ordinary sight'. Another way of phrasing this is to ask how indeed it is possible to see with the ordinary faculty of sight, that is, to maintain a necessary realism about the conditions of existence, *and* to see beyond these conditions, that is, to overleap reality. Or, how do women live in the world as men have defined it while creating the world as women imagine it could be? . . . This means not being crushed by the *contrast* between what the world is and the way it ought to be (Raymond 1985:85).

Feminist community organizers have spent efforts honing their skills in this regard. They point to important reforms for women that began by modest efforts: a group of women gathered in the Railway Room of the House of Commons in 1966 to demand changes for women and a royal commission is formed (Findlay 1987). Or the women of the Tobique reserve in New Brunswick challenge a century of legislated discrimination against married Native women in the Indian Act and help create new law (Bear with the Tobique Women's Group 1991). Or a doctor, Henry Morgantaler, opens an abortion clinic in Toronto in July 1983, and thereafter the debate cannot be ignored (Antonyshyn and Merrill 1988). Or a women's centre begins, then another, and another, and another, and these centres band together to pressure government to create a policy for funding women's centres (Cohen 1993). Or one woman recognizes the injustice in the remarks of a coworker and challenges them.

Many organizers would state that the major skill required is the ability to analyse the injustices of the patriarchal system and demonstrate how these play out on a daily basis in women's lives. Not only are inequalities exposed to those who may be in a position to make changes, women who might not have a feminist analysis are informed about the often subtle but relentless oppression of patriarchal institutions. Thus, in the Downtown Women's Construction Project, women of different cultures, experiences, and opportunities who may have never come together will have the opportunity to work in one place on common issues and begin to ask questions: Why are these women (or why am I) without homes? Why are they exploited? Why does the newspaper not talk about these issues? What can be done?

Care or Cause?

Inherent in the stereotypes of feminist community organizers is a debate about whether there are two unrelated streams of activity, one concerned with nurturing and caring for other women (and children), and the other focused upon social and political analysis and change. Women occupying the first niche are portrayed as filling their traditional maternal duties in the public sphere. Women concerned with broader issues are somehow depicted differently, as fighting not only social inequalities but also the stereotypical image of women. Not surprisingly, these women are often portrayed as shrill, aggressive, and 'masculine'. The REAL Women's Movement in Canada and the US, founded on the erroneous belief that to be a feminist is to be uncaring of home and family, is one obvious expression of this division.

An example of a women's project illustrates the fallacy of the care/cause dichotomy. Recently I heard on the radio a woman speaking from Bosnia about the development of a women's refugee camp. The camp was a shelter for women and children, regardless of their religion or their 'side'. The radio interviewer, like me, wondered how women could live together in the midst of such a bloody religious and sectarian dispute. The woman explained that the differences over which the war was being fought had very little meaning within the camp. While there were occasional feuds among the women, these were understood as emerging from fatigue and concern as much as from anything else. She said that women had to carry on their work, feeding their children, preparing for winter, maintaining some semblance of family life, regardless of the war. They knew that accomplishing these tasks under such appalling conditions and achieving a modicum of safety for themselves and their children could only be achieved if they acted collectively. In the process of overcoming obstacles together, they began to feel that they had some power over their lives. The interviewer inquired whether the woman had hopes that these women's peaceful existence could, in some small way, ameliorate the conditions in her country. The woman thought not. She believed that their shared sense of group empowerment might help them maintain their belief in peace and survive the war, but she could not imagine that they could influence the terrible events happening around them.

Although the women in their camp in Bosnia do not believe that their efforts will make a difference to the larger context in which they live, created as it has been by centuries of oppression and disputes, their very behaviour illustrates to themselves, to other citizens, and to those outside the dispute that there is hope and another vision for their people.

The newspaper account of the Downtown Women's Construction Project portrays this project on the caring side of the continuum with no particular political agenda. Its overall aim is described as providing a safe home and a supportive environment for women, and the story makes no mention of challenging social or political systems. Interestingly, although the women are portrayed as dressing in men's work clothing and pursuing traditionally male occupations, their 'femininity' is underscored: two participants are quoted as saying that this project means a great deal to them because it is concerned with helping other women and there is mention that the residents are fond of animals and that some of the women are mothers.

Although the efforts of the women in this project are described in traditional ways, the story and the photograph, perhaps inadvertently, make a political statement in themselves, not unlike the women in the Bosnian camp. Women who are drug addicts, prostitutes, and poor single mothers are standing together, caring for each other, gaining valued skills, and obtaining public resources. Writing of the development of abortion clinics in Ontario, Antonyshyn and Merrill state that: 'The clinics have succeeded in providing a desperately needed service to thousands of women and, in so doing, have highlighted the failures of the existing system. They have served as a rallying point and an incredibly effective organizing tool for building the movement' (Antonyshyn and Merrill 1988:153).

The portrayal of the dichotomy between care and action has a long legacy. Historians have coined the term 'maternal and social feminists' as one way of describing women's work in the community (Kealey 1979; Struthers 1987a, 1987b). The maternal feminists were supposedly those who believed that women's virtues, such as gentleness, civility, and caring attitudes, should govern public as well as private discourse, and that women's entry into public life would guarantee the promulgation of these values. Charity work apparently provided an obvious calling for Canadian maternal feminists. Here women could set up their own organizations such as the Women's Christian Temperance Union, the Voice of Women, and other such organizations, or at least assume major roles in existing organizations and demonstrate how their natural abilities as women could alleviate the mounting social problems of poverty, homelessness, and unemployment. Social feminists were women who apparently set their sights on changing law and policies that discriminated against women through social action.

In other places I have challenged academics' creation of maternal and social feminists as yet another way of stereotyping women's work in the community and diminishing it (Callahan 1994). Instead I think the care/cause dichotomy hides another essential mission of feminist community organizing:

How do we take the work done in the home for free ('caring work') and make it collective work to be done in public settings and paid for by the public purse ('the cause')? Further, how do we infuse all of our work, whether done in the private or public sphere, with the important values of egalitarian and caring relationships? Unless we tackle this, we are in danger of reproducing inequality, swapping the anathema of patriarchy with yet another oppression, albeit one where women are in charge. Finally, how do we make the public and decision makers aware that some of our so-called caring work is a natural outcome of patriarchal institutions? The issues of wife assault, child abuse, sexual assault, abortion, and elder abuse (to name a few) have been raised in different ways by feminists who speak on the basis of direct experience in caring for those who have experienced such indignities.

Victims or Actors?

The stereotypes of feminist community organizers portray a vastly different perspective of women as victims and actors. In both cases the stereotypes depict women who are capable of acting: the dutiful volunteer and the political activist are both illustrations of independent action, albeit of a very different order. Clearly women who act independently on behalf of those less fortunate than themselves are seen as more feminine than those who act independently on their own behalf. The stereotypes not only divide women on the basis of those who act properly; they establish distance between classes of women: the advantaged who are actors and the disadvantaged, victims of their lot.

There are many tangled webs in these portrayals of women. If all women are so oppressed, then how can they act so capably? Yet if women do not act on their own behalf, then how can they gain their own freedom? As Walker states: 'It does a disservice to both women and our understanding of the structuring, ordering and ruling of society to regard ourselves as having been merely passive victims of historical, social and political processes controlled by a conspiracy of men' (1990:3). However, ironically, as women work together to overcome their oppression, they lose public sympathy: 'They did it, now why can't you?' Clearly, the reporter of the press story has chosen to emphasize the capacity of these women to take action, *in spite of previous difficulties*, which, on one hand, feels respectful. However, at the same time it allows readers to ignore the harm done to these women because of deeply held and pervasive beliefs about women and the unequal social systems that result from these beliefs. Even the headline of the story 'They're Building a Future' makes plain that women can recover from adversity by hard work and joint efforts.

I think that this dichotomy between women as actors and victims is a particularly disabling one for feminist community organizers and for women who eschew feminism because they don't see themselves as victims. One of the most important turning-points for my own understanding of this issue occurred after I read Linda Gordon's (1985) study of child welfare agency case records in Boston over the past 100 years. Gordon began her research sympathetic to the point of view that child welfare agencies serve as vehicles of social control, and that their development at the turn of the century was a result of the need to restructure the family to serve the interests of the new ruling class of industry and manufacturing. However, while she found evidence that supported this perspective, she also discovered that clients sometimes used child welfare agencies to serve their own purposes. In spite of great risks, some women clients contacted the child welfare agencies to report that their husbands were beating them. They used the power of the agency workers to protect them from their spouses and to increase their own power base within the family. Further, many middle-class women helpers understood and aided in this endeavour.

One clear lesson from this study was that it is important to look at the action of so-called victims. Instead of assuming that they are not and have not fought against their oppression, it is a service to illuminate their work, relationships, and communities. In my early days, I did not see the community of Chinese mothers that lived and worked right under my nose. I thought they needed organizing. When Carol Stack began her study of families in an urban housing ghetto, she saw only family disintegration until she asked the women themselves to identify their families (Stack 1974). Only then did she see the logical order of the housing development and the daily reciprocal relationships that defined family and community for these residents. The public may see some women as merely homemakers, other women as victims or clients. The task of feminist organizers is to name these efforts and create further opportunities for their growth. Thus the debate about victims or actors hides the reality that women are both. Most important, it draws attention away from the fact that women are owed reparations for centuries of discrimination in the form of employment equity policies, victim assistance programs, social welfare services, and other concrete reforms. The quest for reparations returns the debate to where it belongs.

Collaboration or Confrontation?

Inherent in the stereotypes of feminist community organizers is contempt for the methods that they use: the dutiful volunteer simply busies herself about her work in a collaborative, even submissive fashion. For instance, the press account of the Downtown Women's Construction Project portrays these women as traditionalists who, without fuss or fanfare, have created something useful in the community. On the other hand, the radical activist is a fanatic willing to use any approach to achieve her ends. Although she often creates commotion, she doesn't seem to leave any lasting legacy for her efforts. Within these stereotypes are powerful messages that keep women separated from one another. Radical women and their actions are ridiculed in the press and everyday conversation. Some women who are deeply committed to improving their lot none the less fear the same censure and distance themselves from activists. Deep within they fear that acting outrageously denies their femininity (and heterosexuality) and an even greater fear that outrageous actions will lead to public humiliation and backlash.

The history of feminist community organizing does not support this dichotomy, and instead is replete with examples of the same women, working within one particular group, on one particular issue, combining the methodical and the outrageous to achieve their goals. Suffragettes chained themselves to public buildings and engaged in hunger strikes, while at the same time collecting signatures on petitions and presenting briefs to Parliament (Cramer 1992). In one case-study of abortion activism in a small city, we found that women worked on several levels, using methods most appropriate for the task at hand (Callahan and Matthews 1992). Short-term organizing, characterized by traditional political strategies such as identifying supporters and getting out the vote to defeat the election of pro-life candidates on the hospital board, were required. At the same time, women organized education sessions, speakouts, coffee-houses, demonstrations, and other similar activities.

The debate about collaborative and confrontational approaches disguises the real contributions of feminists to organizing. Most important, women have vigorously pursued the development of alternative organizations (Staggenborg 1989; Weeks 1994) and team-building strategies, which are now finding favour in business and government. Although these inclusive methods and flat structures are also reflected in many other community development approaches, feminist community organizers view these as actual outcomes of their work, not just processes whereby other goals will be achieved. They believe that achieving particular and important results using traditional patriarchal methods defeats the overall victory because it does not forge new approaches or a new vision of social relations. Feminist collective organizations are also distinguished by their insistence that individuals do not have to leave their private selves at home when they enter public realms and work on collective issues.

The Better Beginnings project in Sudbury illustrates how these aims are put into action within the organization (Reitsma-Street and Rogerson 1995). Six management processes in collective organizations were identified in the operations of the project: (1) promoting forums for participation, (2) creating egalitarian work relationships, (3) nourishing dailiness, (4) caring for the caregivers, (5) expanding the capacity to act powerfully, and (6) nurturing partners and networks. The idea of nourishing dailiness is interesting and speaks to the attempt to unite the public and private realms: 'Management processes attentive to dailiness start with the bodies, fears and uniqueness of people within the minutiae of every encounter—whether a meeting, an event, a workspace, and long-term planning exercises. . . . Concrete attention to dailiness is expressed through food, space and time for visiting (Reitsma-Street and Rogerson 1995:9–10). The struggle to develop new methods of working collectively yet at the same time achieving some success in changing a world that seems to respond most to 'tough' measures is ongoing.

Feminists have made other contributions to the science of organizing that are hidden by the collaboration or confrontation debate. Finding approaches so that those who experience the problem or issue get to define it is one of these. For instance, women have used their development of sexual assault centres to name sexual assault, to describe it in all of its forms, to hear many women from different stations describing its effects, to watch as their meanings are appropriated by institutional processes (Walker 1990), and to begin the process of defining it again. The principal method for defining issues has been the consciousness-raising approach, pioneered in the early stages of the movement. Most consciousness-raising groups followed a similar process, originating with the New York Radical Feminists (Cohen 1993; Shreve 1989). A topic was introduced to a group of women, each of whom was allowed 'free space' to talk as long as she wanted. Most groups were leaderless except for the organizer of the meeting, most stayed together for considerable time, and some moved beyond their internal dialogue to connect with other groups and take action. The notion of needs assessment, so central to community development, is greatly enlarged by the contributions of feminist organizers.

Volunteer, Independent, or Paid State Services?

Another feature of feminist community organizing apparent in the stereotypes is the notion of women receiving remuneration for their organizing work. Both the dutiful volunteer and the radical organizer work for free, one from a sense of duty and knowledge of her proper place, the other because of deeply held passions and commitment. The fact that neither is paid rein-forces the idea that the work has little importance. The press story is typical in that it makes no mention of payment for any of the women involved in the project, although the students may receive some subsidy (at least they have left behind income assistance).

In reality, the situation is much more complicated. Most women do not get paid for their organizing work, not because they do not want or need wages but because most women's organizations have few financial resources. Women's organizations have always had to struggle for funds, lacking well-heeled benefactors willing to donate money to groups seeking to overthrow the very system that created these wealthy benefactors in the first place.

Feminist community organizers feel that such a portrayal of their work is highly diminishing and inaccurate. The tasks involved in the Downtown Women's Construction Project—contacting and selecting street women for a complex work placement, cobbling together funding from different govern-ment ministries, and gaining the commitment of business and community leaders—require highly skilled organizers. Implying that women can do it in their spare time without any special training or skills is to ensure that it remains poorly regarded and in the realm of traditional volunteer work.

However, receiving payment for organizing work brings other problems. It can put distance between participants and workers, volunteers and paid staff, and lead to the hierarchies that are anathema to feminist community organizing. For instance, the press story also contains at least five different individuals or groups of women: the participants who are the women expe-rienced in the problem, the organizer, a teacher in charge of carpentry skills, a counsellor, and a politician. Although there is a strong message of self-help in the article (the women 'pull themselves out of poverty . . . turn[ing] a downtown house into a shelter for their sisters') and their efforts are featured first in the story, it is also clear that skilled professional women are in charge and are variously described as 'project co-ordinator' and 'training team leader'. Much has been written about the irony of recreating class and race inequalities within the very structures set up to challenge them. In response, feminist organizers have experimented with flat salaries and shared jobs.

However, the pay issue uncovers the other more substantial one, the degree to which accepting government funding compromises the agenda of feminist organizing. Two well-known examples include the decision by the Saskatchewan Action Committee, Status of Women to terminate funding by the Secretary of State's Women's Programs in 1983 in large part because of the 'Program's insistence reserving the right to approve the political strategies of funded groups' (Schraeder 1990) and a similar decision by the Vancouver Rape

Relief Society to forgo funding from the provincial Department of the Attorney-General on the basis that the government wished access to agency files deemed confidential by the organization. However, while these two incidents are important, the fact is that the development of women's community services in Canada has been largely funded by the state in the last three decades. Three federal government programs in the early 1970s (Opportunities for Youth Program, Local Initiatives Program, and the Secretary of State's Women's Programs) provided funds for most of the first women's centres and transition houses in the country.

Without doubt, government funding has brought demands for more hierarchical and bureaucratized systems within grassroots organizations (Shragge 1990). Schraeder's (1990) study of the Secretary of State's Women's Programs, the largest and earliest government funding source for grassroots feminist groups, concluded that government funding had deleterious effects. It changed feminists working within government from advocates to mediators, while those working in grassroots organizations gradually tailored their own needs to coincide with government priorities. However, Schraeder concludes:

> . . . state funding should be recognized as a legitimate gain for women, and evidence of the impact of struggle. As we have seen, funding carries a risk of co-optation, but it has also permitted feminists to engage in numerous political activities and to deliver badly-needed services to women in crisis. The essence of co-optation is one of progressive groups being induced to buy into a state defined agenda with the illusion of having secured power. On the contrary, real power lies in our political clarity and ability to challenge the political positions of the state (Schraeder 1990:197).

Feminist community organizers maintain that the debate between community and state actually begins with the analysis by Schraeder (1990) and Ng, Walker, and Muller (1990). It is counterproductive to view the community as benign and the state as evil, as such a debate obscures the need for a critical analysis of both. The community as a site for women's work bears critical analysis. Without women's efforts, there would be few child care services and drop-in centres. Communities have turned a blind eye to the violence in families. The existence of transition houses and sexual assault centres are evidence that women's homes and neighbourhoods are often not safe places. Communities can be confining for women who sometimes use their community work to escape and create another public sphere beyond the community where they are the actors and decision makers. Canadian farm women created locally based organizations to connect with other isolated women and then connected these organizations to provincial and national ones to provide them with a voice in agricultural and social policy. The United Nations conference in Beijing in 1995 attracted more than 35,000 women from thousands of community-based organizations.

The need for an analysis of state policy is also evident. For instance, many provincial governments are devolving health and social services to community in the name of community control and empowerment. Feminist analysis raises questions, not just about 'off-loading' to community but about who in the community may actually bear the brunt of community control measures. It will be women, working in the home for free and in low-paid care jobs in community agencies.

Thus for feminists the community-state debate is actually a red herring. The real issue is how can women at all stations gain an analysis of so-called reforms and work together for progressive changes. Rather than define 'good' feminists as those who eschew government funds and government jobs, women have determined that creating bridges among women's groups and between community groups and women within government is sensible and productive. Pitting 'grassroots truth' against 'political clout' has not been useful when both, in fact, are needed. Women have raised questions about whether they should accept the boundaries between state and community that have been drawn by others and instead chart the map differently according to who can help them with their work. The usefulness of coalition building is evident in the press story. Poor women, community organizers, and a government minister (presumably with the involvement of her bureaucrats) have joined forces to create change. The government minister who heads the only ministry dedicated to women's issues in the country is there by dint of feminist community organizing.

While many feminist organizers believe in this notion of coalition building, they are also aware of another reality. Women working outside formal government and community organizations and who are sharply critical of both are an essential part of the action. These women, sometimes gathered in small teams and informal groups within the community, take stark positions and ruffle feathers of many community members, including feminists. Yet inherent in their unwillingness to compromise their position or move in from the margins of the feminist movement is their strength. They provide the basis for debate and change within the feminist movement. Theirs can be the bedrock position from which those attempting change through compromises can measure how far they may have strayed. While these are the women most ridiculed in the media and community, it is important for other feminists to acknowledge their contribution to the movement. Otherwise we support the notion that there are indeed different kinds of feminists. The 'good' feminists are the collaborative ones, at least according to those in power. To those on the margins, the 'good' feminists are those who are not co-opted. We are weakened in the process.

Only Feminists or All Women?

The final debate—whether feminist community organizing is only done by feminists or whether it represents the full range of women's community work—is the most contentious. In fact, the degree to which women working in the community hold a feminist analysis of their work varies greatly. Interestingly enough, women who may disagree with the overarching analysis of women's oppression often work diligently at the community level to change unfair policies and practices affecting women and become more convinced of women's oppression in the process.

However, this dichotomy is at the heart of the marginalization of feminist community organizing. Some say that if it can only be done by feminists, then it is an exclusive activity that works against the inclusive principles of community development. In my experience, this debate is not prevalent in contemporary practice, although it shaped a few arguments in early feminist organizations in the 1960s. In one, members of a sexual assault centre broke away from the existing centre and began their own organization because they felt that the original centre had lost its feminist roots. However, this kind of controversy has been the exception in my experience. What distinguished one project from others was not the feminist credentials of the participants but the desire to work with women on their behalf to improve their collective lot.

A more contemporary issue focuses upon the issues of women, class, and race. To what extent has feminist community organizing been a pastime of White middle-class women, leaving out the issues of poor women and women of colour? Women from the Black feminist collective describe their struggles in attempting to work with all of their people for social justice and, at the same time, work within the Black movement to eradicate sexism (National Film Board 1991). They labour to convince their Black brothers that sexism is linked to racism and both must be addressed. At the same time, they do not feel that the complexity of their struggle is understood by White feminists who often view it as one of 'dual discrimination', being both Black and female in a White world. While problematic, Black women state that the issues of being Black and female in a 'Black' world adds even more difficulties. Moreover, women of colour are raising questions about feminist analysis of domestic and community life, citing the creation of 'homeplace', the world created by Black women where they took their conventional role 'and expanded it to include caring for one another, for children, for black men, in ways that elevated our spirits, that kept us from despair, that taught some of us to be revolutionaries able to struggle for freedom' (hooks 1990:44).

Herein lies the important challenge for feminist community organizers: revealing the range of experiences of women of colour, ableness, sexual orientation, class, and others; appreciating how, given present circumstances, women oppress other women, yet, at bottom, understand their common cause as women struggling within a patriarchal culture. The Downtown Women's Construction Project illustrates how some common agendas can be created through doing work that benefits all participants, construction workers, and future residents as well as organizers.

Conclusion

This chapter has challenged the typical notions of feminist community as either one kind of endeavour—the short-term, caring for others, volunteer, traditional activity carried out by women—or the other—the long-term, action-oriented, paid activity carried out by feminists. Instead, I argue that it is neither one, nor is it necessarily just both. Instead feminist community organizing is better understood by examining specific examples and discovering the issues that women have identified through their work together. In this chapter I have identified a different set of challenges that do not fit the stereotypes of the work. These can be illustrated as follows:

Devoted Volunteers	Feminist Community Workers	Radical Organizers
• short term/small scale	• illuminating oppression	• long term/large scale
• caring for others	• transforming caring work	• working on a cause
• women as victims	• establishing reparations	• women as actors
• collaboration	• organizing collectively	• confrontation
• volunteer community	• analysing power	• paid state
• all women	• joining race, class, gender	• only feminists

The Downtown Women's Construction Project is not a group of 'do-gooders' saving fallen women nor 'flaming radicals' using the plight of disadvantaged women to trumpet the failings of patriarchy. It is the creation of a women's community using a different map. Members of the community are working together in different but valued stations, all are receiving resources from the state in one form or another: the politicians, the teachers, the students, and the organizers. As such, the project is as much a state service as a community one. Women are using government support for their own needs and to create facilities and opportunities previously unavailable to them. They are mapping their own course according to their own definitions of need, which change over time (consider the addition of the dog kennels in the Downtown Women's Construction Project). They are unwilling to do without, to do it for free, or to let government off the hook. They differ in class and race, a feature of the patriarchal culture around them. These differences will not be overcome easily even in the creation of women's communities, yet they are trying to understand their divisions. By banding together, they speak for another way of living. This is the essence of feminist community organizing.

I have suggested that feminist community organizing has remained on the margins of community development because it challenges the oppressive nature of communities and because it has been misconstrued and stereotyped. I would go further. I think that feminist community organizing also remains on the margins of some contemporary thinking, including some feminist thinking, because it raises the value of communitarianism. Most of the gains made by women in recent decades are those that affect individual rights, given the strongly individual nature of our society. The theory holds that as a few women get better education, better jobs, and better breaks overall, so will all women benefit over time. Feminist community organizing challenges this trickle-down theory of social progress. Instead it argues that all social institutions, be they public business or private families, should embrace notions of collective well-being rather than simply serve as sites for individual opportunity. For some women, particularly those who have benefited individually from the feminist movement, the collective message is unwelcome and unnecessary. It is considered a voice from the past, old-style feminism. Thus this chapter, 'Postcards from the Edge', is written to these women as well as others interested in community development.

References

Antonyshyn, L., and A. Merrill.
  1988. 'Marching for Women's Lives: The Campaign for Free-Standing Abortion Clinics in Ontario'. In *Social Movements, Social Change: The Politics and Practice of Organizing*, edited by S. Findlay et al., 122–44. Toronto: Between the Lines.

Bear, S., with the Tobique Women's Group.
1991. 'You Can't Change the Indian Act?' In *Women and Social Change: Feminist Activism in Canada*, edited by J.D. Wine and J. Ristock, 198–220. Toronto: James Lorimer and Co.

Callahan, M.
1994. 'Stereotypes of Women in Social Work'. Unpublished doctoral thesis, Faculty of Social Science, University of Bristol.

———, and C. Matthews.
1992. 'Abortion Advocacy in a Canadian Community: Organizing to Gain Control of Abortion Policy and Services'. In *Communities and Social Policy in Canada*, edited by B. Wharf, 124–50. Toronto: McClelland and Stewart.

Cohen, M.
1993. 'The Canadian Women's Movement'. *Canadian Women's Issues*, vol. 1, edited by R. Pierson et al., 1–31. Toronto: James Lorimer and Co.

Cramer, M.
1992. 'Public and Political: Documents of the Women's Suffrage Campaign in British Columbia, 1917–1971: The View from Victoria'. In *British Columbia Reconsidered: Essays on Women*, edited by G. Creese and V. Strong-Boag, 123–38. Vancouver: Press Gang Publishers.

Cunningham, F., et al.
1988. *Social Movements, Social Change: The Politics and Practice of Organizing*. Toronto: Between the Lines.

Dauphinais, P., S. Barkan, and S. Cohn.
1992. 'Predictors of Rank-and-File Feminist Activism: Evidence from the 1983 General Social Survey'. *Social Problems* 39, no. 4:332–45.

Dominelli, L.
1990. *Women and Community Action*. Birmingham: Venture Press.

Donnermeyer, J., and G. Passewitz.
1991. 'A Retrospective on the *Journal of the Community Development Society*: Authors and Methods'. *Journal of the Community Development Society* 22, no. 1:98–105.

Findlay, S.
1987. 'Facing the State: The Politics of the Women's Movement Reconsidered'. In *Feminism and Political Economy: Women's Work, Women's Struggles*, edited by H. Maroney and M. Luxton, 31–49. Toronto: Methuen.

Garlick, B., et al.
1992. *Stereotypes of Women in Power: Historical Perspectives and Revisionist Views*. New York: Greenwood Press.

Gilmore, K., and W. Weeks. 1995. 'How Violence Against Women Became an Issue on the Social Policy Agenda'. *Australian Social Policy*, edited by W. Weeks, 76–94. Sydney: Allen and Unwin.

Gordon, L.
　　1985. 'Child Abuse, Gender and the Myth of Family Independence'. *Child Welfare* LXIV, no. 3:213–24.

hooks, b.
　　1990. 'Homeplace: A Site of Resistance'. *Yearning: Race, Gender and Cultural Politics*, edited by b. hooks. Toronto: Between the Lines.

Kealey, L., ed.
　　1979. *A Not Unreasonable Claim: Women and Reform in Canada, 1880s to 1920s*. Toronto: Women's Educational Press.

Kuyek, J.
　　1990. *Fighting for Hope*. Montreal: Black Rose Books.

National Film Board.
　　1991. *Sisters in the Struggle*. Ottawa: National Film Board.

Ng, R., G. Walker, and J. Muller.
　　1990. *Community Organization and the Canadian State*. Toronto: Garamond Press.

Raymond, J.
　　1985. 'The Visionary Task: Two Sights Seeing'. *Women's Studies International Forum* 8, no. 1:85–91.

Reitsma-Street, M., and P. Rogerson.
　　1995. 'A Management Style for Community Organizations: Report Presented to the Sudbury Better Beginnings, Better Futures Association and Laurentian University'. Unpublished.

Sachs, W.
　　1992. 'The Discovery of Poverty'. *The New Internationalist* (June):7–11.

Schraeder, A.
　　1990. 'The State-Funded Women's Movement: A Case of Two Political Agendas'. In *Community Organization and the Canadian State*, edited by R. Ng, G. Walker, and J. Muller, 184–202. Toronto: Garamond Press.

Shragge, E.
　　1990. 'Community-Based Practice: Political Alternative or New State Forms?' In *Bureaucracy and Community*, edited by L. Davies and E. Shragge, 137–73. Montreal: Black Rose Books.

Shreve, A.
　　1989. *Women Together, Women Alone*. New York: Viking.

Stack, C.
　　1974. *All Our Kin*. New York: Harper and Row.

Staggenborg, S.
1989. 'Stability and Innovation in the Women's Movement: A Comparison of Two Movement Organizations'. *Social Problems* 36, no. 1:75–92.

Struthers, J.
1987a. '"Lord Give Us Men": Women and Social Work in English Canada, 1918–1953'. In *The Benevolent State: The Growth of Welfare in Canada*, edited by A. Moscovitch and J. Albert. Toronto: Garamond Press.

———.
1987b. 'A Profession in Crisis: Charlotte Whitton and Canadian Social Work in the 1930s'. In *The Benevolent State: The Growth of Welfare in Canada*, edited by A. Moscovitch and J. Albert. Toronto: Garamond Press.

Walker, G.
1990. *Family Violence and the Women's Movement: The Conceptual Politics of Struggle.* Toronto: University of Toronto Press.

Weeks, W.
1994. *Women Working Together: Lessons from Feminist Women's Services.* Melbourne: Longman Cheshire.

Wine, J.D., and J. Ristock, eds.
1991. *Women and Social Change: Feminist Activism in Canada.* Toronto: James Lorimer and Co.

Wolfe, N.
1993. *Fire with Fire.* Toronto: Random House.

Woods, M., J. Nelson, and T. Bliss.
1989. 'Eighteen Years of the *Journal of the Community Development Society*: Where Have We Been? Where Are We Going?' *Journal of the Community Development Society* 20, no. 1:55–63.

Chapter Eleven

Community Action as a Practice of Freedom: A First Nations Perspective

Kathleen Absolon and Elaine Herbert

Introduction

Community action as a practice of freedom requires a critical awareness of many factors that affect communities. For First Nations peoples, community action begins with understanding the residual effects of colonialism. Community action towards a practice of freedom requires examining and understanding how the White supremacist beliefs and values of Canadian society subordinated and oppressed First Nations peoples through the Indian Act and other racist and sexist discriminatory laws and policies. Hence the 'context' of community action includes knowledge that speaks to and addresses the political, cultural, social, and economic conditions of First Nations communities.

This context also recognizes that while the colonization process dehumanized First Nations, it also dehumanized the perpetrators. The way Euro-Canadian society is structurally arranged supports and perpetuates oppressive ideologies based on race, class, gender, age, and sexual orientation. Collectively we (both mainstream and minority) are simultaneously socialized by and into the 'isms', although at opposite ends of a superiority/inferiority continuum (Gilchrist 1994). As a result, mainstream and minority are kept politically illiterate and silenced (Adams 1989; Carniol 1995; Freire 1970; Howse and Stalwick 1990). We assume that social workers have not been exposed to enough critical information to readily put Aboriginal peoples' issues into a context of colonization as a consciously structured oppression. Until these perspectives permeate all socialization structures, we must continually search for authentic explanations of our reality.

Defining language is an important element in our discourse on community action. We have adopted the phrase 'action as a practice of freedom when the goal is to liberate' from the work of bell hooks (1994) and Paulo Freire (1970). The title of this chapter emphasizes what we believe is the essence of community practice. Community action becomes a practice of freedom when the goals of practice are directed towards liberating people from external and internal oppressive forces. Liberation is sought through mechanisms of critical examination, education, dialogue, and deconstructing internalized oppression/racism.

Community action occurs when people have an investment in change. For example, a group of First Nations women in Ontario built housing for women in their communities experiencing violence. These women took the necessary training, built the apartments, and when the men laughed at them and told them their building would fall down, they were not discouraged, nor did the building fall down.

The socio-economic conditions in many First Nations communities leave little doubt that social work practice needs to move beyond the conservative, pathology-based practice of blaming the victims to practice that helps to eradicate structural racism, heals the symptoms of colonial rule, and works towards rebuilding healthy communities. Community action as a practice of freedom comes closest to describing the nature of community work in First Nations communities in Canada that we believe clearly needs to occur.

Community action (and organization) for growth and change, as opposed to community development, denotes active participation and ownership of planning from conception to the implementation of a project. 'Community development' models from the past create images of 'outsiders' coming into a community and voyeuristically engaging in some form of community manipulation. Community development also implies that 'underdevelopment' exists, and that 'development' must occur in ways similar to those in the Third World. This implication of 'underdevelopment' is an example of how language from the dominant society implies superiority over the 'developing' subordinate community that needs help.

Paulo Freire, a Brazilian community activist and educator, writes that 'all domination involves invasion—at times physical and overt, at times camouflaged, with the invader assuming the role of a helping friend. . . . invasion is a form of economic and cultural domination' (1970:150). In the First Nations context, invasion has been camouflaged by the concept of needing development, which is steeped in racist ideology, colonial mentality, and an assimilation perspective directed at 'civilizing' the 'Indian savage'.

Development, for the most part, has not left communities with skills to grow independently, nor have First Nations communities had access to education that would foster decolonization and the unlearning of internalized racism. A structural understanding of colonial oppression, critical thinking, and questioning skills have been systematically omitted in Native communities. The paradox is that we must use our oppressors' language to pave the path towards liberation. To eliminate this element of colonization, we must stringently critique the use of language and its meaning.

The chapter presents perspectives of community action through the works of Paulo Freire (1983) and bell hooks (1994), two leading educators whose work critiques colonialism. Concepts of consciousness raising, liberation and oppressor/oppressed contradictions, popular education, adult education principles, and cultural and feminist approaches are recreated through a First Nations critical lens and cultural perspective. Also, we draw on examples from our own experiences as community practitioners to illustrate various concepts or ideas. Throughout the chapter we reiterate the importance of history, race, power, and oppression as dynamics that should guide analysis and practice. The traditional practices and integration of a 'cultural' component needs to be community-controlled, owned, and directed, and will vary depending on the community and nation(s) in community practice. In this sense, we do not attempt to integrate cultural practices into the perspective. Rather, culture exists within our perspective because of who we are and what we do.

Because dialogue is so integral to community action, we have used our dialogue as the central example from which we begin examining the 'contexts' in which we live. In our dialogue we 'locate' ourselves and demonstrate how we have begun to develop a conscious understanding about where we come from and where we need to go. We critique our experiences and speak about all the challenges we face personally and professionally, as women, educators, community members, and practitioners. We draw from personal and practice examples to bring some life into our discussion. Hence we examine some of our experiences through a lens that is critical, structural, feminist, and cultural. We perceive our dialogue as a process of breaking silence as we establish a discourse towards a healing process. Through the dialogue, a critical Aboriginal perspective as a practice of freedom begins to form a basis for community action.

Further, critiques of the issues that diminish community action as an authentic practice of freedom are identified in our conclusion, with an emphasis on their structural source. We appeal for continued development of Aboriginal models of practice that authenticate, liberate, and continue to address theory and practice of critical education contextualized by the First Nations in Canada. There is a craving for material written by and about Aboriginal peoples that recount their experiences from their perspective. Seeking the truth, as hooks (1993b) affirms, is a necessary part of a journey to recovery.

A Critical First Nations Perspective of Community Action

Transforming of a reality by which they are oppressed, requires transformative action. The people must have a fundamental role in the transformative process (Freire 1983:120).

Useful Theories

We propose to apply a First Nations feminist lens to four theories. The theories are: Freire's concepts of oppression and liberation; hook's analysis of power, race, sexism, and patriarchy; the structural analysis of society developed by Moreau and Carniol; and the Anishnabek First Nations Medicine Wheel concept. In doing so we create a perspective that reflects First Nations experiences with our own history, spirituality, and identity, our own rules and decisions, limits, inner logic, and our own intellectual paradigms and blind alleys (unknowings). The perspective will demonstrate how our language, experiences, values, and beliefs provide a basis for community action. These theories assist us to examine critically the oppression of First Nations, which leads to creative ways of achieving social change. Freire (1983) concluded that education was not neutral and domesticated people rather than liberated them. In Canada the residential school is an example of transforming First Nations peoples into images of what non-First Nations people believed First Nations should be. The emphasis was on teaching girls to cook, clean, and sew so as to be good, quiet housekeepers and housewives. (Many girls were placed in non-Native households as housekeepers and child care workers.) On the other hand, boys learned to farm and ranch. Education was not a priority in residential schools, but assimilation and developing a compliant and cheap labour pool were.

bell hooks is a Black woman and scholar with First Nations roots. Her feminist analysis of race, power, popular culture, sexism, and patriarchy within Black communities provides a framework for First Nations to examine these same issues. In her article 'bell hooks Speaking About Paulo Freire: The Man, His Work' (1993a), she positioned Freire in her mind and heart as a challenging teacher whose work furthered her struggle against the colonizing process—the colonizing mind-set. hooks succinctly contextualized Freire's work for many people seeking a language of liberation when she remarks that 'I came to Freire thirsty, dying of thirst (in that way that the colonized, marginalized subject who is still unsure of how to break the hold of the status quo, who longs for change, is needy—is thirsty), and I found in his work . . . a way to quench my thirst'. In her book, *Sisters of the Yam: Black Women and Self-*

Recovery (1993b), hooks provides an example of Black women's recovery from internalized oppression (racism, sexism, and patriarchy), which is a useful model in analysing the experience of First Nations women within colonization. First Nations women's groups are beginning to deal with recovery issues by seeking their own truths and breaking silences, talking to one another, sharing stories, confronting stereotyped images, and organizing coalitions, yet First Nations women have a lot of work to do in reclaiming power to influence their own lives. There are many structural and attitudinal barriers to overcome within our own communities. Through *Sisters of the Yam* (1993b), hooks validates the strength, struggles, and powerlessness of Black women, and illustrates a constructive process for First Nations women to engage in. We want to note that the work of feminist Aboriginal writers—such as Paula Gunn Allen (1986), Sharon McIvor (1995), and Theresa Nahanee (1995)—expands the perspective of the effects of colonization on Aboriginal women.

Structural theory of oppression is a compilation of ideas and practices from five social workers—Moreau (1990), Carniol (1992), Dominelli (1988), and Howse and Stalwick (1990)—who have begun the work of using a structural and Freirian analysis to understand First Nations issues. This analysis challenges the idea that social work is not political. Structural analysis provides a way of examining how structures and institutions in Canadian society promote and perpetuate oppression. For example, rather than identifying individuals as unmotivated and lazy, a structural analysis of poverty in many First Nations communities reveals the systemic barriers that create and perpetuate poverty. Structural analysis reveals the lack of access to educational, social, and political opportunities for First Nations peoples and identifies the institutional omission of our culture. An example of structural racism is the Indian Act, a federal policy governing every facet of the lives of First Nations peoples. It has instituted barriers to financial and land equity, use of resources, memberships and identity. It outlawed critical social structures, songs, ceremonies, dances, and forms of governance. In doing so, the Indian Act has perpetrated many dehumanizing acts.

First Nations peoples whose nations have a Medicine Wheel philosophy, such as the Anishnabe nation, are beginning to recreate their life philosophies into theoretical models of practice. Some Aboriginal scholars have begun the task of searching for explanations and solutions to their experiences and histories through the use of the Medicine Wheel (Absolon 1993; Dumont 1993; Nabigon 1993). A Medicine Wheel model is also used to analyse critically our experiences as First Nations peoples in relation to all of creation. The Medicine Wheel has been used for centuries and is an indigenous model of community practice. For example, the concepts of sitting in a circle, sharing stories, and learning from one another is akin to equalizing power differences, finding mutuality, and creating safety in a group setting. The four directions of the Medicine Wheel provide guidance towards a holistic and balanced picture of any given situation, with varying levels of depth and understanding. In organizing community, for example, some First Nations will use the Medicine Wheel as a practice model to ensure that the spiritual, emotional, mental, and physical aspects of healing are recognized and incorporated into an action plan. It can also guide people in understanding their roles, responsibilities, and accountability to the whole community. Some Aboriginal peoples, who are natural community practitioners, receive cultural direction and guidance by gaining a solid knowledge base in their own cultural teachings, such as those of the Medicine Wheel.

Taken together, these theories provide a framework to examine the oppression and subjugation of First Nations in Canadian society, which in turn leads to understanding what First Nations have internalized about themselves. Knowing where to begin without blaming the victim is an important first step, and recreating these theories into our own context provides a process for decolonization, which is described as:

> . . . [an] act of confrontation with a hegemonic system [White supremacist capitalist patriarchy] of thought; it is hence a process of considerable historical and cultural liberation. As such, decolonization becomes the contestation of all dominant forms and structures, whether they be linguistic, discursive, or ideological. Moreover, decolonization comes to be understood as an act of exorcism for both the colonized and colonizer. For both parties it must be a process of liberation; from dependency, in the case of the colonized, and from imperialist, racist perceptions, representations, and institutions which, unfortunately, remain with us to this very day, in the case of the colonizer. . . . Decolonization can only be complete when it is understood as a complex process that involves both the colonizer and colonized (Samia Nehrez as quoted in hooks 1992:1).

Decolonization for First Nations means discarding the bonds of colonial oppression and challenging the dominant forms and structures that continue to suppress our reality. It is imperative, therefore, that theories used in working with First Nations communities acknowledge or include the roots of oppression, the *history* of colonization and racial oppression, First Nations distinct world views, and the geographical disparity and distinct nature of First Nations across Canada.

We suggest that the process of decolonization be an integral part of what First Nations define as a holistic model of practice, which is based on the

Medicine Wheel philosophy. Holistic practice involves examining the spiritual, emotional, physical, and mental aspects of the individual and/or community. We believe that holistic practice needs to take into account our authentic past, articulate the realities of our present, and critically challenge and move towards an *authentic and self-determining* future. Authenticity in this sense is about being 'real' and not disguising our truth and reality with lies or myths. Authenticity challenges us to examine our situation with honesty and courage, and to have truth inform practice in a manner that gives dignity and integrity back to the people. Anything else might be false and, as Gilchrist (1994) cautioned, we must not set ideal images for ourselves. If we derive our solutions and actions from an inaccurate (externally determined) past, the solutions themselves become inaccurate.

One problematic example of how First Nations idealize and romanticize culture is the unquestioned role of elders. Traditionally, elders of the community were those we looked to for assistance and guidance. This practice has been revitalized in recent years to the benefit of our communities. However, there have been reports of abuse by elders, which has caused confusion within the community because of the unquestioned belief that elders must be respected and listened to. Hodgson writes that:

> . . . respect for elders has been confused with condoning abuse by older people. Consequently, when an older person is the perpetrator of physical, emotional or sexual abuse, our community is more reluctant to disclose that violence. This is not because violence is cultural, but because respecting elders is (Hodgson 1990:36).

The process of decolonization includes First Nations' ability to examine critically the reality of our lives, to understand how the oppression we have experienced has been integrated into our lives, and how we sabotage our recovery process because of our internalized oppression. While it is imperative that Euro-Canadians understand how colonization was a process of cultural genocide, it is also imperative that First Nations recognize the extent of the damage this process has done to our lives and how we can begin to change that. We cannot unquestionably accept what may be presented as a traditional value and/or belief. Our cultures have been so permeated with Euro-Canadian values and beliefs that it is impossible to experience tradition in its purest sense. We offer the following principles that we believe work towards a process of decolonization and a practice of freedom: consciousness raising, critical thinking, and critical education. All three principles are woven together and foster the same thinking.

Consciousness raising occurs when one begins to think critically about self and identity in relation to one's political circumstance (hooks 1993a:147). One example of this process is examining sexism in First Nations cultures. In *Aboriginal Women and Treaty Making* (Absolon, Herbert, and MacDonald 1996), the women interviewed believed that their traditional role of decision making in their communities was usurped by the sexist assimilative policies and practices of the Indian Act and is still being perpetuated by the current politics of Aboriginal communities. Only 20 per cent of the chiefs in BC are women, which is related to the fact that First Nations women could not vote or run for position on council in their own communities until 1951. Another sexist policy that has significant implications for women is the lack of division of property rights for women on reserve upon the dissolution of marriage. The women who participated in the study believe they can begin to change these sexist policies by having equal representation at the treaty-making tables, either by mandate or legislation that would include women both on and off reserve.

Critical thinking and analysis require us to examine our locations (where we sit in relation to power), our disempowerment, and how we participate in abuse of power (Pinderhughes 1989). Critical thought proposes that we question self, community, policy, and actions. Critical thinking involves the ability to ask crucial questions or else maintain oppressive silences. Critical thinking involves examining where we place ourselves and how we participate on a continuum of privilege/oppression and superiority/inferiority.

For example, when First Nations communities take steps towards sobriety, acknowledging this as a first step in striving for community sobriety is important, but it is not the end. We need to continue examining and dealing with other accompanying issues, such as child welfare, sexual abuse, violence, etc. The process of recovery should be examined and questioned. Despite the first steps towards recovery, communities will remain indoctrinated and colonized if the issue of alcoholism is not understood within the larger framework of colonization. For many years, alcoholism has been regarded as a pathology, which is the basis of the disease model, Alcoholics Anonymous, and, more recently in Aboriginal communities, the adult children of alcoholics. What these present, particularly for Aboriginal peoples, is the notion of a predisposition to alcoholism. Utilizing a structural model, it is possible to take this notion of predisposition and analyse it within the context of the effects of colonization. We will probably find that many people utilize alcohol and drugs to cope with the experience of being a residential school survivor, with poverty, or with being battered. Internalized beliefs that alcoholism is a character flaw and a genetic weakness of Aboriginal peoples can hold the community hostage because of the disempowerment this kind of analysis of alcoholism conveys. Sobriety is only part of the recovery process and the action that follows is just as crucial as the action that precipitated community sobriety.

Critical education is another fundamental component of community action as a practice of freedom. What we need to do is engage in dialogue and break the silence of our colonization, come out of isolation, and tell our stories to each other and anyone else who is willing to listen and learn (Howse and Stalwick 1990). The dialogue following this section illustrates a beginning to the process. Many Aboriginal communities are bringing people together for a critical education process culturally, socially, economically, and politically. Examples of such events are Aboriginal women and wellness conferences, men's wellness gatherings, elders and/or youth conferences, economic development education, and community-healing ceremonies. These events cover areas relevant to Aboriginal history; cultural practices and teachings; social, political, and economic issues; decolonization; and many others. There are public events that recognize the inhumanity First Nations have experienced from racist government policies and practices, and they, too, play a part in critically educating the public. For example, in June 1996 in Victoria, BC, a community-healing ceremony was conducted between the Ministry of Social Services and the local First Nations communities in acknowledging their participation in the cultural genocide of Aboriginal families. People shared their stories, along with their grief and loss, and an open dialogue was created between the ministry and First Nations.

This information, however, is not publicly available nor is it taught in the schools that, for the most part, educate and socialize our youths. We cannot assume that the adults in our communities know and understand what their oppression is about. Community action must include critical collective education so that identification, planning, and action can be validating and empowering. Education is critical because it involves looking at our history from our perspective and can be used as an essential tool to determine our own future.

We believe that unless one consciously engages in critically examining structural oppression, one cannot begin to eradicate it. Oppression is not necessarily overt. Silent compliance to racist policy perpetrates structural oppression. Ideologies of racism, sexism, heterosexism, and classism each has its own history and should be deconstructed so we can question their use as justification for privilege and oppression. Deconstructing ideologies as a basic component of critical education can provide meaningful information for a community education plan.

Our perspective of community action attempts to reveal *power* imbalances in race, gender, class, sexual orientation, age, or ability. First Nations women need to be acknowledged for the crucial roles they have in their communities. White people need to be willing to examine racism as power inequity, and First Nations men must be willing to examine the power imbalances between men and women in many First Nations communities. First Nations women's groups have endeavoured to point out the connection between these factors and violence. However, many of these women are threatened, silenced, and viewed as traitors.

When people are not included and consulted in community work, the action is impaired. An example of community action that was impaired and consequently stopped was the South Vancouver Island Justice Education Project in British Columbia. This was a community initiative to provide cross-cultural education to government agencies and community members and to grant diversion alternatives and sentencing interventions to Coast Salish citizens in conflict with the law. Some women in the community wanted an inquiry into this justice initiative after a case of sexual assault in which:

> . . . significant pressure was placed upon the victim(s) to have this matter treated in a traditional way. . . . It failed to address the critical needs of the victim(s) while raising the alleged offender to 'preferred status'. The serious nature of the alleged offence (sexual assault with multiple victims), the lack of resources to ensure public safety, and the lack of any defined principles or practices of the proposed 'Tribal Justice System', increased the concern among citizens (Clark et al. 1995:53).

An inquiry into the project found that there was very limited consultation with the community regarding the initiative from development to implementation. Seventy-two per cent of the community members surveyed believed that the project did not effectively provide justice in their communities (Clark et al. 1995). Collective action has the power and mandate to effect change in most cases. However, as the South Vancouver Island Justice Education Project demonstrated, the whole community must be mindfully and respectfully represented. Individual action leaves people isolated and often personally wounded and burned out.

In addition to critical education and structural analysis, the framework for community action must include a consideration of culture. *Culture* includes our traditional practices that guide and enhance social, spiritual, economic, and political development. The cultural practices must be owned, identified, and integrated according to one's nation and geographic location. The cultures across Canada represent our diversity—the Micmac in the east, the Inuvialuit in the north, the Chippewa in the south, the Haida Gwaii in the northwest, the Coast Salish in the west, and many other interior, coastal, woodland, and prairie peoples. Communities will determine their cultural model and how it will be integrated into community action. At this point, community members can examine and discuss how the cultural model works towards a process of decolonization. How does this model educate and help the people out of their present condition? How does this model validate and enable all the voices of the community to be heard?

Culture and cultural practices are integral in community work because they provide the basis of who the community is. The aspects of culture within First Nations communities that sustain them are those beliefs and practices that have been remembered despite the efforts of the Church and the government to eradicate them. Unfortunately, other aspects of culture that are now part of these communities are negative, such as alcoholism and violence. Culture is constantly changing, and First Nations communities require new information and education because revitalizing culture alone will not release us from the grip of our colonial masters.

The Context of Our Reality: Personal and Political

This next section of the chapter is our dialogue. We chose this method to translate the principles of community action through our experiences. Through this dialogue we engage with each other and explore our different ways of knowing, interpreting, and relating to the world.

> KA: *Oni*, Elaine. I'm honoured to be working with you here. Establishing our beginnings is crucial in determining where we place ourselves today and in understanding how we got here. It's all about my identity and where it comes from—our history. For example, my perspective is derived from my experiences, which reflects a combination of knowing and understanding both my privilege and oppression. I grew up rural, in the bush, isolated from urban life and somewhat from reserve life. There are five siblings and two parents, and our identity combines both Ojibwa and European ancestry. As a result of my geographic and racial in-betweenness, I have located myself in both privilege and oppression, never fully in either. My 'bush' socialization allowed me to feel a sense of freedom. I have come to believe that as a result of this particular socialization, my spirit was allowed to thrive and experience liberation in a very unique way—this is a part of my privilege. My privilege in accessing both cultural and academic teachings, and the oppression and racism I experience as a First Nations woman have together created a unique place for me to work as a scholar, educator, community person, and healer.

For the past four years, I have been the First Nations educator in a school of social work and a community builder within the urban First Nations community. As an educator, I have brought my personal experiences into my work, the community, and the classroom. I have been able to *learn out of* inferior feelings by talking about my experiences within a *context of decolonization*. My process of learning is moving from strengthening my mind towards strengthening action and practice. As a community worker, I need to be involved with the people and feel connected to the community. I am a natural builder, and I love being with my people. I have been intimately involved with organizing Aboriginal women and community, and I thrive on the notions of bringing people together to build community.

'Community action' begins with me working towards a holistic balance. I believe that healthy communities need healthy individuals who can work in a way that promotes wellness. I yearn to question and understand the roots of my pain and our collective pain as Aboriginal peoples. It was not until I engaged in a process of consciously examining my historical development in my family, community structures, and society that I began to learn about the reasons for the diseased symptoms of our communities. I did not understand the degree to which my life and socialization were affected by racism and sexism, and as a result I internalized the many messages of inferiority about who and what I was. These experiences for me occurred ever since I can remember, and were perpetuated in education, through the media, the literature, and many other structures I came in contact with throughout my life. In this sense, I guess I was taught to walk 'in fear' about my identity.

Making connections between my personal, political, and structural reality helped liberate me. My experience tells me that the omission of our reality and history, coupled with negative stereotypes, result in a widespread ignorance that fosters fear and hate. To me this is treatable and preventable for many First Nations peoples and non–First Nations people in Canada. My path of unlearning and relearning (as I have come to describe it) and finding my truth evolved out of finally understanding that 'it' didn't just happen to me. I was not alone. This, I believe, is where my passion in collective and community action comes from: the essential need to come out of isolation, name our reality, and break the 'culture of silence' as expressed by Brazilian writer Paulo Freire. The writings of Paulo Freire had a significant impact on me, as did other writers, such as bell hooks. These influences led me to immerse myself in community practice and reflect in thinking and action as a community builder. I have chosen to leave academia and move fully into community practice where I will be working with several communities in my home territory. This change is critical for me if I am to continue to feel and experience my people and our issues. I feel ready to do this now because I have begun to decolonize my mind, and it is stronger and clearer about who I am and where I come from. All these things fit together for me and it's difficult to speak to my *context* briefly. There are many levels at play in my life. What about you, Elaine? How would you begin to 'locate' yourself?

EH: I want to begin this conversation, Kath, by saying that it is a privilege and honour to write this paper with you. I believe that we are an example of the diversity of Aboriginal peoples in Canada because of our backgrounds, yet we share common values and beliefs that have made it easy to combine our ideas in this paper. Like you, I have found in my personal and work experiences that a sense of identity is crucial to the healing process of individuals and community. We chose a format common to most First Nations to introduce themselves as belonging to a particular First Nation. This format is for the benefit of the reader to get a sense of who we are as the authors. I want to begin by saying that my privilege as an academic scholar and teacher is balanced by the experience of growing up in a small rural reserve community. Growing up poor (by mainstream Canadian standards of living) but happy, my childhood instilled in me an identity of who I was and where I belonged, which even the Indian Act was unable to sever. I am a member of the Bonaparte band, Shuswap nation. I spent my formative years living with my grandparents in this small rural reserve. I am currently a doctoral candidate in the interdisciplinary program at the University of BC, combining a study of law, social work, and education. I bring practical work experiences that inform this discussion, experiences that range from working in rural and urban First Nations organizations in capacities as management as well as staff member; social science researcher for academic and government contracts; and instructor at the Aboriginal community and university level. I am somewhat of an idealist in terms of believing in change. This paper has helped me to articulate some of my thoughts about community change, which I know from experience needs to begin with the self.

KA: I agree with you, Elaine, our diversity is evident and real, and I would like to add that my questioning arose from not understanding why some parts of my environment and childhood had so much pain and grief, and why my Ojibwa relations did not talk with pride about being Indian. I have since come to understand that my roots are buried in institutional racism. My reserve community existed only as a document and a statistic. Our community has many challenges to face because most of us are all geographically separated, and there is a lot of interracial mixing and strong patriarchal forces governing our issues. I believe, though, that we are living in an era of transformation, and as I strengthen, I, too, work for change, envisioning similar ideas that we are discussing, Elaine.

EH: Yes, I believe that it is important for the reader to understand that because we understand the effects of colonization on Aboriginal peoples from personal experience. We are passionate in our refusal to continue to be colonized. Our formal education is an experience we share, as well as the social and political understanding of our shared oppression (race/gender), which has brought us together to write this chapter. One of the most important concepts we bring to this dialogue of community action as a practice of freedom is an understanding and practice of decolonization. My experience of this process began in 1984. I had an opportunity to participate in a seminar that was led by Paulo Freire at the University of BC. This was an experience of consciousness raising for me when I realized I could actually make sense of the effects of colonization. I had finally found the words that freed my thinking. Paulo's work was a form of liberation for me.

I travelled to Brazil a year later with a group of graduate students who were continuing to study Freire's work. However, reading hooks's work was like taking Freire's work one step further. I was able to understand how the sexist policies and practices of the Indian Act are still being practised against First Nations women today, and that many First Nations communities ignore this fact. hooks's work also helped me to understand that it was okay to be a feminist, not just any feminist, but a First Nations feminist, which includes analysing racism and sexism within the context of colonization. Through both of these writers I was able to develop a critical analysis that helped me to critique Aboriginal culture as well as Euro-Canadian culture. For me, decolonization is the praxis that Freire talks about when he says that it is not enough to be conscious about your situation. You have to take action, reflect upon that action, and act again. Our lives must be a living example of our politics.

KA: Decolonization at the individual level is obviously easier than at the collective level of a community. This is one of the reasons for our dialogue, which is to provide examples of what we experienced in our own process of decolonization. At a personal level, my action stems from a holistic point of view in my process of becoming human again. I say this knowing that my socialization has dehumanized me as an Indian person. I will try and describe my current awareness.

As a woman, I need to keep in touch with this knowledge as a mobilizer for unlearning and decolonizing myself. Spiritually I have to ground my identity in truly understanding who I am and where I came from. I have done this through my Anishnabe culture and by learning from my teachers and elders. Emotionally I have to learn about and understand the nature of my pain, anger, grief, and loss, and actively find my strengths and gifts. I have done this through personal therapy and cultural healing. Mentally I have had to strengthen my mind, raise my consciousness, understand the political context of my socialization, unlearn internalized racism, and engage in a critical analysis and dialogue about the authentic roots of our oppression. My process at this level has been through education, attending university, researching critical literature, engaging in critical dialogue, and finding mentors to guide, validate, and support me. Physically I have had to build up my stamina and endurance to work within our struggle for authentic action, and I have had to maintain a clean and clear body, mind, and spirit throughout. I maintain this by abstaining from alcohol and drugs, and exercising and participating in cultural ceremonies. As I mentioned earlier, I need to *act* and move beyond a theoretical place to practice, and this is the direction I am emphasizing now by leaving social work education to work in communities. I believe this is a practice of action and reflection. From these levels of holistic action with self, my relationships with others (such as family, community, and larger structures nationally and internationally) are affected. Within these relationships is my inherent relationship to the land, Mother Earth, and the Creator. I feel that when I am committed to my own health and well-being, I can relate to things outside myself in a manner that promotes wellness. I also feel that our realities are complex, and that the dimensions of our relationships external and internal to our communities are critical. Given this, we cannot take for granted that our realities are as they once were precontact.

For example, I worked with a group of Aboriginal women in an urban community for about two years, organizing a provincial women and wellness conference. The experience was incredible, the work exhausting, and the diversity among the women evident. Somehow I was on automatic pilot, and I *assumed* the work would be all fun and easy because we were all Aboriginal women. Well, our diversity in thinking and working around many issues surfaced shortly after the initial politeness ended. I was surprised by our diversity and initially feared it, so the practice was quite different from what I intellectually understood. I surprised myself in not being prepared for our own differences, though most of us came with a strong determination to see the project through and to care about our own process. We wanted to bring hundreds of Aboriginal women together to share and learn from one another. We always had meetings that began and ended in prayer and circle check-ins, which helped us to connect with each other amidst the pressures of making tough decisions and organizing the details of a major event. We made a commitment to care and respect each other, and I embraced our process and soon ended up celebrating our diversity as a community of Aboriginal women. The experience was rich, that's for sure.

EH: You raise an important point of how the renaissance of First Nations cultural beliefs and practices is contributing significantly to community change and cultural action. Many communities are experiencing social changes, such as the sobriety movement away from alcoholism and drugs. Many more First Nations are discovering that cultural beliefs and practices are helping to keep them sober. These are good things that are happening, but they are not enough. Treatment methodologies need to move beyond the medical model definition of alcoholism and consider that the use of alcohol and/or drugs is usually symptomatic of other problems. My experience of working with First Nations women in an out-patient addictions program is that these women are using alcohol and drugs to cope with childhood sexual and physical abuse, battering, poverty, and loss of their children to the Ministry of Social Services. I use treatment methodologies that I consider part of the process of decolonization by helping them understand how racism and sexism contributed to their circumstance of abuse and neglect instead of believing that a character flaw within themselves caused the addiction. We have so much internalized oppression already; we do not need more people telling us that it is something within us that is flawed. I believe it is crucial for those of us who are helpers to continue to evaluate our practice and understand how we are helping or hindering our clients. For those of us who use First Nations ritual and ceremonies in our practice, we need to evaluate how these practices are helping or not helping. We cannot assume that everyone wants to participate in these practices just because they are Aboriginal.

KA: Community action then is a practice that frees people. We need to experience liberation from internalized racism, sexism, and oppression. We need critical education and consciousness raising. At the end of the day, the people must be able to ask critical and proactive questions about issues that affect their community. As well, the people must have an understanding beyond themselves of the structures that affect them so they can take constructive action that is authentically theirs.

EH: I was thinking, Kath, as I read your last statement, that the reader is probably wondering how all of this happens, assuming that it makes sense. This process of understanding and unlearning the effects of colonization will take time, hopefully not as long as it took to create the situation. In terms of utilizing these concepts in community work, there are many possibilities. However, one of the hurdles we have to overcome in community work is the idea of a quick fix. Many people, either Aboriginal or non-Aboriginal, have offered a quick fix to community problems that do not work; at best, they offer only temporary relief. It is important for community members to ask critical and proactive questions when these quick-fix people show up and tell everyone that they can remedy the community problems in three days. It is not possible, even if they came back for another three days. Based on my own experiences with some of these methods, I believe that what are utilized in these situations are adaptations of growth therapy. Participants are involved in a process whereby they engage in an emotional catharsis, releasing feelings, which in and of itself is therapeutic— at least in the short term. The problem with this method is that this usually takes place over two or three days, and the helpers leave without helping the participants fully understand or resolve their feelings. I have witnessed this happening when an individual 'lets it all out' by publicly purging his or her emotions about the same situation again and again. For Aboriginal peoples, the next step is for someone to help them make sense of the feelings released in the context of the rest of their life, which includes the social and political environment. First Nations communities need to be cognizant of quick-fix artists, whose main priority is to make a fast buck at the expense of people's pain. It will require community activists, who themselves are in a process of decolonization, to be able to help in a constructive way.

KA: Your example, Elaine, reminds me of how our communities are still being taken advantage of by people like Euro-Canadian consultants, lawyers, and therapists, who are still the neocolonial experts who know what First Nations peoples need. First Nations peoples and issues have become a source of revenue for many 'experts'. Of course, we have to acknowledge that it is First Nations peoples who hire them, which raises the question of their own internalized oppression. Colonialism is not dead, and we challenge the notion of 'postcolonialism', which implies that colonization is over. Given what you've just stated and what I understand, we are not out of a colonial era. We are still in it, and the term 'postcolonial' implies that it is history and in the past, but it's not. We are still struggling with the government and Euro-Canadian institutions in a battle for self-determination for the return of stolen land. Our lives are still dictated federally by Indian Affairs, provincially by ministries, and locally by municipalities. Women are still oppressed and silenced, not only by Euro-Canadian patriarchy but now by First Nations patriarchy. I'm really glad you raised these points.

EH: This process of dialogue is exciting and empowering, but also kind of scary. We have shared parts of ourselves that many people will be able to read about. I am not sure how I feel about that. I know we struggled through many aspects of writing this paper, Kath, believing that we could make a contribution to the literature on community work. I believe we accomplished what we set out to do, which was to offer some ideas for people to think about and try. It is important for people to know that we do not believe we have all the answers. We wanted to demonstrate through our dialogue how important it is to communicate and articulate your thoughts and ideas. I hope that this information can help people begin to discuss the same things we have been talking about. This reminds me of the dialogue we had on the child/family services organization that I chair. I have endeavoured to model a more equal level of working instead of the structural hierarchy of the board. We try to communicate and discuss things in healthy ways, but sometimes it is hard to overcome old patterns. We have come a long way from the problems of the previous board and staff. We always have to remember that our organization is supposed to teach families healthy ways of coping with their problems. The point that I believe is important here is that community action begins with the self. It is difficult to help or interact in a group if you do not have a good sense of your self and identity. I speak from an experience I had many years ago when I first worked for my band. I helped to organize a group of women who wanted to get involved in community activities. When these women wanted to engage the chief and council in a dialogue over some of the decisions being made, they were quickly disbanded and I was fired. I did not have the skills or knowledge to help these women (many of whom were my relatives, as were members of the council) challenge the neocolonial authoritarian power that the Indian Act gives the chief and council.

Nine years later, the Ministry of Social Services was going to terminate the contract of the Child/Family Services board that I chaired. The board was successful in stopping the termination and it still exists as a well-functioning organization today. Two things had changed from the first situation. I had changed by engaging in a process of decolonization that sustained a stronger sense of self and identity, and, secondly, I was also supported by a group of people who shared the same passion, which was to provide Aboriginal child and family services in Vancouver. I want to complete this thought, Kathy, by saying that change is a process that involves everyone. I remember that in one social work class I taught, I listened to Euro-Canadian students tell me that after fourteen years of schooling, they did not know anything about residential schools. I remember that after class I felt an intense rage and then sadness as these students did when they realized they had been taught a fraudulent history. We have both shared experiences like these in classrooms when we had to listen to students make racist statements with no understanding that they were racist. It would have been impossible to continue hearing this stuff if we had not been able to debrief our experiences and support each other. This is an example of what Paulo Freire is referring to when he says that education is political and never neutral. So is community work.

KA: Your example of how we supported each other while working within an institution is very relevant to the purpose of community work and is absolutely critical. Community work is more than providing a service and helping peoples become organized. It is about our life and survival as peoples on this land, and our existence is connected to economic, social, political, and cultural self-determination. Our issues are about us coming into an 'action' that focuses on how we, the First Nations of Canada, engage in community action with each other. We need to engage in our own perspectives of practice that incorporate our true realities (we are peoples with many different truths), combined with our cultural identity and spiritual practices. Community development must be transformed into a community action that comes from the people, with intrinsic dialogue that works to liberate, not domesticate, First Nations peoples. Before we close our dialogue, Elaine, I just want to acknowledge the exciting, stimulating, supportive, and scary aspects of what we must begin talking about. My hope is that, through our dialogue, we have begun to model a small part of a much larger process. This has been both a pleasure and an education. *Meegwetch*, Elaine.

Conclusion

In all cultural revolutions there are periods of chaos and confusion, times when grave mistakes are made (hooks 1994:33).

Community action as a practice of freedom embodied in this chapter calls for some fundamental change in how community development is presented in Aboriginal communities. We introduced some theories, practices, ideas, and, most important, some new language. We have asked you to view the process of colonization as a deliberate act of racism driven by an ideology held by Euro-Canadians who believed they were superior to Aboriginal peoples, who used capitalism to exploit and destroy Aboriginal social and economic systems, and who changed or destroyed cultural values and beliefs by imposing the Church and state on our nations. We offer the theory of decolonization for not only Aboriginal peoples but non-Aboriginal people as well.

It will be a constant struggle to deconstruct the domination and oppression history has left us with, and we must be conscious of the remaining neo-colonial forces that work against community action strategies (Foley and Flowers 1992). In addition to inadequate and racist government policies and programs, there are factors that create barriers to progressive and radical movement. One factor is the lack of coordination and clarification in existing government-sponsored programs for Aboriginal populations. The lack of jurisdictional clarity between federal and provincial governments and between national and provincial Aboriginal organizations is another.

Many of the existing programs are reactive and inappropriate, and have evolved out of the governments' desire to allocate dollars for a particular problem or issue. Aboriginal peoples face pressure to adapt to Euro-Canadian models of working, and are often trained in mainstream settings and therefore lack the critical and organizational skills to create an authentic model of change. Currently many Aboriginal organizations are faced with poorly funded programs and a lack of community support, coupled with unrealistic expectations. Quite often we see a few people doing all the work, with minimal attendance and participation by community members. There simply is a lack of professionally trained Aboriginal peoples to foster community planning and action. This relates to the inaccessibility and irrelevance of secondary and postsecondary education.

Some of the most important community initiatives in BC and throughout Canada are the First Nations child welfare programs, which face all of the abovementioned problems. Federal and provincial governments are encouraging First Nations band and tribal councils to assume responsibility for child welfare, yet both are reluctant to provide adequate funding. A recent study of BC First Nations child welfare programs (Herbert 1995) found that they have insufficient resources to provide innovative and preventive services, and many end up replicating the crisis model of intervention practised in the provincial ministry responsible for child welfare.

The jurisdictional dispute between the federal and provincial governments provides an excuse for both to evade responsibility for assisting First Nations peoples to develop community-governed and culturally appropriate services. Given the tragic history of child welfare provided by provincial child welfare agencies to First Nations peoples, which was a disaster second only to the residential school experience, a more supportive attitude and more generous funding should characterize government policies.

We continue to appeal for ongoing developments of Aboriginal perspectives and models of practice that are based in a critical analysis of Aboriginal Canada. We also want to acknowledge the work currently taking place in regions across Canada through writers such as Howse and Stalwick (1990) and Morrissette, McKenzie, and Morrissette (1993). There is a great need for those who are willing to take the risks, brace their fear, and blaze the trails to know that, to some degree, they are creating a path for others. We are at a time when self-determination across all spheres of our lives is vital to put an end to our oppression. Women are beginning to voice their concerns, youths are giving us strong messages, elders are taking their place, and our communities are beginning to have hope. Remember, the approach needs to be balanced and include all the dimensions that make up our realities: our history, racism, sexism, the impact of colonization, critical education, political literacy, self-recovery, community, and cultural ownership.

References

Absolon, K.
1993. 'Healing as Practice: Teachings from the Medicine Wheel'. A publication in process prepared for the WUNSKA network, Saskatoon, Saskatchewan.

_____, E. Herbert, and K. MacDonald.
1996. 'Aboriginal Women and Treaty Making in BC'. A research document prepared for the Ministry of Women's Equality, Victoria, BC.

Adams, H.
1989. *Prison of Grass*. Saskatoon: Fifth House.

Allen, P.G.
1986. *The Sacred Hoop*. Boston: Beacon Press.

Carniol, B.
1992. 'Structural Social Work: Maurice Moreau's Challenge to Social Work Practice'. *Journal of Progressive Human Services* 3, no. 1:1–19.

_____.
1995. *Case Critical: Challenging Social Work in Canada*, 3rd ed. Toronto: Between the Lines.

Clark, S., et al.
1995. 'Building the Bridge: A Review of the South Vancouver Island Justice Education

Project'. Victoria: Ministry of the Attorney General, Department of Justice and the Solicitor General of Canada.

Dominelli, L.
1988. *Anti-racist Social Work*. London: Macmillan.

Dumont, J.
1993. 'Justice and Aboriginal People'. In *Aboriginal Peoples and the Justice System*, edited by the Royal Commission on Aboriginal Peoples, 42–85. Ottawa: Canada Communication Group Publishing.

Foley, G., and R. Flowers.
1992. 'Knowledge and Power in Aboriginal Adult Education'. *Convergence* XXV, no. 1:61–73.

Freire, P.
1970. *Cultural Action for Freedom*. Harvard: Harvard Educational Review.

———.
1983. *Pedagogy of the Oppressed*. New York: The Continuum Publishing Corporation.

Gilchrist, L.
1994. 'Aboriginal Communities and Social Science Research: Voyeurism in Transition', Saskatchewan Indian Federated College. A publication in progress prepared for the WUNSKA conference, Chase, BC.

Giroux, H.A.
1993. 'Paolo Freire and the Politics of Postcolonialism'. In *Paulo Freire: A Critical Encounter*, edited by P. McLaren and P. Leonard, 177–88. New York: Routledge.

Herbert, E.
1995. 'An Overview and Analysis of First Nations Child and Family Services in BC'. Prepared for the Gove Inquiry into Child Protection.

Hodgson, M.
1990. 'Shattering the Silence: Working with Violence in Native Communities'. In *Healing Voices: Feminist Approaches to Therapy with Women*, edited by T. Laidlaw et al., 33–44. San Francisco: Jossey-Bass.

hooks, b.
1992. *Black Looks: Race and Representations*. Toronto: Between the Lines.

———. 1993a. 'bell hooks Speaking About Paulo Freire: The Man, His Work'. In *Paulo Freire: A Critical Encounter*, edited by P. McLaren and P. Leonard, 146–54. New York: Routledge.

———.
1993b. *Sisters of the Yam: Black Women and Self-Recovery*. Toronto: Between the Lines.

————.

1994. *Teaching to Transgress.* New York: Routledge.

Howse, Y., and H. Stalwick.

1990. 'Social Work and the First Nations Movement: Our Children, Our Culture'. In *Social Work and Social Change in Canada*, edited by B. Wharf, 79–113. Toronto: McClelland and Stewart.

McIvor, S.

1995. 'Aboriginal Self-Government: The Civil & Political Rights of Women'. A thesis submitted to the Faculty of Law, Queen's University, Kingston.

Moreau, M.

1990. 'Empowerment through Advocacy and Consciousness-Raising: Implications of a Structural Approach to Social Work'. *Journal of Sociology and Social Welfare* XVII, no. 2:53–67.

Morrissette, V., B. McKenzie, and L. Morrissette.

1993. 'Towards an Aboriginal Model of Social Work Practice'. *Canadian Social Work Review* 10, no. 1:91–108.

Nabigon, H.

1993. 'Reclaiming the Spirit of First Nations Self-Government'. In *Rebirth: Political, Economical and Social Developments in First Nations*, edited by A. Mawhinney, 136–45. Toronto: Dundurn Press.

Nahanee, T.

1995. 'Dancing with the Gorilla: Aboriginal Women and the Inhumanity of the Canadian Criminal Justice System'. Master of Law thesis, Queen's University, Kingston.

Pinderhughes, E.

1989. *Understanding Race, Ethnicity and Power.* New York: Free Press.

Chapter Twelve

From the Ground Up: Community Development as an Environmental Movement

Frank James Tester

Roots

Nothing is more fundamental to human survival than the integrity of the planet's ecosystems. The claim that our social beliefs and industrial practices are threatening planetary survival is a strong one, increasingly well researched, documented, and debated internationally.[1] While concern for natural systems parallels the 200-year growth of modernist assumptions and a history of industrialization, since the mid- to late 1960s environmental concerns have become an essential element in the political and social life of all Western liberal democracies.

Commencing in the mid-1960s, four social movements have had a profound impact on the Canadian liberal welfare state and community development in Canada, whether 'community' is defined geographically or by interests ('virtual' communities).[2] The contemporary women's movement, the peace movement, the Aboriginal peoples' movement, and the environmental movement have developed as significant social forces. They have changed how Canadians see themselves, confronting them with issues that had been obscured for decades by traditional assumptions about development and inaccessible institutions.

In the 1990s virtual communities are redefining themselves using the 'politics of identity'. Thus the women's movement is, in fact, a composite of movements and political expressions defined by race, class, and even geography, as in women of colour, Aboriginal women, women in the garment industry, associations of rural or farm women, and so on. Similarly, the environmental movement embraces a wide range of philosophical identities, such as social ecology, animal rights, ecofeminism, and so on.[3] These developments challenge the modernist assumptions of liberal theory: that a modern society is consensual, that a particular grand theory of democracy (liberal pluralism) is a satisfactory model for guiding the activities of groups, communities, and even nation-states. The recognition of multiple realities, in some measure, is the practice of postmodern politics.

As Jim Lotz notes in Chapter 2, the roots of community development in Canada are commonly identified with the work of Moses Coady, the Antigonish Movement, and social action to address regional economic disparities, especially in the Maritimes and the Prairies. But by the 1950s, in the presence of a rapidly expanding economy and previously unheard of responses to matters of human welfare—that is, the creation of a liberal welfare state—community development efforts focused on the notion of 'citizenship'.[4]

The experiences of the depression and of the Second World War had a profound effect on a generation of civil servants, planners, and community workers, who were convinced that 'difference' gave rise to social conflict. While addressing differences in material circumstances was not irrelevant to these efforts, the creation of a Canadian culture of shared values, aspirations, and social objectives was the focus of community development practices that were heavily influenced by liberal notions of welfare and social justice. These efforts are typified by the community development perspectives of Murray Ross (1955).

The commitment to creating a Canadian community of shared interests, habits, and values is obvious from attempts, in the decades following the Second World War, to assimilate Aboriginal peoples. This was often undertaken with the best intention of providing them with the same rights of citizenship accorded all Canadians. Civil servants, social workers, and others worked within the theoretical assumptions available at the time. Community development officers often played a critical role in these initiatives (Tester and Kulchyski 1994:337–9). Sparked by the Liberal government's 1969 'White Paper on Indian Affairs', assimilationist policies were increasingly challenged by an emerging militant and contemporary Aboriginal peoples' movement.

Paradoxically, this was given impetus by creative attempts in the late 1960s to practise community development within the Department of Indian and Northern Affairs. As a result of these efforts, Aboriginal peoples' tactics changed from unsuccessful appeals to the state to address their social and economic circumstances to militant protests. Community development efforts also contributed to the genesis of contemporary Aboriginal peoples' movements.[5] It is therefore not surprising that by the late 1960s the department had moved dramatically to rein in the community development workers it had assigned to Indian reserves across the country.

Throughout the 1970s and 1980s community development initiatives identified with traditional sites of practice: the neighbourhood houses and agencies often funded by the United Appeal. Practice commonly focused on issues of child welfare, welfare rights, and, to a lesser extent, on a general concern for the distribution of social and economic power in Canadian society. Increasingly in the 1980s practice developed around emerging social movements as they challenged the state and addressed new social issues, such as youth unemployment, immigration, housing, gay and lesbian rights, and the erosion of rights won by organized labour and women's issues.

By the late 1980s, according to public opinion polls, environmental issues had replaced jobs and the economy as the major concern of Canadian electors. This forced the Conservative government of Prime Minister Brian Mulroney to initiate policies and make promises, which left some impression that environmental issues were being taken seriously.[6] What followed—an acid rain treaty with the United States, the Canadian Environmental Protection Act passed in June 1988, the introduction of a federal 'Green Plan' in 1990 (which was abandoned five years later), and other initiatives—were arguably of questionable substance.[7] They originated from a government committed to developmental ideas firmly located within modernist assumptions about economic growth, wealth generation, and 'the idea of progress'.[8]

A relationship between environmental issues and concerns for social justice was first articulated by the peace movement in the late 1960s and 1970s. Greenpeace, which is now an international environmental organization, originated in Vancouver with a group protesting the presence of nuclear-armed ships and submarines in Canadian waters and nuclear arms testing. Nuclear issues have focused international attention on human rights. Historically, nuclear testing has exploited the land and the indigenous peoples of the South Pacific. The mining of uranium in Saskatchewan and the processing of nuclear materials in the United States is a history of the abuse of Native lands. Nuclear power plants and waste disposal facilities have typically been located in areas occupied by indigenous peoples and the poor.

By the late 1980s cynicism about grand-scale policy solutions to environmental problems was common within the movement. However, since the 1970s more had happened than merely identifying environmental issues as subjects for policy making. Environmentalism was an increasingly radical critique of modernist assumptions, including that of traditional politics and economics, and the positing of alternative economic, social, and political forms. Aboriginal peoples facilitated much critical thought, which is also reflected in the writings and work of ecofeminists, others working in the bioregional movement,[9] and some dissident economists, among them Herman Daly, former senior economist with the World Bank (Daly and Cobb 1994). There are, therefore, important points of convergence among the peace movement, Aboriginal peoples' movement, women's movement, and environmental movement.

The renewed women's movement and the development of vocal and action-oriented environmental groups in the late 1960s were symptomatic of a decreasing respect for authority and expertise, which has historically characterized much of Canadian culture. (This culture, associated with the hierarchy and formality of British institutions and the staunch Protestantism and conservative Catholicism of Upper and Lower Canada in the late 1800s, was given new form through the military and paramilitary service experienced by many Canadians during the Second World War.) Faith in traditional authority declined in a population that was better educated and informed about global events than any previous generation. In the 1960s and 1970s social and environmental issues were of increasing concern for citizens sceptical about the extent to which corporations and governments accounted for their interests.

There are many reasons for these changes in the relationship between civil society and government, among them the pace and increasingly obvious consequences of the social and environmental changes of the 1960s, which challenged such modernist assumptions as the idea of 'progress', the inviolate nature of expertise, and the benevolence of development.[10] Robert Paehlke characterizes the consciousness of the new environmental movement as one in which 'The symptoms of environmental problems, arising from interactions between human communities and built and natural environments, may be measured biologically, but the disease itself lies in our socioeconomic organizations, and the solutions are ultimately political' (Paehlke 1989:36). Described this way, environmental problems, arising from interactions between human communities and built and natural environments, are among the most important for community development practice.

The significance of these interactions is threefold. First, community development has increasingly focused on movements as well as geographically defined communities. Secondly, unlike the 1950s, community development initiatives have increasingly challenged rather than served the state's interests. Finally, the peace movement, the Aboriginal movement, and the women's movement are now giving direction and focus to the environmental movement as it focuses on matters of social justice and human rights, linking these matters to struggles over ownership, control, and relationships with land and resources. In the 1990s geographically specific issues, such as logging in Clayoquot Sound, Vancouver Island, and low-flight training in Labrador, etc., have received national attention. These and other events increasingly unite those concerned about human rights, Aboriginal peoples, and environmentalists in a common cause. Issues, such as the logging of old-growth forest, ultimately point to concerns at the core of the environmental movement: how production and consumption are practised in Western cultures.

Environmental Practice in Urban Landscapes

Rural and so-called 'natural' environments are not the only focus of the contemporary environmental movement. Environmentalists also have much to say about urban landscapes. By the late 1960s, children born in the small, semirural towns surrounding the major urban centres of southern Ontario were watching the conversion of farmland to acres of subdivision. The middle-class affluence of the 1960s added miles of freeways, many suburban shopping centres, and strips of highways lined with many automobile dealers, fast-food services, and discount retail stores. The logical progression of modern capitalist economies fostered criticism of the culture of consumption (Tester 1994: 85–6; Wachtel 1989).

In Vancouver, as in the urban centres of Ontario, residents watched a relatively new phenomenon appear on the urban skyline. High-rise apartment towers often created 'neighbourhoods' in which residents scarcely saw and hardly knew who was living next door (Gillis 1983). Mid- to low-income families' demand for housing gave impetus to cooperative housing initiatives. The oil boom of the 1970s recreated this explosion of urban landscapes on the Prairies, especially in Calgary and Edmonton, Alberta.

Residents of inner city neighbourhoods, particularly those characterized by lower incomes and older housing stock, were subjected to urban renewal. Century-old neighbourhoods became the targets of a form of 'development', which linked physical form to social problems. Epitomizing modernist assumptions, urban renewal swept away the chaos and clutter of old Victorian communities and replaced them with the predictability and clean lines of an expanding culture of business and technology. Opposition to these forms of urban development (much of it facilitated by community organizers and activists) generated new attempts to accommodate Canadians whose housing needs were outside market logic. These included experiments with socially mixed housing and the development of False Creek in Vancouver and the St Lawrence neighbourhood in Toronto (Pendakur 1987).

Other changes in the country's economic base profoundly affected community development. Typical of these changes was the rapid expansion of the British Columbia resource-based economy. By the late 1960s, the skyline of downtown Vancouver was inundated with office towers occupied by a new generation of young professionals, hence the progressive gentrification of Kitsilano, a neighbourhood on the south side of English Bay within easy access of the downtown core. Development plans for the neighbourhood ran up against 'the generation and the values which had fed counter-culture social movements' (Hasson and Ley 1994:243).

Most of this activity—much of it concerning the impact of changes to the physical landscape on neighbourhoods—developed independently of a rapidly expanding environmental movement.[11] While the themes for community development were many—poverty, housing, children's rights, community-based social services, community economic development, etc.—the underlying assumptions were derived from principles of and convictions about social and redistributive justice.

The status of community development work at the time is illustrated by reference to the content of *Community Work in Canada* (Wharf 1979). The categories used to organize the text (locality development, social action, and social planning) reflect a humanist agenda emphasizing the important role of human-centred convictions and social action in addressing the social needs and conditions of many Canadians. These needs were not met and were even exacerbated by the organization of power and the control of wealth in Canadian society (Buckbinder 1979). In the late 1970s the concerns of the environmental movement—which was engaged in battles against water and industrial pollution, acid rain, the proliferation of nuclear power, parks protection, and energy conservation—seemed peripheral to a community development focus on the distribution and redistribution of scarce social and economic resources.

However, throughout the 1980s the environmental movement increasingly considered urban landscapes. In 1995 the *New City Magazine*, a popular journal that has dealt with environmental considerations, planning, and community development in urban settings since 1973, described the urban environment to which its contributors are committed:

> The New City which we can consciously evolve from our present urban realities will be based upon the morality which can be derived from ecological principles and applied to preserve both its environmental and social integrity. It is not an objective construct to be achieved, but a comprehensive set of social, ecological, cultural and political processes . . . which are derived from the available local models of natural ecological processes (*New City Magazine* 1995:1).

The concept of sustainability thus provides a logical basis for planning (and community development) in urban and rural environments. This raises fundamental questions about urban/rural relationships, for example, the use of rural communities as disposal sites for urban refuse.

Environmental Constructs for Community Development

In the 1990s the integration of environmental considerations with all aspects of community development has new urgency. Not surprisingly, the expansion of Canadian capitalism has increasingly united issues of social justice and environment. Social justice can be increasingly regarded as a matter of environmental justice. This suggests that not only must we as workers, neighbours, ethnic minorities, women, poor people's alliances, etc., deal with questions of redistributive justice, we must do so in relation to the problem of sustainability (Gardner and Roseland 1989).

What principles, what sets of relations will ensure not only our survival and human development but the integrity of ecosystems and a future for our children? Where do community development workers locate themselves in relation to economic development projects that provide jobs but contribute to the destruction of old-growth forest or to air and water pollution? Will the community centre include activities and information that will assist neighbourhoods in protecting natural ecosystems, promoting sustainable lifestyles, and supporting practices consistent with ecological principles? In the interests of employment and alleviating poverty, as well as funding social programs, should the antipoverty and labour movements advocate a reduction in interest rates or the value of the dollar to promote forms of economic growth that are destroying the planet?

In the 1990s environmental realities highlight new and important concerns for community development initiatives. They also suggest a need for new theories linked to practice. While community development, which is grounded in theories of social justice, has historically failed to recognize ecological principles and the environmental limits of development, ecologically based community practice has struggled to integrate consideration for social relations and social justice with environmental realities. The 'jobs versus environment' debate and the development of sustainable practices in communities dependent on primary production are illustrative. Nowhere is this more evident than in the Canadian forest sector.

Similar relations require attention in urban settings. Roseland notes that 'Inequities undermine sustainable development, making it essential to consider the distributive effects of actions intended to advance sustainable development' (Roseland 1994:77). His observations on the outcome of community development practice, aimed at changing urban planning practices in the United States, are illustrative. He notes the effects of ordinances in the United States that were intended to protect environmental amenities. In some cases they drive up housing prices. Developments often 'leap-frog' over preserved open space, resulting in the creation of less expensive communities. The result is more commuting, traffic, and air pollution, which threaten the amenities that were originally meant to be protected.

Attempts to relate concerns for social justice to ecological realities are evident in some of the basic tenets of bioregionalism.

1. Biologically and culturally defined regions—bioregions—offer the best opportune spatial scale within which a great variety of forms of human governance and development can be practised;
2. Human governance within a bioregion should be democratic and responsible to local control, should nurture a high quality of life, and should be judged on its ability to achieve social justice;
3. Economic development within a bioregion should be locally regulated, use appropriate technology, focused on self-reliance with limited value-added export manufacturing, and should expand only to the extent that resident ecosystems can sustainably support exploitation[12] (Aberley 1993:9).

Further attempts to integrate principles of social justice with environmental considerations are being developed using critical theory and feminist scholarship. Carolyn Merchant, professor of environmental history, philosophy, and ethics at the University of California, summarizes these considerations as follows:

> The domination of external nature by internal nature exacts a cost. The unrestrained use of nature destroys its own conditions for continuation, as the inexorable expansion of capital undercuts its own natural resource base. Similarly, the repression of human emotions and animal pleasures leads not to human happiness but to anguish. But the tighter the rein, the greater the potential for rebellion. The revolt of nature is thus contained within the enlightenment project. Internal nature rebels psychically, spiritually, and bodily. External nature revolts ecologically. Here critical theory and the ecology movement intersect (Merchant 1994:4).

Internal nature also revolts politically. Documenting the historical role of men in this domination and articulating the recovery of human emotions and spirituality with regard to nature are concerns of ecofeminists and others within the environmental movement.[13] Men's domination of nature parallels their domination of women, an observation that provides the base for ecofeminist practice. As suggested by Merchant's observations about nature and critical theory, there are logical reasons why human development and social justice—concepts that have guided community development since the 1920s and the contemporary women's movement—must now, in an age of ecology, be joined with environmental principles.[14]

The concept of environmental justice bridges some of the differences in these theoretical foundations. A statement of 'Principles of Environmental Justice', produced by the First National People of Colour Environmental Summit in Washington, DC, enriches the social justice perspective, which has informed much community work in Canada. Commencing with a preamble that notes the environmental injustices that have particularly affected ethnic and racial minorities as well as the poor,[15] some of its tenets are:

> Environmental justice mandates the right to ethical, balanced and responsible uses of land and renewable resources in the interest of a sustainable planet for humans and other living things.
>
> Environmental justice demands the right to participate as equal partners at every level of decision-making including needs assessment, planning, implementation, enforcement and evaluation.
>
> Environmental justice affirms the right of all workers to a safe and healthy work environment, without being forced to choose between an unsafe livelihood and unemployment. It also affirms the right of those who work at home to be free from environmental hazards.
>
> Environmental justice opposes the destructive operations of multi-national corporations.
>
> Environmental justice calls for the education of present and future generations which emphasizes social and environmental issues, based on our experience and an appreciation of our diverse cultural perspectives (Hofrichter 1993:237–9).

The examination of community development experiences that integrate principles of social justice with environmental realities reveals the possibilities of redefining community development work in Canada. Two case-studies from British Columbia are illustrative.

Strathcona Community Gardens

The Strathcona community gardens are located in a neighbourhood south of Vancouver's downtown east side. In terms of income and tenancy, the area is an extension of the downtown east side, a neighbourhood that has been described as a 'landscape of marginality' (Hasson and Ley 1994:174).

Strathcona was named after Lord Strathcona, a founding director of the Canadian Pacific Railroad.

The neighbourhood continues to be a major site of Chinese settlement in Canada, with origins in the building of the transcontinental railway. The district, which is also home to many retired industrial workers and low-income families, also attracted Jewish and Ukrainian immigrants as well as other working-class people from eastern Europe. Strathcona is among the most culturally mixed and historically interesting neighbourhoods in Vancouver. It is also among the poorest. Hasson and Ley report that in 1986, which was the end of a deep recession in British Columbia, the census tract at the core of the district revealed that the male unemployment rate was 29 per cent, and that 80 per cent of unattached individuals were classified as low income (Hasson and Ley 1994:114–15).

The Strathcona community gardens are at the centre of an area formerly occupied by industrial warehouses and working-class housing. The site had been an industrial dump that was closed by the city but never cleaned up. In 1984 residents (mostly women in the community) approached the city's parks board to use the area for community gardens after tests revealed that there were no hazardous soils on the site. They were granted a one-year lease, which was extended to five years and has since been renewed.

Entering the garden is a remarkable experience. In addition to individual plots, the area includes a large orchard, herb garden, and a composting operation, which uses wastes from local organic restaurants and the Carnegie Centre, a community centre that serves the poor and transient populations in the downtown east side. The Carnegie Centre has its own plot in the garden along with over 100 others used by local residents. There is no fence around the site, which is liberally dotted with benches. The gardens give local residents a peaceful haven in the core of the city. The gardens are operated by a non-profit society whose board of directors uses a consensus model of decision making.

The whole experience of gardening—understanding and rehabilitating the soil, banning the use of herbicides and pesticides, dealing with a not entirely sympathetic city council, and linking the gardens to other centres and activities in the community—has put participants and organizers in touch with a host of other important community issues that they have subsequently addressed. The gardeners helped develop a coalition that killed plans to build a high-tech, environmentally unfriendly garbage-processing plant in Strathcona. Participants played a major role in stopping the spraying of herbicides in all Vancouver parks (Strathcona Community Gardeners 1992:118). The gardens have prompted the community to ask many other essential questions about modernity, such as how food is produced, how the ability to meet basic needs is necessary for individual and community well-being, and how socially and environmentally sustainable relations between people and the environment can be developed.

The Village of Hazelton

While the experience of the Strathcona community gardens illustrates the role of ecological principles and community action in an urban setting, the experience of the village of Hazelton demonstrates their relevance in a setting typical of many Canadian communities. The Canadian economy's commodity-based nature suggests the importance of considering environmental realities in community development practice.

Hazelton is a small, resource-dependent community of about 500 people at the centre of the Upper Skeena region of northwestern British Columbia. The region is mountainous and the surrounding area is the subject of a well-known land claim by the Gitksan and Wet'suwet'en peoples. The politics of the area have been described as ranging 'from arch-conservative to direct-action militant. Sometimes it is perceived that the word anarchy was invented to describe the curious blend of cooperation and friction that is the hallmark of local political interaction' (Maitland and Aberley 1992:93).

The history of Hazelton, like countless small communities across the country, is tied to the forest industry. In the 1950s modernization closed many small, locally owned sawmills and larger operators took over. These have sustained the community through periods of economic boom and collapse and noticeably increased resource exploitation. In the 1960s and 1970s the effects of clear-cutting became noticeable on surrounding slopes, and local people (especially the Gitksan and Wet'suwet'en) had their traditional lands and other activities in the bush threatened by a scale of logging that focused on maximizing production and short-term profit.

With the destruction of the community's central sawmill in the late 1960s, Hazelton began examining forestry practices in the region, which culminated in the realization that local control and management of the resource were important. In Hazelton, the 1970s gave rise to activism and dissent among the Gitksan and Wet'suwet'en. The non-Aboriginal community was also aware that the landscape was increasingly disfigured by clear-cutting and logging practices that adversely affected streams in the area. The Ministry of Forests' attempts to consult the community and accept feedback from an advisory committee on logging conditions were inadequate. Dissatisfaction with the use of resources and the development of the local economy increased when a local sawmill was closed and a timber license was awarded to a Prince George company for the region north of Hazelton in a process that bypassed the local chief forester.

Hazelton is a case of the local village council taking an active role in community development. With the assistance of a community planner committed to the principles of bioregionalism, the 'Forest Industry Charter of Rights' (later called 'A Framework for Watershed Stewardship') was developed, revised, and distributed within the region and throughout the province. This effort corresponded with other activities that addressed similar concerns, notably the development of the Forest Stewardship Act by the Tin Wis Coalition, a group representing Aboriginal peoples, labour, and environmentalists in the province.

Hazelton moved to change its municipal boundaries to incorporate the area's only sawmill so that tax revenues could be used for social and other purposes. The 'Framework for Watershed Stewardship' took an ecosystems approach in managing all forest-related resources (air, soil, and water). It proposed that the control of resources be done on a bioregional basis through the creation of watershed authorities. In response to public input, the document was later revised to include seventy-five principles of natural resource stewardship. These guided decisions affecting resources and activities in the region and enumerated principles of citizen involvement in determining how those resources should be managed. Similarly, the Forest Stewardship Act put forward by the Tin Wis Coalition advocated replacing the traditional top-down system of forest management with a new regime centred on elected community boards (Tester 1992:36).

Community development activities in places like Hazelton and groups like the Tin Wis Coalition have contributed to significant changes in the management of British Columbia's forests and in the processes for settling land disputes. As an exercise in community development, the Commission on Resources and Environment (CORE) has involved community and regional interests in attempts to resolve long-standing disputes about land use and conservation. The Forest Practices Code of British Columbia Act, which was passed in July 1994, fell short of the ideal of extreme decentralization contained in community initiatives. However, it reflected many of the sensibilities resulting from years of community organizing over forest practices in the province, including a summer of protests and 800 arrests over forest management practices and old-growth logging in Clayoquot Sound in 1993.

The new code moved the focus of forest management from fibre production consistent with a modernist agenda to a recognition of the diverse values and relationships with forest ecosystems in the province. The preamble to the legislation commits the province to the sustainable use of forests and, among other things, defines sustainable use as 'providing stewardship of forests based on an ethic of respect for the land, [and] balancing productive, spiritual, ecological and recreational values of forests to meet the economic and cultural needs of people and communities, including First Nations . . .'

While the impact of such legislation on actual practices remains to be seen, community development work on forestry issues in British Columbia has had a significant impact in changing the attitudes and practices of an industry that is at the core of British Columbia's society and economy. Community organizing over land use and forest issues has been relatively successful in helping to change human/environment relations.

Conclusion

These experiences illustrate many of the observations made earlier in the chapter. In the case of Hazelton, changes in the rural landscape alerted the community to issues that required their attention. The role of Aboriginal peoples, their land claims, and their alternative vision of what constitutes a forest contributed much to the debates and explorations within the community. As in the case of Strathcona community gardens, organizing over environmental concerns reveals not only features of material production that are often hidden from view but suggests that alternative social relations are essential to addressing social and environmental problems. Both are an important focus for community development practice.

The experience with community gardens in Strathcona and logging in Hazelton demonstrate 'that community empowerment comes not only from struggling against injustice, but also from proposing viable alternatives' (Maitland and Aberley 1992:98). At a community level, this self-identification of needs and solutions addresses what community developer John McKnight regards as the authoritarian definition of needs and the colonization of our individual and collective lives by institutionalized and state services (McKnight 1994:3–6). While the libertarian tone in McKnight's work raises questions about state responsibility for collective well-being, his observations suggest that community development in Canada, rather than merely defending existing social programs and initiatives, should continue to question how and by whom they are delivered. There are many alternatives that address issues of social justice and environment. The development of urban agriculture can address the basic food needs of the urban poor. Projects that encourage young people to map the environmental and social amenities in their neighbourhoods and communities can contribute to developing a sense of community and a responsibility for it. Citizens' groups are needed to monitor the impacts that transnational corporations (including those in the retail sector) are having on employment and the environment in communities across the country. The development of local currencies, credit, and labour exchange systems offer alternative possibilities for keeping resources, labour, and employment opportunities in local communities (Swann 1992:110–17).

The health of the country depends on how we relate to the resources from which Canadians make a living and whose revenues fund social and other programs. Social and community development workers should play important roles in mediating, organizing, and advocating over the management and allocation of natural resources and the nature of commodity production in the country. Commodities still form the base of the Canadian economy. In dealing with forest management, for example, community workers' skills are relevant in mediating among environmental groups, First Nations, and labour, and in organizing alternative forms of employment and advocating for community control of the resources upon which local populations depend. These skills can be exercised by working within environmental groups, participating in round-table discussions and other public processes, as well as contributing to the design and delivery of processes for public education and involvement.

The relative affluence and lifestyles of the 1980s have been hard on food and other cooperatives. However, with household incomes dropping in the 1990s while income disparities increase, cooperatives continue to offer important alternatives for the provision of food, shelter, and employment. The cooperative movement needs rejuvenation in the face of the economic realities in the 1990s. We must learn from historical experience. At the retail level, Bridgehead, Oxfam Canada's alternative trading and retail operation, models forms of trade and production that take environmental and social standards seriously. Bridgehead markets goods produced by suppliers in developing countries who manufacture them according to a code that respects the environment, justice, and human labour. Fair trade initiatives to label domestic and international goods in a manner respectful of the environment and human labour need to be organized. Public support for these initiatives and public education about the social and environmental effects of current production and consumption are critical in community development practice.

Underlying these initiatives is a critical need to change the way in which men relate to power and resources. There is also a need to address the terrifying domination of nature that characterizes the current global environmental crisis. The democratization of communities and management of the resources upon which we all depend—materially, socially, and spiritually—must reflect the imperative of redefining how we relate to one another, and how we relate to the planet upon which our survival depends.

Acknowledgements

Thanks to Roopchand Seebaran of the School of Social Work, University of British Columbia, and to Angela Smailes of Vancouver's Eco-City Network for comments and suggestions.

Notes

[1] A consistent source of readable information on the global environment is *State of the World* reports, published by the Worldwatch Institute in Washington, DC. Edited by Lester Brown and others, this series of yearly reports reveals the impact that global economic systems continue to have on the planet's ecosystems.

[2] For a brief history of citizen participation in Canada, especially the environmental movement as an important aspect of that history, see Tester (1992).

[3] Writing in *Ecofeminism*, Mies and Shiva borrow from a definition of ecofeminism provided by King, who writes: 'Ecofeminism is about connectedness and wholeness of theory and practice. It asserts the special strength and integrity of every living thing. [Devastation of the Earth and her beings is the result of] the same masculinist mentality which would deny [women] right to [their] own bodies and [their] own sexuality, and which depends on multiple systems of dominance and state power to have its way' (Mies and Shiva 1993:14). Mies and Shiva go on to acknowledge and discuss the tensions between spiritual and political expressions of ecofeminism.

[4] Perhaps state responses to the problems anticipated at the end of the Second World War should not be seen as 'unexpected'. In light of the dismantling of the welfare state in the 1990s, social workers and others should perhaps re-examine its origins. Within the confines of liberal pragmatism, the welfare state can be seen as a necessary adjunct to problems of capital accumulation at a particular historical moment and less relevant at other times (see Finkel 1977). This is why the Liberal Party can be responsible both for its development in the period 1945–71 and its dismantling in the 1990s.

[5] Several articles written by a *Globe and Mail* reporter, George Mortimore, document the impact of this approach. Writing in 1967, Mortimore began one of his articles entitled 'What Next?' with the line 'Canada's quiet long-suffering Indians are beginning to take a tougher line.' He continues:

> A federal community development officer had been working in Hay Lakes; … [the officer] had been encouraging the people to think, talk and decide what they wanted.

> This kind of encouragement is one reason for the new militancy. But there are drawbacks.
>
> Ottawa's Indian Affairs Branch says it wants Indians to take the initiative, but when the Indians do act vigorously, Government officials are inclined to panic. The Hay Lakes march, for example, touched off an official backlash that stripped federal community development workers of much of their independence (Mortimore 1967a:10).

[6]There are many indicators that by the late 1980s, environmental issues had become a major concern to most Canadians. A Gallup poll taken in February 1985 revealed that 51 per cent of Canadians believed pollution was a very serious problem. By March 1986 cuts to the budget and staffing of Environment Canada had generated 15,000 letters of protest (*Globe and Mail* 1986:A5). An Angus Reid poll in September 1988, prior to the federal election in November, indicated that 82 per cent of those surveyed wanted water pollution addressed, and 77 per cent of the same wanted stricter antipollution laws.

[7]While a new Clean Air Act was signed in the United States in November 1990, Canadian and American groups' lobbying of the US House of Representatives and Congress had far more to do with the outcome than the then Canadian prime minister's lame attempts at personal diplomacy with US President Ronald Reagan. The Canadian Environmental Protection Act had provisions for up to $1 million in fines and jail sentences for polluters, but the legislation was laced with ministerial discretion. In the seven-month period after it was passed, three firms were charged, one receiving a fine of $500, while over 300 companies had been found in violation of its provisions (*Toronto Star* 1989:A20).

Similarly, Ottawa backed away from the financial commitments made when the Green Plan was first announced, and by the time it was dropped by a subsequent Liberal administration, only a fraction of the money originally committed to addressing environmental issues had been spent. It has been suggested that the Green Plan contained surprisingly few measures to actually protect the environment, the majority of initiatives being to generate and disseminate information (Hoberg, Harrison, and Albert 1993:1).

[8]The 'idea of progress' in a Canadian context is examined by Robert Wright (1993). Wright's thesis on Canadian economics is important background for community development practice in Canada. Drawing upon the work of novelist Margaret Atwood, economist Harold Innis, and painter Alex Colville, Wright identifies those elements of Canadian cultural experience (local knowledge) that are essential to understanding both the possibilities and problems associated with community practice in Canada in an era that challenges modernist agendas and assumptions.

[9]In *Boundaries of Home*, Doug Aberley defines bioregionalism as 'a utilitarian mouthful of syllables [designating attempts] to wed dynamic human populations to distinct physical territories defined by continuities of land and life' (1993:3).

[10]The pivotal work often cited to illustrate growing recognition of the impacts of modernism on ecosystems is Rachel Carson's *Silent Spring* (1962). It dealt with the systemic implications of pesticides on the environment.

[11]An exception is energy-related concerns, triggered by OPEC's increase in the price of oil in 1973. This focused the attention of many environmentalists on urban design (housing and transportation systems).

[12]Limiting value-added production for export runs contrary to the suggestions put forward by other environmentalists and economists who advocate increasing the value-added component of production in the forest sector to maximize the jobs and benefits derived from timber production. Reconciling ecological considerations (countering policies that encourage exploitation through development of an export-oriented economy) with social considerations (maximizing employment) is not easy. Such considerations challenge community development workers attempting sustainable development within the logic of capitalist economic systems.

[13]Communal aspects of these relationships are illustrated in *Circles of Strength: Community Alternatives to Alienation*, edited by Helen Forsey (1993). The book focuses on intentional communities in which people have consciously chosen to live and work together, bound by mutual agreements and commitments to a particular place.

[14]In 'In an Age of Ecology: Limits to Voluntarism and Traditional Theory in Social Work' (Tester 1994) I have further explored the relevance of critical theory to social work practice and environmental issues. Domination is not the only relevant concept. A 'sense of place' is important to human health, safety, and identity—all concepts relevant to human development and considerations important to community development. Modernism alienates us from particular landscapes. 'The absence of [a locus in which I can be myself]—being constantly infused with a world made by Others—implies the loss of self, of safety, identity—an image that is truly my own' (Tester 1994:84). The emphasis in the bioregional movement on 'place' is thus critical to human development and ecologically informed community practice.

[15]An indication of the extent to which poverty, race, and class relate to environmental degradation can be found in an insightful collection of statements from citizens' groups across the United States (Highlander Research and Education Centre 1994).

References

Aberley, D., ed.
1993. *Boundaries of Home: Mapping for Local Empowerment*. Philadelphia, PA/Gabriola Island, BC: New Society Publishers.

Buckbinder, H.
1979. 'The Just Society Movement'. In *Community Work in Canada*, edited by B. Wharf, 129–52. Toronto: McClelland and Stewart.

Carson, R.
1962. *Silent Spring*. Boston: Houghton Mifflin.

Daly, H., and J. Cobb.
1994. *For the Common Good*. Boston: Beacon Press.

Finkel, A.
 1977. 'Origins of the Welfare State in Canada'. In *The Canadian State*, edited by
 L. Panitch, 344–70. Toronto: University of Toronto Press.

Forsey, H., ed.
 1993. *Circles of Strength: Community Alternatives to Alienation.* Philadelphia, PA/Gabriola
 Island, BC: New Society Publishers.

Gardner, J., and M. Roseland.
 1989. 'Thinking Globally: The Role of Social Equity in Sustainable Development'.
 Alternatives: Perspectives on Society, Technology and Environment 16, no. 3:26–34.

Gillis, A.
 1983. 'Strangers Next Door: An Analysis of Density, Diversity and Scale in Public
 Housing Projects'. *Canadian Journal of Sociology* 8, no. 1:1–20.

Globe and Mail.
 1986. 'Resource Extraction, Environmental Protection Both Urged' (13 March):A5.

Government of British Columbia.
 1994. *Forest Practices Code of British Columbia Act* (Bill 40, Chapter 41, Assented 8 July
 1994). Victoria: Queen's Printer for British Columbia.

Hasson, S., and D. Ley.
 1994. *Neighbourhood Organizations and the Welfare State.* Toronto: University of Toronto
 Press.

Highlander Research and Education Centre.
 1994. 'Environment and Development in the USA: A Grassroots Report for UNCED'.
 New Market, TN: Community Environmental Health Program of the Highlander
 Research and Education Center.

Hoberg, G., K. Harrison, and K. Albert.
 1993. 'The Politics of Canada's Green Plan'. Paper presented at the Annual Meeting of
 the Canadian Political Science Association, Ottawa, 6–8 June.

Hoff, M., and J. McNutt, eds.
 1994. *The Global Environmental Crisis: Implications for Social Welfare and Social Work.*
 Aldershot, UK: Avebury.

Hofrichter, R.
 1993. *Toxic Struggles: The Theory and Practice of Environmental Justice.* Philadelphia,
 PA/Gabriola Island, BC: New Society Publishers.

McKnight, J.
 1994. 'Ideas: Community and Its Counterfeits'. CBC Radio (Ideas) transcript, 3, 10, 17
 January.

Maitland, A., and D. Aberley.
   1992. 'Watershed Stewardship: The Village of Hazelton Experience'. In *Putting Power in Its Place*, edited by J. Plant and C. Plant, 91–9. Philadelphia, PA/Gabriola Island, BC: New Society Publishers.

Merchant, C., ed.
   1994. *Ecology: Key Concepts in Critical Theory.* Atlantic Highland, NJ: Humanities Press.

Mies, M., and V. Shiva.
   1993. *Ecofeminism.* London: Zed Books.

Mortimore, G.
   1967a. 'What Next?' *Globe and Mail* (28 October):10–11.

———.
   1967b. 'Caught between Cultures'. *Globe and Mail* (28 October):7–9.

New City Magazine.
   1995. 'Ecological Citizenship in the Bioregional Community: A Statement of Principles'. *New City Magazine* 16, no. 1:1.

Paehlke, R.
   1989. *Environmentalism and the Future of Progressive Politics.* New Haven/London: Yale University Press.

Pendakur, R.
   1987. 'Policy Analysis: Canadian Housing Policy and the Issue of Social Mix'. Master's thesis, Environmental Studies, York University, Toronto.

Roseland, M.
   1994. 'Ecological Planning for Sustainable Communities'. In *Futures by Design: The Practice of Ecological Planning*, edited by D. Aberley, 70–8. Philadelphia, PA/Gabriola Island, BC: New Society Publishers.

Ross, M.
   1955. *Community Organization: Theory and Principles.* New York: Harper and Brothers.

Strathcona Community Gardeners.
   1992. 'Gardening for a Change: Strathcona Community Gardens'. In *Living with the Land: Communities Restoring the Earth*, edited by C. Meyer and F. Moosang, 113–19. Philadelphia, PA/Gabriola Island, BC: New Society Publishers.

Swann, R.
   1992. 'The Need for Local Currencies'. In *Putting Power in Its Place*, edited by J. Plant and C. Plant, 110–17. Philadelphia, PA/Gabriola Island, BC: New Society Publishers.

Tester, F.
   1992. 'Reflections on Tin Wis: Environmentalism and the Evolution of Citizen Participation in Canada'. *Alternatives, Perspectives on Society, Technology and Environment* 19, no. 1:34–41.

————.

1994. 'In an Age of Ecology: Limits to Voluntarism and Traditional Theory in Social Work Practice'. In *The Global Environmental Crisis: Implications for Social Welfare and for Social Work*, edited by M. Hoff and J. McNutt, 75–99. Aldershot, UK: Avery.

————, and P. Kulchyski.

1994. *Tammarniit: Inuit Relocation in the Eastern Arctic, 1939–63*. Vancouver: University of BC Press.

Toronto Star.

1989. 'Only Three Firms Charged in 7 Months under Ottawa's "Tough" Pollution Law' (6 February):A20.

Wachtel, P.

1989. *The Poverty of Affluence: A Psychological Portrait of the American Way of Life.* Philadelphia, PA/Gabriola Island, BC: New Society Publishers.

Wharf, B., ed.

1979. *Community Work in Canada.* Toronto: McClelland and Stewart.

Wright, R.

1993. *Economics, Enlightenment and Canadian Nationalism.* Montreal and Kingston: McGill-Queen's University Press.

Chapter Thirteen

Campaign 2000 to End Child Poverty: Building and Sustaining a Movement

Rosemarie Popham, David I. Hay, and Colin Hughes

Introduction

In July 1996 the prime minister proudly announced the fact that, according to the United Nations, Canada again ranked number one in human development (United Nations Development Programme 1995). A month earlier, government silence was deafening when UNICEF reported that Canada was the seventeenth out of eighteen countries in the rate of child poverty (UNICEF 1996). The two reports from internationally recognized organizations make it obvious that while poor children live in poor families, they do not necessarily live in poor countries. Canada is failing its most vulnerable segment of the population—poor children. In doing so, we are failing to invest in our future.

Campaign 2000 is a Canadian social movement advocating for national policies to end child poverty in Canada. Since 1991—through research, advocacy, political lobbying, media events, partnership with a major retail business, and public education activities—Campaign 2000 has focused public attention on the more than 1.4 million poor children in Canada, one of the wealthiest countries in the world (Statistics Canada 1994).

In 1989 members of the House of Commons unanimously committed themselves 'to seek to achieve the goal of eliminating poverty among Canadian children by the year 2000' (House of Commons 1989). This chapter tells the story of Campaign 2000, a coalition of forty-nine organizations across Canada committed to the full implementation of the 1989 House of Commons all-party resolution.

Campaign 2000 is made up of nineteen national partners located in Ottawa or Toronto and thirty community partner organizations in every province. The forty-nine partners represent just about every interest in the not-for-profit sector, such as antipoverty groups, children's groups, housing, food banks, religious organizations, social planning, health, and immigrant women's organizations. All partners support the mission statement, principles, and goals of Campaign 2000; distribute information about child poverty produced by Campaign 2000; and hold public education events and take part in political lobbying around the time of the release of the *Child Poverty in Canada* report card on 24 November of each year, which is the anniversary of the all-party resolution to end child poverty.

We tell the story of Campaign 2000 as a conversation among three partners. We try to answer three questions:

1. What are some key strategies of Campaign 2000?
2. As there are only three years left before the year 2000, what has Campaign 2000 done to ensure the implementation of the all-party resolution?
3. Did we follow basic community development values?

Each of us has been involved with Campaign 2000 since its early days. We are: Rosemarie Popham, director of social action for the Family Service Association of Metro Toronto and national coordinator for Campaign 2000; David Hay, senior research associate for the Social Planning and Research Council (SPARC) of BC, a Campaign 2000 provincial partner; and Colin Hughes, a community worker with the Children's Aid Society of Metro Toronto and the chairperson for Metro Campaign 2000, a community partner. We wrote this article by telephone, fax, 'travelling discs', and e-mail. This typifies the long-distance collaborative work of the campaign. Although we have been part of this same campaign for five years, the three of us have never met together. While this chapter has three voices, it still greatly understates the complexity and vitality of community development in a cross-Canada social movement. Campaign 2000's partners across Canada would each have unique stories to contribute. We also omit a number of strategies. For simplicity—and consistency with all partners' annual commitment—we have chosen to talk about strategies that focus on 24 November, the date on which all partners agree to draw attention to child poverty.

Campaign 2000 is a functional community (or a community of interest) rather than a geographic community (or a community of locale). The partners are committed to addressing the issue of child and family poverty and believe that the federal government has a responsibility to honour the all-party resolution to end child poverty.

Community development involves people (directly or through organizations) taking democratic control by participating in planning, bottom-up decision making, and community action. The process and outcomes of community development reflect common values, conflict, and compromise, and the shifting of power to the community. Community development values include equality, caring, sharing, and a commitment to social justice (SPARC of BC 1995).

What Are Some Key Strategies of Campaign 2000?

Five strategies provide examples of the unique character of Campaign 2000, both in their impact and their reflection of community development values. These are:

- developing a community partners network

- establishing a crossnational, annual event on 24 November

- forming a partnership with Body Shop Canada in a public education campaign

- organizing a public education campaign during the 1993 federal election

- sending a letter from high-profile Canadians to Prime Minister Chrétien

Developing a Community Partners Network

After years of public education and lobbying the federal government by groups like the Child Poverty Action Group, the Canadian Council on Social Development, and the Canadian Council on Children and Youth, a resolution was finally passed unanimously in the House of Commons of Canada to eliminate child poverty in Canada by the year 2000. Representatives of the three official parties spoke passionately to the resolution. It was moved by Ed Broadbent, leader of the New Democratic Party, seconded by the Progressive Conservative Minister of Youth Jean Charest, and defended eloquently by Liberal Member of Parliament Lloyd Axworthy. At the time the economy was strong, unemployment rates were the lowest they had been in two decades, and average incomes were slowly rising (Child Poverty Action Group et al. 1994). Economists were optimistic that we were embarking on a boom period. However, we were at the end of an economic recovery and on the brink of a recession.

Shortly after the 1989 all-party resolution, several organizations with long histories of commitment to child poverty developed a plan to focus public attention on the government's commitment to end child poverty. They agreed that it was essential to build a coalition beyond the handful of national groups traditionally associated with child poverty, hence it was decided to develop a network of grassroots, community-based groups committed to public education and political action against child poverty. The development of the network was significant for a number of reasons:

- Canadians had become sceptical of large organizations, whether they were business, labour, government, or the voluntary sector.

- We could create an echo effect regarding child and family poverty if local organizations across the country were clearly committed to the same goal, regardless of their provincial or sectoral affiliations.

- A broad-based coalition would add to our legitimacy and prevent the campaign from being dismissed by politicians as a single 'self-serving interest group'.

To build the network of community partners, and to agree on policy directions and national action, Campaign 2000 representatives held thirteen policy soundings. The soundings provided an opportunity to hear the views of agency representatives and poor people regarding child poverty and the federal government's role in addressing it. In July 1991 SPARC agreed to convene a BC policy sounding, facilitated by a Campaign 2000 representative. Campaign 2000 provided funds to cover expenses of the meeting. People experiencing poverty or interested in poverty issues and representatives of groups working on poverty issues participated. BC participants outlined a number of issues:

- There were hungry children in the school system.

- The loan system for funding university students threatened 'perpetual debt' for poorer families.

- The nature of employment was changing (i.e., more unstable, low-wage, part-time employment), as well as family structure (i.e., more single-parent families).

- The public provision of health and social services was threatened by federal cut-backs.

- There was cynicism about the federal government's policies and direction (e.g., free trade and social benefit 'harmonization' with the US).

At the same time, participants agreed on the conditions that would be essential if children and their families were to fulfil their potential: control over their own lives; adequate and equitable family incomes; access to housing, food, and health care; community sustainability; and the restoration of hope, purpose, and dignity to the lives of all Canadians. Participants also had suggestions for Campaign 2000:

- Involve children as spokespersons.

- Make materials accessible and easy to understand.

- Have materials that dispel the myths about poverty and poor people.

- Promote collaboration among social service/social policy 'professionals' and low-income people.

- Involve low-income people in decision making and communication roles.

- Focus energies on education and action, not on more research.

- Make it clear that the campaign's focus on child poverty does not deny the importance of eliminating poverty for *all* Canadians.

The Metro Action Group on Child Poverty organized a local Campaign 2000 sounding in September 1991. No community development story begins at a precise moment, and this was particularly true for Campaign 2000 in Metro Toronto. The Metro Action Group had formed earlier as a network of organizations and volunteers to address the child poverty issue locally. Campaign 2000 offered the potential for these organizations to work within a more broadly based strategy.

About twenty people from various parts of the voluntary sector attended the Metro sounding. Most of them had not been previously involved with the Metro Action Group. They urged the campaign to include low- and middle-income adults, children, and youths from all cultural groups. They also advocated for national policy initiatives, including full employment, progressive taxation, universal child benefits, housing, and access to postsecondary education and child care.

The Metro Action Group merged with other interested people from the community sounding to form Metro Campaign 2000. Sustaining Metro Campaign 2000 has involved considerable outreach, education, and network-building activity.

The BC and Metro soundings were two of thirteen that took place across Canada. After each sounding, a report was sent back to participants for verification and revision. A summary document was then sent to all participants as a basis for a national policy sounding, to be held in Ottawa in October 1991. Representatives from each of the local soundings were invited. An invitation to prospective participants stated that the objectives of the national policy sounding were threefold: (1) to move from local perspectives and to discuss and agree on national policy directions for the eradication of child and family poverty; (2) to determine how the network members would communicate and work with each other; and (3) to decide on strategies for public education and action on child and family poverty.

Campaign 2000 was able to provide money for two people from each province to attend. The BC group felt that two low-income people without other financial resources should be funded. Four additional people attended with other funding sources. As all thirty participants were deeply committed to the issues, and as this was the first time the group had ever been together, anxieties arose over how and by whom decisions would be made. Although the sources of these anxieties were broad and diffuse, two areas—policy content and direction, and the management of campaign funds—provided grounds for the most lengthy debates.

For example, some community participants from BC were concerned about new policy directions developed by professionals that may not incorporate the perspectives of low-income people. With regard to funding, community participants who did not have other resources to participate in the provincial and national soundings felt uncomfortable asking that their expenses (e.g., child care, buses, taxis) be covered by the organizers. They felt that professionals didn't understand the realities of life for low-income people. As is common with endeavours of this kind, we underestimated the costs of getting the campaign off the ground. It was clear that if we were to involve low-income people as partners in Campaign 2000, these people had to feel comfortable and confident about their contribution to the direction of policy statements being developed, and especially about their financial situations, if they were to be fully involved.

As well as understanding realities for low-income people at the local level, we also needed to be aware of the culture and realities of national voluntary sector organizations. Each national partner involved in the national policy sounding brought its own issues, mandates, and constituency needs to the sounding. Each was also responsible for reporting back to its board, which introduced a further layer of accountability, bureaucracy, and ownership.

Our attempts to develop a policy agreement among thirty people and organizations at the national policy sounding in Ottawa were indeed challenging. Despite extensive consultation over the summer, preparation of drafts based on community soundings, participation in workshops, and meetings of the entire group in plenaries over two days, disagreement limited the consensus we could establish.

The conflict reflected locally and regionally specific concerns, commitment to short- versus long-term solutions, divergent views of the roles of various levels of government and community, the newness of the venture and the lack of trust between people who shared a concern but had no history as a coalition, and different views of how government resources should be used. For example, one disagreement between professionals and representatives of poverty groups was over universal versus targeted programs. The former favoured universal, while the latter felt this approach was wasteful and that funds should be targeted to the poor. Each of these factors attested to the reality that policy formation is extremely complex, involves many participants, takes place over a long period, and usually consists of innumerable decisions. Given all of these challenges, it was heartening that we were able to agree on a declaration whose goals and principles have become the touchstone of the work we have done since. The goals of the campaign on which we all agreed were to:

1. raise and protect the basic living standards of families in all regions of the country, so that no Canadian child would ever live in poverty
2. improve the life chances of all children in Canada so they can fulfil their potential and nurture their talent, and become responsible and contributing members of Canadian society
3. ensure the availability of secure, adequate, affordable, and suitable housing as an inherent right of all children in Canada
4. create, build, and strengthen family supports and community-based resources in order to empower families so they can provide the best possible care for their children (Campaign 2000 1991).

The most telling moment of tension between low-income people and participants was when, after many hours of working together, just before the final agreement on the declaration, a low-income participant asked, 'Tell me again who you are and what you know about poverty.' Ultimately, there was a healthy pragmatism that dominated, a feeling that we were all in this together, and that we all have skills and experience to contribute. This was a vital community development experience for Campaign 2000. While we could not agree, for example, on whether children should be required to wear uniforms to school in order to eliminate pressure on low-income parents to buy designer clothes, we did agree that no idea would be shelved because of who put it forward, and that no idea would go forward without general support. A culture of respect and a shared vision was established.

BC's decision to involve lower-income people who were active in social change points to the value and challenge of building broader alliances and perspectives. We need many other 'cultures' (e.g., self-advocacy groups, labour, faith, parents, youths etc.) or perspectives to build a policy community. We also need to value, and have valued, our own perspectives as workers (who are as much a job loss away from poverty as anyone), or as child care workers (who are among the lowest paid occupations), and as parents.

From a community development perspective, building trust among the partners in Campaign 2000 was crucial. It was important to give people time to get to know each other. We also tried to build quickly on our areas of agreement, as taking action on areas of mutual concern helped to build cohesion.

The national policy conference of Campaign 2000 took place the weekend before a major conference in Ottawa called Canada's Children, organized by the Child Welfare League. Canada's Children attracted 350 delegates from across Canada from all sectors and all levels of government. This venue was an opportunity for Campaign 2000 to build broader networks and to test some of our ideas with others. The final meeting with MPs on Parliament Hill, to whom the conference recommendations were presented, was also the first opportunity to hold the MPs publicly accountable for the 1989 all-party resolution.

Establishing a Crossnational, Annual Event on 24 November

On 24 November 1991, the second anniversary of the all-party resolution, we sent each MP a copy of our Campaign 2000 declaration, and in a media conference at the House of Commons we announced our intention to monitor the implementation of the 1989 all-party resolution. Gerald Caplan of the *Toronto Star* captured the chronic dilemma of any group seeking media attention—competition with other issues that are deemed by print editors and electronic producers as more newsworthy. Alluding to the resignation of the cochair of the Constitution Committee on the same day as the launch of Campaign 2000, Caplan wrote:

> The competing announcement (the news of Claude Castonguay's resignation) the same day as the launching of Campaign 2000 to end the 'national disgrace' of child poverty in Canada was deemed far less newsworthy, in fact barely newsworthy at all. Which makes one wonder: What are the priorities of this Canada we're trying so hard to save? (*Toronto Star* 1991).

With supporting material from the national office of the campaign, SPARC took the lead role in the BC network and distributed a media release announcing the launch of Campaign 2000 to Vancouver papers, provincial radio stations, and community papers and radio stations in other parts of the province. The strong media coverage was the result of the BC network's links to the national campaign. Having a local angle to a national story was a persuasive media hook.

On 24 November 1991 Metro Campaign 2000 participated in the launch of Campaign 2000 by holding a fax-a-thon. After the national partners released the Campaign 2000 declaration at a news conference and to MPs in Ottawa, Metro Campaign 2000 developed a simple letter for constituents to send to their MPs. The letter asked the MP to send the constituent a copy of the Campaign 2000 declaration and tell the constituent what he or she thought about it. In this way the MPs would be encouraged to read the declaration, comment on it, and help distribute it. This seemed a feasible activity. The letter was distributed widely through our networks so that most MPs received at least one letter, and some responded. Follow-up with MPs did not occur due to breakdown in preliminary plans and lack of resources.

Early in 1992, members of the BC Campaign 2000 network met to update people on the status of the campaign, and to discuss how BC participants wanted to focus their energies. BC participants noted that although their organizations were working on issues of poverty every day, they felt that it was important to stay involved with Campaign 2000. People could easily recognize the success of Campaign 2000 activities to date.

However, BC participants also noted that indicators of success in community development have to include the process as well as the result. They felt that the ongoing development of Campaign 2000 could be strengthened. In particular, they felt that the policy development process could be further democratized and have greater involvement from low-income people. As well, particular attention had to be given to the need for adequate resources to achieve the objectives of the campaign, especially to fund broad community participation.

This was the resource reality. Campaign 2000 was (and still is) operating on a shoestring budget. Every penny is required to maintain the involvement of the partners, ensure information flow between national and community partners, and monitor and report on child poverty each 24 November. After extensive consultation between partners, we decided that having a product for public education was a priority. Unless we were able to monitor and report on child poverty, the coalition would have no use, regardless of the level of shared trust, caring, and commitment.

In a memorandum from the national partners to all community partners in February 1992, a new direction for the campaign was proposed. We would develop a social report card of key trend indicators to illustrate the economic, social, health, education, and housing status of families with children in

Canada. As well, policy targets would be developed to address the direction needed to change the status of poor families with children. A proposal for a Campaign 2000 newsletter completed the central elements of the new direction. Community partners were asked for their comments.

At the time the BC network was less than thrilled with the focus of activities outlined in the proposal. We were concerned that a social report card approach would place too great an emphasis on monitoring the status quo and less emphasis on developing policy proposals that would lead to the alleviation of poverty. What we failed to recognize then (but appreciate now) is the value of the report card, which was ultimately developed to promote credible research findings for supporting the work of Campaign 2000.

To try to ensure a respectful community development process among the partners, early in 1992 we hired a part-time community partners coordinator whose position was funded for fifteen months. She invested time in building the community partner network through a newsletter called *Campaign 2000 Countdown*, regular phone calls to the thirty community partners to support them in their work, and facilitating the information flow between national and community partners.

The national coordinator, the only ongoing paid staff person for Campaign 2000, builds and sustains the partners' network; staffs the national partners' meetings four times a year; fundraises, promotes and coordinates media contacts; responds to public enquiries; arranges and staffs all meetings with politicians and bureaucrats in Ottawa; prepares briefs and presents them (with partners) to federal standing committees and international bodies; does public speaking; writes articles related to child poverty; coordinates the report card development with the Centre for International Statistics; and oversees events related to 24 November and the release of the report card. All this is done in two days per week! Since funding for the community partners coordinator ended, the nurturing of the partners has received short shrift. The vitality, which still exists among the partners, is a result of the solid preliminary work we did together, the clarity of our mission, and our shared commitment to 24 November when we all participate in a child poverty-related event in our own communities. The campaign would have foundered many times if the partners had not gone out of their way to use their own expertise, time, resources, and persistence to keep the issue of child poverty in the public eye.

National Report Card, 1992

The first national report card on child poverty was released on 24 November 1992. Partners were encouraged to issue a local press release about child and family poverty and to release the 1992 report card to their members and supporters. By this time, we had increased our national partners from three to thirteen and had established a stable base of thirty community partners.

Report cards are researched by the Centre for International Statistics at the Canadian Council on Social Development. They are based on the most recent data regarding levels of poverty, international comparisons, life expectancy, food bank use, employment rates, etc. Our target audience for 40,000 report cards consists primarily of academic, religious organizations, professional, and government representatives. Each partner receives report cards for distribution within its own sector or constituency.

Media response to the 1992 report card was extensive, and child poverty in Canada was the lead story on CBC Radio and CBC and Global Television News nationally. The *Financial Post*, the *Globe and Mail*, the *Toronto Star*, the *Ottawa Citizen*, the *Vancouver Sun*, and many other daily newspapers covered the report card on 25 November.

Metro Campaign 2000 Report Card, 1993

Metro Campaign 2000, together with MPs from the federal subcommittee on poverty, organized a community forum and approached the Council of Metropolitan Toronto to pass a resolution in support of the 1989 federal resolution. Council passed a resolution, and referred it to Metro's Community Services to develop a blueprint for addressing child poverty.

The blueprint has never been developed, even though we have contacted the policy people at Metro. Part of the reason may be that the recession and the cap on the federal Canada Assistance Plan was starting to take its toll on Metro, resulting in huge costs to the province and Metro as a result of escalating welfare caseloads. Metro was more interested in reducing costs and cutting its budgets than addressing the human costs of child and family poverty. Metro is now, however, organizing a task group on children.

Metro Campaign 2000 participated in local media coverage of the first national report card. We had a fact-sheet on child poverty with indicators culled from a variety of sources. Our estimates for Metro were higher than national estimates, which drew local interest. However, the estimates were based on outdated and perhaps debatable information. Rather than waiting for 24 November 1993, Metro Campaign 2000 decided to design a local report card (similar to the national one) using local indicators of child poverty to draw attention to child and family poverty in the federal election slated for October 1993 and to report on the voting records of Metro's MPs on key social policy bills. To finance the production and printing, we approached local organizations involved with the campaign for donations and raised about $2,500.

It is amazing how little useful information we have on the well-being of families with children. This probably reflects the view that family life is largely a private matter. Despite all the money that goes into income support, social services, etc., there was very little data to contribute to community understanding at a Metro level. With the able research assistance of the Metro Social Planning Council, we found that unemployment in Metro had increased two-and-a-half times in the past five years, and that waiting lists for day care had increased over five times, but the most interesting finding was that, by 1993, as many as one in three Metro children living at home lived on social assistance.

The policy side of the Metro Campaign 2000 report card had pictures of Metro MPs and their voting records on bills regarding the Canada Assistance Plan, unemployment insurance, child benefits, and child care. It explained the programs and the impact of the cuts. The Metro report card was released at a news conference during the federal election and received substantial media coverage. About 10,000 report cards were distributed to all politicians through networks, at all-candidates meetings, and even in subways and under the windshield wipers of cars.

The Body Shop Canada's Public Education Campaign, 1993

The Body Shop makes and sells non-animal-tested skin and hair products. It prides itself on being a responsible corporate citizen and, until 1993, had conducted extensive in-store public awareness campaigns on environmental issues. Following the release of the 1992 report card, The Body Shop approached Campaign 2000 to ask if we would be interested in being a partner in a public education campaign on child poverty. While there was no doubt that The Body Shop cared about the issue, the president of The Body Shop Canada was also on the board of the Family Service Association of Metropolitan Toronto, one of the partner organizations in the campaign, and was therefore familiar with the work and credibility of the research we undertook. For The Body Shop in Canada, this would be their first campaign focusing on a social issue; for Campaign 2000, the offer presented a huge opportunity as well as a conundrum.

Partners had different views on forming partnerships with business. There was a healthy debate among national, provincial, and community partners over such questions as who would be supporting whom, how the partnership would work, and what the campaign hoped to accomplish. Partners were cautious of the voluntary, 'cash-strapped' sector allowing ourselves to be exploited by the corporate, 'cash-rich' sector. Partners did not want Campaign 2000 to be used to boost the profile of a business to increase its sales. Again, the issue of trust arose and partners were wondering if The Body Shop was really concerned about poverty.

Ultimately, partners in all areas with The Body Shop stores took part in the two-phase public awareness campaign. Called the Light a Fire campaign, activities included displaying two mammoth window posters for three weeks each. T-shirts with the slogans 'I Am Your Future, You Are Mine' and 'Light a Fire under the Powers That Be' were sold in all of the stores. Each store linked up with a child poverty organization in its community, and $2 from the sale of every t-shirt was donated to this local group. The second phase of the campaign was timed to coincide with the federal election. Postcards in all stores were filled out by customers and sent to elected representatives at all three levels of government, urging them to act on the issue of child poverty.

BC network members worked closely with The Body Shop stores on a wide range of activities. All the activities were public participation events that involved speakers and displays on the issue of child poverty. Representatives of business and government, low-income people, and many people from community organizations working on poverty issues participated. For example, SPARC worked with The Body Shop store in a prominent downtown Vancouver mall to stage an afternoon tea with speakers on poverty issues and a focus on low-income, single (mostly teen) mothers. As well, media releases, information tables in shopping malls, postcard signings, and 'letters to your MP' campaigns were all undertaken.

The Body Shop/Campaign 2000 partnership was valuable for its public education potential, and for involving business in the network of education and action on poverty. Campaign 2000 received letters, phone calls, and even donations from people who stated that before The Body Shop campaign, they had not thought about child poverty in a country as wealthy as Canada. Today, many employees of The Body Shop continue to be involved in volunteer work with local organizations serving poor children.

MPs bombarded with postcards from their constituents were forced to acknowledge child poverty and to respond to their local constituents with much greater attention than they would have otherwise to a faceless, national, Ottawa-based organization.

The Body Shop/Campaign 2000 partnership provided national media exposure for child poverty, which we could not have garnered on our own. CBC Radio's 'Morningside' program interviewed Margot Franssen, The Body Shop president, about corporate social responsibility. Campaign 2000 and child poverty issues were a prominent part of the discussion between Franssen and 'Morningside' host, Peter Gzowski, whereas our own efforts to appear on 'Morningside' had never resulted in even mild interest in child and family poverty. Having corporate interest in the issue was an advantage we had lacked. Metro Campaign 2000 was intrigued with the novel partnership between The Body Shop and Campaign 2000, and participated by getting the word out and having people sign postcards.

The 1993 Federal Election and the Public Education Campaign

Like every other public interest group, Campaign 2000 hoped that the 1993 federal election would be an opportunity to draw public and political attention to our issue. We provided each Campaign 2000 partner with a federal election kit, which included suggestions for working with the media during the election campaign and holding an all-candidates meeting with a focus on child poverty. Local partners in Campaign 2000 also asked each candidate to sign an endorsement of the 1989 all-party resolution. One of the Campaign 2000 community partners was a guest on the televised leaders debate. In that forum she asked Jean Chrétien, the Liberal leader, how he would address child poverty. Mr Chrétien referred back to the Red Book's promise of jobs as the solution.

The week after the election of the Liberal government, The Body Shop delivered 80,000 postcards to the new government in front of the House of Commons. They brought a specially painted bus filled with staff and postcards to the event, which provided great 'visuals' for the media. While our poster campaign with The Body Shop Canada ended at that point, they have continued to support Campaign 2000, and in 1995 provided a grant through The Body Shop Foundation, which was crucial for the production of the 1995 national report card. This report card, the bleakest yet, indicated that child poverty had increased 55 per cent since the 1989 all-party resolution. In 1995, in addition to the report card, we also released an eight-minute video, which brought the report card to life. All partners received a copy of the video to help them with local outreach and education.

Development of a Policy Perspective, 1994

After the release of our 1993 report card, it became abundantly clear that if Campaign 2000 was to be more than a reactive national lament, we needed to be more specific about our policy solutions. Consequently, in 1994 the Child Poverty Action Group developed a policy perspective, which was adopted by

Campaign 2000. This document, entitled *Investing in the Next Generation*, was released on Canada Day, 1994. It proposed a life-cycle strategy for families with children, advocating for initiatives that would benefit vulnerable, modest-income families, as well as the poor. It also proposed a social investment fund to pay for these programs. The fund would include revenues from existing government programs for families with children, employer taxes, corporate taxes, and an additional citizen tax (Campaign 2000 1994). The print media publicized the release with headlines such as, 'More Young Growing Up Poor' (*Ottawa Free Press*), 'Canada's Future in Peril Because of Child Poverty' (*Vancouver Sun*), 'Child Insurance Pushed for Canada' (*Halifax Chronicle Herald*). In addition, each partner had a twenty-page document outlining Campaign 2000's solutions, which built on the original principles and goals agreed to by the partners in 1991. This document has provided a framework to move into the policy arena with some assurance. In 1994 the document became a focus of our policy solutions presented in the 1994 report card.

When we released the 1994 national report card, we were old hands at it, but we were also in danger of becoming 'old news'. As Karen Webb of CBC TV remarked, 'An increase in child poverty isn't news. A year ago social policy ideas might have been news, but with social security reform [of the federal government] everybody's [coming up with ideas for solutions]'.

The report cards are in high demand by governments, students, professional organizations, media, and people who hear about us in indirect ways. They have been a critical tool for Campaign 2000. At both the local and national levels, our advocacy and policy work needed real data to back up our arguments for change. Without the data (sometimes even with the data), we were in danger of being branded as a special interest group with an axe to grind, and would lose credibility.

Metro Campaign 2000 Report Card, 1994

In Metro, in addition to other media work, we assisted a *Toronto Star* team with a special eight-page insert on child poverty, which appeared the weekend before the release of the 1994 report card. They were also put in touch with other community partners in Ontario. With the support of a provincial teachers' association for production and distribution, we also developed a brochure for educators on child poverty related to the UN Convention on the Rights of the Child, and suggested activities to mark the fifth anniversary of the 1989 federal resolution.

The 1994 Metro report card included new indicators, the impact of the federal social security review, and noted the contradictory response by all levels of government in addressing child poverty. In Ontario, for example, the then NDP government was reaching the end of its term and was stalling on important reforms, especially regarding child care and social assistance (which were never carried out). The Metro report card received considerable media coverage. There seemed to be interest in the local dimensions of the national issue of child poverty. For example, the 24 November article in the *Toronto Star* was headlined 'Child Poverty Exploding in Canada, Activists Say'. While the headline dealt with the national report, the content and analysis was focused primarily on Metro findings. Also, the *Globe and Mail* coverage quoted both SPARC and Metro Campaign 2000.

Metro Campaign 2000's Report Card, 1995

In Metro Toronto throughout 1995 and spring 1996, the prospects for children became dimmer as federal and provincial politics took a radical swing to the right. The deceitful federal strategy of equating social policy reform with deficit reduction was carried to new heights in Minister of Finance Paul Martin's 1995 budget. In a single budget he had managed to gut and forever change Canada's national social security system. There was an Ontario election that resulted in a Conservative government committed to implementing radical cuts to welfare recipients' benefits and social services, instituting workfare, and creating huge tax breaks benefiting the most wealthy. From a social policy perspective, these developments are ugly and dispiriting. But over this time there has also been increased policy activism and greater awareness of the dangers these policy directions pose to children and communities.

In Metro Campaign 2000's 1995 report card—for which *Today's Parent* magazine provided the artwork and layout at no charge—we highlighted the massive withdrawal of the federal government from the social policy field, and the terrible impact of the provincial government's policies on children. On the flip side of the report card (which is in a poster format) we have a picture of children and a simple message stating 'We Can't Afford Child Poverty'. The poster has been displayed by sympathetic allies throughout Metro. The content of the report card has been cited in editorials, in Metro Hall, and the Queen's Park legislature.

For the release of the report card, we organized and held a news conference at Queen's Park, which was immediately followed by a full day of community hearings on public policy directions, child poverty, and the UN Convention on the Rights of the Child. The rationale was simple. In the absence of any sense of moral obligation among Canadian politicians towards children, we invoked the international Convention (to which Canada and the provinces are signatories). In the absence of any domestic mechanism to implement and monitor the provisions of the Convention (which includes, among many rights, the right to an adequate standard of living) we invented a mechanism at the community level. We brought together a panel from UNICEF Canada and flew in the senior adviser on children's rights from New York. About twenty presentations were given by children, parents, community leaders (including the mayor of Toronto), and academics. We compiled the presentations into a brief of over 100 pages and sent it as a grievance to the Centre for Human Rights in Geneva and to the federal and provincial governments. UNICEF noted that this was the first hearing of its kind in any industrialized nation. The event and report card received good news coverage, including an article in the 25 November 1995 *Globe and Mail*, which had the headline 'Rights Violated, UN Adviser Says'.

Metro Campaign 2000 has been increasingly active in 1996 with deputations, workshops, news conferences, letters and submissions on Metro, and provincial and federal policy developments. We have new allies, including the municipalities who are concerned about the impact of cuts.

BC Campaign 2000

Although limited resources in BC and nationally have not facilitated the broader participation of low-income people in Campaign 2000 activities, SPARC has continued as an active partner in Campaign 2000. Throughout 1992–5, the BC Campaign 2000 network acted as an information support and distribution link between individual members and organizations, and as an information and advocacy source for the media, students, academics, government, community organizations, and the public at large. SPARC also served as the contact for BC contributions to *Campaign 2000 Countdown*, the campaign's newsletter, and remains an important contact for work with the national office.

SPARC continues to promote awareness of child and family poverty through media releases, print, radio and television interviews, and speaking engagements with community groups; commentary on federal and provincial budgets; a presentation to the Parliamentary committee hearings on social security reform, etc.

In 1995 the BC Campaign 2000 network joined forces with First Call, a provincial child and youth advocacy coalition. First Call wanted to increase public and political awareness of child and family poverty. The BC Campaign 2000 network is now a larger, more diverse and committed group working on child and family poverty issues. The pervasiveness of poverty's effects throughout society is gaining wider recognition, accompanied by an increased realization that urgent action is required.

For the first time, BC Campaign 2000 produced a BC provincial report card to coincide with the release of the 1995 national report card on 24 November. For the BC report card, we sent a letter to all BC federal members of Parliament, asking them to endorse the 1989 House of Commons resolution, and to specify at least one action that their party is taking to end child poverty in BC. The MPs' replies to the letter are documented on one side of the BC report card, with BC child poverty-related statistics on the other.

BC Campaign 2000 held a news conference to release the 1995 Campaign 2000 report cards. At the conference we presented an overview of both the provincial and national report cards, and gave brief presentations on child poverty perspectives (i.e., from parents, youths, teachers, and a journalist). Linda McQuaig, best-selling Canadian author and journalist, was in Vancouver to speak about her latest book. She generously agreed to participate in our news conference, and presented her perspective on child poverty.

Energetic preconference work by network members generated substantial media interest, and over a dozen major media outlets (print, radio, and television) attended the conference. As a result of our news conference, network members were interviewed for news clips, and participated in radio and TV interviews and radio call-in shows. A number of articles on Campaign 2000 and child poverty also appeared over the following week.

BC Campaign 2000 is planning another news conference with both BC and national report cards for November 1996. We are also producing a Campaign 2000 community action kit, which will include the report cards and information on Campaign 2000, as well as ideas for organizing a Campaign 2000 work group in people's own communities.

Letter from High-Profile Canadians to Prime Minister Chrétien

When it was time to release the 1995 report card, we felt we needed a demonstration of support to persuade Prime Minister Chrétien to commit to federal leadership in combating child poverty. We asked fifty accomplished Canadians across the country to sign a letter asking the prime minister to make ending child poverty a priority. Thanks to their provincial networks, the partners were invaluable in persuading people as diverse as Andrew Coyne of the *Globe and Mail* editorial board (from central Canada), David Suzuki (from the West Coast), and Dr E. Epperley, president of the University of PEI, to sign the nonpartisan letter, which we released along with the report card. While it is impossible to measure the success of any single initiative in the prime minister's office, there is no doubt that the impact of receiving a letter signed by high-profile Canadians across the country was not lost on Prime Minister Chrétien.

Two months later, Paul Martin, minister of finance, noted in an interview in the *Ottawa Citizen* (12 January 1996) that child poverty was his number-one priority—if only he had the money. In February 1996, after much internal lobbying from the Liberal child poverty caucus, Martin announced a doubling of the work income supplement. Then in June 1996 Prime Minister Chrétien announced that the federal and provincial governments had agreed, at a first ministers' conference, to find a joint strategy to address child poverty.

Support for Campaign 2000

Over the past five years we have engaged in many strategies. We have described just some of them. None of these would have worked without the following:

1. Initial leadership from organizations like the Child Poverty Action Group, which was an early proponent of a national coalition.
2. The support from Family Services Association of Metropolitan Toronto (FSA), where Campaign 2000's national coordinator works, has been superlative. The FSA's board of directors and executive director have made clear that, based on the population we serve, child and family poverty must be a priority.
3. Financial support from foundations—Children's Aid Society, Laidlaw Foundation, Toronto Hospital for Sick Children, The Body Shop Canada, Trillium Foundation, Canadian Teachers' Federation, Federation of Women Teachers' Associations of Ontario, and Save the Children Canada—have kept us afloat from year to year.
4. Campaign 2000's partners have a broad and genuine sense of ownership. In 1996 national partners committed $10,000 to keep the campaign going, and have also provided approximately $100,000 worth of in-kind support. This includes translation, faxing and distribution, helping with presentations to government committees, printing, providing meeting space and lunches, supporting fundraising, providing extensive unpaid staff support, as well as all-day working sessions with twenty professionals four times a year. Almost without exception, community partners have persisted despite significant cuts to many of their own organizations in the past four years. They are creative, responsive, and the source of highly credible education on child poverty and political influence.

5. There is also a broad sense of ownership for what we stand for. The report card is produced by the Centre for International Statistics at the Canadian Council on Social Development, but vetted and reworked many times by the national partners before it is released each year. As a result, there is a broad identification with the contents of the report card and its distribution. As well, many community partners use it as a basis for a local report card relevant to their own communities.

Did Campaign 2000 Influence the Federal All-Party Commitment?

There are certain techniques of language and debate used in public discourse on contentious social issues (Richardson et al. 1995). For example, increasing public awareness of poverty in Canada prompted the Parliamentary Committee on Poverty in 1992 to focus its work on the *definition* of poverty rather than on its mandate, the elimination of poverty. The committee (with 'assistance' from groups like the Fraser Institute and from media such as the *Globe and Mail*) worked at reducing the official poverty line as a way to 'eradicate' poverty in Canada. At times, Campaign 2000 was forced into technical discussions on defining the poverty line. We pointed out that the poverty line was created by Statistics Canada, that it was a tool comparable to poverty lines used by other industrialized countries, and that regardless of the tool used, child poverty was increasing. Our decision was to meet the technical challenge, but not to let it sidetrack the real debate.

Involvement in an advocacy movement in the 1990s is like working out when you're over fifty. No matter how bad it seems (the country or your physical shape), you have to remind yourself that it would be a lot worse if you did nothing. Politicians inevitably take the public pulse before acting on an issue. Polls, surveys, media coverage, and contacts from constituents all reflected concern about child poverty.

In July 1994 89 per cent of Canadians felt that child poverty must be a priority for the federal government (Angus Reid 1994). Over the past five years, MPs have received 80,000 of The Body Shop postcards from their constituents, letters from local Campaign 2000 partners, eight editions of our newsletter, and copies of all report cards. Child poverty has gained and maintained an awareness in the minds of Canadians.

In 1994 the federal government undertook to reform social security. We were heartened that tackling child poverty was central to its objectives, and that the responsibility for reform was given to Lloyd Axworthy, minister of human resources development, who had spoken eloquently in defence of the 1989 all-party resolution. It seemed that our efforts to remind the federal government of its responsibility to honour its commitment to tackle child poverty was being taken seriously.

Across the country many Campaign 2000 partners responded to Axworthy's discussion paper, which set out options for social policy reform. Many partners echoed the policy perspectives put forward in Campaign 2000's *Investing in the Next Generation* document. Partners also used a letter developed centrally to urge their own MPs to reject a consolidated block fund for social programs. Despite high hopes, it was clear by January 1995 that the minister of finance was driving social policy reform, *not* the minister of human resources development.

While Campaign 2000 partners have been successful in cultivating media contacts, the results are never predictable. Often our input is cut in the editing, or our stories are bumped by more dramatic events. For example, the story of the 1993 report card was originally slated for discussion on an interview on 'Canada AM', a major morning television show. However, that morning there was news of a guilty verdict for two boys in Britain in the death of a three-year-old boy. The producer of 'Canada AM' offered to go ahead with the Campaign 2000 report card story *if* we could make a connection in the interview between the boys in Britain and child poverty. We refused.

The budget for Campaign 2000 is so small that the campaign does not have its own telephone line as it is cheaper to use Family Services Association's number, yet its work is referred to (though not always applauded) by established public policy organs like the Fraser Institute, the *Financial Post,* and the *Globe and Mail.* Campaign 2000 and the issue of child poverty has garnered significant media attention in terms of inches of print media, air time on popular programs, and requests for responses to new stories.

Campaign 2000 zeroed in on the persistently high level of child poverty. This was a strategic decision on our part because we thought that a focus on child poverty would be the most effective way to capture public attention in a short period of time. Our challenge now is to avoid the emerging political drift that will pit the deserving versus the undeserving poor, in essence pitting children against their parents and other poor adults. On several fronts, including public awareness, media attention, and corporate support, Campaign 2000 has had an impact. Tragically, there has been a 55 per cent increase in child poverty since the all-party resolution. Despite concern reflected in the polls, there has been little outcry from Canadians about the federal government's failure to address child and family poverty.

Did We Follow Community Development Values?

Community development values—equality, caring, sharing, and social jus-tice—have helped to guide the process of working within the Campaign 2000 partnership. We have assumed that each partner brings resources and will make a valuable contribution. There was ample conflict and compro-mise in our discussions about the original content of the declaration and in determining if and how we would participate in The Body Shop campaign. In terms of the community development goal of shifting power to the com-munity, Campaign 2000's national partners (of whom there are now nine-teen) operate in a non-hierarchical, shared decision-making model. They continue to meet about four times a year, and have had very significant input into the design, content, and use of the report card. National partners also make very significant contributions: translation, meeting space, production costs, lending their organizational expertise to the campaign, and so on. However, having a non-hierarchical structure with significant shared owner-ship is different from shifting power to local groups. Community partner participation in decision making has been much more limited since funding for a community network coordinator terminated in 1993. This has meant that much of the communication to community partners has consisted of sharing information and ideas, not involving them in decision making nor assisting them in their local community development efforts. None the less, the coalition has not fractured. The cohesion reflects the clarity of our focus, our commitment to action on 24 November each year, the pride that part-ners have in our annual report card, and our firm belief that Canada must address child poverty.

The Metro Campaign 2000 network was built by pulling together vari-ous community groups and organizations and promoting the legitimacy of and capacity for social action. Though we promote activism within the net-work and publicize our message, finding resources to enable greater and more direct citizen involvement over the long term remains a challenge. Significant in-kind support has been provided by voluntary sector organizations that have given staff time and administrative support (including Colin's time from the Children's Aid Society, David's from SPARC, and Rosemarie's from Family Services Association). An important but often overlooked aspect of commu-nity boards is their willingness to be involved and flexible in issue organizing and policy advocacy. Without in-kind support from various community orga-nizations, voluntary action, and the judicious use of foundation funds, Metro Campaign 2000, like the national campaign, would not exist.

Like the Metro Campaign 2000, the BC Campaign 2000 network has had no paid staff to develop and carry out plans, so the skills individual members bring to developing the community have been critical. Partners have had no shortage of ideas, but it is one thing to have an idea and another to have the ability to carry it out. While an important function of community is to build skills through the participation of its members, activities should match abilities.

Where Do We Go from Here?

As partners in Campaign 2000 we are committed to a strong federal role in income security for families with children. We are aghast at the 1995 federal budget, a budget that slashed funding for health care, postsecondary education, and social and income security payments for families and children; reneged on a federal election promise to increase child care; reduced funding for unemployment insurance; and failed to produce a strategy for job creation. In short, federal support for areas needed to eliminate child poverty have been dismantled with the exception of the child tax benefit, which, while far from adequate and not indexed, at least remains (as of summer 1996).

1996 will be a watershed year for Campaign 2000. Issues of child poverty have again risen to the top of the social agenda. The 1996 budget doubled the work income supplement for working poor families, although it did nothing to assist those on welfare. The mood towards poor families receiving welfare is mean and punitive, and in the United States (as we write) President Clinton has announced the end of guaranteed federal assistance to children. People are understandably sceptical of the government's commitment to provide more than lip-service to children. As we begin to gear up for a federal election anticipated in 1997, we are reminded that a promise made in 1989 has so far not prevented 428,000 more children from falling into poverty.

Despite its remarkable influence and contributions, Campaign 2000 will not achieve its goal if Canada does not take action to end child poverty, but, however tempting, it will be misleading to conclude that the campaign was unsuccessful if judged by this criterion alone. This chapter has illustrated the power of community development as an approach to social change. Campaign 2000 has strengthened the information, understanding, and connections of the social policy activists and community developers involved. Campaign 2000 has created awareness among Canadians about the issue of child and family poverty and contributes to the fact that the issue remains squarely on government agendas.

As social policy activists and community developers, we bring our values to work. Campaign 2000's work is about applying those values—social justice, caring, sharing, and a commitment to equality—to the problem of child and family poverty. These days we're frustrated that social policy and social justice concerns are overlooked. The *government* agenda seems to have become the *corporate* agenda—an almost single-minded pursuit of policies that support business and capital accumulation. Business and corporate leaders would be quick to point out that many more government policies and programs would have to be changed or eliminated for a corporate agenda to be truly apparent, and this may be the case. However, it would seem that government policy certainly incorporates business concerns *first*.

The fact remains that the political, public, and media interest in children developed and sustained locally and nationally by Campaign 2000 has been considerable. This may not be enough to turn the tide, but it illustrates what we should be doing. Relative to other areas of social work practice, policy activism is an *extremely* limited practice in social organizations. Many activists have acted as though the consensus that brought about constructive social policies in Canada would last without our close involvement in sustaining community understanding and support, or in protecting it from more powerful and advantaged interests. This assumption has been wrong. The prospects for children are getting dimmer. Hopefully this will compel Campaign 2000 partners, social organizations, and all those people concerned about child and family poverty to work harder and more effectively for action. If the people of Canada, through the policies of our government, do not live up to the national and international commitments to children—despite being prodded, urged, and briefed on how to do so—at worst, Campaign 2000 will be viewed as a noble failure.

References

Angus Reid.
1994. 'First Wave'. Report to Human Resources Development.

Campaign 2000.
1991. *Declaration*. Toronto: Campaign 2000.

———.
1994. *Investing in the Next Generation*. Toronto: Campaign 2000.

Child Poverty Action Group et al.
1994. *The Outsiders*. Toronto: Family Services Association of Metropolitan Toronto.

House of Commons.
1989. *Debates*. Ottawa: House of Commons.

Ottawa Citizen.
    1996. 'Child Poverty Can't Wait' (12 January).

Richardson, M., et al.
    1995. 'Language and Power: The Alpac Case'. *First Reading* 13, no. 1:20–1.

SPARC of BC.
    1995. *Building Community Alliances.* Vancouver: Social Planning and Research Council of BC.

Statistics Canada.
    1994. *Income Distributions by Family Size.* Ottawa: Statistics Canada.

Toronto Star.
    1991. 'A Lousy Week for Canada, Especially for Children' (12 December).

UNICEF.
    1996. *The Progress of Nations.* New York: UNICEF.

United Nations Development Programme.
    1995. *Human Development Report.* New York: Oxford University Press.

Chapter Fourteen

Who Participates? Citizen Participation in Health Reform in BC

Joan Wharf Higgins

Introduction

This chapter is the story of three communities implementing a provincial health reform policy and their efforts to engage citizens in community development work to identify health priorities and goals. The information required to tell this story was gathered by qualitative methods: ethnographic study of three community health planning groups, interviews with citizens[1] (both those who participated and those who did not), and documentary review. The purpose is to recount the experience of fostering public participation in developing a community health plan, to understand the strengths and weaknesses in engaging constituents, and to identify the lessons we can learn from this experience.

Over twenty-five years ago, Sherry Arnstein (1969) depicted citizen participation as a categorical term for citizen power. Arnstein's eight-rung ladder begins with no citizen participation and control, and concludes with complete citizen control. The findings from this study suggest that a sense of personal power or control, and being valued as a citizen, constitutes a necessary primary but usually forgotten element in gaining the participation of citizens. A loss of citizenship prevents substantial numbers of citizens from participating in community life. The motivation to participate, the benefits and costs of becoming involved, and the satisfaction of participating are also interwoven with the notion of power and being valued.

The chapter begins with an introduction to the context of the community development work, followed by a brief look at the citizen participation literature. A discussion of the membership and work of the health planning groups is presented. The discussion is punctuated with the perspectives of both participants and non-participants, and with connections to the community development literature. The chapter concludes with recommendations for fostering broad-based participation in community health reform initiatives.

The Context: Participating in New Directions

British Columbia, like many other provinces, is restructuring its health care system in the face of rising expenditures and an aging population.[2] The health reform policy, New Directions, evolved from the 1990 Royal Commission on Health Care and Costs, which concluded that the health care system, although one of the best in the world, was fragmented and unable to evaluate adequately the outcomes of its services. The centralized structure for decision making and resource allocation resulted in poorly managed and uncoordinated health care. Not all British Columbians enjoyed reasonable access to the health system, and health inequities existed. An important conclusion of the royal commission was that there is enough money in the health care system, but it needed to be carefully and better managed. Local management and decision making, along with an emphasis on health promotion and disease prevention, was the thrust of the 1991 commission report, entitled 'Closer to Home'.

Two years later, the provincial Ministry of Health released its response to the royal commission report, 'New Directions for a Healthy British Columbia'. To revitalize the health care system, five new directions and thirty-eight priority actions served to guide the implementation of health reform:

1. The document recognized that the determinants of health must be addressed in order to achieve 'Better Health' of British Columbians in a holistic sense. Issues such as housing, education, employment, the physical and social environment, as well as lifestyle, genetics, and health services, were acknowledged as affecting the state of health. As such, health becomes not only the responsibility of the Ministry of Health and health care providers but also that of other levels and ministries of government, the community, schools, and companies and industry whose activities indirectly or directly influence health.

2. To ensure that services are appropriate and health needs are being met, and to assist people to make informed decisions about their health care, 'Greater Public Participation and Responsibility' was emphasized as an important component of the health reform strategy. In order to achieve this second direction, opportunities for citizens to participate in local decision making must be made available.

3. The centralized health system was frequently criticized for being insensitive to local health issues and inequitable in its allocation of resources and services. Through establishing community health councils (CHCs) and

regional health boards (RHBs), local communities and regions will 'Bring Health Closer to Home' and gradually assume control over planning, resource allocation, management, and delivery of health care services. CHCs and RHBs are the vehicles through which greater public participation will be achieved. 'Communities will take the lead in developing proposals to establish councils, boards and health centres. Implementation will be at a pace that meets communities' needs and allows us to learn from experience' (British Columbia Ministry of Health and Ministry Responsible for Seniors 1993a:16).

4. In acknowledging the unpaid support that volunteers and family caregivers provide to the system, 'Respecting the Care Provider' became critical to revitalizing the health system. Such respect requires providing adequate support, appropriate training, and good working environments.

5. Finally, 'Effective Management of the New Health System' is necessary to ensure ethical and financial accountability. There is also a need to establish a closely coordinated system in which citizens, particularly the traditionally underserved client, 'do not fall through the cracks' (British Columbia Ministry of Health and Ministry Responsible for Seniors 1993a:18).

Guided by these five new directions, communities throughout the province began restructuring the health care system. In the Capital Regional District (CRD), the transition began in spring 1993. The CRD encompasses several communities from Port Renfrew to the southern Gulf Islands, covering almost 1,000 sq. mi. (2,590 km²) on the southern end of Vancouver Island. The 1994 population was an estimated 321,580. When compared to other Canadian metropolitan areas, the CRD has the largest percentage of residents over sixty-five years of age. The average 1991 family income was $45,941. With 9.8 per cent of the regional population classified as low-income families, the CRD has almost 2.5 per cent fewer low-income households than the rest of the province (despite the fact that three municipalities in the region are above the provincial low-income family average). CRD residents are slightly better educated than other British Columbians, and the region is also characterized by small households with an average size of 2.6 persons. With Victoria as the capital of the province, the government is the largest employer sector in the CRD, followed by the retail trade and the health and social services industry.

The health reform process was facilitated by the Capital Health Board (CHB), the designated regional health board for the CRD, which established seven health planning groups throughout the region to facilitate and ensure community input into the development of community health plans and priorities. A precedent for the CHB structure had evolved from the Victoria Health Project, an earlier regionwide collaborative effort to improve planning and delivery of health services to seniors. Thus the foundation for a community consultation process was well in place. Unlike other regions in the province that had ministerial New Directions transitional staff to assist volunteer health planning groups, the CHB had dedicated, experienced staff who nurtured the community development process in each of the seven geographical clusters of the region. Each health planning group provided two representatives to sit on the CHB to contribute towards the regional health planning process and maintain a two-way flow of communication.

The CHB initiated the process with newspaper advertisements inviting citizens to attend health planning group meetings in the seven municipalities. For the first few months, CHB staff facilitated the evening meetings, but with a view to engendering leadership from within the group. Gradually, chairs (in some instances co-chairs) were elected in the groups. My involvement began in February 1994 when I noticed an advertisement in the regionwide newspaper inviting citizens to attend a regional forum on citizen participation in health reform. At the time, I was a doctoral student studying citizen participation in community-based heart health projects, and went to the forum out of personal and professional interest. Shortly thereafter, I regularly attended the monthly meetings of the health planning group in my municipality.

The health planning groups were established to create community awareness and foster broad-based participation. The process was outlined in the ministry document 'Processes, Benchmarks and Responsibilities for Developing Community Health Councils and Regional Health Boards', which included a checklist of various community groups and organizations that the health planning groups were to contact. The document also suggested a variety of ways to reach citizens, from traditional techniques of surveys and forums to kitchen-table discussions and meetings with already established interest groups. The document encouraged health planning groups to evaluate their efforts at communicating and reaching out to the public, including identifying the successes and challenges.

By spring 1994, I realized that the context of the health planning groups provided a rich data source for studying citizen participation and shifted my research focus to citizen participation in the health reform process. With an articulated commitment by the CHB to having a process that was participatory, inclusive, and that embodied the grassroots voice, the implementation of health reform in the CRD provided an ideal context in which to document the experience.

In fall 1994, with the consent of three other health planning groups in the area, I began the ethnographic part of the data collection: observing and participating in health planning group meetings and activities in the community designed to attract and engage citizens in the health planning process. I followed this process until the groups submitted their application for designation as community health councils in June 1995. In June I conducted personal interviews with health planning group members to record their perspective and experience of the process. To explore the viewpoint of those citizens who had not participated in New Directions, a colleague and I conducted focus groups. These group interviews were with citizens who are traditionally underrepresented at the participation table, and, for the most part, were absent from the membership of the health planning groups. A brief look at the citizen participation literature will help to set the stage before discussing the experiences of participants and non-participants.

Please, in My Back Yard: A Brief Look at the Citizen Participation Literature

From the diverse and voluminous interdisciplinary literature on public/citizen/community participation, we know that it is a highly touted, valued, and idealized concept considered integral to the 'health' of a democratic community, yet one that has been realized only in a limited sense (Checkoway and Van Til 1978). The principle of participation is valued by the disciplines of community development, health promotion, public health, community psychology, adult education, nursing, urban planning, and social work, just to name a few. Participation is espoused as engendering ownership of programs and services, rendering them more appropriate to local needs. It is proposed as a means to foster self-determination of problems and solutions, as a strategy for redistributing power and equity, and as a means of empowerment.

Lomas and Veenstra (1995), in their examination of who came to rural and urban Ontario town hall meetings to participate in decision making in health and social services, found participants to be better educated and three to seven times more likely than the general population to be employed in the health and social services field. They warned readers not to 'pretend that the current consultation technologies really attract the general public' (Lomas and Veenstra 1995:40). Despite the importance of recruiting citizens who represent all segments of society, participants in a variety of activities are characterized by their wealth, education, confidence, and skills. Moreover, not everyone participates when given the opportunity to do so. If participation is such a good thing, why don't more people participate (Norton et al. 1993)?

Several researchers from a variety of disciplines (e.g., Anderson et al. 1994; Bermejo and Bekui 1993; Hunt 1990; Potapchuk 1991; Sherraden 1991; Syme and Nancarrow 1992; Wolf 1993) have criticized the design flaws of traditional participation techniques, including the economic and sociocultural barriers that make public forums inconvenient and inaccessible, the intimidation of citizen advisory meetings that require educational and financial resources, and an overreliance on superficial opinion surveys. Traditional techniques have failed to foster broad-based public input. These barriers, note Kathlene and Martin (1991), contribute to keeping the traditionally voiceless silent.

In her chapter, 'Matching Method to Purpose: The Challenges of Planning Citizen-Participation Activities', Rosener (1978) suggested that the participation techniques used are often inconsistent with the interests and capabilities of the citizens: 'So while public officials claim apathy, citizens claim inequity' (1978:114). Recently, studies in public administration have confirmed Rosener's assertion, suggesting that a citizen interested in participating in local activities might not find the structure or opportunity to participate very inviting (Farr 1992; Persons 1990; Wolf 1993). Issues of child care, transportation, language, and timing of meetings may be irrelevant to the 'professional' volunteers, but without addressing such barriers and employing diverse forms of outreach, initiatives will fail to reach the constituents and hence ignore their views.

The American Health Decisions organization (Crawshaw 1994) has conducted research to determine the reasons why people in ethnic communities attend meetings, given their limited discretionary time and resources. Meetings are held in ethnic neighbourhoods at familiar venues (e.g., churches), at various times (with child care provided), and held in the language of the neighbourhood in an attempt to reach those who lack the discretionary time, money, and access to political power. Similarly, Norton et al. (1993) and Wandersman (1994) have suggested the need to investigate barriers to participation for lower-income and underrepresented groups, which may begin with the opportunity to become involved. Having greater resources probably makes it easier to participate in the traditional mechanisms of meetings and committees.

Consequently, although better-educated people tend to participate more in public involvement programs, this may not necessarily reflect a lower degree of interest among others in the community. It may be that the procedures adopted by those who design public involvement programs are not suitable or are distasteful to the rest of the community. It may be that, given alternative public involvement techniques, representative samples of the population can be encouraged to participate. One of the prevailing patterns in the citizen participation literature suggests that the average person does become involved in community initiatives to protest against something he or she perceives as negative—a jail, a halfway house, a nuclear waste plant, or a highway in their neighbourhood. This is NIMBY, the Not In My Backyard syndrome. Perhaps these same people might also participate in other community activities if the opportunity is in their backyard.

Finally, Smith, in reflecting on his experiences with a community development project with the Simcoe County District Health Council, noted that:

> Given the multidimensional factors in health the need for a new way of thinking and planning has become essential and must be reflected in the structure of the planning authority. We have accepted the WHO [World Health Organization] definition of health but the structure of planning does not reflect this holistic view. The community development approach to planning requires this holistic view (Smith 1995:102).

Thus, despite the eclectic assortment of research in the field, one conclusion stands out: the difficulty of enlisting participants from a broad base of citizens. The search for innovative and accessible devices for fostering participation continues (Buckwalter et al. 1993; Potapchuk 1991) in the face of 'uncertainty as to how best to encourage active health alliances and community interest in health initiatives' (Macallan and Narayan 1994:18).

The Health Planning Groups: Textbook Participation

> What I see in the health planning group, almost exclusively, is White Anglo-Saxon Protestant. It's the power group—the same power group all the time ...When I look at who's on the proposed community health council—who's interested in being on it—it's the same scenario. And, from that point of view, there's a lot of work we need to do (Health planning group member).

Only the Powerful Participate

To a great extent the membership and work of the health planning groups mirrored the citizen participation literature. Most members, if not health or health-related professionals or providers (or retired from the profession), certainly possessed the financial, discretionary, and personal resources that enabled them to attend evening meetings, weekend forums, and devote a large amount of time and effort to the process (ranging from six or seven hours a month to forty hours a week). Most meeting locations required the use of a vehicle. Familiarity with the health language was also a prerequisite. Although the groups operated on a consensus model of decision making, being familiar with meeting protocol and etiquette was definitely an advantage. These findings are compatible with the bulk of citizen participation research: participants were well educated, well spoken, and well off (Beatley et al. 1994; Lomas and Veenstra 1995).

In addition to their socio-economic status, however, the findings from this case-study also reflected the importance of an individual's perceived control to participating in health reform. Fundamental beliefs about power influence people's decisions about whether and how to participate in community life (Hill 1991). The research reported in the literature demonstrates that citizens who participate in community organizations often feel more empowered (Israel et al. 1994; Schulz et al. 1995; Smith 1995), or have a greater sense of control (Chavis and Wandersman 1990) than non-participants prior to embarking on the participation experience. These citizens have a sense of efficacy or belief in their personal abilities and become involved when they believe that the possibility for making a difference exists (Berry, Portney, and Thomson 1993; Chrislip 1995).

Empowerment expresses itself 'at the level of feelings, at the level of ideas about self-worth, at the level of being able to make a difference in the world around us' (Rappaport 1985:17). These expressions were obvious in the voices of participants. In addition to their wealth of experience and skills, participants enrolled in the health planning groups with a sense of confidence that they would contribute and make a difference. One of the health planning groups' chair articulated this most clearly in our interview: 'When I originally looked at who I thought were involved, and why they were involved, it was because of an active care about health care. But when I look at it, I think the issue that really stands out is personal power. It's not just the interest in the field, but how much personal power a person feels they have in terms of making a change and making a difference.'

Some health planning group members did not resemble the typical participant profile (I interviewed a person with a mental illness, a person with a physical disability, and a single parent), yet each believed herself to have something meaningful to contribute to the community development process. For example, one health planning group member became involved to ensure some equity in the decision-making power: 'I like my voice to be heard. I have a valid perspective of what's being needed. It is crucial that people with disabilities are involved because for too many years able-bodied people have been making the decisions about health.' Similarly, one participant, who dubbed herself the 'token mental health consumer', attributed her purpose for involvement as, 'I just think [that] through life experience, I'm valuable.'

As with previous experiences in the literature, involvement was attractive to the participants because, to some degree, it served their needs and interests (Kelly and Van Vlaenderen 1996). Analogous to participation experiences in Healthy Cities (Mhatre and Deber 1992), Healthy Communities (Wharf Higgins 1992), and other communities implementing New Directions (British Columbia Ministry of Health and Ministry Responsible for Seniors 1993b), those with 'concentrated interests' (the professionals and providers) were more involved than those with 'diffuse interests' (the general public). Other reported reasons for participants' involvement were representing their profession or occupation, which reflected a mix of professional and personal interests: 'I realized that I had some major concerns about the heavy involvement of acute care in the health planning group. That's when I decided [that] whether I had time or not, I had to be there.'

People also participated out of a sense of duty or sense of community. Previous research (e.g., Berry, Portney, and Thomson 1993; Chavis and Wandersman 1990; Davidson and Cotter 1989; Smith 1995) confirms that a sense of community or belonging functions as both an antecedent to, and consequence of, participation. Involvement has been commonly viewed as the natural expression of an underlying sense of community (Chavis et al. 1986). This has led several scholars to argue that personal empowerment encompasses not only self-perception of power and control but a sense of connectedness to others (Lord 1994; McCarron, Tenenbein, and Hindley 1994; Sheilds 1995). Riger (1990) criticizes much of the research on personal empowerment as neglecting and overshadowing the importance of connectedness in human life. Her argument is that both connectedness and empowerment 'are integral to human well-being and happiness and to well-functioning communities, and that both ought to be objects of our study. However, little work has been done to integrate the two ideas' (Riger 1990:287). A more inclusive model of empowerment should incorporate factors such as sense of community and communion in addition to control (Nelson et al. 1995).

Most of the participants interviewed had experience in previous or concurrent volunteer community initiatives or professional efforts. These experiences gave them a repertoire of skills and knowledge that they could draw on to contribute effectively, such as skills that enabled them to run a meeting, write briefs, speak in public, facilitate group discussions, interpret research, and absorb a great deal of written material. They brought with them knowledge of the health care system and other service industries, they knew the identity of key provider and community players to contact, and had a great deal of experience from previous professional or community work. Participants who represented consumer interests in the health planning groups also had an extensive resumé of volunteer community work, ranging from Little League to Kiwanis to neighbourhood associations. Participants' membership had been initiated either by personal invitation or referral, further validating the participants' sense of worth in contributing to the process.

Hold a Meeting and They Will Come

The health planning groups engaged in traditional forms of participation (such as their evening meetings), organized public forums and meetings, and distributed surveys. As with other experiences in the literature, the opportunities to participate were structured so that it discouraged many in the community from participating (Gilbert 1987). In fact, the response rates for these methods were disappointing at best. In a series of six public forums in one community, only forty-eight people out of a population of 58,100 attended. This same community received 122 completed surveys mailed to 22,000 households. The chair of that health planning group acknowledged that 'I don't think there's a whole lot more people that want to participate.' Another health planning group organized a Saturday public forum to assess community health concerns. Attendance at this forum represented less than 0.2 per cent of the population. Health planning groups had a much better response when volunteers with questionnaires approached residents at a series of summer events, a regionwide health fair, and at the local mall, activities and venues that provided a ready-made audience.

A related and oft-repeated concern of the health planning group members and the participants I interviewed was the need to include the grassroots (representative) community voice, despite a lack of consensus on how to achieve it. Certainly the health planning group members were cognizant of their lack of community representation, and for some that provided the biggest disappointment of all. Each participant I interviewed, whether a chair of the group or a former participant, admitted that the group foundered in efforts to garner broad-based participation, but were divided as to whether the group membership reflected the diversity of their constituency. The discussions around the health planning group tables often centred on the means by which interest and participation in the health reform process could be generated. Participants were also well aware of the difficulties they might encounter in attempting to consult with the public: '[I] think the danger is that we will get frustrated by trying to mobilize the public and just give up

on it . . . and get into that kind of [attitude that] if they don't want to participate, screw 'em, we know what's better for them.'

In some instances, health planning group members presented information at existing community network and organization meetings. At times,
however, the health planning groups anticipated that representatives from
other community groups would join them. Others realized from the outset
that meetings precluded citizen attendance by the very nature and logistics of
the meeting structure: 'darkness, driving, [lack of] day care are all barriers to
coming to a meeting [like this]'. A few recognized that participation could
not be defined as simply attending a meeting, but included other means of
enlisting involvement: 'From my perspective, I don't believe that going to the
meetings is the only way to participate. I think there's all sorts of different
ways [to participate], and not necessarily formalized ways.'

Some health planning group members blamed a lack of individual interest in health as a reason for low participation rates, while others cited the dis-
mal level of public awareness of New Directions as an explanation.
Participants were cognizant of the time and financial barriers inherent in
health planning group meetings, and were also critical of the complexity and
packaging of information in discouraging inclusive participation.

> They [double-income families] are so taxed for time and here is yet one
> more demand on their most precious resource, and they decide, no, I can't
> participate, I have other things to do.

> The next door neighbour can't relate to the health jargon, for one thing,
> and don't see where they fit in with New Directions, if they've even heard
> of it. They don't hear of or know of the meetings or anything like that.

Some of these reasons were corroborated to a great extent in our discussions with non-participants. Most non-participants were vaguely, if at all, familiar with New Directions. The information they had gleaned through the press
and media was negative: 'It's [coverage about New Directions] the negative
things. It's the cuts, what's wrong, not what we can do to create something better or not what is available. Just what's not going right.' The descriptions of
health reform in government publications were found to be loaded with jargon, perplexing, and, most telling of all, perceived to be a way for the dominant group to maintain power: 'It's like they want to make it [New Directions]
so hard you can't get it—the control thing—don't want them to know too
much, and write it in a different language. Then they [the general public] really won't understand.' Yet the majority of non-participants defined health in a
holistic sense, and grasped the need for integrated and coordinated services.

The Benefits: Membership Has Its Rewards

Some research in community psychology suggests that participation in voluntary organizations is a means of engendering psychological empowerment (Chavis and Wandersman 1990). People experience feelings of greater control over their own lives and increased competence following active involvement in groups (Kieffer 1984). Although by no means disempowered at the beginning of the process, participants reported gaining skills, knowledge, experience, and personal insight as a result of their involvement, attributes that certainly contribute to people's sense of control in their lives.

The chair of one health planning group reported, 'I have done things in the last year and a half that I never could [have] imagined doing—never, [like] facilitating workshops. I had never facilitated anything in my life before.' One woman, even after a brief involvement with a health planning group, reported that she learned more about group dynamics and 'how to chair meetings . . . and you can draw from that experience without going to a workshop itself for that'. Others spoke of learning more about the health system, their community, and of achieving a sense of control over some aspect of their lives: 'I'm less scared. I feel safer.'

Overwhelmingly, participants mentioned the benefit of meeting others ('I've met a lot of nice people') and sharing with them a vision for better health, indicating a sense of belonging and enjoyment from the personal relationships among the participants. 'I think it [participating in the health planning group] utilizes a lot of my background. It's nice to be able to use all of that and find I'm in a group that appreciates my being part of the group.' For some, enhancing their sense of community was also part of the benefits reaped: 'something else I've got out of this is a sense of belonging and sense of community'. Previous research has indicated that such solidary benefits sustain the participatory act (Norton et al. 1993; Prestby et al. 1990). As well, the data from participants support the contention that communion and connection are integral components of personal empowerment, in addition to a sense of mastery and control (Riger 1990). Here the data corroborate the literature: empowerment functioned as an antecedent to, and consequence of, participation. The empowered became more empowered.

The Costs: Membership Has Its Dues

By contrast, and not unexpectedly, the sense of belonging and being able to contribute effectively was missing (at the group level) for those people who dropped out of the health planning groups. One former health planning group participant had dropped out of the process because she felt unwelcome by the group, and because her abilities were not being put to use: 'I didn't feel useful. I think you need to feel useful and part of the group. I felt like it was their group, and [I] was just visiting.' Moreover, she sensed her contribution (to serve as a liaison to the medical community) was not valued by the group because 'they never followed up on my work'. A third drop-out, after devoting almost a year to the process, came to the conclusion that the process was flawed and refused to return: 'I didn't see that anything we did was worthwhile or useful.'

The inventory of costs in the participation literature range from personal costs of time, effort, and relinquishing other obligations, to those associated with group processes (personality conflicts, sluggish progress, disagreement over goals) (Prestby et al. 1990). These costs were evident in participants' experiences, yet a more profound and potent price took its toll on health planning group members: a loss of social worth and respect. For some, this loss was a personal assault on their contribution to the work of the group as an equal and respected member. A direct assault on personal value as a professional participating in the process can be seen in this quote from one health planning group member, who recalled:

> . . . the times that I felt [like quitting] most . . . weren't the times the process just seemed to be going on and on. It was the times when people were actively confronting me in a very negative way, saying 'Health care professionals are out to make their money. Why do we want to survey health care professionals, or why do we care about what they think? We're out to make the health of the community better. They don't know anything about it. They don't want to deal with it. . . . They're just out there to make their money, and after all, it's in their best interest to keep us ill'—that sort of stuff, and I just thought, I don't need this.

However, the most frequently cited cost for participants was their loss of control over the implementation of decentralized decision making. New Directions might well be described as a top-down provincial directive to reorganize the health care system from the bottom-up. 'It [New Directions] is a ministry-organized and directed initiative, but it is being sold as a grass-roots reaction; there wasn't anything grassroots about it', complained a former health planning group member. Said another: 'The government has carefully orchestrated us to be herded. I feel that we have been blind-sided.'

During the two years that participants worked to implement New Directions, seemingly subtle and inconspicuous actions by the provincial government began to add up to what felt like, according to participants, a conspiracy against the work of the health planning groups. At the heart of the participants' uneasiness with their relationship to the Ministry of Health was the designation of community health councils in the CRD and the fate of the health planning groups. Despite applications for six CHC designations in the region, the minister designated only one, the group that had been negotiating for self-governance prior to the birth of New Directions. The remaining six health planning groups were restructured into three community health planning and advisory committees, with no legal authority for decision making. In addition, the minister ordered the CHB management and governance structure revamped, its membership replaced, and its mandate revised.

Looming large over the entire implementation of New Directions was an upcoming provincial election, a prediction that another party would take office, and the uncertain implications for the future of the health reform process. Reminiscent of the lip-service paid to citizen participation by political élites during the US War on Poverty (Berry, Portney, and Thomson 1993) and the provincial government's reform of social services in the 1970s (Clague et al. 1984), provincial staff who might sabotage health planning group efforts were another source of concern for participants. Bureaucrats uncommitted to New Directions—intolerant of decentralization and fearful for their jobs—were wary of sharing their authority with others: 'What I fear is that the minister and deputy minister have demonstrated that they're so incapable of managing the people down below them who are not happy with all of this, and are very skilled at fighting their own kind of battles, will put the whole thing at risk.'

While the participants felt they had been promised decision-making authority in the beginning and could influence implementation of local governance structures, health planning group members felt that their work had not been taken seriously. To many participants, the final result smacked of tokenism. In the end, despite the advice and efforts of participants, the government did what it deemed best. The Ministry of Health, in dismissing the recommendations of health planning group and CHB members, challenged the participants' notion of equality and threatened their ongoing involvement. As one participant remarked, 'What trust do I have in the system now? I don't know if I can continue working on [health reform] under these circumstances.'

Not surprisingly, interviews with participants revealed that the most negative aspect of their involvement stemmed from government roadblocks to their efforts. Wearied by their perception of the ministry changing the rules midway, participants felt a sense of powerlessness over the outcome. One participant remarked that this tendency left her with a 'haunting feeling about the process. Did it manipulate us to come to where we are, or did we arrive where we are because we were remaining true to a community development process?'

Participants also felt somewhat deserted by the provincial government when they found themselves trying to foster participation in relative obscurity. Participants felt burdened with the responsibility of raising public awareness about New Directions without the expertise, sufficient funds, or resources to do so. In fact, most of the publicity generated in the local media was negative, emphasizing cuts in patient services, and was sensationalized by the official opposition party in waging a political battle. This left the health planning groups fighting a campaign loaded with political baggage.

A more localized implementation frustration with the group process spawned a sense of impotence when the pace plodded along, when the group was indecisive, or when participants perceived the goals as ill defined and their tasks unclear. When one participant was asked in the interview if she planned on continuing her involvement, she replied, 'I need a clearer picture of what's involved. I don't want to spend all those hours meeting if nothing comes of it.' One former participant became disillusioned with the group process when she perceived that citizens were not responsible for implementing New Directions: 'We got into these work study groups that were "make work", and they were just a complete waste of time. I got terribly frustrated.'

These implementation challenges contributed to the frustration that hinged on the participants' sense of losing control over the process, leading them to feel a sense of futility and to question the value of their efforts: 'I think there is a certain cynicism that we're spinning our wheels. We're going through all of this and doing a heck of a lot of work, and is anybody going to take any notice?' This experience of the participants' inability to make a difference in how health services were managed and delivered in their community influenced empowerment at the group and community level. Organizational empowerment is characterized by providing opportunities for individual growth, the pursuit of mutually defined goals, and access to shared decision-making processes, as well as affecting the policies and decisions in the community (Israel et al. 1994). Participants in health planning groups also shared common goals, strategies, and decision-making authority within the group, and perceived themselves to have both the individual and collective competency to establish five CHCs in the region. Yet to be truly empowering organizations, the health planning groups needed more than competent members. They had to be successful in their bids for change: 'People must be able to see themselves in the governing process if they are to feel connected. . . . [Government] must reflect [the] voices in the community' (Chrislip 1995:22).

It is difficult for ordinary citizens to know in any objective sense who won and who lost in most public policy matters. However, their perception of who won and lost affects their sense of whether government is fair and open to all. . . . Moreover, such perceptions affect individuals' calculus as to whether or not it is worth their while to become involved in politics (Berry, Portney, and Thomson 1993:102).

Thus individuals were empowered by the health reform experience, but collectively their ability to influence the implementation of their vision of New Directions in the CRD was negligible.

The Traditionally Voiceless Citizens

I'm feeling like I'm not being heard, and this is a really big issue for me (Person with a physical disability).

While dimensions of personal empowerment were present in the narratives of health planning group members, the non-participants told decidedly different stories. Rappaport (1985) suggests that empowerment is difficult to define but easy to recognize, and more easily understood (Jones and Meleis 1993) in its absence—powerlessness, alienation, loss of a sense of control over one's life—concepts that were evident in the voices of non-participants. The First Nations groups spoke of their long history with colonization and their mistrust of the government: 'We've been hurting now for 150 years. They [the government] haven't followed through with any of their promises. I'm very leery anytime we're offered something and wonder what they'll take.'

For some, this meant feeling abandoned and alone; as one street youth remarked, 'We don't have nobody telling us it is going to be okay.' One individual with a mental illness commented: 'You go through life where there are times you feel that you've lost control and you don't know why.' For this woman, getting out of bed in the morning was a daily struggle. Negative self-perceptions of power have previously been shown to limit the power of low-income residents in changing community conditions (Checkoway 1991).

Beyond the powerlessness of the non-participants' voices was another dimension: they did not feel equal as citizens. The notion of 'citizen' implies equality of status and respect as a member of society and being accorded the same rights as everyone else (Moon 1988). For Marshall (1977), citizenship is comprised of three rights: (1) civil and legal rights (the rights of free persons), (2) political rights (the rights to vote and to hold office), and (3) the social rights (rights of economic and social well-being). The basis for these rights is what Marshall refers to as the equal social worth of all members of society:

'to be accepted as full members of society, that is, as citizens . . .' (1977:8). Equal social worth means that a minimal level of resources will be available to everyone—a safety net ensuring a minimum of education, income, health, and housing—that enables individuals to maintain a place in the community. Equal social worth is a necessary condition for the full exercise of civil and political rights. As Marshall argued, without the rights guaranteed by the welfare state, gross inequalities in wealth, education, and status render civil and political rights largely theoretical (Brown 1989; Gorham 1995).

Yet the non-participants' accounts of the treatment they received from government services and society generally chronicle consistent disrespect, and suggest they were being recast from citizens to recipients (Hoatson, Dixon, and Sloman 1996): 'At social services, I feel like I am begging', commented an individual with a mental illness. Similarly, a person with a physical disability pleaded, 'What do you have to do to get the respect, to get the help that you need?' Perhaps due to their experiences with advocating for self-government, Aboriginal citizens demanded 'to be approached as First Nations governments and to be treated with respect. We need to enter on an equal footing.'

Moreover, McKnight suggests that such services 'tend to be pathways out of community and into the exclusion of serviced life' (1992:62). Many of the services designed to enhance life for disadvantaged people have unintended iatrogenic effects (Rappaport 1985), including dehumanization, oppression (Merzel 1991), and humiliation (Sen 1994), thus harming the recipients they are supposed to help. Lord (1994) and with Hutchinson (1993), as well as with Culpitt (1992), discuss the consequences of prolonged dependency on social service systems as low self-esteem and limited practice in decision making, factors that contribute to the experience of powerlessness and estrangement. The role of expert reinforces this minimization of citizenship, taking decision making away from citizens and putting it in the hands of professionals (Roche 1987).

Further, Pateman (1988) argues that employment has become the key to citizenship, and good citizens support themselves. Self-supporting means that an individual is a citizen of equal worth to, and deserving of respect from, other employed citizens. The street youths were well aware of their status: 'People are taught that you're shit if you don't work and pay taxes.' Some non-participants—particularly those with a physical disability or mental illness, and (to a lesser extent) single parents, First Nations, and street youths—were unable to be self-supporting citizens and hence depended on social or human services for survival. Yet the very act of depending on welfare and social services can be stigmatizing in and of itself, despite the right to receive such benefits (Moon 1988): '[Going to social services is] a very demeaning experience. They ask you "Well, why are you here?" I had enough problems on my plate at the time to have to go through that as well. It is scary just to ask for help.'

Indeed, marginalized people—second-class citizens—have received an 'undeserved exile' from society (Moon 1988; Pateman 1988). The irony is that receiving services from the very institutions established to help them eroded their confidence and confirmed their sense of stigma. Relying on social services that, as citizens, non-participants had a legitimate civil and political right to access ('A socialized system is supposed to help everybody', commented a street youth), stripped some sense of their personal dignity and independent living skills, eroded a sense of full citizenship (Bryson 1992), and disempowered them (Gorham 1995). These citizens were not recognized by fellow citizens as being of equal worth. Such recognition is basic to democracy and to participation in that democracy. While, in theory, all citizens are created equal, some are more equal than others (Brown 1989), thus generating two classes of citizenship (Gorham 1995). The experiences of non-participants suggested that, as a result of circumstances and attributes beyond their control (a mental illness, a physical disability, the inability to live at home, their ethnicity), they felt in some way mistreated by and disenfranchised from society. Their value as citizens in society had gradually, inadvertently slipped away.

Just as a sense of communion is a dimension of empowerment, its absence is synonymous with powerlessness and non-participation. Citizens must sense that they are part of the community if they are to participate (Smith 1995). Cousineau suggests that 'It is an essential condition of any well-functioning community that its members sense that they belong. As a community, we should be prepared to do what we can to ensure that our institutions encourage the sentiment of being a valued member of the collectivity' (1993:150).

The sense of belonging or not belonging is derived from the actions of the state or the citizens around them. When people feel that they belong or do not belong in a collectivity, it is because the larger group has done something to engender the sentiment: 'Somehow [the health system needs to be] set up so that the consumer has some tool because, as it is set up right now, the consumer has no tool. That is why I really felt disenfranchised, very much on the outside.' Lacking a sense of belonging engenders feelings of disconnection and alienation, which are disempowering (McCarron, Tenenbein, and Hindley 1994).

To foster the sentiment of being valued requires that professionals need to forsake the 'language, mannerisms and organizational structures [that] maintain power over people' (Lord 1994:217) and concentrate on understanding the context of people's lives. This notion of connectedness was not lost on focus group members:

I think that what is fundamental to humans is we live in communities. You have to promote that sense of community in everything. If you start doing that in some way—by having the leaders, as that is who the community health board is in a sense—they are looked at as leaders of your community health program . . . You get this feeling they are not a faceless board. Perhaps more people will start saying, 'Perhaps I would like to be on that board' or 'I am interested in [doing] this.'

Exploring participation in a South African community health project from the participants' perspectives, Kelly and Van Vlaenderen's findings led them to 'believe that the nature of participation is strongly determined by existing relations within the society and these are interpolated into participatory processes within projects' (1996:1243). Thus if focus group members perceived themselves as less than equal to other citizens as a result of their experiences in society, they may have correctly anticipated that similar circumstances would occur within the health planning group structure. It would seem that a loss of citizenship prevents substantial numbers of residents from participating in community life.

Viewing Participation from the Margins

A common and consistent theme among members of the focus groups was that involvement in committee meetings, public forum and meetings, and surveys did not fit with their reality. Nevertheless, these people invited the health planning group members to experience a slice of their reality:

Come join us, walk with us. If you want a real insight into how we are, go put your grubbiest clothes on, grab yourself a backpack, and spend maybe a day on the streets. . . . It would give them [the health planning group] a better idea of what we're going through to sit with us and pan one day and see how many people step over you and look at you and go 'Ugghh'.

Somebody share with us. Give him [a health council member] his $529 and say, 'Okay, get out. Live for a month. Get out there and find out what you can have and what you can do. And also, here's your symptoms and see what you can find out in the way of getting help for those.'

It has got to be more involved—[more] participation for them. Let them understand more what their decisions [to fund] may take away or help.

When understanding participation from these citizens' perspectives, it becomes clear that there are multiple realities in which the opportunity to participate exists. Relying on a limited repertoire of participation techniques that demand attendance at public forums and meetings will only make sense for, and be relevant to, a select few. Surveys, questionnaires, and presentations to advisory committees are convenient and accessible means of participation for socio-economically advantaged citizens because the *community comes to them.*

The same logic needs to be applied to people for whom being valued, not to mention surviving, is a major struggle every day. In order to participate in 'traditional' structures, these people would have to be treated as 'traditional' citizens, with the full citizenship rights and respect accorded the privileged. Clearly, the focus group members perceived that they were not regarded as equals.

The challenge that the health planning groups faced in fostering broad-based citizen participation was not solely an issue of apathy or of increasing awareness but foremost, as Rosener (1978) suggested, one of inequity. The participation opportunities offered by the health planning groups were inconsistent with and irrelevant to the interests and capabilities of focus group members. The design flaws included more than meeting locales and times— the very idea of a meeting itself was meaningless for non-participants. Marginalized citizens can also accuse the power group of being uninvolved, uncaring—indeed, egocentric and smug—in their view of participation, so they, too, can ask that if participation is such a good thing, why more people do not participate. The suggestions from focus group members also support Smith's (1995) contention that a new way of thinking about, and structuring participation in, health planning requires a holistic view.

Indeed, in their case-study of community participation in South Africa, Kelly and Van Vlaenderen (1996) found the nature of participation to be differently understood and experienced by different participants. These researchers found that a local community's 'experiential' knowledge and professional knowledge represented two distinct frames of understanding. Acknowledging that other domains for participation exist does not discount the contribution of the health planning group members nor their conventional structures for participation. It may be through 'the contributions of both community and professional knowledge, an intimate understanding of the realities and needs experienced in the context, and an understanding of specific professional competencies and possible services' that a holistic view emerges (Kelly and Van Vlaenderen 1996:1243).

A look at the evaluative research in citizen participation suggests that how participation efforts are structured do not in and of themselves guarantee the success of projects in recruiting a wide breadth of citizens (Berry, Portney, and Thomson 1993; Poulin and Kauffman 1995). Merely offering a menu of opportunities to participate does not bring people out of the woodwork. The daily burdens of marginalized citizens are powerful dynamics that contribute to an overwhelming sense of inadequacy and alienation, feelings that are not simply ameliorated by being offered easier avenues for participation.

However, rethinking what participation means for a variety of constituents, and restructuring the opportunity to participate so that it is 'closer to home', begins to acknowledge the experience and needs of citizens and their equal social worth as members of society. In turn, it may begin to restore the sense of community and belonging that seems fundamental to participation.

As other scholars note (Lord 1994), it is important for isolated and powerless people to be able to make a contribution to their communities, a contribution that is unlikely to be realized in contexts that have little meaning and relevance for marginalized people. Having access to valued social roles is also part of the empowerment process (Wolfensberger 1983), as it can reduce isolation and heighten feelings of self-worth. One non-participant with a physical disability feared he lacked the qualifications to become involved: 'I would love to participate in some way . . ., but my problem is not having the skills and tools. . . . How smart do you have to be to be on a board?' It may be that citizens *are* interested in health and *do* wish to influence the quality of health in the community, but do not feel they really can (Kubiski 1990), or have not had the chance to (Berry, Portney, and Thomson 1993) in contexts that are meaningful to their lives.

The traditional approach to participation in New Directions (health planning group meetings, public forums, and community surveys) was simply unable to accommodate and reflect how people viewed and understood their lives. The opportunities to participate only met the needs of the well-heeled (and perhaps well-healed) citizen. Becoming involved in the lives of traditionally underrepresented citizens as a form of participation for health planning group members begins to acknowledge their experiences, needs, and value as part of society. Lord's (1994) research confirms that listening to and observing the lives of disempowered citizens provides the strong sense of value that was lacking early in the transition from powerlessness to power. It also means we have to pay attention to power relationships. How the opportunity to participate is structured maintains power over people rather than sharing it with them.

Summary: Fostering Grassroots Participation

Structuring the opportunity to participate is a significant variable in fostering broad-based citizen involvement, although not merely for convenience's sake. Going into local backyards signifies that all citizens are valued for their contribution, and acknowledges that not all residents possess the discretionary resources and sense of control to participate in 'foreign' territory. By virtue of moving the structure of participation to local turfs and backyards, the value of participation becomes more visible to citizens. Continued reliance on traditional participation techniques symbolizes an apathetic attitude on the part of officials.

Riger (1990) has criticized the concept of personal empowerment as emphasizing the masculine aspects of mastery and control. She argues for a feminist version to include a sense of community and communion as equally important aspects of empowerment. Participation can be empowering in the feminist sense of 'power to' rather than 'power over' (French 1986). Our focus group members echo that sentiment, suggesting that lacking a sense of community or connection to the collectivity precludes participation in community organizations, thus denying citizens the benefits of the participation experience, particularly personal empowerment. Being valued is a precursor to empowerment when participation is the means.

The lessons learned from the community development experience in health reform suggest that fostering broad-based citizen participation in identifying and planning health priorities and plans can be enhanced by the following recommendations:

1. Go to their turf. Spend some time in different neighbourhoods and experience the reality of the diverse constituents in the community. This gesture not only validates the experiences of others and engenders a sense of communion but demands that the participation issue be viewed from a different perspective. Extending a personal invitation to citizens also communicates that they are valuable to the process.

2. Nurture, weed, and fertilize the process. It takes time to build trust with marginalized citizens. Respect the integrity of the practice of participation by allowing a long enough time frame for the process to develop. It is important to provide participants with feedback and act on their input, so they can see that their contribution is not token. I returned transcripts of the personal interviews and focus group discussions to each individual and granted him or her editorial power. They had control over the data. Only three people out of a total of forty declined the opportunity to review the transcripts, and the changes were corrections of grammar.

As evidenced by the macro implementation issues discussed earlier, it would also be wise to ensure that policy goals and objectives are clearly stated so as to avoid or minimize ambiguous interpretation.

3. Meaningful citizen participation demands that it be respected and valued by both citizens and government (Berry, Portney, and Thomson 1993). As borne out by the experiences of health planning group members, token and 'rubber-stamped' participation can occur in all socio-economic classes. Volunteer efforts require the support of paid staff, training for citizens, and other resources that the government (or other funding body) needs to recognize as integral to a community development initiative. The effort and work of the citizenry must be honoured, otherwise the most effective grassroots ventures will become artificial.

The final point is particularly salient. If indeed a sense of value can be nurtured in disenfranchised citizens through participation opportunities that respect their life experiences, we must be very sure that their work will be honoured and utilized before we encourage the process. Dismissing the efforts of citizens will, at the very least, dissuade further involvement. It may also breed greater isolation and mistrust among those whose sense of belonging has not yet taken root.

Note

[1] I would like to acknowledge that these data were collected in collaboration with the citizens of the Capital Regional District. I would also like to thank Nancy Reed for her assistance and collaboration in organizing and conducting the focus groups, transcribing the focus group data, and for her commitment to the purpose of the research.

[2] In the summer of 1996, and under the leadership of a new minister of health, the regionalization of New Directions was temporarily suspended pending a review of the process of New Directions. The team assessing the process is composed of four members of the legislative assembly and three regional health administrators. As of November 1996, the prognosis of the regionalization process remained uncertain, despite ministerial assurance that 'community involvement continues to be a cornerstone of health reform' ('MLA Review Team Appointed', *Capital Health Board Update* 2, no. 7 [1996]:1–8).

References

Anderson, M., et al.
1994. 'Public Participation: An Approach Using Aerial Photographs at Ashford, Kent'. *Town Planning Review* 65, no. 1:41–58.

Arnstein, S.

1969. 'A Ladder of Citizen Participation'. *American Institute of Planners Journal* (July):216–24.

Beatley, T., et al.

1994. 'Representation in Comprehensive Planning'. *Journal of the American Planning Association* 60, no. 2:185–96.

Bermejo, A., and A. Bekui.

1993. 'Community Participation in Disease Control'. *Social Science and Medicine* 36, no. 9:1145–50.

Berry, J.M., K.E. Portney, and K. Thomson.

1993. *The Rebirth of Urban Democracy*. Washington, DC: Brookings Institute.

British Columbia Ministry of Health and Ministry Responsible for Seniors.

1991. 'Closer to Home: Summary of the Report of the British Columbia Royal Commission on Health Care and Costs'. Victoria: British Columbia Ministry of Health and Ministry Responsible for Seniors.

———.

1993a. 'New Directions for a Healthy British Columbia'. Victoria: British Columbia Ministry of Health and Ministry Responsible for Seniors.

———.

1993b. 'Communities Putting New Directions into Action'. Victoria: British Columbia Ministry of Health and Ministry Responsible for Seniors.

———.

1994. 'Processes, Benchmarks and Responsibilities for Developing Community Health Councils and Regional Health Boards'. Victoria: British Columbia Ministry of Health and Ministry Responsible for Seniors.

Brown, C.

1989. 'Citizens' Rights'. *New Statesman and Society* (April):28.

Bryson, L.

1992. *Welfare and the State*. London: The MacMillan Press.

Buckwalter, D., et al.

1993. 'Citizen Participation in Local Government: The Use of Incentives and Rewards'. *Public Management* (September):11–15.

Chavis, D., et al.

1986. 'Sense of Community through Brunswik's Lens Model: A First Look'. *Journal of Community Psychology* 14:16–23.

———, and A. Wandersman.

1990. 'Sense of Community in the Urban Environment: A Catalyst for Participation and Community Development'. *American Journal of Community Psychology* 18, no. 1:55–81.

Checkoway, B.
1991. 'Neighborhood Needs and Organizational Resources'. *Nonprofit and Voluntary Sector Quarterly* 20:173–89.

———, and J. Van Til.
1978. 'What Do We Know About Citizen Participation? A Selective Review of Research'. In *Citizen Participation in America*, edited by S. Langton, 25–42. Lexington: D.C. Heath and Company.

Chrislip, D.
1995. 'Pulling Together: Creating a Constituency for Change'. *National Civic Review* (Winter):21–9.

Clague, M., et al.
1984. *Reforming Human Services: The Experience of the Community Resource Boards in British Columbia*. Vancouver: University of BC Press.

Cousineau, M.
1993. 'Belonging: An Essential Element of Citizenship: A Franco-Ontarian Perspective'. In *Belonging: the Meaning and Future of Canadian Citizenship*, edited by W. Kaplan, 137–51. Montreal and Kingston: McGill-Queen's University Press.

Crawshaw, R.
1994. 'Grass Roots Participation in Health Care Reform'. *Annals of Internal Medicine* 120, no. 8:677–81.

Culpitt, I.
1992. *Welfare and Citizenship: Beyond the Crisis of the Welfare State?* London: Sage Publications.

Davidson, W.B., and P.R. Cotter.
1989. 'Sense of Community and Political Participation'. *Journal of Community Psychology* 17:199–25.

Farr, C.
1992. 'Fostering Diversity on Appointed Boards and Commissions'. *Public Management* (July):14–17.

French, M.
1986. *Beyond Power: On Women, Men & Morals.* New York: Ballantine.

Gilbert, A.
1987. 'Forms and Effectiveness of Community Participation in Squatter Settlements'. *Regional Development Journal* 8, no. 4:56–80.

Gorham, E.
1995. 'Social Citizenship and Its Fetters'. *Polity* 28, no. 1:25–47.

Hill, L.

1991. 'Power and Citizenship in a Democratic Society'. *Political Science and Politics* 24, no. 3:495–8.

Hoatson, L., J. Dixon, and D. Sloman.

1996. 'Community Development Citizenship and the Contract State'. *Community Development Journal* 31, no. 2:126–36.

Hunt, S.

1990. 'Building Alliances: Professional and Political Issues in Community Participation. Examples from a Health and Community Development Project'. *Health Promotion International* 5, no. 3:179–85.

Israel, B.A., et al.

1994. 'Health Education and Community Empowerment: Conceptualizing and Measuring Perceptions of Individual, Organizational and Community Control'. *Health Education Quarterly* 21, no. 2:149–70.

Jones, P.S., and A.I. Meleis.

1993. 'Health Is Empowerment'. *Advances in Nursing Science* 15, no. 3:1–14.

Kaplan, W.

1993. 'Who Belongs? Changing Concepts of Citizenship and Nationality'. In *Belonging: The Meaning and Future of Citizenship*, edited by W. Kaplan, 245–64. Montreal and Kingston: McGill-Queen's University Press.

Kathlene, L., and J.A. Martin.

1991. 'Enhancing Citizenship Participation: Panel Designs, Perspectives and Policy Formation'. *Journal of Policy Analysis and Management* 10, no. 1:46–63.

Kelly, K.J., and H. Van Vlaenderen.

1996. 'Dynamics of Participation in a Community Health Project'. *Social Science in Medicine* 42, no. 9:1235–46.

Kieffer, C.

1984. 'Citizen Empowerment: A Developmental Perspective'. *Prevention in Human Services* 3, no. 16:9–35.

Kubiski, W.S.

1990. *Citizen Participation in the '90s: Realities, Challenges and Opportunities.* Winnipeg: Institute of Urban Studies, University of Winnipeg.

Lomas, J., and G. Veenstra.

1995. 'If You Build It, Who Will Come?' *Policy Options* (November):37–40.

Lord, J.

1994. 'Personal Empowerment and Active Living'. In *Toward Active Living*, edited by H.A. Quinney, L. Gauvin, and A.E.T. Wall, 213–18. Windsor, ON: Human Kinetics Publishers.

_____, and P. Hutchison.

1993. 'The Process of Empowerment: Implications for Theory and Practice'. *Canadian Journal of Community Mental Health* 12, no. 1:5–23.

Macallan, L., and V. Narayan.

1994. 'Keeping the Heart Beat in Grampian: A Case Study in Community Participation and Ownership'. *Health Promotion International* 9, no. 1:13–19.

McCarron, G., S. Tenenbein, and P. Hindley.

1994. 'Communication, Belonging and Health'. In *The Determinants of Population Health*, edited by M. Hayes, L. Foster, and H. Foster, 57–72. Victoria: University of Victoria.

McKnight, J.

1992. 'Redefining Community'. *Social Policy* (Fall/Winter):56–62.

Marshall, T.H.

1977. *Class, Citizenship and Social Development*. Chicago: University of Chicago Press.

Merzel, C.

1991. 'Rethinking Empowerment'. *Health/PAC Bulletin* (Winter):5–6.

Mhatre, S.L., and R.B. Deber.

1992. 'From Equal Access to Health Care to Equitable Access to Health: A Review of Canadian Provincial Health Commissions and Reports'. *International Journal of Health Services* 22, no. 4:645–68.

Moon, J.D.

1988. 'The Moral Basis of the Democratic Welfare State'. In *Democracy and the Welfare State*, edited by A. Gutmann, 27–52. Princeton: Princeton University Press.

Nelson, G., et al.

1995. 'Psychiatric Consumer/Survivors' Quality of Life: Quantitative and Qualitative Perspectives'. *Journal of Community Psychology* 23:216–33.

Norton, S., et al.

1993. 'Perceived Costs and Benefits of Membership in a Self-Help Group: Comparisons of Members and Nonmembers of the Alliance for the Mentally Ill'. *Community Mental Health Journal* 29, no. 2:143–59.

Pateman, C.

1988. 'The Patriarchal Welfare State'. In *Democracy and the Welfare State*, edited by A. Gutmann, 231–60. Princeton: Princeton University Press.

Persons, G.A.

1990. 'Defining Public Interest: Citizen Participation in Metropolitan and State Policy Making'. *National Civic Review* 79, no. 2:118–31.

Potapchuk, W.R.

1991. 'New Approaches to Citizen Participation: Building Consent'. *National Civic Review* 80, no. 2:158–68.

Poulin, J., and S. Kauffman.

1995. 'Citizen Participation in Prevention Activities: Path Model II'. *Journal of Community Psychology* 23:234–49.

Prestby, J.E., et al.

1990. 'Benefits, Costs, Incentive Management and Participation in Voluntary Organizations: A Means to Understanding and Promoting Empowerment'. *American Journal of Community Psychology* 18, no. 1:117–49.

Rappaport, J.

1985. 'The Power of Empowerment Language'. *Social Policy* (Fall):15–21.

Riger, S.

1990. 'What's Wrong with Empowerment?' *American Journal of Community Psychology* 21, no. 3:279–93.

Roche, M.

1987. 'Citizenship, Social Theory and Social Change'. *Theory and Society* 16:376–7.

Rosener, J.B.

1978. 'Matching Method to Purpose: The Challenges of Planning Citizen-Participation Activities'. In *Citizen Participation in America*, edited by S. Langton, 109–22. Lexington: D.C. Heath and Company.

Schulz, A.J., et al.

1995. 'Empowerment as a Multi-level Construct: Perceived Control at the Individual, Organizational and Community Levels'. *Health Education Research* 10, no. 3:309–27.

Sen, R.

1994. 'Building Community Involvement in Health Care'. *Social Policy* (Spring):32–43.

Sheilds, L.

1995. 'Women's Experiences of the Meaning of Empowerment'. *Qualitative Health Research* 5, no. 1:15–35.

Sherraden, M.S.

1991. 'Policy Impacts of Community Participation: Health Services in Rural Mexico'. *Human Organization* 50, no. 3:256–63.

Smith, D.

1995. *First Person Plural: A Community Development Approach to Social Change*. Montreal: Black Rose Books.

Syme, G.J., and B.E. Nancarrow.

1992. 'Predicting Public Involvement in Urban Water Management and Planning'. *Environment and Behavior* 24, no. 6:738–58.

Wandersman, A.

1994. Personal communication.

_____, et al.

1987. 'Who Participates, Who Does Not and Why: An Analysis of Voluntary Neighborhood Organizations in the United States and Israel'. *Sociological Forum* 2:534–55.

Wharf Higgins, J.

1992. 'The Healthy Communities Movement'. In *Communities and Social Policy in Canada*, edited by B. Wharf, 151–80. Toronto: McClelland and Stewart.

Wolf, M.

1993. 'Involving the Community in National Service'. *Social Policy* (Fall):14–20.

Wolfensberger, W.

1983. 'Social Role Valorization: A Proposed New Term for the Principle of Normalization'. *Mental Retardation* 21, no. 6:235–9.

Zimmerman, M.A., et al.

1992. 'Further Explorations in Empowerment Theory: An Empirical Analysis of Psychological Empowerment'. *American Journal of Community Psychology* 20, no. 6:707–27.

Chapter Fifteen

Lessons and Legacies

Brian Wharf and Michael Clague

This concluding chapter addresses the objectives of the book outlined in Chapter 1. First, we sought to describe the beginnings of community development in Canada, which, to some extent, has been achieved. Certainly the beginnings in Quebec are chronicled in detail, but the chapter on the history of community development in anglophone Canada represents an overview of significant events rather than a province-by-province review. While it would have been desirable to include chapters on the beginnings in Atlantic Canada, Ontario, the Prairies, and BC, as well as Quebec, this would have turned the book into a history of community development to the exclusion of other objectives.

A second objective was to tell the stories about a number of state-sponsored activities that occurred in the 1970s, and a number of significant initiatives are chronicled in chapters 6, 7, and 8.

A third objective was to report on current community development activities. Some of these are known as social movements, and we explore the meanings attached to community development and social movements later in the chapter. Whether conceptualized as community development or social movement, organizing to bring about changes in the environment, for women, and in First Nations communities represents some of the most vibrant change efforts occurring now.

A fourth objective was to determine if the case-studies could shed light on a number of troubling dilemmas that have and continue to bedevil community development. Most of this chapter is devoted to addressing these dilemmas, but first we need to acknowledge that while all of the above objectives have been met to some extent, we encountered considerable difficulties in tackling a fifth objective. We asked chapter authors to consider whether their case-studies revealed the use of building-blocks in terms of theory or previous practice. For example, were frameworks such as those developed by Rothman or Dominelli used? If so, were they helpful or were they a distraction? While some commented on the utility of frameworks, others did not.

Dilemmas in Community Development

1. What has been, is, and should be the relationship between community organizations and the state?

2. What is community development and can any unique characteristics be identified? What are the differences between community development and social movements?

3. Did the initiatives reported in the case-studies change the ordinary and grand issues of social policy?

4. How is community development funded?

5. Are the existing conceptualizations of practice useful? Are new ones required?

6. Is community development an appropriate and acceptable term?

As a way of concluding the book, we address perhaps the most difficult dilemma of all: in these unsettled times, can we create caring communities and, if so, how?

The Relationship Between Community Development and the State

The case-studies reveal a wide range of activities aimed at bringing about change, and all of them bring communities into contact with the state. The extent and complexity of the relationship is illustrated by the experiences of community groups in Quebec. In a letter to the editors, Deena White commented on this relationship as follows:

> It is important to understand how central the concept of the state is in Quebec as the representation of the 'nation', where perhaps the Catholic Church had played the dominant role prior to the 60s. With the state serving as a kind of magnet for all society building (to avoid saying 'nation building') and community action groups seeing themselves as contributing to the development of the society, a state/community dynamic emerges, which makes community action in Quebec exciting and allows for some influence in both directions (White 1995).

Community groups in Quebec have taken on a number of activities. They deliver services designed and funded by the state, while at the same time reserving the right to criticize the rationale and objectives of some of these services. Thus while a number of organizations, including the provincial welfare rights organization, have argued against workfare programs, some agencies have taken advantage of provincial funds to establish workfare programs for recipients of social assistance. A not inconsiderable consequence of these programs has been to strengthen the voluntary sector. In Chapter 4 White claims that 'Community action is now most likely to be kindled by the convergence of grassroots and government strategies, in spite of their different objectives.'

The relationship between the state and communities differs in a number of ways, but most importantly on the dimension of autonomy. What degree of autonomy do communities have in their attempts to bring about change? Five variations of this relationship can be identified, and these are arranged in an ascending order of community autonomy in a manner similar to the well-known ladder of citizen participation (Arnstein 1969). To avoid confusion, it should be noted that the following discussion focuses on the relationship between community organizations and the state, and not on the process of community development. We note further that mutual aid and self-help are contained in all of these variations of autonomy.

1. Agent of the state
2. Partner with the state
3. Campaigning against the state
4. Independent of the state
5. Challenging state institutions and values

Agent of the State

In this function communities implement plans conceived elsewhere. The most extreme form of the agent role occurs when senior levels of government off-load responsibilities to communities without a commensurate transfer of resources. Off-loading represents the policy position of neoconservative and neoliberal governments. This position neatly combines their determination to reduce the deficit and cut back on social programs with an ideology that regards families, friends, voluntary agencies, and churches as the most suitable institutions to provide help. Although there are no chapters dedicated to off-loading, criticism of this policy is evident in many chapters.

Communities often welcome the role of agent if adequate resources are provided in order to tackle troubling issues such as unemployment. Thus the chapters on the Company of Young Canadians and the Opportunities for Youth and Local Initiatives programs describe how communities responded to and carried out programs designed by departments of the federal government. Although these programs were conceived outside the community, they had both short- and long-term contributions, some of which we describe in the section on the impact of community development.

As a matter of principle, we are opposed to off-loading and indeed to the role of agent for communities. We believe that those responsible for implementing policy must have some voice in designing the policy. This principle holds both with respect to direct-service staff in organizations and to communities implementing the policies of senior levels of government. The research on policy implementation supports our contention that separating the responsibility for design from that of implementation is a recipe for failure (see, among other sources, the collection of articles in the special issue of the *Policy Studies Review* 7, no. 1, 1987).

Partner with the State

The role of partner brings communities into a more proactive stance in which community institutions collaborate with senior levels of government to design and implement policies and programs. Some examples of the partner role include the Children's Aid Societies in Ontario, the regional and local health and welfare centres in Quebec, and regional school boards in many provinces. Nevertheless, given their control over resources and legislation/policy, federal and provincial governments are, without doubt, the senior partners. They can dissolve any community agency or school board that they regard as incapable of fulfilling its responsibilities, as happened recently in BC where elected members of the North Vancouver school board were dismissed.

The role of partner requires community agencies to engage in social planning and advocacy functions. Indeed, some school boards and agencies like the Ontario Association of Children's Aid Societies have developed the capacity for quite sophisticated research and planning, and on the basis of these activities can and do criticize provincial and federal policies.

Campaigning Against the State

In its advocate function, community development represents the disadvantaged and argues for additional resources from the state. This is, of course, the function described in Chapter 1 as social action with Saul Alinsky (1971), the best known and certainly the most colourful practitioner. The advocacy experiences described in this book do not have the flair and dash of Alinsky's style of organizing, and indeed only the First Nations and environmental movements resort to confrontation as part of their strategies. The antipoverty movement—as represented by the National Association Against Poverty, Campaign 2000, and many local groups—relies mainly on a social planning strategy based on research and culminating in testimony to legislative committees and briefs to provincial and federal governments.

Independent of the State

Autonomous community organizations develop and control services with little or no interference from the state. The autonomous community represents the antithesis of off-loading since the community has the initiative and control.

This role represents the dream of old community theorists like Murray Ross (with Lappin 1967), who argued that developing community capacity was the overall objective of community development. Yet as John McKnight (1987) argues, rather than developing the capacity of communities, professionals have developed a service industry whose best clients are themselves. By contrast, McKnight claims that communities can take care of their own, and his argument is supported in this book by the determination of First Nations communities to regain health and independence.

In our view, the case for community independence is compelling, and it is the role we favour for providing out-patient health, social, and recreational services. Community autonomy ensures that those affected by social policies will be central in the development of these policies. However, as we have noted in previous works (Wharf 1992), it can lead to the condition of 'acute localitis' (Montgomery 1979). This condition refers to the domination of community affairs by an élite few and to the establishment of values and norms of behaviour that are different from and not supported by the larger community. We are reminded by feminists, who point out that, like families, communities can become closed, conservative, and critical of views from outside (see Chapter 10 by Callahan in this book).

We are also reminded that many of Canada's most progressive social policies came from federal and provincial governments, and despite our disenchantment with the current federal government's neoconservative philosophy (and in particular that of its immediate predecessor), we continue to believe in the case for national policies in health and social welfare.

A crucial component in this discussion of community independence is the notion of caring. Can communities become caring places and, if so, what are the requirements? Using Warren's framework outlined in Chapter 1, it seems that not all communities have an innate capacity for caring. Indeed, initiating and nourishing this capacity will be extremely difficult in transitory and anomic neighbourhoods, which lack both identity and interaction (Warren 1980). We contend that caring communities require both national/provincial policies and local institutions around which caring activities can cluster.

Challenging State Institutions and Values

In this function community development challenges the accepted norms and the boundaries of what is seen as permissible in society. While in one sense the state represents these norms and establishes the boundaries, many changes go beyond altering state priorities and policies. The intent of social movements is to change the public's perceptions with regard to such differing matters as the prevailing attitudes to gays and lesbians, how we define work, and what kinds of work should be paid from the public purse. The work of the feminist and environmental movements provide examples of successful challenges, although both acknowledge that their work is far from finished.

Like all typologies, the boundaries in this classification are permeable, and the experiences chronicled in the case-studies slide between categories. Thus a community group or agency may act as a partner with the state, while at the same time advocating for change and thinking of ways to alter societal norms and attitudes.

What Is Community Development? How Does It Differ from Social Movements?

In Chapter 1 we outlined some of the more well-known definitions and descriptions of community development. Here we review this discussion using the insights obtained from the preceding chapters. It is clear that the chapter authors affirm the view that community development is a strategy of change grounded in an ethos of equality and social justice. It is a process anchored in the conviction that all affected by a particular action or decision should have an opportunity to participate. Yet as we will argue in a later section of the chapter, despite this noble intent and some considerable achievements, community development has thus far failed to alter significantly the grand issues of social policy.

A number of chapters suggest that participating in community development activities represents one of the few ways for ordinary people and consumers of health and social services to bring about change. That said, we are reminded by the chapter on health reform that the invitation to participate is typically taken up by the well-off, the well spoken, and the well educated.

While Chapter 14 deals with a provincial initiative in health reform, the task of securing participation was assigned to regional and local groups. The chapter sets the challenge to find more appropriate ways to involve consumers and marginalized people in community activities.

From his review of the history of English-speaking Canada in Chapter 2, Lotz makes the point that community development occurs when communities are in trouble, when the state or the market has failed to provide jobs or housing. Lotz puts the point in a cogent fashion:

> Community development has too often been seen simply as a process or an approach for dealing with the problems of marginalized and disadvantaged groups and peoples. Seldom is it recognized as a way of coping with the central government's failure to understand ordinary people's needs and aspirations and institute the structural changes required to meet them.

In their description of the beginnings of community development in Quebec in Chapter 3, Panet-Raymond and Mayer make a similar case for the contributions of community development: 'With the help of social animators and financial assistance from the Church and the United Way, tenants, consumers, and the unemployed organized themselves into committees. They advocated for rights to housing, work, health, leisure, and recreational facilities, especially for children and families.' A combination of state and community forces are required to assist in the development of caring communities.

We turn now to a discussion of community development and social movements. Given the intent of community development to strive for social justice, what distinguishes community development from social movements? Indeed, the term social movement is usually applied to organizing initiatives in feminist and First Nations communities and with respect to the environment. Is community development a movement? If so, it is rarely identified as such in the writings on social movements. Two of the most recent books on social movements in Canada contain only fleeting references to community development (Carroll 1992; Cunningham et al. 1988).

For its part, the literature on community development emphasizes the process of bringing about change and gives particular attention to such matters as organizational auspices, resources, and professional skills (Brager et al. 1987; Lee 1986). Since we have devoted considerable space to defining and describing community development, we now identify the salient characteristics of social movements.

Carroll and colleagues identify two forms of social movements. The earliest conceptualization is known as resource mobilization theory.

On the basis of felt grievances stemming from shared interests, the constituents of a movement pool their resources and secure other resources in order to pursue collective goods such as higher wages, universal day care and Native land claims. The strengths of this perspective lie in its focus on the social organization of collective action. The weaknesses are the absence of ideology and the similarity to pressure group politics (Carroll 1992:7).

A more recent conceptualization favoured by Carroll and colleagues is described as New Social Movements.

New Social Movements are viewed as instances of cultural and political praxis through which new identities are formed, new ways of life are tested and new forms of community are prefigured. Social movements are determined by the extent to which actions challenge or break the limits of a system of social relations (Carroll 1992:10).

Given these definitions, the similarity between social movements and community development is readily apparent. Resource mobilization resembles those community development activities that press for new resources on behalf of disadvantaged groups. The more recent perspective challenges accepted ways of governing and behaving in society. A clear example of confronting the existing pattern of social relations comes from Chapter 4, which describes how community organizations in Quebec challenged the conception of mental illness as defined by psychiatrists and other professionals.

Even the most progressive civil servants rarely shared the ideological convictions of the grassroots activists. While the councils often supported psychiatric hospitals that wanted to create support structures in the community for their deinstitutionalized patients, the activists ultimately wanted to *remove* the psychiatric establishment and *eliminate* narrow medical treatment.

Social movements are characterized by outrage, commitment to a cause, and leadership from charismatic people. These characteristics are found in many community development initiatives. The chapters on Quebec and BC present evidence of the vibrancy and commitment of community development activities. In Chapter 3, Panet-Raymond and Mayer contend that 'Community development is really a social movement in Quebec, which explains its impact.'

In view of the similarities between community development and social movements, why are they treated separately in the literature and indeed in common parlance? Several reasons are advanced here.

First, community development has traditionally been an arena for professional practice for social workers, adult educators, and others. Whether the action took the form of Alinsky's conflict tactics or Ross's cooperative style, much of the analytic and strategic work was performed by paid professional staff. Indeed, Alinsky often claimed that one of his trained workers could organize any community to deal with a troubling issue. While the theory of community development demanded that these experts be 'on tap and not on top', and while in many instances the professionals worked to do local communities' bidding, they were nevertheless pivotal to the unfolding of community action. These were the days when texts such as the influential *Dynamics of Planned Change* (Lippitt et al. 1958) spoke unabashedly about the role of the planned change expert, who in effect became a therapist and change agent for communities.

The professional's role has changed significantly in recent years. In the feminist and First Nations movements, and in organizations like the BC Association for Community Living, members develop the agenda and determine what kind of advice and support they need. They have redefined the relationship between helper and client and replaced it with mutuality and partnership. Campaign 2000 illustrates this development in which poor people, community workers, and others have joined together in a national movement to end child poverty. Nevertheless, as the chapter on community economic development makes very clear, there is still a role for professionals who provide information and training about specific activities.

A second reason for the distinction between community development and social movements is that the history of community development is firmly grounded in communities of place and in activities, such as advocating against the construction of high-rise buildings and campaigning for new health and social services. Given the strength of this history, many still see community development as having a firm connection to neighbourhoods and other localities, whereas social movements transcend local issues and are national and even international in their scope.

A third reason was noted in the first chapter and concerns the historical baggage of community development. In Chapter 11, Absolon and Herbert argue that for First Nations peoples, community development has been a disaster, as it destroyed their culture and lifestyles.

However, as Tester notes in Chapter 12, the distinction between community development and social movements is fading: 'community development has increasingly focused on movements as well as geographically defined communities . . . unlike the 1950s, community development initiatives have increasingly challenged rather than served the state's interests.' He supports the argument with the two vignettes in the chapter. Strathcona community gardens is a local initiative that transformed an industrial dump site into community gardens, but residents did not leave the initiative as a purely local effort. Rather, convinced of the case for banning pesticides and concerned about their use elsewhere in municipal parks, they took their case to city council and won. The second illustrates a community take-over of a logging operation, which has changed clear-cutting into environmentally friendly logging.

We return to the question raised at the beginning of this section: What is community development, and can any unique characteristics be identified? In the view of many chapter authors, community development is dedicated to changing the status quo and to bringing about a more just and equal society. Community development provides a vehicle for ordinary citizens in low-income neighbourhoods to articulate their needs and priorities. Given the barriers that prevent these citizens from taking an active role in the democratic process, such participation becomes an important way to exercise the democratic franchise.

Perhaps the most important characteristic of community development is the ethic of solidarity, of wanting to belong to and be supported by a group. For some, belonging involves attachment to a place and to neighbours. For others, particularly those who have the resources to travel outside their place of residence, common interests provide the reason for attachment, as White describes in Chapter 4.

> In all cases the principal difference between these projects and those programs implemented by, for example, public ('community') health professionals lies in the significance attached to '*la vie associative*': conviviality, or ways of 'being together', are the very essence of the 'intervention'. This seems to be true not only of those organizations initiated by activists but also of less politically conscious, local self-help projects, such as collective kitchens and thrift shops. The 'community' in this form of action is often embodied in the organization itself, consisting of both workers and users for whom the organization *becomes* their community.

The Impact of Community Development

The case-studies reveal rich legacies of community development. In the following discussion, we summarize some of the most important ones. Many chapters identify agencies and programs that were established by community development initiatives and still exist today. It is not our intent to repeat the impacts recorded in the various chapters, and we emphasize only the most substantial impacts.

The Opportunities for Youth (OFY) and Local Initiatives Program (LIP) represent the agent rung in the ladder of community participation. Although community advisory councils were established, it is clear that communities played a role in a plan conceived at the federal level. OFY and LIP were designed by federal bureaucrats, albeit creative ones, funded by the federal government, and then implemented in local communities. But even in this conception of a federally designed plan, one objective of LIP, according to a briefing paper quoted by Keck and Fulks in Chapter 6, was 'to test whether state intervention can take the form of supporting groups of unemployed or sub-employed individuals to seek solutions to their problems . . .' Hence we see here the intent to provide opportunities for communities to resolve troubling issues, but such an intent requires much more than an invitation. As the chapters on health reform, regional planning, and community economic development make clear, most state interventions (however positive in intent) will experience difficulties, if not outright rejection, if they are parachuted into communities. In Chapter 9, Lewis outlines the case for 'social scaffolding', which includes involving local and important institutions and gaining widespread community support.

It is also clear that these programs reflected the context of the times. Untroubled by the now-omnipresent issue of the deficit, the federal government was able to allocate large sums of money to resolve unemployment among the young and the seasonally employed. Significantly the unemployment rate was 4 per cent in contrast to the 1996 rate of 11 per cent, yet at that time, a 4 per cent rate was seen as sufficiently serious to warrant large-scale intervention by the federal government.

Despite the essentially passive role for communities, these programs did have demonstrable impacts. First, they created services, such as transition houses, which are now an accepted part of the many social services in all communities. Second, these programs commenced the difficult task of altering societal attitudes. That they achieved some success is illustrated by the remarks of an influential columnist. In a 1975 *Toronto Star* column, Anthony Westall wrote that paying women to do social service work was beyond the pale! In Westall's opinion, this contributed to unemployment rather than solving it! In 1996, while a few ardent neoconservatives support the notion that women should return to the kitchen, only the most foolhardy would campaign for its adoption.

The Company of Young Canadians (CYC) was also designed and funded by the federal government. Yet from the beginning, the staff of CYC were assigned to work *for* communities, and, at least in the view of the authors of Chapter 7, the CYC can be seen as an early experiment in a partnership between the state and communities. The CYC launched one of the first and still successful comprehensive community health centres in Ottawa–Carleton, and made a substantial contribution to First Nations communities. For example, CYC was instrumental in starting cultural education centres in Yellowknife and Alert Bay, and established Aboriginal radio stations.

One of the most significant contributions of the CYC was to recognize the importance of community economic development, and it can be regarded as a pioneer in community economic development. In its later years, over half of its projects had an economic component. Finally, we note Brodhead, Goodings, and Brodhead's claim (in this book) that the CYC established the right to organize on a local basis: 'Above all, the status quo had been challenged, sometimes successfully, and the establishment had been put on notice.'

The second rung of the community autonomy ladder is that of partner in which communities take on a more active and creative role. Chapter 5 on the turbulent years in BC documents the design and implementation of the Local Area Approach, which represented the efforts of community development workers and social planners to resolve the vexing issue of coordinating and integrating services. While it lacked legislative clout, the approach encompassed much of the reasoning that eventually formed the foundation of the Community Resource Board Act. As Clague notes in Chapter 5, this act had the potential to alter substantially the landscape of health and social services in BC. However, the act was short-lived. The 1975 election of a Social Credit government, which embraced a neoconservative approach to social policy, resulted in the neglect of these initiatives. They remained as stalled ventures until the re-election of the NDP government in 1991.

Fortunately, this has not been the case in Quebec, and as the chapters on the history and recent events in that province make clear, the contribution of community groups has been substantial on all rungs of the autonomy ladder. These chapters are replete with examples of the number and variety of community groups and provincial associations. Their accomplishments have ranged from the establishment of a number of programs, such as women's shelters and centres for homeless youths, to influencing the content of provincial policies in mental health.

The role of challenging norms and values is illustrated by community economic development, which is in the process of changing some fundamental conceptions of the economy and work. Community economic development practitioners argue that communities can create employment, can own and govern economic enterprises, and can distribute rewards in a just and equitable fashion. The environmental movement has entered into the jobs-versus-environment debate, and as Tester argues in Chapter 12, the challenge is to 'integrate principles of social justice with environmental considerations'. The feminist and First Nations movements have substantially altered societal perceptions of women and First Nations people.

The overall impact of the initiatives reported here can be summarized as follows. Community development activities have been and can be effective in advocating and developing new arrangements in community care. They can challenge accepted norms and values, which requires commitment, resources, and imagination over a long period. However, community development activities have failed to alter the grand issues of social policy on the distribution of power and income, and, as the chapter on Campaign 2000 makes abundantly clear, the grand issues are inordinately difficult to change. We return to this example in a later section of the chapter.

An Alternative View

It is apparent that most of the case-studies represent a very positive view of community development. Many of the authors invested years of their lives in community development activities and, despite disappointments, cherish optimism about community development as a strategy for change. The optimism is firmly supported by many chapters, particularly the Quebec chapters, which document the significant changes that have occurred as a consequence of the efforts of community groups at both local and provincial levels.

Yet these views are by no means unanimous. Other writers have criticized community development as a strategy for change. From her review of community development's accomplishments, Dixon claims that 'CD has been generally an intervention imposed from outside for the good of those inside—it has been a paternalistic intervention' (Dixon 1989:88). To this observation others would add that community development has not only been paternalistic but patriarchal (Callahan in this book), racist (Absolon and Herbert in this book), and classist (Ng et al. 1990).

In contrast with the very positive tone of Chapter 7 about the accomplishments of the Company of Young Canadians, a review by a First Nations writer arrives at a very different conclusion:

> While the CYC was not created to serve any particular ethnic group in Canada, a large part of its program was aimed at native communities. These young, instant experts on things Indian were, like community development officers, supposed to motivate the people to use their own initiative. Instead,

bumbling and stumbling through community after community with little or no sensitivity to the feelings of the people they were going to help if it killed them, these dedicated amateurs discouraged and weakened Indian organizations. . . . The net result of their eager (and quite truly most of these young people meant well) fumbling was to weaken the base through which the Indian could express his needs and through which he had the best opportunity to press his case (Cardinal 1969:400).

Indeed, similar criticisms are launched against many community development initiatives. Left-leaning critics argue that community development addresses only minor matters, and in doing so diverts attention from the grand issues of social policy, thereby allowing the unequal distribution of wealth and power to continue (Lemann 1988). In this view, the main purpose of community development is to smother dissent.

How Is Community Development Funded?

Financial support for community development activities has always been sparse and difficult to acquire. Community organizations raise funds in a variety of ways, and indeed many complain that they spend so much time in fundraising that they do not have time to get on with their work. Given the difficulties in obtaining financial support, the establishment of the Secrétariat à l'action communautaire in Quebec is both a welcome and innovative initiative.

But as many chapters point out, receiving funds from the state is a double-edged sword since a continuing relationship with the state may blunt the radical edge of community groups. According to Panet-Raymond and Mayer, 'the dilemma facing community development in the 1990s is how to become a viable partner while not losing its original mission'.

In addition to its strong tendency to co-opt community groups into its agenda, the state can be a fickle funder. Since the election of Lucien Bouchard as premier of Quebec, the *sécretariat* has been awarded a new mandate to develop *l'économie sociale*. This mandate represents a substantial change from the original purpose of government support for community action to one of funding community agencies, which provide services and, in particular, develop the social economy of Quebec.

We should add that the *sécretariat* is not without precedent. In its early days, the Welfare Grants Division of the then department of National Health and Welfare created a program that allocated funds to community organizations and even to radical welfare rights groups. These groups brought together recipients of social assistance and demanded increases in the amount of assistance and in the ways in which it was administered. The program proved to be contentious, particularly when welfare rights groups launched demonstrations against organizations like the Salvation Army. Over time the Welfare Grants Division changed its priorities and, prior to its demise in 1995, funded only 'safe' and 'respectable' research.

The Canada Assistance Plan (CAP) was an additional source of funding and support for community development activities for many years. CAP was conceived primarily as an instrument of federal leadership to promote similar standards among provincial social assistance and child welfare programs. By contributing half of the costs of these programs, the federal government was able to exercise considerable influence in setting standards and eliminating provincial residency requirements. CAP also contributed to the cost of community development programs initiated by municipal and provincial governments. Regrettably, from our point of view, CAP was cancelled in 1996 and, aside from Canada Futures noted in Chapter 9, the federal government provides no funding for community development activities.

Is There a Conceptual Base of Practice?

As noted at the beginning of the chapter, authors were asked whether conceptualizations of practice informed their work or the work they were describing. Were any of the concepts and frameworks outlined in Chapter 1 useful in thinking about and writing their chapters? There were two types of responses. Some academics based their work in the literature. Thus Panet-Raymond and Mayer noted the influence of Rothman and a number of francophone theorists; Absolon and Herbert indicated the usefulness of the work of Freire, hooks, and Moreau; and Callahan built on the conceptualizations of feminists like Dominelli in constructing a new approach to feminist organizing.

But practitioners like the Brodheads, Goodings, and Lewis anchored their work in a cause: to bring about change untrammelled by theory and concepts. Certainly their work had a vision and was purposeful, yet the strategies emerged from thought and discussions rather than from conceptualizations of practice.

The point is not new. In an earlier work, Wharf wrote about the connections between theory and practice in community organizing as follows:

> The demands of practice are such that community workers are hard pressed to find time to read and keep up with the literature. Unless one received a thorough grounding in theory while at university and then used concepts

and frameworks in practice, theory simply takes a back seat. To be used theory has to be useful and the case studies suggest that practitioners have not found this to be so (Wharf 1992:221).

One concept we did not introduce in Chapter 1 is the notion of convergence of interest, but over the years it has captured our attention as a useful framework for thinking about and analysing practice, the convergence of interest (Sower 1957). Convergence occurs when an issue has currency and potency, when it is an issue whose time has come, when resources are available, and when dedicated champions lead the charge. For example, consider the difference between the successes achieved by the environmental movement in the 1990s and the work of Campaign 2000. Prior to its recent successes, the environmental movement had struggled for years to establish its cause as legitimate. Its early struggles were contemptuously dismissed as the ravings of hippies and discontented academics who did not understand the realities of economics. The new movement won some battles only when its proponents kept environmental issues on the policy and community agendas, gained the support of respected people, and made clear the logic of their argument and the barrenness of opposing arguments.

By contrast Campaign 2000 is taking place in a context dominated by national and provincial deficits. In addition, the clever but false claims of neoconservative politicians and their business allies that the debt has been brought about by excessive spending on social programs makes it extremely difficult to argue for additional resources to eliminate child poverty. Hence Campaign 2000 confronts a hostile attitude that is reinforced by the perception that Campaign 2000 is led by professional poverty activists and social workers who, like their earlier counterparts in the environmental movement, lack social standing, credibility, and any understanding of politics and economics.

Indeed, Campaign 2000 is striving for a virtual revolution. It is trying to reverse a strongly held belief that parents are solely responsible for the care of their children. This belief is most firmly held by upper-class and conservative people who are, of course, in the fortunate position of having the resources to support both their children and their ideology. In one fell swoop, Campaign 2000 confronts well-established beliefs and the influential people who cherish them.

To challenge these beliefs, Campaign 2000 will require sufficient resources and influential allies. With the help of these allies, it may then be able to advance prominently and persistently the arguments of Linda McQuaig and others that the real reasons for the deficit are high interest rates and low taxation rates for corporations and the wealthy (McQuaig 1993,

1994). It may also draw attention to the costs of child poverty by revealing the impact of poverty on health, education, and employment. Indeed, with resources and allies, Campaign 2000 may develop into a social movement, but it will need to be a very powerful one to overcome the barriers of power and privilege that presently keep children in poverty.

The notion of the convergence of interest applies just as neatly to small-scale neighbourhood efforts, such as building a community garden or bicycle routes. Convergence of interest enables citizens to assess commitment and timing, match resources against resistance, and identify appropriate strategies.

To Develop or Organize?

We now review the definitional issue of community development. The two terms are so intertwined and embedded in our vocabulary that it may be impossible to 'kill them off' (Mayo 1994:65). However, we take seriously the point made by Absolon, Herbert, and others who contend that development is an offensive term. If change efforts are to include and respect organizers and workers in First Nations communities and in the feminist movement, we must eradicate vocabulary that is offensive.

Along with Miller, Rein, and Levitt, we prefer the term organizing to development (Miller, Rein, and Levitt 1990). They note that organizing can occur in a variety of locales and around several issues. In Chapter 10 Callahan, too, uses organizing as her term of choice in discussing feminist community organizing. Organizing encompasses the efforts of neighbour-hood residents to free their areas from crime (Wilson and Kelling 1989), of First Nations communities to resurrect traditional methods of healing and governing, and of groups determined to change societal perceptions. With organizing as the key term, we can talk about organizing in neighbourhoods, in interest groups, and in social movements.

We also want to identify characteristics of organizing that will assist groups in preserving the mission of reform rather than being captured by the state. In dismantling the stereotypes of feminist organizing in Chapter 10, Callahan has proposed activities for feminist workers that might well serve as an example for all organizers. These activities are based on analysing power to illuminate oppression, to bring about reparations for the disadvantaged, to transform caring work into a valued and paid activity, and to work towards a more just and equal society.

These activities are similar to the tasks of advocacy, developing new arrangements in community care, and challenging the accepted notions of social policies and institutions identified at the beginning of the chapter. However, the feminist terms give an added bite or edge and leave no doubt as to whose side organizers are on.

Some additional advantages of substituting organizing for development should be noted. It is a plain, simple term that is readily understandable to all. We organize in order to bring about change. As a neutral term, organizing does not have the shades of meaning associated with terms like social action, social planning, and locality development. These shades of meaning have, of course, resulted from the Rothman framework. It is a tribute to the influence of Rothman's work that, despite his plea to the contrary, strategies of change tend to be associated with the models of social action, social planning, and locality development. Thus social action carries the connotation of Alinsky's conflict orientation, social planning involves research and rational persuasion, and locality development is essentially a benevolent grassroots approach to change.

As many of the chapters make abundantly clear, groups use a variety of strategies sometimes sequentially and sometimes simultaneously. Most strategies require a base of relevant research and clear thinking in order to decide on the most advantageous strategy. A useful and simple conceptualization of strategies comes from Warren, who distinguishes between consensus, campaign, and conflict strategies (Warren 1969). Consensus strategies are used when there is agreement between the state and the group pressing for change. These strategies take the form of research, briefs, and rational arguments. Campaign strategies occupy the middle ground when the state does not regard the issue as high priority. Strategists then try to bring the issue to the public's attention and use both public education and arm-twisting sessions with key people. Conflict strategies come into play when the parties disagree, and values clash, as exemplified by the feminist, First Nations, and environmental movements, which often mount demonstrations, marches, or other public displays of discontent.

An additional advantage of organizing is that it sends a clear message to those of a neoconservative bent. Organizing in communities is distinctly different from developing communities so that the state can off-load its responsibilities. As Callahan notes in Chapter 10, it is women who bear the brunt of off-loading despite the rhetoric of 'community empowerment'.

The chapters have made abundantly clear that organizing is most often directed at changing the priorities of various levels of government. Organizing is an option open to people who are not often among the ranks of elected politicians, and hence represent another set of views about issues and governance. While politicians in senior levels of government are elected to represent the views of their constituents, they are, by and large, upper- and middle-class conservative males and represent the values of conservative Canada. If we wish to have a more open and participatory style of policy making, we should recognize that the views of groups like the National Anti-Poverty Organization and its provincial and local counterparts can make significant contributions. They are familiar with issues such as poverty, inadequate housing, and unsafe neighbourhoods, and they can offer illuminating information about policy debates on these issues. We should note, too, that while low-income and marginalized groups are frequently dismissed as special interest groups, hardly anyone hurls similar charges at the Canadian Chamber of Commerce or the Business Council on National Issues. Such groups are seen as dedicated to national interests rather than to their own and particular interests.

Towards the Caring Community: Citizenship and Community

If we as a nation are to accomplish the daunting challenge of expecting communities to care for their residents, we must recognize that this challenge requires four crucial components: (1) strong national/provincial socio-economic policies, (2) establishing caring neighbourhood institutions, (3) municipal governments dedicated to community caring, and (4) an ethic of solidarity among residents. We deal with these four components in turn.

Strong National/Provincial Socio-economic Policies

In our view, the caring capacity can be created and nourished in many Canadian neighbourhoods and communities only if they are supported by progressive federal and provincial socio-economic policies. While some communities (like those of the Amish) are isolated from the rest of the world and manage to be caring places, their culture and style of living is vastly different from those that characterize Canadian communities. Most Canadian communities require support from senior levels of government, which have the mandate to redistribute income and wealth equitably and develop universal programs in education, health, and social welfare. We only have to look to the US to recognize the essential barrenness of the residual approach to social policy. The US spends more on its splintered health care programs than Canada does and yet thousands of citizens lack coverage for health. Despite being the richest and most powerful nation in the world, the US has the highest number of children living in poverty among the industrialized countries (UNICEF 1996). Residual policies create divisions, set neighbour against neighbour, and erode the sense of citizenship.

The classic case for strong national policies that create and nourish citizenship was argued by Marshall and is discussed in some detail in Chapter 14. In essence, in order to accept the responsibilities of citizenship and behave in a supportive fashion to family members and neighbours, people must feel secure. Only if they are confident that they can support themselves and their families, or if they are assured of an income in the event they cannot do so, can they act generously and assist neighbours and friends. If people lack such confidence, they become threatened and preoccupied with survival. In our society the responsibility for preparing people to be good citizens rests with families, schools, communities, and the state, but only the state, together with the corporate sector and the trade union movement, can establish the basic condition of economic security through employment creation, retraining, and income replacement when jobs are not available.

Ironically, for those who eschew leadership from the state, our first step in building caring communities is to have strong national policies. These policies must be based on a commitment to the kind of economic development described in Chapter 9 where economic growth occurs within a context of community governance and social justice. These policies must also include a commitment to tax reform and to strategies for debt reduction that do not involve sacrificing social programs. In advancing this case, we echo the arguments of academics such as Leo Panitch and Neil Brooks, journalists like Linda McQuaig, and social policy organizations, including the Canadian Council on Social Development, the National Council of Welfare, and the Caledon Institute.

Establishing Caring Neighbourhood Institutions

The second step in building caring communities is to identify, establish, and support the kind of community institutions that facilitate caring. Many acts of caring are carried out in an informal way by neighbours looking after each other, but in addition to informal caring, some recognized, legitimate community structures are required. Some examples of these structures include community schools, health centres, and churches.

We want to signal here the contributions of neighbourhood or settlement houses as powerful agencies for providing care and developing community capacity. Neighbourhood houses offer a variety of programs, such as respite care for parents, recreational programs for all ages, and meeting rooms for self-help and other types of groups. In addition to these direct services, neighbourhood houses engage in social planning and advocacy activities. They can identify and track local needs, and suggest ways of meeting them.

Since these agencies are open to everyone, and since they do not offer programs that stigmatize people, they are a structure around which the community can organize.

Since neighbourhood houses are governed by residents, they provide an opportunity for citizens who otherwise would have few (if any) chances to participate in the process of making decisions. In this way and through their organizing activities, neighbourhood houses enable residents to take up the responsibilities of citizenship.

Municipal Governments Dedicated to Community Caring

The third component is the need for municipal governments to support community organizing. Certainly one of the most prominent examples of enlightened municipal leadership comes from the city of Seattle, which has made a commitment to enhance the quality of life in neighbourhoods. To implement this commitment, the city established the Department of Neighbourhoods, which has created neighbourhood service centres. These centres provide seed money for neighbourhood-initiated projects and, if requested, lend community development workers to staff these projects. The results have been outstanding: neighbourhoods have established community gardens and recreational programs, they have cleaned up blighted areas, and, most important, they have gained a sense of control over their areas and their lives.

An Ethic of Solidarity Among Residents

Caring communities require caring people who, as we have argued earlier, have the support of strong national policies and local structures. In addition, caring people are characterized by what White has termed (in Chapter 4) the 'ethic of solidarity'. The ethic can also be described as a deep sense of belonging to a place where the attachment is so great that participating in and contributing to neighbourhood affairs is more joy than obligation. Since women have been in the forefront of these activities, it will come as no surprise to women readers that the only writers to include community care as an essential component of community work are feminists (Callahan in this book; Dominelli 1989).

As a concluding note, we recognize that despite the optimism and idealism in many of the case-studies, the current climate established by neoconservatism and the control exercised by multinational corporations over national economies suggest that the immediate future of organizing for social change is bleak at best. However, as noted repeatedly throughout the chapters, community organizing thrives in bleak times. Perhaps an unintended contribution of neoconservatism will be to provide a context and ammunition for a variety of groups to organize and change not only the ordinary but the grand issues of social policy.

We can also take heart in the widespread interest in rediscovering community. While this interest includes contradictory motives (the abdication of state responsibilities versus empowering people), it does indicate people's collective yearning to have more control over their lives in unsettled times. This is an opportunity for community organizing to challenge the dominant economic and political power structures. By advocating a renewed commitment to social justice, community organizing in all its varied forms can bring credence to the old and neglected notion of the good citizen. In the socially just community, entitlements and obligations, rights and responsibilities, are distributed equitably.

Several of the case-studies suggest that one aspect of community organizing's heritage is no longer helpful. Community development (and we use the term development purposefully) has been imbued since its inception with Western ideas about progress. Minority groups, other cultures, and environmentalists have pointed out that these ideas have led to materialistic excesses and destruction of the environment. Today we must recognize that community organizing should not be wedded to a particular notion of human progress, although we argue strongly that human rights are a bedrock of community work in all cultures. There are many ways in which people can live and work together to nourish the best in all of us and what we can become. Community organizing is both optimistic about human nature and its potential and realistic about our limitations. Recognition of this duality enables us to get things done, and there is much we have to do.

References

Alinsky, S.
  1971. *Rules for Radicals*. New York: Random House.

Arnstein, S.
  1969. 'A Ladder of Citizen Participation'. *Journal of the American Institute of Planners* 4:216–24.

Brager, G., et al.
  1987. *Community Organizing*, 2nd ed. New York: Columbia University Press.

Cardinal, H.
  1969. *The Unjust Society*. Edmonton: Hurtig.

Carroll, W.K., ed.
    1992. *Organizing Dissent*. Toronto: Garamond Press.

Cunningham, F., et al.
    1988. *Social Movement and Social Change*. Toronto: Between the Lines.

Diers, J.
    1992. 'Generating Power by Removing the Dam Barriers'. Paper presented to the
    Waking Up the Neighbourhood Conference, Victoria.

Dixon, J.
    1989. 'The Limits and Potential of Community Development for Personal and Social
    Change'. *Community Health Studies* XIII, no. 1:82–91.

Dominelli, L.
    1989. *Women and Community Action*. Birmingham: Venture Press.

Lee, B.
    1986. *Pragmatics of Community Organization*. Mississauga, ON: Common Act Press.

Lemann, N.
    1988. 'The Unfinished War. *The Atlantic Monthly* 262, no. 6:37–56.

Lippitt, R., et al.
    1958. *The Dynamics of Planned Change*. New York: Harcourt Brace.

McKnight, J.L.
    1987. 'Regenerating Community'. *Social Policy* 17, no. 3:54–8.

———.
    1992. 'Redefining Community'. *Social Policy* (Fall/Winter):56–62.

McQuaig, L.
    1993. *The Wealthy Banker's Wife*. Toronto: Penguin Books.

———.
    1994. *Shooting the Hippo*. Toronto: McClelland and Stewart.

Mayo, M.
    1994. *Communities and Caring*. New York: St Martin's Press.

Miller, S.M., M. Rein, and P. Levitt.
    1990. 'Community Action in the United States'. *Community Development Journal* 25,
    no. 4:356–68.

Montgomery, J.
    1979. 'The Populist Front in Rural Development or Shall We Eliminate Bureaucracies
    and Get On with the Job?' *Public Administration Review* (January/February):58–65.

Ng, R., et al.
    1990. *Community Organization and the Canadian State*. Toronto: Garamond Press.

Ross, M., with B. Lappin.
1967. *Community Organization: Principles and Practice.* New York: Harper and Row.

Sower, C.
1957. *Community Involvement.* Glencoe: The Free Press.

UNICEF.
1996. *The Progress of Nations.* New York: UNICEF.

Warren, D.I.
1980. 'Support Systems in Different Types of Neighborhoods'. In *Protecting Children from Abuse & Neglect*, edited by J. Garbarino and H. Stocking, 61–93. San Francisco: Jossey-Bass.

Warren, R.
1969. 'Types of Purposive Social Change at the Community Level'. In *Readings in Community Organization Practice*, edited by R.M. Kramer and H. Specht, 205–22. Englewood Cliffs, NJ: Prentice-Hall.

Wharf, B.
1992. *Communities and Social Policy in Canada.* Toronto: McClelland and Stewart.

White, D.
1995. Personal communication to B. Wharf.

Wilson, J.Q., and G.L. Kelling.
1989. 'Making Neighbourhoods Safe.' *The Atlantic Monthly* 263, no. 2:46–52.

Abbreviations

ADDSMM	Association pour la défense des droits sociaux du Montréal métropolitain
ARDA	Agriculture Rehabilitation and Development Act
BAEQ	Eastern Quebec Planning and Development Office
BCACL	BC Association for Community Living
CAP	Canada Assistance Plan
CDC	Community development corporation
CDÉC	Corporation de développement économique communautaire
CED	Community economic development
CELDIC	Commission on Emotional and Learning Disorders in Children
CHB	Capital Health Board
CHC	Community health council
CLCS	Centre local de services communautaires
COM	Conseil des oeuvres de Montréal
CORE	Commission on Resources and Environment
CRB	Community resources board
CRD	Capital Regional District
CUSO	Canadian University Service Overseas
CYC	Company of Young Canadians
DACUM	Developing a Curriculum Process
DREE	Department of Regional Economic Expansion
ETF	Evaluation Task Force
FRAP	Front d'action politique
GMAPCC	Greater Montreal Anti-Poverty Coordinating Committee
HRDA	Human Resource Development Association
HRDC	Human Resources Development Canada
IMCC	Inter-Ministerial Child and Youth Committee

LIP	Local Initiatives Program
MCM	Montreal Citizens' Movement
MSS	Ministry of Social Services
NEEI	Nisga'a Economic Enterprises Inc.
NHW	National Health and Welfare
OFY	Opportunities for Youth
POPIR	Projet d'organisation d'information et de regroupement
RAJ	Regroupement autonome des jeunes
RÉSO	Regroupement pour la relance économique et sociale du Sud-Ouest de Montréal
RDC	Rural Development Council
RHB	Regional health board
SUPA	Student Union for Peace Action
VOP	Vancouver Opportunities Program
VRB	Vancouver Resources Board

Contributors

Kathleen Absolon, program coordinator, B'saanibamaadsiwin Native Mental Health Program, Muskoka-Parry Sound

Dal Brodhead, consultant, New Economy Development Group, Ottawa

Mary Brodhead, consultant, New Economy Development Group, Ottawa

Marilyn Callahan, associate professor, School of Social Work, Victoria

Michael Clague, Clague Consultants, Vancouver

Wayne Fulks, computer technology consultant, Sudbury

Stewart Goodings, executive director, International Affairs Branch, Human Resource Development Canada, Ottawa

David Hay, senior research associate, Social Planning and Research Council of BC, and provincial partner, Campaign 2000

Elaine Herbert, doctoral candidate, School of Social Work, University of BC, and consultant in First Nations issues

Colin Hughes, community worker, Children's Aid Society of Metro Toronto, and chair of Metro Toronto Campaign 2000

Jennifer Keck, assistant professor, School of Social Work, Laurentian University

Michael Lewis, executive director, Centre for Community Enterprise, Port Alberni

Jim Lotz, consultant in community development and freelance writer, Halifax

Teresa MacNeil, assistant to the president, St Francis Xavier University

Robert Mayer, professor, École de service social, Université de Montréal

Jean Panet-Raymond, professor and director, École de service social, Université de Montréal

Rosemarie Popham, director of social action, Family Service Association of Metro Toronto, and national coordinator, Campaign 2000

Frank Tester, assistant professor, School of Social Work, University of BC

Brian Wharf, professor, Faculty of Human and Social Development, University of Victoria

Joan Wharf Higgins, assistant professor, School of Physical Education, University of Victoria

Deena White, assistant professor, Department of Sociology, Université de Montréal

Index